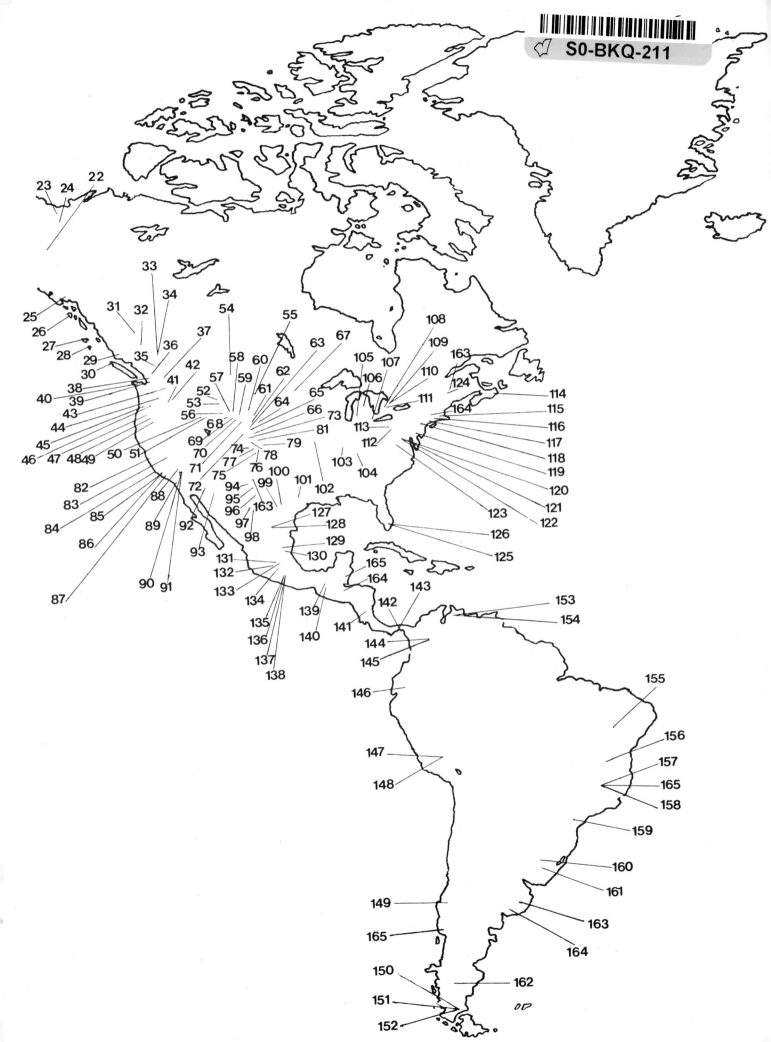

Early Man in the New World

Early Man in the New World

Edited by
Richard Shutler, Jr.

SAGE PUBLICATIONS
Beverly Hills / London / New Delhi

ᕐᖗ

For information address:

SAGE Publications, Inc.
275 South Beverly Drive
Beverly Hills, California 90212

SAGE Publications India Pvt. Ltd.
C-236 Defence Colony
New Delhi 110 024, India

SAGE Publications Ltd
28 Banner Street
London EC1Y 8QE, England

Printed in the United States of America

Library of Congress Cataloging in Publication Data

Main entry under title:

Early man in the New World.

    Bibliography: p.
    1. Paleo-Indians—Addresses, essays, lectures.
2. Indians—Origin—Addresses, essays, lectures.
3. America—Antiquities—Addresses, essays, lectures.
I. Shutler, Richard, 1921-
E61.E2 1983   970.004'97   82-24102
ISBN 0-8039-1958-1
ISBN 0-8039-1959-X (pbk.)

FIRST PRINTING

Cover design by Brenda Baker

CONTENTS

*It is with a deep sense of personal
and professional appreciation that
we dedicate this book to
H. MARIE WORMINGTON*

LIST OF TABLES

LIST OF FIGURES

RICHARD SHUTLER, Jr.

1 Introduction

At the American Anthropological Association meetings held in San Diego, California, November 18-22, 1970, I organized a symposium titled "Early Man in North America, New Developments: 1960-1970." The symposium was designed as an attempt to synthesize the information gained from a large number of Early Man sites excavated in North America from 1960 to 1970 in regard to their chronological placement, environment, technology and typology, geographical distribution, and the lifeways of those who inhabited them. The time period under consideration was before 5000-6000 B.C. This symposium was later published in *Arctic Anthropology* (Vol. 8, 1971).

The favorable reception of the symposium both at the meetings and in the published form suggested that the information in the various articles by recognized experts in the field served a useful purpose.

Accordingly, I decided to organize a sequel to the 1970 Symposium at the Society for American Archaeology meetings held again in San Diego, California, in April 1981 to present the advances in our knowledge of the many aspects and problems in the Early Man in America field that had occurred between 1970 and 1980.

The 1981 Symposium was also composed of recognized experts in the Paleoindian field, some of whom had taken part in the 1970 Symposium. This recent symposium was sponsored by the Society for Archaeological Sciences, which was meeting jointly with the Society for American Archaeology. All of the chapters in this book are revised editions of the papers prepared for the 1981 SAA meetings in San Diego.

The subject matter of the 1981 Symposium and of the subsequent publication is directed at a wide-ranging audience: the interested layman, the student, and the professional archaeologist.

The time of the earliest arrival of people in North America is a very contentious subject. There is no consensus among specialists in this field beyond that of accepting that man was definitely in the New World by 12,500 years ago. While field work during the past 10 years has provided additional information on many of the problems concerning the time of arrival and the lifeways of the first Americans, few of these problems have been solved. This lack of agreement as to arrival times, routes taken into continental North America, and related problems is apparent among the authors of this book. While there is no consensus at this time on some of these major problems, we do know a good deal more about the artifact complexes and lifeways of these earliest peoples than we did ten years ago.

In my own view, probably the most significant advancement in the Paleoindian field during the past decade is that we can now place the minimum time for the first occupation of North America at 20,000 years ago, with some probability of this important event having occurred 30,000 years ago, and the possibility that it occurred as long ago as 50,000 years. From the Meadowcroft Rockshelter Site in Pennsylvania we have the most conclusive evidence for the presence of man in North America 20,000 years ago.

All of these very important and controversial subjects are discussed in the following chapters. As was the case in the 1970s, the next ten years will certainly produce more information on these problems of when and how people first entered North America, and will provide additional evidence about their environment, technology, and lifeways. I doubt, however, that the most important question of when man first arrived on this continent will be settled to everyone's satisfaction during the 1980s, if ever.

Acknowledgments

As the convenor of the Early Man Symposium, I wish to thank all of the participants for taking time from their busy schedules to prepare their papers for presentation at the San Diego meetings, and to revise them for publication. To Irv Taylor, President of the Society for Archaeological Sciences at the time of the 1981 meetings, I express my thanks for that organization's sponsorship of the symposium. Particular thanks are due to James Hester, who wrote the back cover appraisal and provided many useful suggestions for the final revision of the manuscript. To Jamie Evrard, who either redrew or drafted from the start most of the maps and illustrations, I cannot adequately express my appreciation. Without the devotion of Mary Quirolo, who spent so many hours checking and correcting all the many details that go into getting a multi-authored book ready for publication, and for organizing and typing the bibliography, this book would not have happened. To Monica Deutsch and Penny Scharf go my special thanks for the many hours they spent typing the manuscripts. I appreciate Brenda Baker's drafting the inside cover site maps and creating the cover illustration. To Roy L. Carlson, Chairman of the Publication Committee of the Department of Archaeology at Simon Fraser University, I am indebted for advancing the funds necessary to prepare this book for publication. And finally, it is with pleasure that I express my deep and sincere gratitude to H. Marie Wormington for synthesizing all the papers in the final chapter of this book. I have valued Marie's friendship and professional advice for over twenty years. Included in our professional collaborations, which I value greatly, are Tule Springs, the 1970 San Diego Symposium, and various exciting visits to archaeological sites and museums from Hokkaido, Japan, to the Outback of Australia.

KNUT R. FLADMARK

2 Times and Places: Environmental Correlates of Mid-to-Late Wisconsinan Human Population Expansion in North America

The initial entry of humans into the New World remains one of the major unsolved problems of American archaeology. This problem is complex and multifaceted, including not only resolution of the date of the first arrivals, but also understanding of whole Quaternary cultural-ecological systems operative at the time of the first American colonization. What was the range of adaptive options first transplanted into North America? Was the ability to cope successfully with a wide range of environments already established among the first arrivals, and if not, where and when were such specializations developed? Were initial cultural adaptive strategies already capable of supporting relatively large populations and relatively complex societies? Did Late Pleistocene environmental parameters, at specific times and places, encourage or inhibit human dispersal and survival? What were likely cultural adaptive strategies if man moved into and/or through North America at certain times? This chapter is an attempt to approach these problems by putting aside for a moment specific archaeological hypotheses in order to focus on paleoenvironmental information pertaining to the Late Pleistocene. Four temporal scenarios spanning 60,000 years (Mid-Wisconsinan; Advance phase, Late Wisconsinan; Late Wisconsinan maximum; and Recessional phase, Late Wisconsinan) will be discussed in terms of major environmental factors that might have limited, pro-

hibited, or shaped human dispersals or adaptations in North America.[1]

The overall time frame considered in this chapter is restricted to the Mid-to-Late Wisconsinan for two reasons: (1) While a very few sites and proponents may suggest the presence of pre-60,000 B.P. man in North America, the bulk of researchers and data strongly argues for an initial main occupation during the Mid-to-Late Wisconsinan; and (2) paleoenvironmental data are vastly more detailed and assured for the Mid-to-Late Wisconsinan than for earlier stages. Any specific discussion of Early Wisconsinan environmental parameters significant to human occupation would be so speculative as to be essentially meaningless.

Late Pleistocene environmental factors that must have controlled or constrained human occupation include glaciations and associated changes of sea level and drainage. Most information about Pleistocene glaciation and associated environmental effects is derived from Quaternary geology, a discipline much more like archaeology than most archaeologists know, and than most geologists are willing to admit. While most paleobiologists, phytogeographers, and archaeologists have apparently been content with available geological information, in some cases they have found themselves in uncomfortable disagreement with geological interpretation.

AUTHOR'S NOTE: An earlier version of this chapter was submitted to a number of Quaternary scientists for comment. I am very grateful to J. J. Clague, D. R. Grant, D. M. Hopkins, R. W. Mathewes, and V. K. Prest for their thorough and thoughtful reviews. I have tried to incorporate all their comments and suggestions, but if any inaccuracies or misinterpretations occur, I alone am responsible.

A well-known example of such disagreement is the "nunatak" controversy (see Ives, 1974, for a review). This debate involves strong biological evidence for biotic refugia in mountainous coastal regions like Scandinavia, eastern Canada, and the northern Pacific Coast, which conflicts with geological assumptions that Late Pleistocene ice totally covered these regions. Part of this conflict arises from geological insensitivity to the type and quality of data needed by other disciplines (for example, Ives, 1974; Lindroth, 1969). While some geologists are satisfied with generalized overviews of regional glacial coverage, small ice-free areas, obscured by such coarse-grained perspectives, might be of great significance to biologists or archaeologists. A second problem is a relative scarcity of directly dated evidence for past glacial limits. This is particularly serious in mountainous regions, where most upper-level glacial indicators are undated. A simplistic assignment of all such indicators to a single, late (and therefore inevitably massive) ice sheet is simply not justifiable.

Today, the nunatak controversy is part of a broader debate in Quaternary geology. This includes a reassessment of the overall magnitude of Late Pleistocene glaciation, as well as speculation concerning rates of Pleistocene environmental change. Many Quaternary geologists can be fitted today into either "maximum" or "minimum" schools of thought regarding the thickness and extent of Late Wisconsinan ice sheets. Implicit membership in one or another of these schools may have a lot to do with whether field workers assign undated surficial evidence of glaciation to a single late "maximum," or are willing to consider relatively thin, late glaciations that have preserved evidence of earlier, more extensive events. Eventual resolution of this debate will have important implications in modelling the feasibility of human occupation in areas near maximum Pleistocene ice-sheet boundaries, and it is important that archaeologists realize that geological thinking on such matters is in flux.

The Wisconsinan stage is seen today as a complex of many stadial and interstadial intervals, of varying intensity and duration, often divided into three main parts or substages: (1) Early, (2) Mid, and (3) Late (see Figure 2.1). Most available information pertains to the latest phase of the Wisconsinan, since earlier periods are far less well known.

The Mid-Wisconsinan

The Mid-Wisconsinan nonglacial interval, from about 60,000 to 25,000 B.P., is now recognized in most of the northern hemisphere (Dreimanis and Raukas, 1975) by extensive glacial retreat and the establishment of biota well within maximum ice-sheet boundaries. In the Old World, the Mid-Wisconsinan equivalent (Mid-Weichselian; Mid-Würm) was important to human physical and cultural evolution, witnessing the replacement of *Homo sapiens neanderthalensis* by *Homo sapiens sapiens* and the development of Upper Paleolithic technologies (Bordes, 1968; Jelinek, 1980). The same period encompassed the arrival of man in Australia and Japan (White and O'Connell, 1979; Pearson, 1978), and may have seen the first significant human penetrations of Eastern Siberia (for example, Powers, 1973; Mochanov, 1980; Stanford, 1979a). The Mid-Wisconsinan, like its regional equivalents, was a time when man achieved increased cultural specialization and population expansion into previously uninhabited regions. As such, it is a theoretically likely time for initial occupation of at least some parts of the New World. The following sections summarize paleoenvironmental data on the Mid-Wisconsinan for northern North America and the potential for humans in the western hemisphere at this time.

Beringia

Matthews (1974) reports a birch-alder semi-open scrub vegetation near Fairbanks with rare spruce, 35-32,000 B.P., while Colinvaux (1967) indicates a herbaceous tundra from the Bering Strait coastline of Alaska, 30-25,000 B.P. Matthews (1975) uses fossil insect assemblages to reconstruct a significantly lower treeline circa 32,400 B.P. at Old Crow, in the Northern Yukon, with the Old Crow locality itself essentially treeless, although Ritchie (1980) notes that the central Yukon had a spruce forest for at least a portion of the Mid-Wisconsinan. However, Hopkins et al. (1981) suggest that spruce was absent or very scarce in Alaska between about 30,000 and 11,500 B.P. Murray (1980) indicates balsam poplar 25,870 ± 1,470 B.P. on the Alaskan Arctic slope, and larch is also dated 25,500 ± 100 B.P. and 29,200 ± 2,000 B.P. near Prudhoe Bay (Sheppard and Chutters, 1976). Some thawing of permafrost occurred in central Alaska during a portion of the Mid-Wisconsinan (Péwé, 1975a, 1976), while sea-levels probably reached about –20 m circa 30,000 B.P. (compare Hopkins, 1973). At this elevation, Norton and Kotzebue Sounds were still dry land, although Bering Strait would have been breached by a narrow seaway (Hopkins, 1979). In the St. Elias Range of the southwest Yukon, Denton (1974) defines the Boutellier nonglacial interval (<49,000 to >29,000 B.P.) as the local equivalent of the Mid-Wisconsinan. During most of this time, glaciers were probably completely withdrawn from lowlands and valleys, although a small-scale glacial readvance may have occurred at one or more intervals. Herbaceous pollen from the St. Elias region, dated 30-38,000 B.P., indicates a relatively cooler climate (Schweger and Janssen, 1980), although the sample includes rare arboreal species, interpreted as products of long-distance transport. This supports Rampton (1971), who suggests a sedge-moss tundra, followed by shrub-tundra, 31-27,000 B.P., with rare alder, birch, and spruce just north of the St. Elias Range.

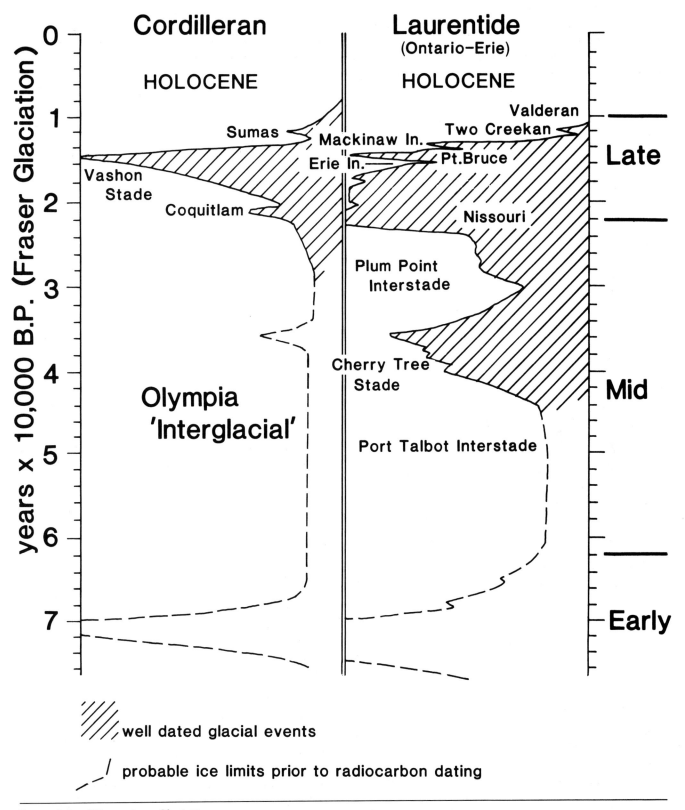

Figure 2.1   Wisconsinan Glaciation

A significant proportion of all directly dated Pleistocene faunal specimens from Beringia lived during the Mid-Wisconsinan nonglacial period, including mammoth, horse, bison, moose, saiga antelope, short-faced bear, muskox, and American lion (Morlan, 1979, 1980a; Péwé, 1975a, 1975b; Harington, 1980a; Kurtén and Anderson, 1980). This is discussed more extensively in the section titled "Wisconsinan Climax: Beringia."

Cordillera

In southwestern coastal British Columbia, the Olympia "Interglacial" or "nonglacial" interval dates from about 58-24,000 B.P., although some eventually glaciated coastal areas remained ice-free as late as 17-18,000 B.P. (Clague, 1978, 1980, 1981; Clague et al., 1980). In the southern Interior Plateau of British Columbia, the Olympia Interglacial spans >43,800 – circa 19,900 B.P. without any direct evidence of significant glacial advance beyond alpine areas (Clague, 1978, 1980; Fulton, 1971, 1975; Fulton and Smith, 1978). By circa 19,000 B.P., glacial readvances may have begun to block some interior drainages, but portions of the southern plateau remained ice-free until circa 17,500 B.P. (Clague, 1981; personal communication, 1981).

Paleobotanical studies in northwest Washington and southwest British Columbia indicate an Olympia nonglacial climate for the southern Northwest Coast generally similar to the present, although a little cooler, particularly around 30-35,000 B.P. (Alley, 1979; Heusser, 1972, 1974, 1977; Hansen and Easterbrook, 1974; Easterbrook, 1976), with coniferous forests predominating. After 29,000 B.P., Alley (1979) detects climatic deterioration and a lowering treeline. Cooler conditions prevailed in the southern Strait of Georgia by 24,500 B.P., with vegetation similar to modern floodplain bogs and subalpine areas (Mathewes, 1979). By 21,000 B.P., alpine-tundra communities had appeared on southeastern Vancouver Island (Alley, 1979), signaling the advancing Late Wisconsinan ice. During at least the final stages of the Olympia Interglacial, all or part of the Strait of Georgia was occupied by a wide braided river floodplain that probably aided mammalian dispersals between the mainland and Vancouver Island (Clague, 1976; Harington, 1975).

Fulton and Smith (1978) describe the Mid-Wisconsinan environment of the Interior Plateau as being much like at present. In north central British Columbia, pollen in the Babine mammoth site, dated 34-43,000 B.P., indicates a cool, semi-open habitat with some spruce, poplar, birch, and willow, similar to modern treeline vegetation (Harington et al., 1974). Peat samples from Atlin, northwestern British Columbia, dated 31-37,000 B.P. (Miller, 1976), and from the northern Rocky Mt. Trench, dated 25,940 B.P., show nonglacial conditions and vegetation at this time (Rut-

ter, 1976). Besides the Babine mammoth, elephant remains have been dated from 27,400 and 25,800 B.P. in the Peace River Valley; 22,700 B.P. in the lower Fraser Valley; and 17,000 B.P. on southeastern Vancouver Island (Clague, 1980). Harington (1975) also reports muskox, horse, and bison from Mid-Wisconsinan sediments of southern Vancouver Island.

In summary, most major lowlands and valleys within the Beringian and Cordilleran region appear to have been little affected by glaciers during the Mid-Wisconsinan interval; they were vegetated and able to support large and abundant fauna. Climatic reconstructions suggest conditions somewhat cooler and drier, but otherwise similar to the present through most of the interval. After about 29,000 B.P., environmental degradation accelerated in glacial areas, but at least portions of the southern Northwest Coast were not inundated by ice until after 18,000 B.P.

Laurentide and Arctic Regions

The land area destined for eventual burial beneath the Late Wisconsinan Laurentide Ice Sheet experienced much reduced glaciation during most of the Mid-Wisconsinan (Dreimanis, 1977b; Dreimanis and Goldthwait, 1973; Dreimanis and Raukas, 1975; see Figure 2.1). However, geological and palynological studies support one or more glacial readvances between 45,000 and 30,000 B.P., with the Cherry Tree Stade climaxing at about 35,000 B.P., in the Erie Basin (Berti, 1975; Dreimanis and Raukas, 1975). Despite margin oscillations, it appears that the main Laurentide ice mass remained relatively restricted through the Mid-Wisconsinan, centred near Hudson Bay and northern Quebec (McDonald, 1971), although it purportedly covered most of the St. Lawrence Lowlands at some time (Gadd, 1971; Ochietti, 1977). Glacial boundaries were possibly not far north of the Great Lakes even during the warmest episodes (Dreimanis and Raukas, 1975), but Eschman (1980) indicates that most if not all of the U.S. Great Lakes portion "east of Milwaukee" was ice-free during Port Talbot II and Plum Point-Farmdalian (Mid-Wisconsinan) time. Andrews (1974) illustrates a 40,000 B.P. Laurentide glacial margin substantially more extended than that of other authors (Figure 2.2); perhaps this can be taken to represent maximum ice cover during a possible Mid-Wisconsinan readvance.

In Atlantic Canada, Prest (1977) notes a complex Mid-Wisconsinan glacial-nonglacial sequence on Cape Breton Island, suggesting proximity to a fluctuating ice margin, while Newfoundland, New Brunswick, and Prince Edward Island are said to exhibit more homogenous glacial deposits. Incomplete glaciation and partial emergence of portions of the Grand Banks during "Early and Mid-Wisconsinan glaciations" is suggested by Alam and Piper (1977:20), while mastodon and, at another site, temperate

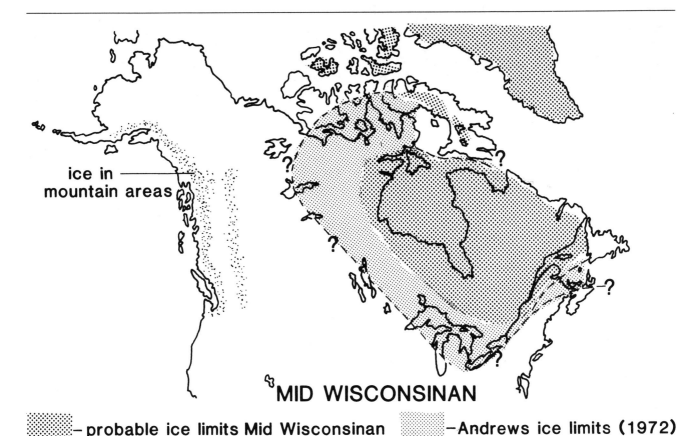

ice in mountain areas

?

?

?

?

?

?

MID WISCONSINAN

░░░ –probable ice limits Mid Wisconsinan   ░░░ –Andrews ice limits (1972)

Figure 2.2   Speculative Mid-Wisconsinan Ice Limits

marine shells dated 31,900-38,000 B.P., indicate some biota in and around Nova Scotia during at least a portion of the Mid-Wisconsinan (Prest, 1977; Wagner, 1977).

Any Mid-Wisconsinan glaciation of the Arctic archipelago was probably restricted to local ice-cap complexes, with intervening unglaciated terrain and sea ice. Nelson (1980) found no evidence for extensive ice cover on coastal Baffin Island for over 100,000 years, although fjord glaciers readvanced 40-60,000 B.P. (Andrews, 1974). Dated samples from a lake on northern Ellesmere Island apparently indicate organic sedimentation from 26,500 B.P. (England, 1976), and Blake (1980) reports marine shells from a buried raised beach on Ellesmere Island at 35,800-41,500 B.P. associated with a rich diatom assemblage, marine algae, and the bone of a dovekie (*Alle alle*). Although such old "finite" shell dates should probably be considered minima, these and a muskox from western Banks Island dated >34,000 B.P. may belong to the Mid-Wisconsinan (Harington, 1980a). Andrews (1974) indicates extensive Arctic unglaciated areas, including all of the island coasts fronting Lancaster and Viscount Melville Sounds at 40,000 B.P., and McDonald (1971) shows a northern Port Talbot ice boundary in Hudson Strait. Here, as

in the Maritimes, increasing evidence for relatively reduced Late-Wisconsinan glaciation suggests that any Mid-Wisconsinan ice cover was probably minor (for example, Ives, 1974).

In the midcontinental area, there is no evidence of glacial cover across Alberta during the Mid-Wisconsinan, and it is likely that any Laurentide margins were generally far to the east (Andrews, 1974; Dreimanis and Raukas, 1975; McDonald, 1971). Jackson (1980a) states that the central "ice-free corridor" area remained unglaciated between circa >50,000-18,000 B.P., while Rutter (1980) feels that the region was accessible until at least 25,000 B.P. This is supported by mollusks from north central Alberta dated 43,500-27,400 B.P., indicating an environment similar to today's (Ritchie, 1980).

Climatic indicators generally suggest alternating warmer and cooler episodes in the Laurentide area during the Mid-Wisconsinan. In Long Island and New Jersey, the Port Washingtonian warm interval at 32-28,000 B.P. supported pine and hardwoods, while pine and spruce dominated the vegetation between 32,000 and 44,000 B.P. and for some time after 28,000 (Sirkin and Stuckenrath, 1980). In the eastern Great Lakes area, Berti (1975) reports a relatively warm interval circa 50-55,000 B.P. characterized by pine and oak, replaced by a cooler, moister pine-spruce-larch forest at 50-22,500 B.P. This is generally supported by Gruger (1972a), who argues for an open, prairie parkland environment in central Illinois 72-28,000 B.P. supplanted by a hardwood pine forest by 28-22,000 B.P. and by a mixed spruce-deciduous forest after 22,000 B.P. Dreimanis and Goldthwait (1973) characterize the climate of even the warmest phases of the Mid-Wisconsinan as cool and boreal in the Lake Huron-Erie region. However, discoveries of grizzly bear and mammoth as far north as Toronto 40-50,000 B.P. (Churcher and Morgan, 1976), rich Mid-Wisconsinan fauna at Medicine Hat and Saskatoon (for example, Harington et al., 1974), and mammoths and probably other fauna in the Peace River area about 27,000 B.P. demonstrate that major biota were able to occupy areas within or near maximum Late Wisconsinan ice boundaries throughout much of the Mid-Wisconsinan.

Mid-Wisconsinan: Summary and Interpretation

Environmental characteristics of the Mid-Wisconsinan (circa 60,000-25,000 B.P.) can be described as variable in space and time but dominated by generally cool (and cooling) temperatures (compare Dansgaard et al., 1971; Morner, 1977). The most common pattern appears to be two periods of much restricted glacierization, separated by a cooler stadial or substadial interval (compare Alley, 1979; Denton, 1974; Dreimanis and Raukas, 1975; Heusser, 1977). Generally cool temperatures are indicated by eustatic ocean levels probably no higher than -10 to -20 m (Field et al., 1979; Hopkins, 1973; Sirkin and Stuckenrath, 1980), although Blackwelder et al. (1979) suggest that sea-levels reached their present elevation about 36,000 B.P. and then fell to -10 to -20 m between 36,000 and 22,500 B.P.

Accepting many data limitations, it is possible to make some general statements about the potential of the Mid-Wisconsinan as a human habitat. First, it seems that through most of the Mid-Wisconsinan interval, almost four times longer than the Holocene, no significant glacial barriers for human occupation existed in central and western North America. With the possible exception of a much-reduced Laurentide Ice Sheet around Hudson Bay (and even it may have disappeared entirely at times), most areas apparently lay open and accessible. People would have had a choice of coastal, mountain, plateau, plains, and even Arctic routes out of Beringia, if only the availability of ice-free terrain is considered – an environmental selection almost as varied as that of the Holocene. Second, as a result of reduced continental ice cover, world eustatic sea-levels climbed well above their glacial minima, attaining a maximum transgression 10-20 m below the present position. This was sufficient to cut the Bering Land-Bridge and to greatly reduce emergent areas of all continental shelves. However, the seaway at Bering Strait was not as wide as

today, and may not have been a serious barrier to biotic transfers between Asia and America, since it was probably frozen solid at least every winter.

It can be assumed that the overall geography of Mid-Wisconsinan central and western Canada was not greatly different from at present. Drainage elements now emptying into Hudson Bay would have drained southward if and when the bay was ice-locked, and lakes may have lain along parts of any remaining Laurentide glacial front. Generally cold and cooling temperatures lowered treelines and displaced altitudinal and latitudinal environmental zones. Deciduous and mixed woodlands in lowland and southern areas probably graded northward into more boreal forests and finally tundra and alpine communities. It is likely that the range of environmental variation at any one time during the Mid-Wisconsinan approximated the biotic diversity of modern North America, although the qualitative or quantitative comparability of environmental zones then and now is not clear. Certainly any human populations traversing the northern half of the continent, from Beringia to the coterminus United States during the Mid-Wisconsinan, must have coped with a variety of environmental conditions, including biotic zones approximately equivalent to contemporary tundra and boreal forests.

In summary, three factors may have presented some general environmental limitations on human activity in the New World during the Mid-Wisconsinan. First, the narrow seaway across Bering Strait may have acted briefly as a seasonal "filter barrier." Second, a generally cool climate, not as cold as the Late Wisconsinan maximum, but substantially cooler than true interglacial or early Holocene climates, may have inhibited arctic and subarctic cultural adaptations. Third, the extent of boreallike forest during the Mid-Wisconsinan may have restricted ease of travel and survival. Although northern and higher altitude areas may have had more extensive tundra than now, this zone was probably not continuous into central and southern latitudes. Thus, people spreading southward through Canada, already tundra-adapted, must also have been forced to develop effective adaptations to boreal forest conditions. The modern subarctic forest is a harsh environment even for ethnographic cultures, and its Mid-Wisconsinan equivalent may have been a significant challenge to initial emigrants from Beringia. Chard (1974) pointed out the possible role of the taiga in limiting human occupation of northeast Asia during interglacials, and a similar constraint might also have applied in northern North America, south of Beringia. It is conceivable that this could have critically slowed human expansion out of northern regions and their "escape" beyond the limits of the impending glaciation.

The Late Wisconsinan – Advance Phase

The traditional model of Late Pleistocene glaciation in North America pictures ice accumulating slowly in two or three major accumulation centers, building toward massive domed ice-caps centered over Hudson Bay (Laurentide Ice Sheet) and the Interior Plateau of British Columbia (Cordilleran glacier complex; see Flint, 1971). This is usually thought to have been a slow process, beginning over 70,000 years ago; weakened, halted, or even reversed during the Mid-Wisconsinan; and vigorously renewed about 25-30,000 B.P.

In contrast, some researchers now advocate a markedly different style, rate, and magnitude of Wisconsinan glaciation. They propose that the Laurentide Ice Sheet formed through the coalescence of a number of independent ice masses; that ice cover was never total in the high Arctic or Atlantic region (England, 1976; England and Bradley, 1978; Grant, 1977; Ives, 1978; Miller, 1980), and that the rate of glacial accumulation could have been much more rapid than previously considered (Andrews, 1980; Barry et al., 1975; England, 1976).

For over ten years, scholars of the Pleistocene have debated various possible models of rapid ice-sheet growth (Andrews and Mahaffy, 1975; Johnson and Andrews, 1979; Lamb and Woodroffe, 1970; Williams, 1978). Flohn (1979) comments on sudden climatic phase changes during the Pleistocene and notes that transitions from interglacial to glacial temperature regimes sometimes occurred in less than 100 years, with cooling rates faster than 5°C per 50 years. Haron et al. (1978) support an average cooling rate of about 10°C per 1000 years, while the Camp Century ice core suggests effectively instantaneous cooling episodes in the last interglacial-glacial cycle (Dansgaard et al., 1971). Such sudden and drastic changes could have been very significant to inhabitants of areas within the ultimately glaciated zone.

The Late Wisconsinan Laurentide Ice Sheet is usually stated to have attained its maximum extent at 22-17,000 B.P. (Bleuer, 1980; CLIMAP, 1976; Cronin et al., 1981; Dreimanis, 1977b; Dreimanis and Goldthwait, 1973; Lamb and Woodroffe, 1970; Mercer, 1972; Stalker, 1980). Southern Cordilleran glaciers, on the other hand (and perhaps the southwestern margin of the Laurentide), reached their greatest extension about 14,500-15,000 B.P. (Clague et al., 1980; Denton, 1974; Morner, 1977). In many cases, the final advance of these ice sheets appears to have been very rapid. Bleuer (1980), Clayton and Moran (1980), and Sugden (1977) all suggest maximum rates of advance of Laurentide outlet lobes up to 1000 m or more per year, while the final 100-150 km of advance of the Puget Sound and Juan de Fuca lobes of the Late Wisconsinan Cordilleran glacier complex took place in less than 2500 years, and perhaps as little as 500 years (Alley and Chatwin, 1979; Heusser, 1973; Thorson, 1980; see Figure 2.3).

Rates of ice-sheet development and associated environmental change could have had significant effects on any

human inhabitants who (hypothetically) might have penetrated into central Canada during the Mid-Wisconsinan. Relatively rapid glacierization or environmental deterioration could have tended to force people back into Beringia instead of southward, while a slow, radial expansion of Laurentide glaciers might have encouraged a gradual displacement of populations in all directions beyond the ice limits. Environmental reconstruction of central and northern North America during the advance phase of Late Wisconsinan glaciation is not simple, since the range and rate of possible effects are theoretically immense. Major climatic, biotic, and drainage changes might have occurred at varying rates, well ahead of the actual ice. Keeping these complicating factors in mind, the following is a tentative reconstruction of the world faced by possible inhabitants of Canada circa 25-15,000 B.P.

Cordilleran Area

The situation in the overall Cordilleran region during the advance of Late Wisconsinan glaciers is uncertain, since only southern portions of the Cordilleran glacier complex have been studied in sufficient depth to provide well-dated information on glacial advances (Clague, 1980, 1981; Fulton, 1971).

Glaciers may have begun to enter the northern Strait of Georgia shortly after 25,000 B.P., but did not extend over southern portions in the vicinity of Vancouver and Victoria until after 17,000-18,000 B.P. (Clague, 1976, 1980, 1981). This slow accumulation expansion of Fraser Glaciation ice in the Strait of Georgia was punctuated by a brief advance of valley glaciers in the southern Coast Range and Cascades about 22,000 B.P., termed the Coquitlam or Evans Creek Stade (Clague et al., 1980). This advance seems to have been confined to mountain valleys and, by at least 19,000 B.P., had retreated an unknown distance into the mountains, leaving the lowlands ice-free until their eventual overriding by the main Fraser (Vashon) glaciers (see Figure 2.1).

Some time after 18,000 B.P., the glaciers filling the Strait of Georgia began a vigorous readvance, with the advent of the Vashon Stade – the local equivalent of the Late Wisconsinan maximum. However, even as late as 17,000 B.P., mammoths were still grazing in the vicinity of Victoria, and glaciers did not reach the west coast of Vancouver Island until some time after 16,700 B.P. (Clague, 1980: 9). Ice did not advance over southern Puget Sound until some time after 15,000 B.P. (for example, Thorson, 1980) and did not attain its maximum position circa 50 km south of Seattle until approximately 14,500 B.P. A similar situation is suggested in the southern Interior Plateau, where Late Wisconsinan ice did not extend south into the United States until about 17,000 B.P. (Clague, 1980). Thus it appears that the critical extreme southern (and possibly western) margins of the Cordilleran glacier

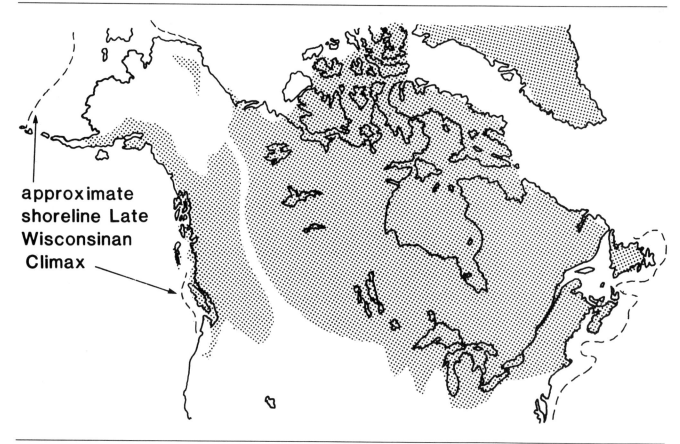

**approximate
shoreline Late
Wisconsinan
Climax**

Figure 2.3   Probable Ice Limits of Late Wisconsinan Climax

complex did not reach their fullest extent until after 17,000 years ago – at a time when at least parts of the Laurentide Ice Sheet had already attained their maximum.

Laurentide Area

Most Laurentide glaciers probably expanded southward, westward, and eastward from Keewatin and Labrador sources. The furthest westward extent of Keewatin ice occurred earliest in the north and progressively later toward the south. Although the latitude at which this maximum westward advance of Keewatin-Laurentide glaciers was first attained is not certain, it was possibly about 55°-60° N. (see Prest, 1969). Ice across this area may have acted as a Late Wisconsinan biotic divide, with flora and fauna (perhaps including people) caught north of the 55°-60° closure" point confined toward the north and west, and biota existing south of the contact, progressively displaced toward the south and west.

Although the ultimate restriction on the habitability of west central Canada was the presence of glaciers, it is likely that other important environmental changes occurred ahead of the advancing ice fronts. Normal drainage into Hudson Bay may have been blocked during at least parts of the Mid-Wisconsinan by ice masses in that area, and

as Laurentide ice expanded westward, further progressive displacement and damming of rivers would have occurred. Ice damming of any individual drainage might have been a relatively sudden event, caused by a single glacial lobe completing final closure of a drainage outlet. In such cases, substantial proglacial pondages might have developed rapidly, tens or hundreds of kilometers ahead of the ice, until at last the pondage basin was overridden or new outlets opened around the blockage. Morlan (1980a) suggests that the flooding of Yukon interior basins by Laurentide ice lobes may have been catastrophic to the local climate and fauna.

Biota of the midcontinental area would have become progressively stressed as Late Wisconsinan glaciers developed and the climate became cooler and perhaps more variable. However, it is not certain that major regions became biotically sterile until actually overridden by ice. Around the Great Lakes there is evidence that Late Wisconsinan glaciers advanced into living pine-spruce-alder forests, as suggested by trees with bark, buried in till, and bent in U-shapes downstream as though still green and fresh when overridden (Berti, 1975; Dreimanis, 1977a; Dreimanis and Goldthwait, 1973). In other areas it is possible that permafrost and tundra developed ahead of slowly advancing ice in response to sharply negative temperature gradients close to the ice front (Dreimanis, 1977a; Rannie, 1977, Richard, 1977). It is likely that much of the periglacial zone immediately along the ice front was an unstable, raw, and unpredictably hazardous terrain due to avalanching mass wastage and sporadic meltwater discharge. Given a multitude of terminal lobes, moving at different rates and directions (see, for example, Clayton and Moran, 1980; Dreimanis and Goldthwait, 1973), perhaps spreading from several accumulation centers, occasional pockets of plants and animals might even have been cut off and exterminated by glacial advances.

Late Wisconsinan Advance Phase:
Summary and Interpretation

The advance phase of Late Wisconsinan glaciation saw diminishing ice-free areas both east and west of the Rocky Mountains at 25-18,000 B.P. Cordilleran glaciers and some Laurentide lobes climaxed at about 14,500 B.P., several thousand years after the usually cited main southern Laurentide maximum at circa 17,000 B.P. Although the rate of ice advance was sometimes rapid, most biota probably responded by gradual population displacement into unglaciated areas. Any human occupants of northern-central North America at this time would have been progressively restricted to diminishing and westward-shifting ice-free areas, although some southern Cordilleran valleys and lowlands may have remained unglaciated longer than most other regions of equivalent latitude. As the Keewatin-Laurentide ice closure climaxed, populations may have been split into northern and southern segments by the creation of a glacial biotic divide at about 55°-60°N. Life along the margin of advancing glaciers was presumably feasible up until the moment of ice submersion, although the immediate ice-frontal zone was almost certainly a very undesirable area.

The Late Wisconsinan Climax

The Late Wisconsinan includes the most extensive glaciations of about the last 60,000 years in North America, but there is disagreement about the detailed glacial boundaries and chronology of this period.

The Laurentide Late Wisconsinan maximum is traditionally assumed to have formed a huge continental ice cap centered near Hudson Bay (compare Flint, 1971; Prest, 1969; CLIMAP, 1976). The ice sheet is sometimes pictured as domelike, with sloping surfaces rising toward central ridges or divides and estimated ice thicknesses of up to 4.2 km (see Sugden, 1977). Andrews (1973) calculates that maximum Laurentide glaciers probably approximated the area of the present Antarctic Ice Sheet (12,653,000 km²). Although a great ice mass with frozen summits thousands of meters high looming over eastern

and central North America is a picturesque concept, and one accepted without much debate until recently, there are several problems with this traditional "maximum" model of Late Wisconsinan Laurentide glaciation.

First is the absence of direct indicators of maximum ice thickness in central areas of the Laurentide Ice Sheet. Traditional estimates of ice thickness are mainly based on theoretical calculations of surface slope trends, assuming a stable glacial regime; measurements of isostatic crustal depression and rates of uplift; and estimates of water volumes removed from ocean reservoirs during the glacial maximum. However, our understanding of crustal and geodetic responses to loading, and the history of world eustatic sea-levels, is far from certain (see Cronin et al., 1981). For instance, Blackwelder et al. (1979) claim that their data determining Pleistocene Atlantic coast sea-levels are more reliable than any previous studies, and their estimates of −60 to −20 m shoreline positions at 17-10,000 B.P. are substantially higher than the −80 to −160 m Late Wisconsinan sea-levels usually inferred, suggesting much reduced volumes of continental ice. A second problem with the classic single-domed ice-sheet model is that the great thickness of ice required in the region of Hudson Bay may exceed any known climatic driving mechanisms that could account for its rapid development and final abrupt disintegration (see, for example, Andrews, 1973; Andrews and Mahaffy, 1975; Lamb and Woodroffe, 1970). Although the rapidity of final recession may be explained by calving into oceans or lakes (Bird, 1973; Thomas, 1977), a more economical solution may be simply to model an initially thinner and more complex Laurentide glaciation.

This interpretation is preferred by Andrews (1980), who argues that the classic concept of a massive, single-ridged equilibrium ice sheet across Hudson Bay is probably incorrect. Instead, he suggests that a much thinner ice cover over northern areas is required to explain increasing evidence for higher eustatic sea-levels during the Late Wisconsinan than previously estimated, and to allow the rapid and extensive fluctuations of Laurentide marginal lobes recorded in many areas. The idea that Late Wisconsinan ice sheets developed through growth and coalescence of partially independent accumulation centers is supported in the northeastern Atlantic by Grant (1977), and in Arctic areas by England (1976), England and Bradley (1978), and Ives (1978). Thus it is possible that the Laurentide Ice Sheet consisted of a complex glacial mass derived from a number of accumulation centers, with initially varied thicknesses of ice and directions of ice movement (Andrews, 1973, 1980), and that the Hudson Bay area was not the center of a smoothly domed ice cap. Opposing models of ice-sheet thickness are critical in evaluating evidence for or against the total and prolonged glaciation of any given area. A thick single-centered ice cap theoretically precludes various ice-free refugia which would be possible given a thinner, more dynamic multicentered ice sheet.

In addition to problems in determining climax ice boundaries and thickness is the fact that the Late Wisconsinan Laurentide maximum was not a single uninterrupted event. Evidence from several areas indicates that the glacial margin oscillated markedly between 20,000 and 14,000 B.P. In the Great Lakes region, Dreimanis and Goldthwait (1973), Dreimanis (1977a,b), and Mercer (1972) interpret the Erie Interstade (Figure 2.1) as a 500-600 km northward retreat of the Erie-Huron lobe, between about 17,000 and 14,500 B.P. Morner (1973, 1977) feels that the Erie Interstade correlates with worldwide climatic amelioration at this time, although Dreimanis (1977a) suggests that the environment may have been too inhospitable in the newly deglaciated terrain for significant biota. Several other important pulses of Great Lakes lobes have been noted, including the Connersville Interstade (a retreat of 40-100 km at 20-21,000 B.P.) and the Mackinaw Interstade circa 13-14,000 B.P. (Dreimanis and Goldthwait, 1973; Dreimanis, 1977a; and Frye and Willman, 1973). Teller and Fenton (1980) suggest several separate ice advances over southeast Manitoba during the Late Wisconsinan and describe a significant recessional episode about 13,000 B.C. Stalker (1980) also indicates a major Late Wisconsinan interstadial at 20-19,000 B.P. in southern Alberta. He notes that interstadial deposits contain abundant mammalian megafauna and that this interval would have been a good time for man to move through the "ice-free corridor."

Irrespective of its possible thickness and complexity, there appears little doubt that the Laurentide Ice Sheet was, as the sum of all its maximum marginal positions, a very extensive ice mass. Between southeastern Alberta and the Atlantic seaboard, a line of dated terminal moraines, till-sheet limits, and other data are relatively firm indicators of maximum southern Late Wisconsinan ice-frontal positions. However, this maximum line is in reality a net or accumulative frontal position, and there is considerable disagreement on the precise timing and synchroneity of advances of individual lobes up to that maximum position in different areas (see, for example, Clayton, 1980; Christiansen, 1979, 1980; Dreimanis and Goldthwait, 1973; Clayton and Moran, 1980; Wright, 1971b). In the continental area, of course, and Beringia, there is no doubt of the existence of unglaciated and biotically productive terrain outside of the ice front, regardless of the precise local position and chronology of glaciers. However, in all other areas immediately peripheral to the Laurentide Ice Sheet, the presence of any potentially inhabitable land during the Late Wisconsinan maximum and initial recessional stages is controversial. In these cases very precise and rigorous determinations of glacial boundaries in space and time become all important. Often such data are lacking, and evaluations of inconclusive evidence frequently reflect merely individual researchers' preferences for "maximum" or "minimum" models of Late Wisconsinan glaciation.

In the following sections, Late Wisconsinan glacial climax paleoenvironmental data will be summarized for Beringian, Cordilleran, midcontinental, Arctic, and Atlantic coast regions. Emphasis will be on the determination of areas potentially suitable for human occupation and their environmental characteristics.

Beringia During Late Wisconsinan Glaciation

The region now generally referred to as Beringia includes unglaciated central portions of the Yukon Territory and Alaska, emergent shelves of the Bering and Chukchi Seas, and the adjacent ice-free segment of Northeast Siberia (see Hopkins, 1979). Although glacial complexes developed in mountains around the central river system of Alaska and the Yukon, most of the interior lowlands remained ice-free. Ice damming caused proglacial pondages in Old Crow and other basins of the northern Yukon (Morlan, 1979, 1980a), but in general the central Yukon basin remained unobstructed throughout the Late Wisconsinan. The unglaciated portion of Beringia constricts progressively toward the southeast, where it is eventually confined to a narrow strip along the Mackenzie Mountains (Hughes, 1972; Prest, 1969; Rutter, 1980).

The Late Wisconsinan vegetation of Beringia has frequently been described as a "steppe-tundra" or "Arctic-steppe" with special characteristics not specifically paralleled in any modern plant community. Apparently dominated by xerophytic grasses, herbs, and shrubs, including a large representation of *Artemesia* (sage), it is usually thought to have been a productive grassland environment much more capable of supporting the complex herbivore communities usually assigned to this period than any existing Arctic biome (see Hopkins, 1979). Archaeologists have focused on the "Arctic-steppe" concept as an environment well suited to the spread of big-game hunting cultures from central Eurasia to North America, but recently the reality and dominance of this vegetational type in Beringia has been challenged. Ritchie (1980) and Cwynar and Ritchie (1980) interpret pollen cores from easternmost Beringia, close to the Laurentide ice front, as showing polar desert or fell-field tundra conditions 14,000 to 30,000 years ago, suggesting that the Late Wisconsinan environment of this part of Beringia was as harsh as the modern high Arctic. (However, see Hopkins et al., 1981). A problem in interpreting Beringian environments is undoubtedly the size and geographic complexity of the area, in comparison to the relatively small number of reported paleoecological studies. It seems improbable that a single vegetational community dominated the entire area (Packer 1980); instead, it is more likely that there was some southwest-to-northeast trend of increasing continentality and decreasing maritime influences (see, for example, Berman et al., 1979).

The apparent richness of Late Pleistocene faunal assemblages has led to a concept of a Beringian mammalian community approximating that of contemporary West Africa, and hence the "need" for an exceptionally rich environment. However, while there is no doubt that many megafaunal species existed for some part of Wisconsinan time, in some part of Beringia, it is not at all certain which belong together in actual life assemblages for any specific place and time. There is a tendency, when describing the mammalian fossils and lithostratigraphy of Beringia, not to distinguish between Mid and Late Wisconsinan deposits and assemblages (see, for example, Péwé, 1975a; Harington, 1980a,b). In fact, when only directly dated fossils are considered, the numbers of finds and diversity of species are much reduced for the Late Wisconsinan glacial climax per se, in comparison to Mid-Wisconsinan assemblages.

In a listing of radiocarbon dates from central Alaska (Péwé, 1975b), *no* animals are directly dated between about 18-21,000 B.P., while only bison, muskox, and perhaps mammoth are reliably dated at 22-15,000 B.P. At Old Crow in the northern Yukon, no faunal remains date from between 22,000 and 14,000, and most are older than 26,000 (Morlan, 1980a). At Lost Chicken Creek and near Dawson City, Harington (1980b) reports only muskoxen (*Symbos* and *Ovibos*) directly dated between 26,000 and 15,000 B.P. A recently reported assemblage of mammoth, horse, camel, caribou, bison, sheep, *canis*, and *lepus* from Canyon Creek, Alaska, apparently dates sometime after 40,000 B.P. (Hopkins, personal communication, 1982), and does not add significantly to this discussion (Weber et al., 1981). While other species found in the same or similar localities are sometimes inferred to be originally associated, this may not be justified, since reworking of older sediments is common in the area.

A review of the last ten years of the files of *Radiocarbon* supports the conclusion that directly dated evidence for a very complex megafauna in Beringia during the Late Wisconsinan glacial maximum does not exist. Instead, Central Alaska may have supported a relatively modest assemblage, including bison, muskoxen, wooly mammoth, and perhaps a few other lesser species, while easternmost Beringia (northern Yukon) may have sustained only muskoxen and smaller mammals for as many as 11,000 years(26-15,000 B.P.). Cwynar and Ritchie (1980) point out the need to understand detailed stratigraphic and chronological relationships of Beringian megafauna before using them to infer past environments and cultural associations, and the wisdom of this recommendation is confirmed above. There seems some cause to revise notions of a Late Wisconsinan hunter's paradise throughout Beringia. Available "big" game in easternmost Beringia may have been limited to a sparse High Arctic assemblage, and available data do not exclude the possibility that *no* major game existed throughout central Beringia around 18-20,000 B.P. Equally intriguing is a hint that mammoths achieved their latest widespread distribution in Beringia dur-

ing the Mid-Wisconsinan interstadial (>23,000 B.P.) and were much reduced in range and numbers later. This might have important implications for hypotheses concerning Beringian origins of North American elephant-hunting complexes.

Sometimes lost in descriptions of Beringia is the fact that the famous land-bridge had coastlines as well as interior plains. Given relatively modest big-game populations inland, the ocean shores may have been very important to human inhabitants, particularly since the unfrozen Pacific coast was presumably a rich zone. Estuaries and lower courses of rivers, such as the Yukon-Kuskokwin, would have experienced major salmon runs (although the upstream extent of spawning salmon may have been limited by turbid waters of aggrading outwash floodplains), while rocky headlands would have been important rookeries for seabirds (compare Hopkins, 1979). It is possible that the productivity of intertidal fauna was reduced by the scouring of seasonal shore-ice (Hopkins, 1979), but this may have been compensated for by changes in sea mammal distributions and migratory behavior resulting from closure of the Bering Strait. Whales and seals, which now migrate into the straits from the Pacific, must have been confined to the southern shore, while walrus and other species now limited to the zone of seasonal sea ice in the Bering and Chukchi Seas were probably also displaced to the southern Beringian coast. Much of the shoreline was possibly a more mesic environment than interior regions, and sheltered habitats, near sea-level, probably supported a more diverse terrestrial flora. Unfortunately, most direct evidence for coastal Beringian environments is now drowned beneath the Holocene marine transgression or obscured by problematical dating (see Colinvaux, 1981).

In summary, Late Wisconsinan environments of Beringia were probably varied, with, speculatively, a significant distinction between coastal and interior habitats. Earlier assumptions of a rich glacial climax herbivorous fauna in central Beringia should be revised to take into account previously unsegregated Mid-Wisconsinan materials. This revision suggests a much more modest Late Wisconsinan faunal assemblage than is often pictured. Particularly in easternmost Beringia, major game was probably rare and limited in diversity. Any human inhabitants entering interior Beringia at this time and moving east toward the "ice-free corridor" would have experienced a progressive deterioration in climate and available fauna, while Beringian Pacific coastal conditions may have consistently been relatively rich.

The Cordilleran Glacier Complex

As indicated previously, Late Wisconsinan (Vashon) glaciation of southwest British Columbia and northwest Washington did not begin to affect southern Georgia Strait lowlands directly until after 18,000 B.P. (Clague, 1981).

By circa 14,000 B.P., the Vashon lobe had reached its maximum southern position *and* retreated over 50 km back north in its final recession (see Thorson, 1980). A tributary lobe in the Strait of Juan de Fuca had advanced about 100 km west of Puget Sound and gone into final stagnation by 14,460 ± 200 B.P. (Heusser, 1973). Ice did not reach the central west coast of Vancouver Island until after 16,700 B.P. and had retreated entirely from southern Vancouver Island before 12,700 B.P. (Clague, 1980). The same Vashon ice left Vancouver close to accumulation centers before 13,000-13,500 B.P. (Armstrong, 1981;Clague et al., 1980). Thus the accumulation, expansion, and final retreat of the last approximately 200-250 km of Vashon ice in the Strait of Georgia, British Columbia, appear to have occurred within a total time frame of less than 5,000 years. Indeed, the final 50-100 km of advance, and possibly retreat, of the Vashon-Puget-Juan de Fuca lobes seem to have taken less than 2,500, and perhaps as little as 500, years, sometime between 17,000 and 14,000 B.P. For the Vashon glaciers of extreme southwest British Columbia, at least, it is difficult to differentiate between prolonged advance, climax, and retreat phases. The whole process was extremely dynamic, with little evidence of stable termini, or significant halts and readvances.

Vashon ice is thought to have attained a thickness of up to 1265 m at the northern end of Puget Sound and further west in the Strait of Juan de Fuca, possibly involving a low gradient ice sheet completely engulfing the uplands of southern Vancouver Island and flowing south on to the Olympic Peninsula (Alley and Chatwin, 1979; Thorson, 1980). The difficulty in accepting this notion is simply that all upper elevation indicators of glaciation are not dated. High elevation straie and erratics used by Alley and Chatwin (1979) and others to indicate a maximum Vashon ice-sheet stage are only assumed to be of Vashon age, but may in fact be considerably older.

More substantial evidence for the rapid advance and retreat of Late Wisconsinan ice occurs in the southern interior of British Columbia, and near the southern margins of the Cordillera glaciation. In this region, Late Wisconsinan ice had not yet advanced into major valleys by circa 20,000-21,000 B.P. (Fulton, 1975; Fulton and Smith, 1978) and was still 120 km north of its maximum terminus by 17,500 B.P. (Clague, 1980; Clague et al., 1980). The same glaciers had retreated from their maximum position by circa 12,750 B.P. (Mullineaux et al., 1978; Porter, 1978). Thus, the southern Plateau Late Wisconsinan glaciation went through most of its growth and recession in less than 8,000 years (20/21,000-12,750 B.P.). Fulton (1975) and Fulton and Smith (1978) advocate a massive ice sheet over at least the southern Plateau during the Late Wisconsinan climax. Tipper (1971) argues for a relatively thin coalescence of ice from several accumulation centers in the northern and central Plateau, while an "intense valley-piedmont glaciation" is suggested for the northeastern Cordillera by Miller (1976). Although the question is not yet

settled given their rapid advance and retreat, it seems probable that Plateau glaciers did not achieve a thick ice cap in the Late Wisconsinan.

In short, available data from the Cordilleran region either indicate, or do not preclude, a relatively short-lived Late Wisconsinan glacial climax, culminating some 14,500-15,000 years ago. It is suggested that the extension and retreat of ice along the southern margin of the Cordilleran region occurred in less than 4,000-8,000 years, between 20-17,000 and 12-13,000 B.P. Before and after this time, large areas of terrain were ice-free and potentially biologically productive. Therefore, regardless of the magnitude of late glacial cover, it is probable that inhabitable areas existed around the periphery of the Cordilleran region for all of Mid and Late Wisconsinan time, with the possible exception of the 8-4,000-year period of climax conditions (compare Mathews, 1979).

In several previous publications, I have argued that the Northwest Coast might have served as a route for early human populations entering North America, even during maximum Late Wisconsinan glaciation (Fladmark, 1975, 1978, 1979). However, the data needed to verify this theory are still not available, and the amount of ice-free terrain open to biotic colonization along the Northwest Coast during the Late Wisconsinan climax is not certain.

The outer coast of Vancouver Island was glaciated at least in part during the Late Wisconsinan (see Alley and Chatwin, 1979; Clague et al., 1980), but the extent of maximum ice cover is unknown. Heusser (1973) suggests that the western terminus of the Vashon-Juan de Fuca lobe was about 100 km wide (from north to south) and, given a 100 m sea-level drop, about 15 km of the ice front would have been tidal, implying unglaciated subaerial terrain around the rest of the terminus. However, this does not take into account possible local isostatic effects. Alley and Chatwin (1979) infer a more extensive ice cover at the western end of the Strait of Juan de Fuca, possibly reaching the edge of the continental slope, but do not describe specific evidence for this conclusion, other than their estimate of a generally thick maximum Vashon glaciation. Carter (1973), Tiffin (1976), and Herzer (1978) all note that portions of the continental shelf off the west coast of Vancouver Island lack evidence for late glaciation. This situation is also illustrated by Clague et al. (1980).

In Queen Charlotte Sound, north of Vancouver Island, there are suggestions of possible ice-free emergent interlobe areas along the outer continental shelf, assuming an 80-100 m relative sea-level drop (Lutenauer, 1972). On the Queen Charlotte Islands, numerous studies have suggested the existence of a major Late Wisconsinan biotic refugium (Fladmark, 1975, 1979). Recent work seems to confirm the presence of terrestrial and aquatic flora on these islands circa 13-15,000 B.P. (Mathewes, personal communication, 1981).

North of the Queen Charlotte Islands, the Alexander Archipelago of Alaska represents a troublesome gap in

Quaternary environmental data. Earlier speculation concerning Pleistocene refugia in the region is neither proved nor refuted by more current information (Fladmark, 1975; Heusser, 1960). Evidence for multiple Late Pleistocene glaciation exists (for example, McKenzie and Goldthwait, 1971; Miller, 1976; Swanston, 1969), but maximum ice boundaries and thicknesses are not well known. Estimates of 900 m thick ice in the center of the archipelago (Swanston, 1969) suggest that the maximum late glacial event was insufficient to form an ice sheet completely overriding the islands, and was probably restricted to valley and coalescent piedmont stages. In this case, it is likely that the outer headlands and slopes of Chicagof, Baranof, and Prince of Wales Islands remained unglaciated, although possibly separated by ice lobes reaching the Pacific through major cross valleys. Near Juneau, Miller (1973) has recorded radiocarbon dates of 12,800 ± 500 B.P. and 12,730 ± 500 B.P. in raised deltas only 8 km from the terminus of the present Mendenhall glacier, indicating that the ice had left the valleys before that time (Miller, 1975).

In Adams Inlet, near Glacier Bay, glaciomarine organic sediments may have begun to be deposited as early as 13,960 B.P. (McKenzie and Goldthwait, 1971), which, in combination with the Juneau data, probably means that the ice had withdrawn from the outer coast substantially before 12,500-13,000 B.P. Finally, Miller (1976) states that the maximum Late Wisconsinan glaciation in the Alaska-Canada Boundary Range near Juneau was not as extensive as an earlier event, consisting only of a "confluent mass of mountain and lowland piedmont valley-filling glaciers" with local accumulation centers and nunataks.

Evidence for unglaciated terrain along the coast of Southeast Alaska from Cross Sound to Prince William Sound has been cited previously (Fladmark, 1975, 1978, 1979) and will not be repeated here. In general, the notion of relatively restricted Late Wisconsinan glaciation in this region seems to be accepted by most geologists (Goldthwait, 1978; Péwé 1975a, 1976; Péwé et al., 1965; Prest, 1969; Reid, 1970). In Cook Inlet, the picture is less certain. Karlstrom (1964, 1965) defined the Knik glaciation as a pre- or Early Wisconsinan advance, followed by the Late Wisconsinan Naptowne glaciation, neither of which completely covered upper Cook Inlet. Unfortunately, redating of the crucial Bootlegger Cove clays, originally considered representative of a Mid-Wisconsinan (Woronzofian) marine transgression (Hopkins, 1967a), indicates that this unit is probably a glaciomarine complex no more than 14,000 years old (Schmoll et al., 1972). This means that the overlying Naptowne glaciation must now be considered younger than 14,000 years in age, and the limits of classic Late Wisconsinan glaciation remain undetermined in Cook Inlet (Péwé, 1975a).

In the Lake Iliamna region at the base of the Alaska Peninsula, Detterman and Reed (1973, 1980) define an undated sequence of five Late Pleistocene stades. The oldest (Kukaklek Stade) is correlated with the Early Wisconsinan (>38,000 B.P.). It was the most extensive local glaciation and the only event that had sufficient thickness to form an ice-sheet, probably damming lower Cook Inlet. Later advances (Kvichak, Iliamna, Newhalen, and Iliuk Stades – presumed oscillations of the Late Wisconsinan) were progressively weaker and less extensive. Deposits left by these glaciers cover only 40 percent of the area, but more extensive glacial cover is inferred from undated scattered erratics and grooved bedrock. Maximum ice thickness of the Late Wisconsinan was less than 370 m, which left the uplands ice-free. It is thought that the mouth of Cook Inlet might have been ice-blocked for part of this time, but dated evidence is lacking.

Detterman and Reed (1973) model a relatively limited Late Wisconsinan glaciation, in contrast to other published synopses of the Alaska Peninsula region. Prest (1969), Péwé et al. (1965), and Péwé (1975a: Fig. 6; 1976) all show a huge, uniform "Wisconsin" ice sheet, totally burying the south coast of the Alaska Peninsula and extending to the edge of the continental shelf. Unfortunately, neither their maps nor much of the limited published geological data available for this region clearly distinguish between Early and Late Wisconsinan deposits. The assumption of a huge ice cap centered over Shelikof Strait, which "sent outlet glaciers northwards through . . . the Alaska Peninsula" (Péwé, 1975a: 21), may be an accurate image of pre- or Early Wisconsinan glaciation, but it probably does not apply to the Late Wisconsinan. Karlstrom (1969) specifically ascribes the most extensive glaciation of the northern Gulf of Alaska to pre-Late Wisconsinan events, and Burk (1965: 106) states that there is "no evidence that a broad Pleistocene ice cap existed . . . but the numerous valley glaciers fed debris-laden bergs into the Pacific." The presence of a small biotic refugium on Kodiak Island is demonstrated by Karlstrom and Ball (1969), and I suspect that a potential exists for similar situations on the Trinity and Shumnagin Islands. Although these islands were apparently overridden by ice at some time (Péwé, 1975a), it is unlikely that such an extensive event correlates with the Late Wisconsinan. In the Aleutians, both Black (1973) and Gard (1980) suggest a near total glaciation of existing land areas during the Late Wisconsinan, but dated evidence for marginal positions is not available, and it is not established to what extent Aleutian ice had spread over the continental shelf.

In summary, the available data suggest scattered ice-free areas around the northern Pacific Coast of North America during the Late Wisconsinan climax, but in most cases are inadequate to prove their existence definitely. Major gaps in Quaternary geological information hamper understanding of the limits and chronology of Late Wisconsinan glaciation on the Alaska Peninsula, Alexander Archipelago, and outer coastal areas of British Columbia. However, given the apparently short life of the Late Wisconsinan southern Cordilleran climax and the influence of topography and distance from ice sources, a discontinuous strip of unglaciated outer coastal headlands, uplands, and islands would seem a likely result of what must have been a relatively weak and brief ice advance onto the outer coast. If relatively lowered sea-levels occurred on the outer coast, this might also have improved the overall connectivity of coastal refugia and the productivity of intertidal resources by exposing more low gradient strand-flats.

A chain of outer coastal unglaciated areas remains a reasonable hypothesis for the Late Wisconsinan climax of the north Pacific coast of North America, and a near certainty anytime before 17,000 and after 13,000 B.P. (Mathews, 1979). We can be confident that if Pacific coastal unglaciated areas existed, they would have been capable of sustaining relatively complex and diverse terrestrial flora near sea-level, with decreased arboreal elements grading into tundra with elevation (compare Florer, 1972; Florer and Heusser, 1975; Heusser, 1974). Estimates of glacial July mean air temperatures suggest a lowering by no more than 7°C in coastal Washington (Heusser, 1977), while marine temperatures in the same area dropped about 2-4°C (Moore, 1973; CLIMAP, 1976). This implies conditions near the southern margin of Pacific coastal glaciation approximately equivalent to the present environment of Southeast Alaska (Moore, 1973; Thorson, 1980). If this latitudinal shift is simplistically extrapolated to the entire Pacific Coast, the Gulf of Alaska coastline might have had an environment similar to the present Bering Strait-Chukchi Sea area during the Late Wisconsinan. However, complicating factors are the Pleistocene closure of Bering Strait, which prevented cold Arctic water from reaching the north Pacific during glacial episodes, and the Japanese Current, which would have continued then, as now, to supply warm, subtropical water to the Gulf of Alaska.

No directly dated faunal material can be ascribed to the precise moment of Pacific Coast maximum glaciation, but as noted earlier this was such a short episode that it becomes almost irrelevant in comparison to long periods of reduced glaciation and improved environments before and after. By 12,500-14,000 B.P., maximum isostatic marine transgressions were occurring all along the inner mountainous coast, accompanied by deposits of glaciomarine sediments (deposited by meltwater streams and dropped from floating ice), and incorporating marine mollusks indicative of flourishing near-shore fauna (Andrews and Retherford, 1978; Armstrong, 1981; Clague, 1980; Fulton, 1971; McKenzie and Goldthwait, 1971; Miller, 1973; Schmoll et al., 1972; Spiker et al., 1977). Lodgepole pine forest was growing near Vancouver, B.C., by 12,600 B.P. (Mathewes, 1973), and terrestrial and aquatic flora occupied the Queen Charlotte Islands by at least 13-15,000 B.P. (R. Mathewes, personal communication, 1981).

The north Pacific Ocean did not permanently freeze during the last stadial, although seasonal sea ice possibly formed in sheltered bays and inlets for a time. Thus, any in-

habitants of shoreline refugia would have had access to marine and intertidal resources almost as rich as the historic bounty for which the Northwest Coast is famous. Salmon and other anadromous fish were probably restricted due to degraded spawning streams, but marine species, including sea mammals, may have been more diversified and abundant. Species like walrus and sea-cow were probably more widely distributed around the Pacific rim and, at least in the latter case, could have provided easy prey for human maritime predators (see, for example, Domning, 1972; Hopkins, 1979). Even major terrestrial game may have survived on some of the larger coastal refugia. An example is the Queen Charlotte Island's caribou (Foster, 1965), which could only have reached these isolated islands during a time of lowered sea-levels or extensive sea ice, both conditions implying a glacial period.

More important at the moment than specific environmental details of Pacific coastal refugia – given unglaciated ground at sea-level, biological productivity capable of sustaining man seems certain – is whether any people would have been able to reach such areas, particularly during the short glacial maximum. If the total ice-sheet glaciation traditionally inferred for the Pacific side of the Alaska Peninsula did occur (see Péwé, 1975a), it seems unlikely that even boat-using people could have made it around the approximately 800-km gap between the Beringian coast and the Kodiak refugium. However, if the Alaska Peninsula glaciation consisted of only valley lobes reaching individual termini at or near sea-level, people might have made the trip by moving between headlands by boats, or by crossing glacial termini on foot. In addition, it may have been possible for humans to travel between the main area of Beringia and Pacific coastal refugia, through partly glaciated valleys such as the Iliamna Lake valley, northwest of Cook Inlet. Although this would have involved cross-ice travel, the total distance is less than 150 km.

If man could have made it to the Cook Inlet-Prince William Sound area, by whatever means, there seems little difficulty in allowing a gradual southward movement to other coastal refugia, and to the limits of glaciation and beyond. However, this movement probably required watercraft, at least during the short maximum glacial period. Unfortunately, the age and effectiveness of Pleistocene watercraft are still unknown despite indications that water travel transposed a viable human population to Australia circa 40,000 B.P. (Hallam, 1977; White and O'Connell, 1979).

The Midcontinental Area and "Ice-Free Corridor"

Any human populations infiltrating southward in mid-Canada during the Late Wisconsinan maximum must have been restricted to limited areas of ice-free terrain, or else they traveled over the glaciers. Although the latter possibility is rarely given any serious discussion, it is worth considering momentarily.

Travel across glacial surfaces is well known to modern

mountaineers as hazardous and time-consuming. Crevasses, avalanches, loose morainal material, and meltwater all make modern alpine glaciers well worth avoiding by foot travelers if possible, and probably most earlier peoples felt the same way. However, it is worth remembering that it *is* feasible to travel on glaciers if one is willing to accept the risk and effort – in other words, when there is sufficient motivation. Early man *might* have crossed even relatively broad expanses of ice if he had some reason to do so – a goal ahead, or pressure behind – and thus simply demonstrating the presence of a valley glacier or a coalescent piedmont lobe in a certain area is not absolute proof that people could not have passed beyond it. It is possible, for instance, that staged supraglacial travel allowed people to reach discontinuous refugia in mountainous terrain, particularly if immediate goals were visible in the distance. Migratory animals such as caribou or birds crossing between more distant ice-free areas might have prompted occasional humans to set out in pursuit, particularly if they were sufficiently hungry. It has been demonstrated in the recent history of Arctic and Antarctic exploration that small groups can carry sufficient supplies in backpacks and simple sledges to support them or many weeks of constant travel over polar ice caps, if prepared in advance. While this is not to suggest that viable Paleoindian populations walked over the Laurentide Ice Sheet between Beringia and southern North America, it is intended to point out that limited cross-glacier travel *per se* was probably occasionally a feasible option. It also seems reasonable to suppose that if anyone ever knew how to minimize the risks and costs of such travel, it would have been the people of the Late Pleistocene.

If man did cross Late Wisconsinan glaciers on his way south from Beringia, direct evidence will probably never be found. More satisfying grist for the archaeologist's mill must be sought in known or inferred unglaciated portions of continental North America whose location, age, and characteristics suggest that they could have served as human habitats, and where archaeological data might be preserved. A prime candidate is the so-called "ice-free corridor."

The "ice-free corridor" runs through the minds of most Early Man specialists, if not in reality, like a highway beckoning Paleoindians south from Beringia. Thought to have been formed by incomplete coalescence or early retreat of eastern and western ice along a contact zone paralleling the eastern flanks of the Rocky Mountains, the ice-free corridor has figured prominently in archaeological speculation concerning the initial entry of man into southern North America. Here as elsewhere, however, controversy surrounds the exact limits and chronology of Late Wisconsinan ice advances, with proponents of maximum and minimum glacial models sometimes "staking all" on the interpretation of one of two crucial radiocarbon dates. These problems are complicated in the corridor area by the need to understand the detailed synchroneity and in-

teraction of glaciers from two very different and widely separated ice accumulation centers – the Laurentide on the east, and the Cordilleran on the west.

There is increasing agreement that a significant portion of southwestern Alberta remained ice-free during the Late Wisconsinan, at least as far north as the vicinity of Jasper-Edmonton (approximately 53°N) (Rutter, 1980; Stalker, 1980). Peat beds near Calgary, just above a C-14 date of 18,400 ± 380 B.P., indicate tundralike vegetation (Jackson, 1979, 1980a). In the Jasper-Edmonton area, Roed (1975) identified multiple undated Laurentide and Cordilleran tills. He attributed the three latest advances to successively weaker Late Wisconsinan glaciers, the earliest of which coalesced, causing a southward diversion of the ice flow and depositing the Foothills Erratics Train as far south as the U.S. border. However, the Foothills Erratics till has recently been radiocarbon-dated at >50,000 B.P. (Jackson, 1980a), indicating that the latest coalescence of eastern and western ice in the Jasper-Edmonton area was probably pre-Late Wisconsinan. Further north, a similar revision of stratigraphic correlations may also hinge on one or two crucial C-14 dates.

In the Peace River region of northeastern British Columbia, Rutter (1976) defined a sequence of Cordilleran advances of progressively diminishing intensity. The last three (Early Portage Mountain, Late Portage Mountain, and Deserter's Canyon) were attributed to the Late Wisconsinan and Holocene, respectively, on the basis of a date of 25,940 ± 380 B.P. "estimated" to underlie Early Portage Mountain till (Rutter, 1976, 1980), and a date originally reported of 11,600 ± 1,000 (Bryan, 1969) on a mammoth tusk found near Hudson Hope, in what is interpreted as a terminal moraine of the Late Portage Mountain advance. However, the original age estimate on the Portage Mountain tusk was in fact "greater than" 11,600 B.P., and the same specimen has now been redated at 25,800 ± 320 B.P. (Clague, 1980; Mathews, 1980).

It therefore seems that the limited Late Portage Mountain advance could represent the Late Wisconsinan Cordilleran maximum in this area. The other date of 25,940 B.P. could also be a maximum limiting age for this event, making Early Portage Mountain a pre-Late Wisconsinan glaciation. If this is the case, Cordilleran ice did not coalesce with Laurentide ice during the Late Wisconsinan in the Peace River area, and widespread undated evidence for high-level glaciation, previously interpreted as late, may correlate with an Early or pre-Wisconsinan phase (Mathews, 1980). The possibility that portions of the Peace River district remained ice-free during the Late Wisconsinan is supported by a sequence of dates of >30,000; 17,570 ± 650; 12,650 ± 320; and 10,740 ± 395 B.P. on a pollen core from near Grande Prairie, Alberta, lacking any stratigraphic evidence of glaciation (White et al., 1979). However, the presence of pre-Quaternary pollen indicates that the two older dates are maximum values, subject to an unknown old-carbon error (White, personal communication, 1981). Much may depend on the analysis of other lake cores in this region.

North of the Peace River area, relatively few data are available until about the vicinity of the British Columbia-Northwest Territories border (60°N), where positive evidence of ice-free terrain begins again and continues into the Eastern Yukon portion of Beringia (Hughes, 1972; Prest, 1969; Rutter, 1980).

Thus there is increasing support for a strip of ice-free terrain paralleling the western margin of the maximum Laurentide Ice Sheet, even during the Late Wisconsinan climax, as proposed by Reeves (1971, 1973). Wherever radiometric dates are available, it seems that Late Wisconsinan Cordilleran advances were probably confined to mountain and foothill valleys, and did not abut against Laurentide ice. Widespread evidence for more extensive glaciation, previously interpreted as Late Wisconsinan, is now increasingly suspected of being Early, if not pre-Wisconsinan in age. If Rocky Mountain glaciers were confined to valleys, extensive upland and alpine areas must have remained ice-free along the east side of the continental divide, regardless of the specific coalescence of the Cordilleran and Laurentide glaciers. In addition, uncertainty as to the synchroneity of Cordilleran and Laurentide frontal maxima along the "ice-free corridor" leaves open the possibility of a very complex, laterally expanding and contracting area of unglaciated terrain whose precise margins at any one time and place may not always be within the resolving power of standard geological procedures. If any ice coalescence did occur during the Late Wisconsinan in the "corridor," it is likely to have presented a significant barrier for only a relatively short time during the glacial climax.

Environment of the "Ice-Free Corridor"

People occupying the "ice-free corridor," or any other midcontinental zone close to margins of Late Pleistocene ice sheets, must have coped with a unique and demanding environment. Many specific details of this world can only be approximately reconstructed with current data, since there are no parallels today for the Pleistocene ice sheets that once terminated across the centers of midlatitude continents. The following is an attempt to reconstruct the environment of a midcontinental corridor, modeled as a narrow strip of unglaciated terrain paralleling the Rocky Mountain foothills from southeastern Beringia to the coterminous United States, during the climax of the Late Wisconsinan. Because data directly from the corridor area itself are limited, some inferences will necessarily be drawn from other ice-marginal areas.

Even if we assume that glacial coalescence was not complete at the maximum extent of glaciation, any ice-free terrain in the central region of the corridor (53-60°N) was probably restricted, perhaps to no more than a few

kilometers' width in places. The eastern boundary of the corridor was the Laurentide ice margin itself, stretching from the Mackenzie Mountains to Montana, while western limits were less definitely fixed by valley glaciers and mountains. Physiographically, the ultimate "corridor" was probably a complex region whose exact limits and characteristics varied with time-transgressive and possibly diachronous eastern and western ice margins.

As described for the advance phase of Wisconsinan glaciation, it is probable that the landscape immediately bordering major glacial termini were harsh, raw, and primitive. Anyone who has clambered over loose piles of rock rubble and skirted meltwater streams and ponds to reach the steep crevassed and dripping front of even a small modern glacier probably needs no convincing that massive Pleistocene frontal areas must have been unpleasant and oppressive. The geomorphic instability of periglacial regions in the corridor was probably also coupled with harsh climates.

Bryson et al. (1969) and Dreimanis (1977a) suggest that the high-domed Laurentide Ice Sheet blocked the southward flow of polar air masses, causing relatively warm temperatures close to the southern ice margin. *If* the Laurentide Ice Sheet was of sufficient height, and *if* polar regions were a more dominant source of cold air than the ice sheet itself, this would mean that any low divide between Arctic and southern regions would have funneled cold Arctic air into the Great Plains (as inferred by Bryson et al., 1969, for the early postglacial). The implication that an ice-free corridor was little more than a frigid wind-tunnel does not improve its prospects for early man. However, the possibility that the Laurentide Ice Sheet was thinner than traditionally modeled (see Andrews, 1980) might force revision of this hypothesis. Another theory that finds occasional mention is the possibility of adiabatically warmed air descending off glacial surfaces and raising temperatures along the ice front. Dreimanis (1977a) compares such winds to contemporary "chinooks" of the western plains and suggests that winters along the southern ice front during the Late Wisconsinan maximum could have been warmer than present. Although adiabatically warmed "föhn" winds do occur in and near mountain ranges, where air is rapidly warmed by compression as it is forced over the summit and down the lee side (see Money, 1965), it is not clear what driving mechanisms could account for any significantly warm airflow off the Laurentide Ice Sheet. Instead, it seems more likely that the dominant circulation off major glaciers was a katabatic drainage of cold dense air resulting from direct cooling of the lower atmosphere by ice. Continuous katabatic winds are inferred for the southern Laurentide margin by Lamb and Woodroffe (1970) and locally for portions of Beringia (off glaciated mountains) by Hopkins (1979). Cold airflow into the topographic depression of the ice-free corridor would have helped maintain low temperatures close to glacial fronts, adding to the harshness of what is even today a very continental climate. In addition, isolated topographic basins and interlobe areas might have acted as cold air traps, forming low-level pockets of particularly severe temperatures.

The above suggests a frigid environment directly adjacent to Late Pleistocene ice fronts in the corridor. However, conditions may have improved markedly only a few kilometers from the glaciers. Sugden (1977) calculates Laurentide surface atmosphere mean temperatures of $-20°$ to $-40°C$ over the ice sheet, rising to $-11°C$ to $+2°C$ just outside the margin, depending on latitude. Lamb and Woodroffe (1970), Dreimanis (1977a), and CLIMAP (1976) infer a steep temperature gradient along the southern Laurentide ice front, and this is supported by Rannie (1977), who measured an average $2.3°C$ summer temperature increase between the foot of a modern alpine glacier and a point 1.5 km down-valley. Thus, localities only a few kilometers from a glacier could have been markedly more favorable biotic habitats than the immediate ice-frontal zone. Particularly advantageous would have been areas some kilometers outside of the maximum limit of Late Wisconsinan glacial oscillations where relatively stable unglaciated landscapes could have maintained mature soils. South-facing uplands of mountains and foothills might have been relatively productive portions of the ice-free corridor complex, with maximum insolation, good drainage, and elevations above cold air layers lying on and near glaciers. There is apparent evidence for biota surviving the Late Wisconsinan in alpine refugia of the Southern Rockies (Packer, 1980), and the upland component of the ice-free corridor ecosystem should not be forgotten.

Laurentide glaciation completely blocked normal eastward drainage of west central Canada. While it is difficult to estimate how much water runoff would have occurred during the height of the maximum Late Wisconsinan glaciation, it is probable that there was sufficient seasonal meltwater to form proglacial pondages all along the Laurentide ice front (see, for example, Alley and Harris, 1974; Jackson, 1980a; Mathews, 1980; Roed, 1975). Christiansen (1979) feels that enormous water volumes were being discharged along the southern margins as early as 16-17,000 B.P. Lakes formed during the glacial maximum may have had most of their shorelines abutting against ice and, in some areas, pondages may have filled the "corridor" between the Cordilleran and Laurentide ice fronts. Cold, berg-laden, and probably biologically sterile, with unstable shorelines and fluctuating levels, such early lakes could only have been disadvantageous to any human inhabitants. However, since it is likely that all lakes froze solidly in winter, they probably would not have seriously hampered mammalian dispersals.

Direct evidence of biota in the ice-free corridor during the glacial climax is limited, and environmental reconstruction must depend on data from other regions. As discussed earlier, it is possible that the environment of eastern Beringia was an impoverished high Arctic tundra, perhaps capable of sustaining muskoxen but not much more, during the Late Wisconsinan peak (Cwynar and Ritchie, 1980). Given such conditions in relatively expansive Beringia, the narrow northern corridor, closely adjacent to a continental ice sheet, must have been even more harsh. Considering that a certain portion of the minimum corridor would have been occupied by raw morainal deposits, meltwater pondages, stagnant and buried ice blocks, and rugged mountain slopes, living conditions must have been extremely marginal. Constant cold wind, dust, bare rock, lakes, permafrost, and ice were probably dominant environmental features of at least the northern portion of the corridor. If the area was not biotically sterile, possibly only south-facing slopes and uplands could have maintained sufficient plant growth for even muskoxen. South of about 52-53°N, the ice-free area widened as the Laurentide ice front bends away to the southeast, and near Calgary a peat section directly overlying a radiocarbon date of $18,400 \pm 380$ B.P. indicates herbaceous tundralike vegetation, with sedge, grass, *Artemisia,* and willow shrubs at a time when the Laurentide ice margin was probably close by (Jackson, 1979, 1980a). This assemblage is comparable to the vegetation of central Beringia, raising the possibility of some ecological continuity between more southern ice-free areas and Alaska-Yukon, assuming any biota in the critical northern portion of the corridor. Although other zones close to the southern Laurentide Ice Sheet often possessed a boreal-forest or forest-tundra vegetation during the Late Wisconsinan climax (see, for example, Calkin and McAndrews, 1980; Gruger, 1972a; Lamb and Woodroffe, 1970; Whitehead, 1973; Wright, 1971a; Zant, 1979), there is no dated evidence of arboreal vegetation in the ice-free corridor region much before about 11,400-11,600 B.P. (Lichti-Federovich, 1970; Ritchie and Hare, 1971). This may confirm that the corridor was a harsher region than the lowland areas adjacent to the southern margins of the Laurentide glacier (Figure 2.4).

There are no significant faunal remains dated to the Late Wisconsinan in the critical central and northern portions of the corridor. However, as speculation it is interesting to note that one of the major intercontinental bird flyways currently parallels the route of the corridor, although the age of this pattern is not known. The identification of certain migratory birds in Beringian Late Wisconsinan faunal assemblages might confirm the presence of bird resting and feeding areas along the corridor, and hence a possible motivation for man to enter the area.

The overall question of the inhabitability of the narrow northern section of the ice-free corridor during Late

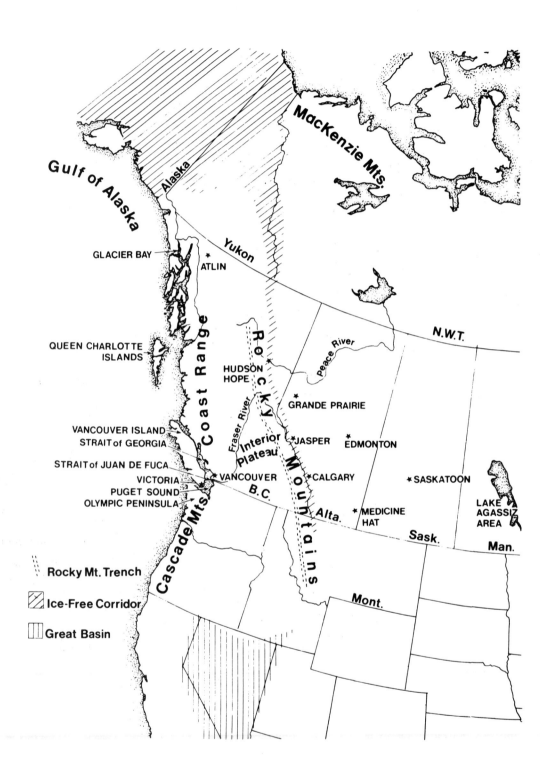

Figure 2.4   Geographical and Political Areas Mentioned in Chapter 2

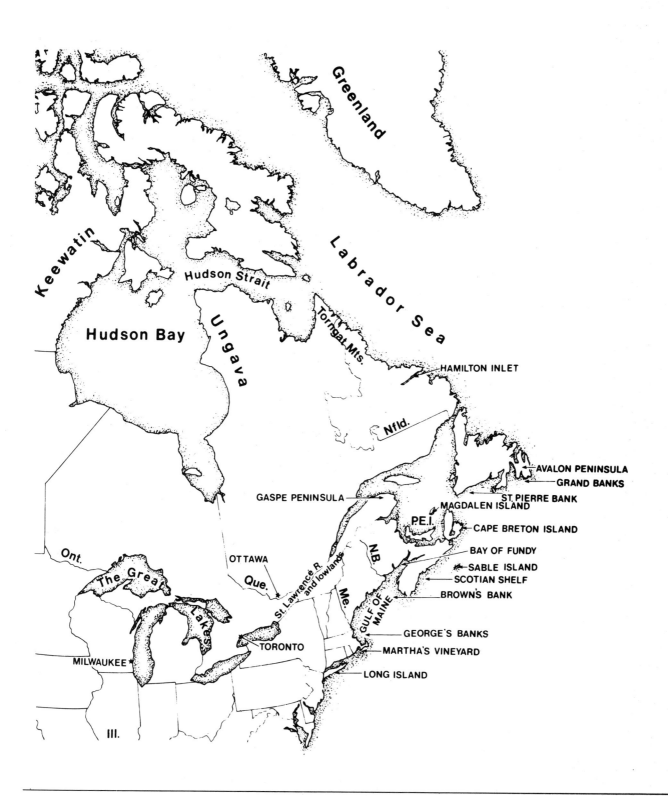

Wisconsinan maxima remains unanswered in any definite sense. We still cannot be certain that a strip of land did remain unglaciated, and if it did, whether it was capable of sustaining human life. If an "ultimate-minimum" corridor is a realistic concept, its human inhabitants must have been thoroughly adapted to squeezing an existence from what was probably one of the most barren and impoverished landscapes ever occupied by man. While perhaps not impossible, this implies a need for a very specialized technology and very strong motivations to move into such a region. Since conditions were probably significantly better just one or two thousand years before and after the glacial climaxes, it is difficult to understand why populations would choose the "worst" time to enter the area.

Arctic and Maritime Areas

In comparison to the relatively warm and productive Pacific coastline, the high Arctic Ocean and Islands must have presented a bleak aspect during the Late Wisconsinan period. Nevertheless, increasing data support a discontinuous chain of unglaciated insulae across the top of the Arctic archipelago and down the Baffin-Labrador coasts to the Maritime provinces. In size, spacing, and distribution, these approximate ice-free areas of the Pacific coast, but much more doubtul is the ability of such Arctic refugia to sustain human life (Figure 2.5).

Vocal adherents to a minimum glacial model for the Maritimes and the Arctic have been Grant (1977) and Ives (1978), who depict glaciers developing from a number of local ice sources and spreading "weakly towards, but in many areas not beyond, the present coast" (Grant, 1977: 247). According to Grant (1977, Fig. 1), potential Late Wisconsinan refugia in the Atlantic provinces include much of the eastern and northern coast of the Bay of Fundy, the northeastern highlands of Cape Breton, the southeastern Prince Edward Island, the Magdalen Islands, some of the coast of the Gaspé Peninsula, and many scattered headlands and promontories around the coast of Newfoundland. Grant (1977) and Tucker and McCann (1980) also see only minor Late Wisconsinan advances onto the south coast of Newfoundland, with ice confined to the valleys. Slatt (1977) and Alam and Piper (1977) find that the Avalon Peninsula ice cap encoached onto just a portion of the Grand Banks, leaving most of the shelf exposed as a "barren plain" crossed by small meltwater streams. Brooks (1977) states that Late Wisconsinan glaciers left extensive upland areas of southwest Newfoundland ice-free, and Prest (1977) confirms that the Magdalen Islands were not overridden by Late Wisconsinan glaciers. However, an ice tongue may have flowed across the western Gulf of Maine, culminating near Martha's Vineyard (Borns and Calkin, 1977; Bothner and Spiker, 1980).

Although Prest (1969) and Flint (1971) see Labrador and Ungava-Quebec as intensely glaciated – indeed, the final center of Laurentide glaciation, with an ice cap remaining in the area as late as 7-8,000 years ago – some data suggest that at least some small portions of Labrador may have remained ice-free throughout the Late Wisconsinan. Fulton and Hodgson (1979) see some support for an unglaciated area in southeastern Labrador, although they feel that coastal glaciation terminated seaward of the present shoreline north of Hamilton Inlet. Vilks and Mudie (1978) and Vilks (1980) use marine pollen deposits as evidence for floral refugia along the southern Labrador coast during the Late Wisconsinan, and suggest that many headlands and islands were left ice-free. However, van der Linden and Fillon (1976) infer repeated Late Wisconsinan ice sheet glaciation of the continental shelf off Hamilton Inlet. Ives et al. (1976) indicate unglaciated refugia in the Torngat Mountains of northern Labrador, and Ives (1977, 1978) also argues for unglaciated refugia along the coast of northern Labrador. Recent radiocarbon dates of 9980 ± 40;10,700 ± 540; 14,040 ± 780; 16,330 ± 330; and 16,975 ± 1,040 B.P. are reported on lake-bottom pollen cores from the central Labrador (Ungava) Peninsula (Stravers, 1980). If these dates can be accepted at face value, they may indicate that the traditional picture of Ungava-Labrador glaciation needs drastic revision. On the other hand, anomalous dates are not uncommon in pollen sections, and the significance of this series is not yet clear.

In the eastern and central Arctic, maximum Late Wisconsinan glaciation is now being increasingly perceived as both significantly weaker and substantially later than southern Laurentide maxima. Today, the bulk of opinion seems to favor a multiplicity of independent ice accumulation centers on the Arctic islands rather than one or more major, thick sheets (England, 1976; England and Bradley, 1978; Ives, 1974, 1978; Miller, 1980), which leads to the conclusion that many marginal and coastal areas remained unglaciated.

Extensive field data indicate that parts of the southeastern and northern coasts of Baffin Island remained ice-free during the maximum Late Wisconsinan, which in this area appears to have peaked about 8,500-11,000 years ago (Andrews, 1974; Andrews and Ives, 1978; Dyke, 1979; Ives, 1974, 1978; Miller, 1980; Nelson, 1980). On Ellesmere Island, Late Wisconsinan glaciation of the north and east coasts may not have been much more extensive than today (Andrews, 1974; England, 1976; Ives, 1974). Studies of northern Greenland and Ellesmere Island indicate that the Late Wisconsinan ice maximum was "extremely limited, leaving an ice-free corridor along Kennedy and Robeson Channels" (England and Bradley, 1978). In addition, some biota may have survived the Wisconsinan in refugia on northern Ellesmere Island (England, 1976; Ives, 1974). Late Wisconsinan glaciation of the Queen Elizabeth Islands was apparently restricted to upland ice caps (England, 1976), leaving coastal strips ice-free (Andrews 1974). Ives (1974) reviews data supporting the survival of mosses and possibly even mammals in Wisconsinan refugia of the Queen Elizabeth Islands, and organic samples from lakes on Axel Heiberg Island have been dated at 16-14,000 B.P. (England, 1976). McLaren and Barnett (1978) note that a Late Wisconsinan ice sheet just reached the southern end of Melville Island from the south, although the rest of the island was possibly affected by local ice caps. Even Prest (1969) and Flint (1971) agree that most of Banks Island remained ice-free during the last major glaciation, while Vincent (1978) detects no evidence of *any* significant Late Wisconsinan glaciation of that island. Even near the center of the Arctic archipelago, Dyke (1978) indicates that the last major glaciation of southern Somerset Island occurred before 38,000 B.P. and still left ice-free upland areas.

If the data described above are correct, there was a discontinuous series of ice-free coastal regions around at least the outer limits of the Arctic archipelago from Banks to Baffin Island and south to Labrador and the island of Newfoundland, the Grand Banks and southern Maritime provinces. It is important to note that Arctic and southern glacial advances may have been markedly diachronous, with northern glaciers culminating about 8-11,000 B.P., several thousand years after the climax of southern Laurentide advances (Andrews, 1974; Miller, 1980). Thus, it is possible that more high-latitude land was ice-free at the time of the southern (Laurentide) glacial maximum than later, when southern Laurentide ice had partly retreated.

The extent to which potential Arctic and Atlantic refugia were affected by late glacial sea-levels is dependent on their proximity to accumulation centers. If Arctic ice masses were still significantly restricted at the time of maximum midlatitude glaciations, eustatically lowered sea-levels might have enlarged and connected some northern refugia. On the other hand, relative sea-levels associated with the latest Arctic glacial climax (8-11,000 B.P.) were higher than at present in all cases (see, for example, Vincent, 1978; Dyke, 1979; Nelson, 1980).

In the Maritime provinces, Grant (1980) shows Late Wisconsinan marine sea-levels as low as − 75 to − 100 m on the outer Grand Banks and Scotian Shelf, where dated shells mark shorelines of 17-19,000 B.P. (Muller and Milliman, 1973). Closer to major ice centers, relative sea-levels up to + 125 m occurred during the late glacial maximum (Grant, 1980). Thus, extensive Late Wisconsinan ice-free areas may have existed off the southern Maritime provinces, in the George's, Sable Island, St. Pierre, and Grand Banks areas, at the same time as much higher sea-levels restricted the extent of northern low altitude refugia (compare Grant, 1977).

To summarize information about northern and eastern North America during the Late Wisconsinan, there is doubt that a single ice sheet totally inundated the landscape in the manner traditionally assumed. Instead, numerous local ice caps probably spread and coalesced, leaving in many

areas unglaciated coastal headlands, islands, and uplands. Some of these were substantial in size (particularly the off-shore Maritimes refugia), although most were probably relatively small and discontinuous. In the Arctic, the lack of synchroneity with southern glacial advances implies that large areas may still have been ice-free during the southern Laurentide glacial climax. Although ice-free Arctic land masses may be proven, their potential suitability for human occupation is far from certain. Few organic remains have been dated as Late Wisconsinan in the high Arctic, and the suggestion that the region then possessed a harsh environment is probably an understatement. It is possible that the Arctic Ocean remained permanently and thickly frozen during the last stadial, although Hunkins et al. (1971) suggest seasonal thawing similar to the present for the last 80,000 years. It is worth noting that several authors have argued for some biotic survival in the east central Arctic throughout the Wisconsinan, including even land mammals (Harington, 1980a; Ives, 1974; McPherson, 1965). However, until sufficient data have accumulated to reconstruct the environment, the significance of such ice-free Arctic regions must remain uncertain.

From Baffin Island southward, an important debate centers around the ice cover of the Baffin Bay/Davis Strait/Labrador Sea area. Johnson and Andrews (1979), Ruddiman and MacIntyre (1979), and Ruddiman et al. (1980) support open water west of Greenland, to account for the rapid build-up of glacial ice and maintenance of the Greenland Ice Sheet during the Wisconsinan. However, van der Linden and Fillon (1976) and Fillon (1980) argue that the Labrador Sea was intensely ice-covered (up to 600 m thickness) 18-10,000 B.P., with meltwater streams discharging over the ice shelf during deglaciation. Their conclusion is directly countered by Vilks (1980), who suggests that Labrador sea-ice conditions have been similar to the present for the last 20,000 years – that is, melting every summer, with local marine productivity at least as high as at present.

In the Maritime provinces and adjacent coastal shelf, potential unglaciated areas are substantially larger than to the north, and thus the probability of feasible human habitats increases. Any glacial climax vegetation in such areas was probably tundralike, as indicated for Labrador (Vilks and Mudie, 1978), Maine (Davis et al., 1975), and Long Island (Sirkin and Stuckenrath, 1975). Meltwater streams probably crossed the exposed banks (Slatt, 1977), and land fauna, including proboscideans, may have occupied George's and Brown's Banks (MacDonald, 1971). The suitability of the Late Wisconsinan eastern seaboard as a potential human habitat seems assured, at least from Nova Scotia southward.

Late Wisconsinan Climax: Summary

Late Wisconsinan glacial maxima probably occurred between 18,000 and 22,000 B.P. for the southern boun-

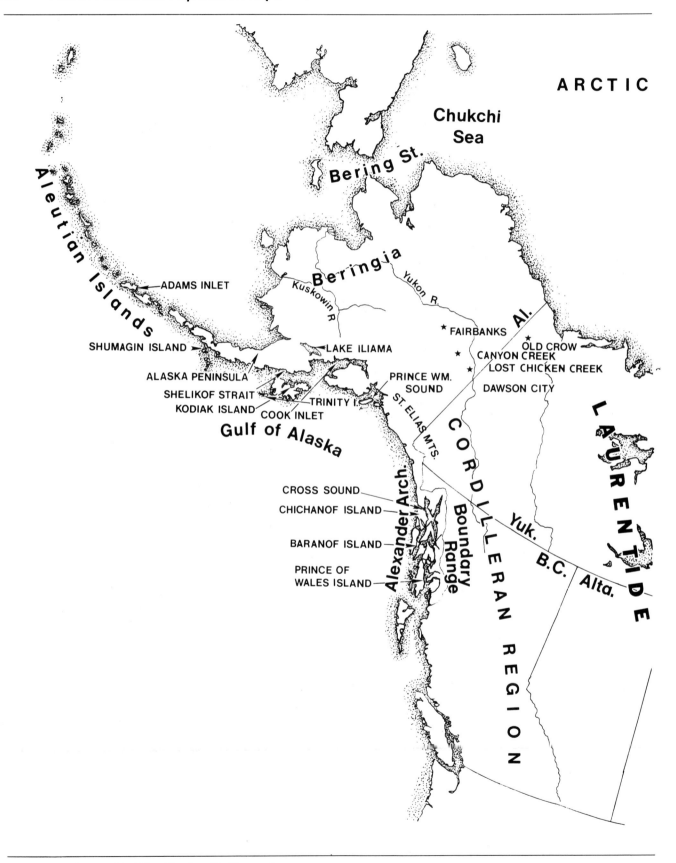

Figure 2.5   Geographical Sites Mentioned in Chapter 2

OCEAN

ROBESON
CHANNEL

KENNEDY
CHANNEL

ELLESMERE ISLAND

AXEL HE'BERG
ISLAND

QUEEN ELIZABETH
ISLANDS

GREENLAND

★CAMP CENTURY

MELVILLE
ISLAND

Baffin Bay

BANKS
ISLAND

VISCOUNT
MELVILLE SD.

LANCASTER SD.

SOMERSET
ISLAND

Davis Strait

Baffin Island

N.W.T.

Sask.

Man.

Hudson

Bay

R E G I O N

dary of the Laurentide Ice Sheet (with a near-maximum terminal position as late as circa 14,500 B.P., particularly in the west); 14,500-15,000 B.P. for the southern boundary of the Cordilleran glacier complex; and perhaps as late as 11-8,000 B.P. in the eastern Arctic. Laurentide glaciers had most effect on restricting available terrain in the central portion of the continent, and at the maximum extent, only three areas of ice-free ground could have been potential pathways for human infiltration beyond Beringia. An Arctic-East Coast Route may be indicated by a chain of discontinuous unglaciated island and coastal areas, but was possibly environmentally incapable of supporting human life in northern areas. The ice-free corridor down the western edge of the Laurentide ice mass is increasingly supported by geological data. However, its biological carrying capacity is unknown, but was probably very limited, particularly in narrow northern portions. Finally, a Pacific coastal route may be indicated by a series of probably unglaciated insulae, but doubt remains as to the accessibility of these areas from the main Beringian land mass. If accessible, there seems every reason to believe that they could have sustained human life, particularly for boat-using, maritime-oriented people.

In all areas, we cannot yet be confident that any route was definitely available for human travel beyond Beringia during the few millenia or centuries of maximum glacial extension; nor can we say with certainty that all gates were closed. Even the inhabitability or desirability of central and eastern Beringia itself may be questioned at the peak of the glacial period. What can be said with some certainty is that the time in which human penetration of northern North America is in doubt, on strictly environmental grounds, is *very short* in comparison to the total duration of the Mid and Late Wisconsinan. Maximum restriction of the midcontinental ice-free corridor probably occurred for short intervals between about 25,000 and 15,000 B.P., and the corridor was inhabitable before and after these events. Southern Cordilleran glaciers achieved their final 100-200 km of extension for only a moment of geological time, sometime between about 17,000 and 14,500 B.P., if dating of the Vashon-Puget-Juan de Fuca lobe is representative. Before and after this maximum interval, environmental quality improved rapidly. Some outer portions of the Northwest Coast remained unglaciated as late as 17,000 B.P. and were certainly again ice-free and available for reoccupation prior to 13,000 B.P. (see Mathews, 1979), if not throughout the Late Wisconsinan. Thus, the Northwest Coast may have been inhabitable longer than the midcontinental area, and at 17-18,000 B.P. may still have been available at a time when the corridor was near maximum closure.

Late Wisconsinan-Early Recessional Phase

The final scenario dealt with in this chapter is the early recessional phase of the Late Wisconsinan, circa 15,000-11,000 B.P. This period is the only one of the four that overlaps with definite archaeological finds and, as a result, human interaction with North American environments is no longer hypothetical.

In the southern Laurentide area, ice margins retreated progressively northward after the Erie Interstade (Dreimanis, 1977a). The Port Bruce advance, which ended the Erie Interstade, was short-lived, culminating about 14,500 B.P., and was followed immediately by another drastic recession termed the Mackinaw Interstade (Dreimanis, 1977a). This involved a glacial retreat of 600 km by about 13,300 B.P. during which plants and animals, including mastodons, probably moved into the deglaciated area. The Mackinaw Interstade signaled a significant weakening of the Laurentide Ice Sheet, and later readvances were far less extensive. In the Great Lakes area, the Mackinaw interstadial was followed by the Port Huron readvance, which culminated about 13,000 B.P. It was a much less extensive event than earlier stades (Dreimanis, 1977a) and was succeeded by the controversial Two Creekan-Valderan (Great Lakean) sequence (see, for example, Black, 1980; Evenson et al., 1976; Fullerton, 1980). Whatever the dating and correlation of the type locality, it seems that the Valderan substage was not as extensive as traditionally pictured, but was a brief and relatively unimportant readvance in an overall trend of rapid retreat (Dreimanis, 1977a).

A drastic retreat of glaciers seems to be registered in many regions of the northern hemisphere circa 13-14,000 B.P., immediately following an extensive advance. This occurs in the southern Cordillera (Clague et al., 1980) and portions of the southwestern Laurentide margin (Dreimanis, 1977a; Jackson, 1980a; Mercer, 1972; Teller and Fenton, 1980; Teller et al., 1980). In New England, ice that remained near Martha's Vineyard as late as 15,300 B.P. had retreated past the present coast of Maine by 13,500 B.P. (Borns and Calkin, 1977), while glaciers abandoned northern New York State between 15,000 and 12,700 B.P. (Calkin and McAndrews, 1980). Also, a calving bay deglaciated the Gulf of St. Lawrence and the river as far upstream as Lake Ontario and Ottawa by about 12,800 B.P. (Borns and Hughes, 1977; Prichonnet, 1977; Thomas, 1977). Hopkins (1979) describes 14,000 B.P. as a time of abrupt, worldwide climatic warming, signaled in Beringia by rapid deglaciation, a rise in sea-level, and a shift toward more mesic vegetation. The Camp Century ice core registers an almost instantaneous transition between glacial and interglacial climates about 13,000 B.P. (Dansgaard et al., 1971; Morner, 1977), a shift that is echoed in a number of northern North American pollen assemblages about this time (Ager, 1980; Maxwell and Davis, 1972; Sirkin et al., 1977; Sirkin and Stuckenrath, 1975; Zant, 1979). From an archaeological standpoint, an age of 13-14,000 B.P. is probably the *earliest* time for permanently ice-free conditions and possible human inhabitants in areas within known maximum Late Wisconsinan ice boundaries. After 14,000 B.P., glacial margins continued their oscillating retreat. By 11-12,000 B.P., sufficient quality of environment to permit human occupancy can be demonstrated well within all maximum glacial boundaries, and by 9-10,000 B.P., Late Wisconsinan ice sheets were greatly diminished (see Prest, 1969).

Coupled with deglaciation was a rapid eustatic rise in world sea-levels. The Bering Strait developed as a narrow seaway around 13-14,000 B.P. and became a significant water barrier by about 12,000 B.P. (Hopkins, 1979). Eustatic transgression along the Atlantic seaboard may have caused rates of up to approximately 3 m of *lateral* shoreline movement annually (Fairbridge, 1977), obviously hampering permanent coastal settlements. I calculate that the Holocene trangression drowned a total land area around North and Central America equal to over 1.5 times the size of Texas, assuming a net rise overall of 100 m.

The Ice-Free Corridor During Deglaciation

Around the western margin of the Laurentide Ice Sheet, the ice-free corridor may have widened significantly by 14,000 B.P. (see Christiansen, 1979; St. Onge, 1980; Stalker, 1980), probably improving its potential as a human habitat. Glacial recession led to large volumes of meltwater forming proglacial pondages and outwash drainages. Christiansen (1979) suggests that most meltwater discharge occurred early in deglaciation, indicating a considerable loss in ice-sheet thickness before significant marginal recession, and that greater meltwater volumes were released in the south than in the north. Immense proglacial pondages did form all along the Laurentide margin during its eastward recession, the largest of which (Lake Agassiz) exceeded the size of the combined modern Great Lakes (Ashworth et al., 1972; Bluemel, 1974; Christiansen, 1979; Elson, 1967; Teller and Fenton, 1980). Lake Agassiz and Lake McConnell further to the north represent final stages of a sequence of shifting, coalescing pondages that migrated across central Canada on the heels of the retreating ice front, beginning with the frigid lakes of the maximum glacial corridor. Virtually all of central and southern Alberta, Saskatchewan, and Manitoba is mantled with lake sediments, reflecting the importance of lacustrine environments during the early postglacial period (Andrews, 1973; Prest et al., 1969).

It seems likely that during the early phases of deglaciation, cold temperatures, high sediment loads, sporadic changes in level and meltwater input, and lack of suitable connections with mature unglaciated drainages would have maintained aquatic ecosystems at very low levels of productivity (see Gibbard and Dreimanis, 1978). Tuthill (1967) identified several species of mollusks and inferred two species of fish for glacial Lake Agassiz, but these cannot be dated specifically. With time, it is likely that more stable pondages hosted increasingly productive ecosystems, particularly as drainage connectivity developed and outwash discharge declined. Although Lake Agassiz was a virtual

inland sea at its maximum extent, and some other lakes were also very large, they all undoubtedly froze firmly in winter and so should not have presented absolute barriers to pedestrian travelers.

Human populations expanding eastward from Eurasia, through Beringia, to southern North America would have encountered major lakes all along their path. The Lake Mansi complex in west central Siberia covered over 1.5 million km² (Grosswald, 1980), while a substantial lake even existed on the emerged Beringian shelf (Hopkins, 1979). The Old Crow, Bell, and Bluefish Lakes continued the pattern in eastern Beringia (Morlan, 1979, 1980a), and innumerable pondages existed through the late glacial and early postglacial stages of the corridor. Further south, in the unglaciated United States, enlarged pluvial pondages of the Great Basin area might be considered equivalent features. Given a widespread occurrence of large lakes during the Late Wisconsinan, it is tempting to speculate about a special role for lacustrine environments in early human adaptations. However, there is little evidence to indicate that such lakes were anything other than features to be avoided by man until stable aquatic ecosystems became established.

Despite a watery landscape, there is reason to be optimistic about the human potential of the midcontinental area after about 13-14,000 B.P. This optimism reflects a sharply increasing probability that the environment could have supported human life by that time. Freshly deglaciated ground would have been bare and raw, but with warming temperatures after 14,000 B.P., a major limitation on plant and animal life lifted, and recolonization probably proceeded rapidly. The presence of spruce forest in the central and northern corridor by 11,600-11,400 B.P. (Lichti-Federovich, 1970; Ritchie, 1980) suggests that the entire area was probably capable of sustaining herbaceous communities well before that time. In many portions of the Laurentide region, freshly deglaciated ground seems to have been initially colonized by herbaceous tundralike vegetation, followed by spruce-dominated forests (Anderson and Davis, 1980; Mott, 1975, 1977; Mott and Farley-Gill, 1978; Richard, 1977; Saarnisto, 1974; Terasmae, 1980; Whitehead, 1979).

The lacustrine landscape of the Plains continued during the Late Wisconsinan recession into the east, where the Great Lakes, St. Lawrence River, and associated systems underwent a complex evolution, including alternating lake levels, replacement of successive meltwater spillways and lake outlets, and marine transgressions (see, for example, Cronin, 1977; Dreimanis, 1977a, 1977b; Fullerton, 1980; Terasmae, 1980). People trying to reach freshly deglaciated terrain north of the Great Lakes-St. Lawrence system would have faced, at certain times and places, large lakes, wide and occasionally torrential meltwater channels and spillways, and an extensive marine incursion well up the St. Lawrence.

Ogden (1977) notes that crossing some of the meltwater drainages of the northeast could have posed a formidable challenge, and that the trans-St. Lawrence area might not have been easily accessible from the south. When we examine Late Wisconsinan North American paleogeography in general, it seems improbable that people could ever have dispersed south of Beringia without some knowledge of practical watercraft to allow negotiation of the broad rivers and lakes. Of course, they may have patiently awaited freeze-up before crossing every significant water body, but it seems more reasonable to expect that watercraft of some type were a basic part of the Paleoindian toolkit.

The Southern Cordillera During Deglaciation

In the southern Cordilleran region, the Vashon-Puget lobe had retreated north of Seattle by 13,650 ± 550 B.P., while the Vashon-Juan de Fuca lobe began downwasting 14,460 ± 200 B.P. (Heusser, 1973; Thorson, 1980). Vancouver was deglaciated prior to 13,000 B.P. (Clague et al., 1980) and lodgepole pine forest was established on adjacent slopes by 12,600 B.P. (Mathewes, 1973). Heusser (1973) indicates that a coniferous forest was established supraglacially on stagnant Juan de Fuca ice by 12-13,000 B.P., a situation paralleled by modern "tilted" forests on glaciers of southeastern Alaska (Post, 1976). Meltwater proglacial lakes followed the retreating ice front northward from Puget Sound until the ocean flooded the basin about 13,000 B.P. (Thorson, 1980). Maximum marine transgressions followed deglaciation of the Fraser Valley and other inner coastal lowlands, with sea-levels briefly up to 100-200 m higher than present. Isostatic adjustment at 13,000-10,000 B.P. sometimes achieved rates that would probably have permitted clear perception of significant vertical sea-level change in a normal human lifetime (see, for example, Armstrong, 1981; Mathews et al., 1970). In interior valleys, deglaciation proceeded by a lowering of glacial surfaces, exposing the uplands first (Fulton, 1967, 1975). Major glacial blocks probably still existed in some southern valleys as late as about 11-13,000 B.P., accounting for the damming of 600-m-deep Lake Missoula in northern Idaho and Montana, and other pondages throughout the southern interior of British Columbia. The Lake Missoula ice dam finally broke shortly after 13,000 B.P., releasing catastrophic floods across central Washington (Easterbrook, 1976; Mullineaux et al., 1978). Although a late glacial readvance seems to be indicated in the Fraser Valley about 11,300 B.P. (the Sumas Stade) (Armstrong, 1981; Fulton 1971), its regional significance was probably minimal, and the overall pace of deglaciation was generally rapid and unbroken by major stillstands and readvances.

In sum, Cordilleran deglaciation was underway by about 14,500 B.P., and significant biotic communities were established along the coast by at least 12,500-13,000 B.P. Human occupation of parts of the outer Pacific Coast by at least this time seems completely feasible given relatively minor postglacial marine transgressions in that area. Minimum dates for initial inhabitability of interior valleys and plateaux are not yet firmly established, but 11-12,000 B.P. for at least the uplands seems a conservative estimate, and it is likely that many areas were available substantially earlier.

Review and Discussion

A review of Mid to Late Wisconsinan environments indicates that natural limitations on human populations infiltrating North America varied considerably in the last 60,000 years. In trying to predict and understand the theoretical range of potential early cultural adaptive systems operative in the New World, it is necessary first to know the range of environmental parameters that might have shaped and controlled cultural options. Such parameters would have been very different between 40-50,000; 15-20,000; or 14-10,000 B.P., and one would expect that cultures reaching unglaciated parts of the New World at any of these times would exhibit adaptive attributes related to the specific scheduling and routing of their passage through northern, ultimately glaciated regions.

The Mid-Wisconsinan nonglacial interval from 60 to 25,000 B.P. was a time when man achieved wide dispersal in other parts of the world and might have been a favorable interval for human population expansion through North America. Certainly glaciation did not present any significant barriers to humans in western and central Canada. However, three other factors, alone or in combination, may have imposed restraints on the extent, rate, and nature of human dispersals and adaptations in the New World. First is the fact that Bering Strait was flooded, at least as a narrow seaway, through part of Mid-Wisconsinan time, not emerging as a land-bridge until the onset of Late Wisconsinan glaciation circa 25,000 B.P. Although the shallow straits of the Mid-Wisconsinan may have lacked the strong tidal currents of the Holocene (compare Hopkins, 1979), minimum water distances of 10-20 km in width would have existed and, while at least seasonally frozen, may have required from man some kind of ability for cross-water travel.

Once in continental Alaska, Mid-Wisconsinan immigrants faced an Arctic environment probably cooler than at present and a mainly tundralike vegetation with scattered arboreal elements. Beringian megafauna were probably richer for at least part of Mid-Wisconsinan time than they were during the Late Wisconsinan. Human populations attempting to spread beyond Beringia in North America would have found no significant glacial barrier to expansion west of Hudson Bay. It is conceivable, therefore, that population elements could have spread some distance south into coastal, mountain, plateau, or plains regions during the Mid-Wisconsinan. Although population expansion along the Pacific coast would have involved no significant maritime ecological transition for people already used to the south coast of Beringia, others moving southward through the interior would eventually have faced new vegetation zones. In particular, they probably encountered boreallike coniferous-mixed forests in considerable depth before passing beyond the ultimately glaciated region of North America. Although this may not have presented any serious difficulty, particularly if the forest was relatively open (see Morlan, 1980a), it is also conceivable that incentives to enter forests were few, in comparison to the rich game resources of the steppe-tundra. Thus, speculatively, man may not have penetrated far from Beringia before the onset of the next glacial phase. Perhaps this accounts for possible evidence of Mid-Wisconsinan man at Old Crow that seems stronger than any equivalently dated materials south of the Wisconsinan ice front.

If Mid-Wisconsinan cultural materials are ever unequivocally identified in northern interior North America, it is likely that they will exhibit adaptation to cold steppe-tundra, littoral, and possibly boreal forest environments. Mandatory equipment for survival in this landscape almost certainly included shelters, tailored hide and fur clothing, watercraft, fire, and group hunting techniques. It is likely that a wide range of animal resources were utilized, including large, medium, and small mammals, as well as fish and mollusks, depending on local availability. It is improbable that plant foods formed any significant part of the diet. If early Beringian maritime-oriented, boat-using cultures existed, they should have been able to live along the entire coast of North America with little difficulty, in the sense of not encountering any radically different marine environments from Beringia to Washington State.

During the advance phase of Late Wisconsinan glaciation, any hypothetical human occupants of northern North America would have faced progressive environmental change or deterioration. The rate at which this occurred is still not established with certainty. However, if various models of "instantaneous glacierization" are correct, environmental degradation of large areas of northern Canada possibly occurred sufficiently suddenly to cause problems for existing fauna. However, it is likely that most mammalian populations, including man, simply shifted their range in response to a relatively slowly diminishing ice-free area in west central Canada. The ultimate impetus for range adjustment would have been the advancing glaciers themselves, and occasionally animals might have continued to occupy regions right up to the ice fronts. Generally, however, fauna probably responded to the indirect factors such as lowering temperatures, ecological degradation, and drainage changes well in advance of actual glaciers.

With time, the Laurentide ice front came close to and possibly coalesced with some Cordilleran glaciers along the Rocky Mountain foothills. The ice may have first achieved this maximum position around 55-60° N, with increasing closure north and south of the original maximum point with time, assuming the usual model of southward and southwestward advancement out of a Keewatin center. Thus the glaciers may have formed a biotic divide across west central Canada, forcing plants and animals to the northwest and southwest of the expanding "bulge" of the Laurentide Ice Sheet. Any people not yet south of 55-60° N may have been displaced back into Beringia as the Laurentide Ice Sheet continued to expand, while populations already south of the glacial biotic divide may have been wedged further southward. If people were in west central Canada during the growth of Late Wisconsinan glaciation, the net effect of the ice advance would have been to force some westward into eastern Beringia (and perhaps British Columbia, depending on the synchroneity of maximum stages) and others southward along the advancing ice margins.

Other environmental attributes of the Late Wisconsinan advance phase include further cooling, which would have heightened the demand for cold-adapted cultures. With the advance of ice sheets, the overall continental area of animal habitat was reduced, and increasing population pressures in small refugia and in areas closest to the ice front may, speculatively, have contributed to unusual predator-prey ratios, and possibly to the short-term advantage of humans. In some cases, fauna and man may have replaced original interior habitats with increasingly coastward locations as glaciation developed, perhaps tending to concentrate more diverse species in the coastal strips. Although cultural adaptive requirements probably remained basically the same as for the Mid-Wisconsinan, relatively rapid environmental change would possibly have demanded development of more flexible or generalized strategies as populations were forced into new and qualitatively different habitats. In addition, the early formation of an icy biotic divide across central Canada might have been the beginning of increasing cultural differentiation between isolated northern and southern populations.

The attainment of maximum glacial conditions in North America apparently occurred at varied dates in different regions. While some of the Laurentide Ice Sheet was already at maximum extent in 22-18,000 B.P., the Cordillera was just starting its major glacial accumulation, and the eastern and central Arctic had not yet begun to experience significant ice build-up. This diachroneity must be reckoned with when comparing the inhabitability of different regions during the Late Wisconsinan.

Although some researchers have emphasized the high carrying capacity of a xerophytic "Arctic-steppe" biome inferred for Late Wisconsinan Beringia, the actual productivity and extent of this zone may be in doubt. Faunal remains dated directly to the Late Wisconsinan suggest a much more impoverished animal assemblage than is usually reconstructed, supporting Cwynar and Ritchie's (1980) concept of a harsh and meager Beringian environment. Probably the richest areas lay along the Pacific coast, with decreasing productivity toward easternmost Beringia.

In the Cordillera, south of Beringia, dated evidence for Late Wisconsinan ice limits is scarce except near the southern limits of the glaciated zone. In this region, Late Wisconsinan ice did not begin to encroach on the lowlands until after circa 18-19,000 B.P. Southern Cordilleran coastal glaciers did not cover their final 100-200 km until sometime between 17,000 and 14,500 B.P. Even during the brief glacial maximum, there is reason to believe that a chain of coastal islands, headlands, and uplands remained ice-free, possibly enlarged by lower outer coast sea-levels, and potentially available as biotic refugia. Given unglaciated ground at sea-level around the north Pacific, its biological productivity and potential as a human habitat seems certain. Less definite is the accessibility of such areas from Beringia, with traditionally extensive models of glaciation on the Alaska Peninsula implying a barrier to coastal travel. However, if dating of the southwestern lobe of the Cordilleran complex is applicable to the whole region, the duration of *maximum* Late Wisconsinan glacial conditions on the Pacific Coast was very short. By at least 13,000 B.P., substantial portions of the outer coast were probably ice-free and potentially inhabitable, as inferred by mollusk-bearing glaciomarine sediments along most of the mountainous inner coast by that time, and by a lodgepole pine forest near Vancouver at 12,600 B.P. Thus, even if the Pacific Coast was impassable during the "instant" of maximum glaciation, there is little doubt of its basic inhabitability shortly before and shortly after 17,000-13,000 B.P.

Increasing geological data also support limited and relatively late glaciation of the high Arctic. Here another chain of ice-free coastal areas stretches from Banks Island in the west to Baffin Island, Labrador, and the Atlantic provinces in the east. This route may have to be considered as a possible means for man entering southern North America from Beringia, if Arctic portions can be shown to have been anything other than polar desert. As noted earlier, some authors have argued for Wisconsinan biotic refugia in the high Arctic, and given people able to cope with the glacial climax environment of eastern Beringia, they might, theoretically, have been able to expand into the eastern Arctic. This hypothesis would be made stronger if it is ever shown conclusively that parts of the Arctic Ocean seasonally thawed during the Late Wisconsinan. While seemingly improbable at the moment, particularly given the apparent recency of even Holocene occupation of polar regions, the possibility of Wisconsinan human dispersals by this route probably should not be discarded completely.

In the midcontinent, any human occupants during 18-15,000 B.P. either lived on the ice itself or scraped a living from periglacial refugia along the "ice-free corridor." While few Early Man investigators have seriously con-

sidered human cross-glacier travel during the Pleistocene, there is no a priori reason to discard this possibility for relatively short distances, where sufficient motivation existed. If anyone occupied the narrow northern confines of the hypothetical glacial-maximum ice-free corridor, they must have lived close to glacial fronts, in what was probably a raw, frigid, and oppressive periglacial environment.

With a dramatic shift to warmer temperatures circa 14,000 B.P., ice masses began to recede rapidly and doubtful refugia of the maximum phase became quickly and assuredly ice-free and colonizable by plants and animals. Thus there is reason to be confident of the inhabitability of a narrow midcontinental strip joining Beringia and the coterminous United States 12-13,000 years B.P., perhaps just a little later than on the Pacific Coast. By this time glacial margins were substantially receded, the climate was warmer than it had been for the last 40-50,000 years, and for a short interval tundralike vegetation *may* have been continuous through the corridor with Beringia, just before the advance of forest.

Coupled with diminishing glacial mass, a great outpouring of meltwater caused short-lived proglacial lakes to form over most of the Prairie provinces. Although similar enlarged pondages were a widespread aspect of the late Pleistocene throughout the northern hemisphere, they were probably mainly negative factors as far as human inhabitants were concerned, since early stages of glacial drainage systems and lakes were biologically unproductive. However, the presence of numerous lakes and meltwater channels suggests that even interior continental hunting cultures would have required a capacity to build and use watercraft.

Along formerly glaciated ocean margins, rapidly rising sea-levels would have forced inhabitants of former coastal refugia up-slope and inland, and possibly prohibited stable coastal adaptations for a time, particularly along low gradient coastal plains. This suggests that coastal cultures may have been under some stress and forced into increased mobility during deglaciation.

Conclusions

During the Late Wisconsinan, only three possible routes existed for human movement out of Beringia, but their actual suitability or accessibility cannot be proven for the glacial maximum per se. An Arctic-Atlantic route seems least likely due to probable environmental harshness. Any cultures capable of survival in this area must have had an extreme level of adaptation to cold, barren environments. A midcontinental corridor seems increasingly supported by geological data, but any ice-free strip directly adjacent to the maximum Laurentide ice sheet would have been a marginal area for human survival. Although Pacific Coast refugia probably enjoyed milder climates and greater biological productivity than the other areas, during the brief glacial climax they cannot be proven to have been accessible from Beringia. If the coast was occupied, the cultural orientation must have been mainly littoral-maritime, including fishing, shellfish collecting, and possibly sea-mammal hunting. Boats of some sort seem mandatory. Unfortunately, people moving by watercraft leave few if any archaeological traces, and theoretically even primitive boats could traverse the entire Pacific Coast of North and South America in less than 10-15 years!

In summary, the Mid and Late Wisconsinans include a wide range of environmental variables, operative at different times and places, that might have affected human dispersal through North America, as well as types of cultural systems that filtered into unglaciated regions. In the last 60,000 years, only a very small proportion of time witnessed any absolute barriers to human infiltration through Canada. However, human expansion during the last glacial maximum (particularly 18-15,000 B.P.) would definitely have been far more difficult than at any other time before or after. Nevertheless, some human movement might have been possible during all or most of the climax phase, particularly via the relatively mild and resource-rich Pacific Coast.

Any interior cultures of the Mid-Wisconsinan, or of advance and climax phases of the Late Wisconsinan, must have been thoroughly adapted to cold Arctic/Polar to Subarctic environments, including the capability to keep warm and fed in some of the harshest landscapes ever faced by man. These were not places for ill-equipped, non-preadapted peoples. Coastal peoples, on the other hand, would have enjoyed at all times the advantage of the continuity of a rich maritime environment around the Pacific rim. Relatively mild climates and easy water travel would have eased the movement of bands of mixed age and sex composition, making the Pacific Coast probably the most attractive route for human dispersals south of Beringia at all times. Here also, there was more possibility for less specialized technologies (intertidal collecting requires little technology at all) in comparison to interior adapations.

The Mid-Wisconsinan may have been a feasible time for initial human entry and dispersal in the New World, par-

ticularly in terms of the absence of significant glacial obstacles and the presence of productive biota. However, unlike the recessional stages of the Late Wisconsinan, Mid-Wisconsinan climates were generally cold, and it is not yet *proven* that human populations existed as far north as Beringia anywhere in the world at this time. Thus, the post-13-14,000 B.P. period seems particularly attractive as a time for midcontinental human population expansion into and through the New World, due to climatic amelioration unequaled in the previous 40,000 years. Shortly after the initiation of deglaciation, a hypothetical interval may have existed in which herbaceous communities formed a continuous ecological link from Beringia to central North America, prior to the expansion of forests. Coupled with warm temperatures, abundant water, and significantly receded ice margins, this might have been an optimum, albeit brief interval (12-13,000 B.P.) for animal and human expansion throughout the continent.

In short, human occupation of North America cannot be proven environmentally "impossible" for any time in the last 60,000 years, although the climax of the last glaciation (particularly 18,000-15,000 B.P.) would seem least favorable. Before or after glacial maxima, human dispersals through North America were much more feasible. Midcontinental cultures prior to 13-14,000 B.P. must have been well adapted to stringent Arctic-type environments. However, on the Pacific Coast, more mesic environments may have permitted greater cultural flexibility within the overall limitations of generalized littoral-maritime adaptations. After 13-14,000 B.P., dramatically warmed temperatures, retreating glaciers, and (brief) biotic continuity probably presented the most optimum conditions for midcontinental human population expansion south of Beringia at any time for the last 60,000 years.

NOTE

1. The first draft of this chapter was completed early in 1981; hence the references cited are most complete up to the end of 1980. Although in later revisions I have tried to incorporate more recent data, this chapter is based primarily on the state of knowledge as it stood at the end of 1980.

R I C H A R D   S H U T L E R ,   Jr.

3 The Australian Parallel to the Peopling of the New World

The model presented here in expanded form (first developed by Macintosh and Larnach, 1976; Larnach, 1974) is that southern China, some 70,000-100,000 years ago, was the dispersal area for the earliest generalized type of *Homo sapiens sapiens*. From southern China, beginning perhaps 70,000 years ago, there was a bifurcation of people radiating north and south. The future Australians leaving mainland China, possibly due to population pressure, moved through Island Southeast Asia, crossing Wallacea, and reaching Australia by circa 50,000 B.P.

During the warm period of Würm I and II, 40,000-50,000 years ago, migrations increased greatly out of southern China, probably due to increasing population problems. The people moving north were evolving into Mongoloids, adapting to cold conditions and reaching the Bering Strait by 30,000 B.P., perhaps earlier.

While *Homo sapiens sapiens* apparently reached Australia before their Mongoloid counterparts crossed Bering Strait into the New World, the Australian parallel is that they both had a common origin in southern China, and both groups entered new continents through restricted entrances at opposite ends of the Pacific Basin a few thousand years apart, where the length of isolation in each area has seen a different pattern of genes, disease germs, and adaptions evolve, distinct from both each other and from present-day Asiatics (Stewart, 1974).

The ancestors of the Australian aborigines would have crossed the dry land of the Sunda Shelf around 50,000 years ago, passing through the Philippines-Malay Peninsula and the area in between and moving across what is now Borneo or Java to the western side of Wallacea. To proceed, as Macintosh (1972: 47) so aptly put it, "they most likely became the world's first mariners." For whichever route they took to cross the Wallacea Deep, they

had to cross a minimum of 65 km of open water. The first immigrants to the New World, on the other hand, depending on when they came, had a broad land-bridge across Bering Strait several times during the Würm (Wisconsinan) glaciation, and a water crossing at other times was certainly feasible (see Fladmark, this volume). Apparently, the Bering Land-Bridge was open twice between 14,000 and 10,000 B.P., and continuously around 50,000 B.P. and between 25,000 and 15,000 B.P. (Hopkins, 1967). The Australian example has shown that water is not a barrier, and some of us feel that the same applies for North America.

The time of crossing to either Australia or North America was crucial to all subsequent events (Stewart, 1974). Fossil *Homo sapiens sapiens* finds in south China and Island Southeast Asia are considered by some to be derived from the Upper Paleolithic ancestors of the Australian aborigines (Larnach, 1974). They include the Tzeyang skull from Nei-Chiang District, Szechwan, a female, 40-50 years old, dated to 20,000-35,000 B.P.; the Liukiang skull, from the Liu-chou District, Kwangsi, a male approximately 40 years old, dated to 25,000-40,000 B.P. Both specimens are considered to be mongoloid (Aigner, 1973). From Island Southeast Asia, we have the Tabon Cave mandible and frontal bone dated at 23,500 B.P., the Niah cave skull, presumably dated at 40,000 B.P., and the Wadjak skulls from Java, poorly dated to between 40,000-10,000 years B.P. (see Figure 3.1).

Present evidence supports the thesis that Australia was first occupied along the coast, and then up the major river systems. This implied adaption to a coastal environment is consistent with a history of crossing islands, as would have occurred in Island Southeast Asia (Bowdler, 1977). While there is some regional variation within Australia to-

43

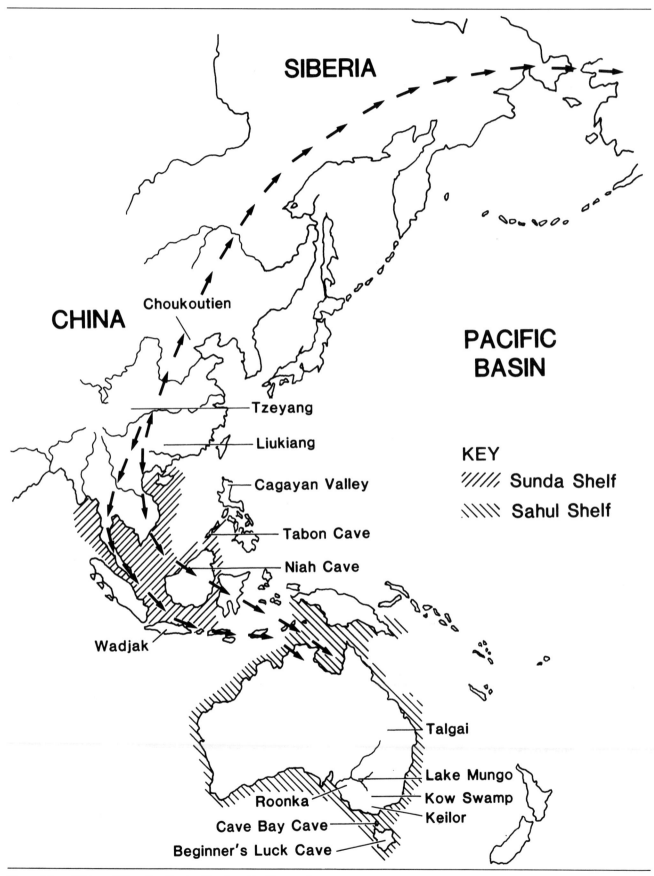

Figure 3.1   Sites and Migration Routes Mentioned in Chapter 3

day, the current weight of evidence indicates that there has been relatively little anatomical variation among Australians for the past 25,000 years, thereby supporting the model of a homogeneous population rather than a multiracial background (Macintosh and Larnach, 1976).

Australian aborigines are clearly distinct from any present-day Asian populations. I mentioned earlier that Australians and New World mongoloids had, over time, become widely divergent in racial characteristics from each other, and from present-day Asiatics. These differences are shown in some blood groups, and although similarities exist, the differences are far more significant. Asiatic mongoloids have the highest known incidence of B and Rh^2, while both are low to nonexistent in Australians and American Indians. Both Asian mongoloids and Australians have high frequencies of A_1, while in American Indians it is quite variable. T. D. Stewart points out that American Indians differ from Asiatic mongoloids in having low frequencies of A_1, B, and Rh^2, but a high frequency of M. The Australian aborigines also have low frequencies of B and Rh^2 but differ from American Indians in having a high frequency of N and no Di^a. It is interesting to note, however, that when the A-B-O frequencies for Asia, America, and Australia were plotted on a map, Stewart found that they grade fairly regularly from Asia, through the points of entrance into America and Australia, and southward. This is especially evident in America, where group B is limited to northwestern North America, group A disappears a little farther southward, and group O is present in the rest of the New World. This blood group distribution is an excellent indicator of entrance into the New World from Asia. The evidence for Australia is also indicative. Group B is limited to an area in the north, and from there on southward, group A increases in frequency to a maximum in the south-central part (Stewart, 1974).

An interesting parallel exists in the presence of shovel-shaped incisors in both Australian aborigines and American Indians. The functional value of shovel-shaped incisors is not known. It may be that the early generalized, evolving *Homo sapiens sapiens* had this trait. Perhaps there was some survival value in the mongoloids retaining this trait, and it is still found occasionally in Australian aborigines because there was no selective pressure to lose it.

For other areas immediately adjacent to Australia, the Tasmanians and Melanesians are variants of one general population pool to which the Australians belong, though the Australians are distinct from them (Howells, n.d.).

We know much less about the earliest New World populations, other than that they were generalized mongoloids. The oldest *Homo sapiens sapiens* skeletal material from North America comprises the Tepexpan, Minnesota, and Midlands skulls, dating possibly to 27,000 B.P. The Laguna Cranium from southern California dates at 17,000 B.P. On the basis of teeth characteristics as determined by Christy Turner, there are three basic groups in the New World: (1) Eskimo-Aleut; (2) Northwest Coast; and (3) all the rest of the New World, with the implication that the Eskimo-Aleut and Northwest Coast people were the last to arrive (personal communication).

It would seem, then, that this model, first proposed by Macintosh and Larnach, has a good deal of support: that the aboriginal Australians, migrating out of southern China some 70,000 years ago, and moving through what is now Island Southeast Asia, were the earliest examples of evolving, generalized, modern *Homo sapiens sapiens* to arrive in their ultimate area of migration.

Coping with the widely divergent environments of the two continents was a totally different problem, and consequently we see the development of distinct cultural patterns at opposite ends of the Pacific Ocean.

RICHARD E. MORLAN

4 Pre-Clovis Occupation North of the Ice Sheets

Intensive field and laboratory work by numerous research-ers during the past decade has greatly increased our understanding and expectations concerning Upper Pleistocene human occupations north of the Wisconsinan ice sheets. The earliest known evidence as of ten years ago (Irving, 1971) comprised a relatively small series of redeposited altered bones from Old Crow Basin. No associated lithic artifacts had been found, although one of the bone artifacts, a caribou tibia fleshing tool, had clearly been made in part by means of stone tools. Furthermore, there existed very little understanding of the stratigraphic contexts from which the bones had been eroded. There arose, and to some extent remain, a number of difficult interpretive problems that constrain the confidence and en-thusiasm of some archaeologists with respect to these early finds.

Recent field investigations in Old Crow Basin have per-mitted the definition of a restricted stratigraphic zone in which *in situ* remains of human activity are likely to be found, while ongoing laboratory studies have placed some of the interpretive problems in the context of a broad taphonomic framework and have shed light on other prob-lems by means of replicative experiments. In addition, both direct and more indirect evidence of flint-knapping and stone tool use has been discovered in some of the Upper Pleistocene sections of the northern Yukon, and both stratigraphy and radiometric dating are now assisting the creation of a chronological framework for some of these finds.

Later periods of the Upper Pleistocene have also been under study, and two new sites – Dry Creek and the Bluefish Caves – are of particular importance, in that they contain lithic tools in primary association with faunal re-mains, including those of extinct large mammals. In both cases, radiocarbon dates, stratigraphy, and paleoecological data are in agreement with respect to chronology and paleoenvironmental setting. At both sites well-integrated, multidisciplinary studies have shed light on several fields of study and on several major historical problems.

These developments of the 1970s will be summarized with reference to some of the larger questions pertaining to the peopling of the New World. Such questions include not only the time of arrival of humankind in the western hemisphere, but also the manner of arrival at Bering Strait, the background and time depth of human adaptation to high latitudes, the capabilities of human societies to cope with the rigors of full glacial environments north of the Arc-tic Circle, and the role of their successors or descendants in the apparently massive extinctions of late Wisconsinan time. Many of these important questions have been ex-plicitly or implicitly addressed by various archaeologists who have spoken or written about the peopling of the New World, and this chapter attempts to interpret the Upper Pleistocene of eastern Beringia (Alaska and the Yukon Ter-ritory) with respect to several themes raised by such statements.

Some of these themes pertain to prevalent but often con-tradictory views of Beringia as a place for human inhabi-

AUTHOR'S NOTE: I wish to thank the Archaeological Survey of Canada, National Museum of Man for support during the preparation of this manuscript and for permission to participate in the symposium. I am most grateful to Jacques Cinq-Mars and John V. Matthews, Jr., for numerous discussions and to Herbert Alexander, Robson Bonnichsen, Alan L. Bryan, and Donald W. Clark for critical responses to an earlier draft of the chapter. We can all thank John Matthews for the keen eyes that spotted the Hungry Creek microflakes and Catherine Craig-Bullen for the keen but tired eyes that saw to the removal of hundreds of them from the samples. This is Contribution No. 4 of the Yukon Refugium Project.

tants, especially during full glacial conditions. For example, the idea has been repeatedly and again recently expressed (for example, Fladmark, this volume) that Beringia might have been inhospitable during full glacial conditions. To some extent this question derives from the ongoing debates among paleoecologists as to the nature of the classical Wisconsinan landscape in eastern Beringia (compare Matthews, 1982; and Ritchie and Cwynar, 1982). To a probably larger extent, this question results from our fundamental ignorance regarding the assemblages of plants and animals, including people, that lived in eastern Beringia at the time. The nonglaciated portions of Alaska and the Yukon Territory comprise an enormous area that is barely explored with respect to paleontology and archaeology. As Giddings (1960: 121) lamented more than twenty years ago, we are too prone to view Beringia as a pathway rather than as a home for human societies. In fact, the critical role of Beringia in the biogeographic history of many plants and animals (Hultén, 1937; Harington, 1978; Lindroth, 1970; Sher, 1974; Youngman, 1975) should warn us that the region might well have been a center for cultural development and human dispersal, as has in fact been demonstrated for several intervals of prehistory (see Dumond, 1977; Laughlin, 1979; Workman, 1980; Anderson, 1980). And when Beringia has been viewed as a pathway, it has often been supposed that the path was open only at certain times in the past, namely during the several periods of Bering Land-Bridge exposure.

In assessing these questions, it is important to remember that all of Beringia (including the western portion in Siberia) is so far north that it could be reached only by human societies that had already developed certain adaptations to northern environmental conditions. Although we do not comprehend it in detail, a technological threshold had to be crossed in order for people to live in the "north" in all seasons. This threshold must have included adequate clothing and shelter for warmth and protection from wind, means of traveling over snow and cold water, and methods of food procurement and storage during the "winter bottleneck," when northern resources can be scarce and difficult to harvest. Such techniques, and the knowledge and technology to realize them and to teach them to one's children, must have characterized human societies long before they reached the vicinity of the Bering Land-Bridge or Bering Strait. In order to enter "mega-Beringia" (see Yurtsev, 1974), human societies had to cross this kind of technological threshold. Hence, we should expect to find the first human inhabitants of the New World already well adapted to northern environments.

Nonetheless, some critical questions remain unanswered: What do such adaptations entail? How are such adaptations manifest in the archaeological record? The speculative "answers" provided by archaeologists reveal a wide range of opinions and attitudes concerning early New World technology. For example, MacNeish (1978: 491; 1979: 3) has characterized the people of his Stage I as "technologically unsophisticated . . . perhaps . . . unskilled as hunters." Alan Bryan (1978: 311) suggests that

> the earliest colonizers of America gradually expanded through northeastern Asia and northwestern North America long before the development of any of the more sophisticated stone or bone flaking technological adaptations (such as Diuktai and Old Crow) to any particular environment had occurred. In other words we should expect to find somewhere in Beringia evidence of a much more basic (i.e., technologically less specialized) stone and bone technology than is represented at Old Crow and in the Diuktai culture. Like the early Australian assemblages, the basic Paleo-American tool kit contained few, if any, standardized stone or bone tool types.

In marked contrast to these positions is a recent assessment by Workman (1980: 129):

> Only cold-adapted and cold-loving steppe hunting cultures could have penetrated the arctic and subarctic in Pleistocene times. Once in Beringia they would have encountered a hunter's paradise . . . . Since only specialized big game hunters with sophisticated lithic technologies could have survived in Beringia, it follows that New World subsistence strategies heavily dependent on vegetal products, insects and small game must represent *in situ* secondary specializations rather than stem cultures. It also appears that lithic industries so crude as to raise legitimate doubts about their human authorship do not have to be taken seriously in the New World.

Other writers have presented arguments similar to Workman's (for example, Irving, 1971: 72), and regardless of one's position on this question, terms such as "standardized," "sophisticated," and "specialized" seem to be given different meanings by various authors.

We cannot expect to gain much insight into the colonization of the New World simply by studying geological charts that depict the emergence and inundation of the Bering Land-Bridge. Not only the colonization of Australia (Hallam, 1977; Shutler, this volume), but also the even earlier crossings of the Straits of Gibraltar (Bordes and Thibault, 1977) show that the ability to make serviceable watercraft has long been within the human ken. Furthermore, a wide variety of conditions have existed at Bering Strait at various times in the past. These range from dry land to open water and, in winter, from shore-fast smooth ice to nearly impassable jumbles of shifting sea ice. We cannot know which of these conditions may have prevailed until we learn from the archaeological record when people first reached eastern Beringia.

Perhaps these misleading themes are partly responsible for the marathon debate that surrounds the subject of "New World origins." Another measure of responsibility must be assigned to the "archaeological oral tradition," which too often replaces published reports as a source of "evidence" concerning the past. For whatever reasons, the numerous reviews of the subject often bear little resemblance to one another, although each purports to be an adequate summary of our state of knowledge (compare Bryan, 1973, 1978; Griffin, 1979; Lynch, 1978; MacNeish, 1978, 1979; Rouse, 1976). Almost predictably, given the climate of controversy, its stormy weather fueled by the circulation of credible and incredible claims, some writers (for example, Jennings, 1974: 76; Griffin, 1979: 44) have been moved to espouse standards for evidence of early human occupation. Although appropriate in principle, their standards threaten to stifle the very investigations they were created to guide. These standards call for an undisturbed, stratified, dated site containing, in addition to artifacts, faunal remains, and human skeletal materials, all the lines of evidence required for a reconstruction of the seasonal local and regional environment, and specialized activities. Unfortunately, we cannot always find such ideal evidence anymore than paleontologists can do all their work on the basis of articulated skeletons and primary death assemblages.

None of the earliest archaeological evidence now available in eastern Beringia meets all of the standards prescribed by some writers for "unequivocal" status. Rather than describing the excavation of an undisturbed archaeological site, I have the more difficult but nonetheless interesting task of describing a complex geological and paleontological record that contains scattered elements of redeposited archaeological evidence of several kinds. Only for final Wisconsinan time have truly undisturbed archaeological deposits been excavated, and these will be mentioned later.

Nearly all of the earliest evidence to be marshaled here has been described more or less completely in recently published reports, or in papers currently in press (Bonnichsen, 1978a, 1979; Harington, 1977, 1978, 1980a; Harington et al., 1975; Hughes, 1972; Hughes et al., n.d.; Irving, 1971, 1978; Irving and Harington, 1973; Matthews, 1975, 1982; Morlan, 1978, 1979, 1980a; Morlan and Cinq-Mars, 1982; Morlan and Matthews, 1978; Schweger, 1982). Among these reports are numerous explanations for the attribution of artificial causes to the interpretation of alterations on some of the vertebrate fossils from various eastern Beringian localities, especially from Old Crow Basin. There is little point in attempting in this short chapter to reiterate these studies, and I must place on the reader the somewhat burdensome task of pursuing this question by consulting the literature cited above. For present purposes, a brief review of geology, taphonomy, paleoecology, and archaeology must suffice to set the stage for a discussion of the meaning of the archaeological record as it is currently understood.

The Earliest Evidence

Geology

Since all of the archaeological evidence to be mentioned in this section depends on the interpretation of redeposited objects, it is especially important to seek in the geological history of eastern Beringia a framework for placing chronological limits on the remains and for understanding certain taphonomic processes that led to the redeposition and concentration of the finds. A detailed review of this subject for the northern Yukon is in preparation (Hughes et al., n.d.), and summaries are already available for Old Crow Basin (Morlan, 1979; Morlan and Matthews, 1978). A number of writers have discussed the geology of the fossiliferous muck deposits in eastern Beringia (Cockfield, 1921; Foster, 1969; Harington, 1977, 1978; Péwé, 1975a; Porter, 1979).

Most of the areas to be considered here were not glaciated during the Pleistocene, although all of them were appreciably influenced by glacial advances and climates. In the northern Yukon, Laurentide ice extended westward to the Richardson Mountains, overrode Bonnet Plume Basin, and diverted regional drainages northward and westward where, augmented by glacial meltwater, large lakes were raised in the interior basins known, respectively, as Bell, Bluefish, and Old Crow (Figure 4.1). There is now some doubt as to how many times such lakes were created, but it is clear that these basins were flooded during a classical Wisconsinan advance of about 12,000-25,000 years ago. Varved and massive clays and silty clays as much as 5 m thick occur near the tops of all intact Pleistocene exposures in the basins and mark the last episode of glacial lake inundation (Figure 4.2). Beneath the clays are relatively thick sequences of alluvial and local lacustrine sediments, often rich in organics, and dated by radiocarbon analyses to approximately 31,000 years ago at the top and more than 54,000 years ago near the base. In the Bluefish and Old Crow basins, thick units of lacustrine sediments underlie the fluvial materials, and the former were originally interpreted as glaciolacustrine in origin, dating to early Wisconsinan or earlier times (Hughes, 1972). It is now known that this lower lacustrine unit in Bluefish Basin is much older and is probably not related to a glacial advance (Hughes et al., n.d.). In Old Crow Basin, available evidence still permits, but does not require, interpretation of the lower lacustrine sediments as glaciolacustrine and probably Illinoian in age. In any case, the long fluvial and local lacustrine sequence lying between these two thick lacustrine clay units probably spans the Sangamon Interglaciation as well as Early and Mid-Wisconsinan times (Figure 4.2, Units 2a, 2b).

The interlacustrine units are very complex, exhibiting rapid lateral facies changes, repeated local shifts in sedimentary environment, and many instances of cutting and filling by meandering streams. At some sections, Unit 2a records the meander scrolls of a single major stream, with vertical relief of about 12-15 m from channel bottom to floodplain. The dipping foreset beds and flat-lying topset beds of this stream are beautifully exposed at Old Crow

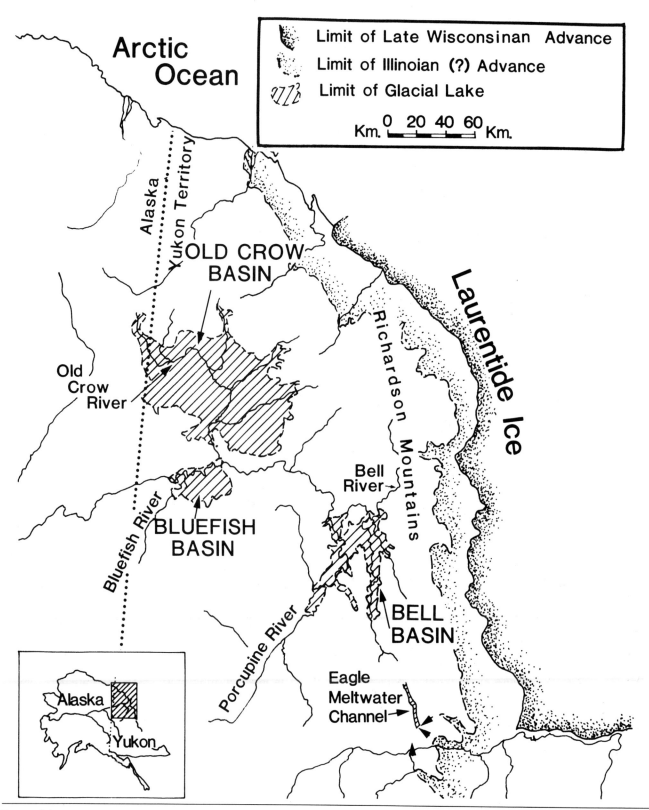

Figure 4.1   Northeastern Beringia: The Yukon Refugium

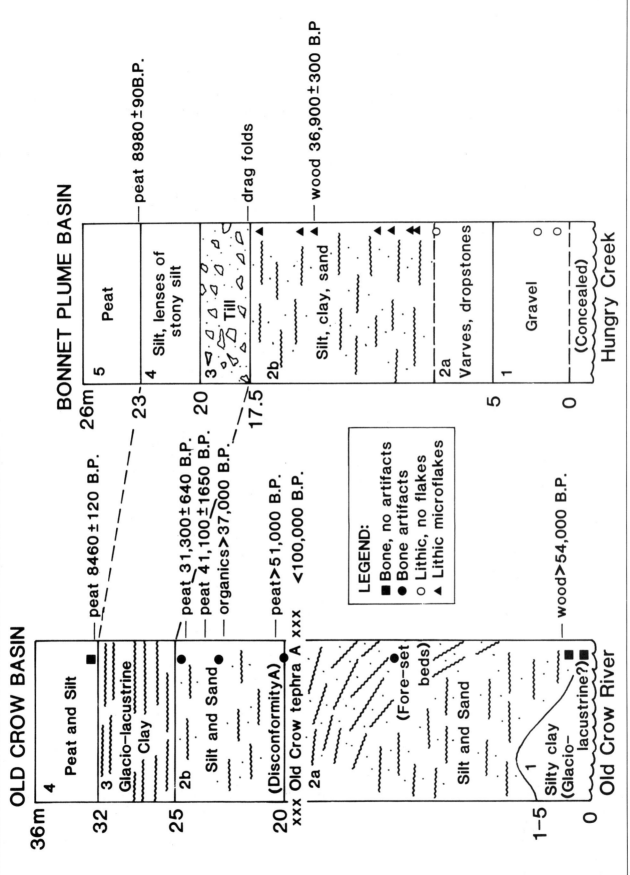

Figure 4.2   Generalized Stratigraphy of Old Crow Basin and Bonnet Plume Basin

51

River Locations 11 and 12, and are suspected at Location 15 and a few other sections. The floodplain of this stream system in Old Crow Basin has been identified as a regional disconformity expressed as an erosional contact at most sections and as a weathered surface at others. That the floodplain was weathered under a cold climate is shown by the frequent occurrence of large ice-wedge pseudomorphs and cryoturbation folds, many of which were truncated by erosion and subsequently buried by cross-bedded alluvial silts and sands. This erosional contact and its correlative surfaces have been labeled Disconformity A, and the correlation of the contacts from one section to another has been aided by the recognition of the Old Crow tephra, which outcrops 50-80 cm below the disconformity in at least five sections in Old Crow Basin. The Old Crow tephra has been fission-track dated by J. A. Westgate and his associates at the University of Toronto (Briggs and Westgate, 1978). A fission track date of <100,000 years ago (the 4-sigma maximum limit) on the tephra and a radiocarbon date of >51,000 B.P. (GSC-2599-2) on peat that grew on a surface postdating the floodplain are bracketing dates for Disconformity A. A more direct chronological estimate has recently been obtained by J. L. Bischoff, U.S. Geological Survey, who computed a uranium-thorium date of 81,068 ± 7500 years ago (1-sigma limit) for a mammoth long bone fragment recovered from Disconformity A. Although none of these dates affords much precision, and none of them has been replicated by duplicate analysis, it is noteworthy that these three dating techniques appear to be in fundamental agreement and correct stratigraphic order for the top of Unit 2a and its contact with Unit 2b.

Unit 2b consists of overbank alluvium, local lacustrine facies, and local reworked loess sequences that alternate with periods of peat growth and soil formation. The top of the unit was weathered in a cold climate and at most sections exhibits ice-wedge pseudomorphs of sizes comparable to those at Disconformity A. The wedges at the top of the unit do not seem to have been thawed and truncated, however, for their tops are intact, and their casts contain peat and other organic sediments deflected downward from the surrounding surfaces. These wedges probably thawed under water or under sediment laid down during the inundation of the basins by the glacial meltwater of the classical Wisconsinan advance. Radiocarbon dates from Unit 2b range from "infinite," on wood believed to have been reworked from older deposits, to about 31,000 years ago, on autochthonous peats that grew on surfaces stratigraphically below the glaciolacustrine clays, but 4-5 m above Disconformity A.

Although archaeological materials will be described in more detail below, it should be noted that bone and ivory artifacts (and possible artifacts) are believed to occur throughout Unit 2b. The largest sample is from Disconfor-

mity A, and a few other examples come from deeper deposits thought to be foreset beds associated with the eroded floodplain. No artifacts are known from the fossiliferous deposits that are found near the base of Unit 2a; specimens reported by Jopling et al. (1981) may not be artifacts, and in any case were recovered from point bar sediments belonging to Unit 2b.

Important geological and possible archaeological evidence has also been obtained from the glaciated Bonnet Plume Basin nearly 300 km southeast of Old Crow. The Hungry Creek glaciation of classical Wisconsinan time was responsible for major stream diversions that supplied much of the water to the glacial lakes just described (Figures 4.1, 4.2). Although originally interpreted as a much older advance (Hughes, 1972), several converging lines of evidence, including a radiocarbon date of 36,900 B.P. under the till of the Hungry Creek glaciation, now show that this advance belongs to the classical Wisconsinan interval (see Hughes et al., n.d.). A series of organic silt and sand samples from fluvial deposits beneath the till have provided an excellent paleoenvironmental record, and distinctive chert microflakes have been discovered in some of these samples.

The water diverted and supplied by the Hungry Creek glaciation flowed through a large trough known as the Eagle meltwater channel (Figure 4.1), and the pathway followed by this discharge entered Bell Basin and then Bluefish and Old Crow Basins. In a southeastern arm of Bell Basin, on the right limit of Eagle River, one exposure has produced a complex sequence of fluvial and lacustrine sands and clays probably attributable to the classical Wisconsinan discharge. Samples of the sands appear to contain rich concentrations of chert microflakes (see below) throughout nearly 8 m of the section; these samples are currently under study.

All of the other localities to be mentioned here with respect to the earliest evidence in eastern Beringia have produced archaeological materials from organic-rich colluvial silts, often known as mucks. Some localities have colluvial units of very great age, but those of interest here are of Upper Pleistocene age, primarily classical Wisconsinan, and represent redeposited loess that became enriched by organics, including vertebrate fossils, during redeposition (see Péwé, 1975a). Among the vertebrate fossils are altered bones, antlers, and tusk fragments, some of which were artificially worked when in a fresh condition.

Taphonomy

Taphonomic considerations (see Behrensmeyer and Hill, 1980) are especially important in identifying and interpreting redeposited archaeological materials. There are two major aspects of this kind of analysis. The first concerns the interpretation of individual bone and antler specimens that may have been altered in many ways and by several processes or agencies. Such interpretations must seek to account for all alterations that have occurred between the death of an animal and the recovery of its fossil or sub-fossil remains, and models depicting the major categories and sequences of alteration have proven useful in the guidance of such interpretations (Clark and Kietzke, 1967; Hanson, 1980; Morlan, 1980a, b). The second aspect concerns assemblage composition, the detection of allochthonous elements, and the reconstruction of primary burial assemblages (taphocoenoses) and death assemblages (thanatocoenoses). This second aspect is a prerequisite for reliable paleoecological analysis, and both aspects are essential for archaeological interpretation. The taphonomy of northern Yukon archaeological materials has been treated elsewhere (Morlan, 1980a), and similar work has been done for one of the muck deposits at Jack Wade Creek in eastern Alaska (Porter, 1979).

Paleoecology

Although not directly germane to the recognition of redeposited artifacts, a paleoecological framework is important to an understanding of the conditions of human occupation, and also contributes to the development of a chronological framework. Paleoecological data can also reveal the existence of disconformities that are sometimes hard to recognize strictly on the basis of lithology and sedimentation.

Sampling in the northern Yukon sections has been directed toward a very broad range of fossil remains, including pollen, bryophytes, vascular plant macrofossils, mollusks, insects, and vertebrates. Details will be presented elsewhere (Hughes et al., 1981), but a general outline for Old Crow Basin will be summarized here. Whether or not the lower lacustrine unit is of glacial meltwater origin, the occurrence of *Mammuthus primigenius* in the upper part of the clays (Morlan, unpublished data) shows that the unit cannot be older than the Illinoian (Maglio, 1973; Harington, 1978; Kurtén and Anderson, 1980). The lowest beds of Unit 2a have produced fossils indicative of local forests perhaps more extensive than now (for example, 30 cm logs at modern treeline) and a few indicators of climate probably warmer than now (for example, *Spilogale* sp., spotted skunk) (Matthews, 1975; Harington, 1978). Forests of some extent and form seem to have been present continuously throughout the interval represented by Unit 2a, but the climate seems to have cooled enough that large logs are not seen on Disconformity A, although well-preserved cones show that spruce still grew on the floodplain.

The ice-wedge pseudomorphs that are truncated by Disconformity A are at least as large as any ice wedges now found in the northern Yukon interior, and they may represent the early Wisconsinan glacial climate that led to the exposure of the Bering Land-Bridge for a few millen-

nia around 70,000 years ago (Hopkins, n.d.). Since these ice-wedge casts are often filled with types of sediment not seen outside the wedges, and since the tops of the wedge casts have often been removed by erosion, it is supposed that the wedges were melted by a climatic warming. If so, the climate might even have been warmer than at present (Matthews, 1980), but regional drainage history could also have been responsible for the thawing of the ice wedges, since Disconformity A represents the floodplain of a large-scale integrated drainage system. In any event, the active layer must have been thicker than at present in order to account for the thawing of the wedges and the occurrence of the deep-burrowing woodchuck *(Marmota monax)*, an animal now restricted to areas south of the zone of continuous permafrost (Brown, 1960; Youngman, 1975).

Above Disconformity A, the pollen and macrofossil records indicate a gradual cooling of the climate, the disappearance of spruce, and a greater predominance of tundra-adapted plants and animals. At least two, and possibly more, generations of ice-wedge growth casts have different forms from those on Disconformity A, although many of them are of comparable size. The tops of the casts are intact, and their fill is comprised of sediments found both above and outside the wedges but deformed into the casts. These wedges appear to have thawed out not because of a climatic change, but because of the inundation of their surfaces by local ponds, and finally by the classical Wisconsinan glacial meltwater lake.

A paleoenvironmental record cannot be derived from the glaciolacustrine sediments themselves, since the clays are nearly devoid of fossils, but a large portion of the classical Wisconsinan interval is represented in lake cores studied by Cwynar and Ritchie (1980; Ritchie and Cwynar, 1982). These cores reveal a treeless environment of considerable severity, but the exact composition of the vegetation has been differently interpreted by various workers as widespread fell field (Ritchie and Cwynar, 1982), or as herbaceous or steppe-tundra (Matthews, 1982).

Cores in the Tanana River valley of central Alaska have also revealed a treeless landscape that was invaded by dwarf birch around 14,000 years ago, and later by spruce forest (Ager, 1975, 1982), and a similar picture has been obtained from the Bluefish Caves site in the northern Yukon (Cinq-Mars, 1979; Morlan and Cinq-Mars, 1982).

The Hungry Creek section, in Bonnet Plume Basin, must be briefly mentioned, since it has produced evidence of locally growing spruce throughout the mid-Wisconsinan, with some of the samples containing plants and insects that have northern limits far to the south today (Hughes et al., n.d.). Perhaps it is not surprising that the sequence does not reveal a marked decline of spruce, since the section was overridden by Laurentide ice during the Hungry Creek advance and therefore contains a significant disconformity at the base of the till, where drag folds show the influence of the ice on the underlying sediment. The underlying sediments containing the chert microflakes represent some portion of the Mid-Wisconsinan during which spruce forests were locally present.

Archaeology

Since most of the artifically altered vertebrate fossils have been recovered from the modern banks and bars of the Old Crow River valley, it is among these redeposited pieces that we can see the broadest range of technological expressions while at the same time clarifying the reasons for supposing them to be of Pleistocene age. Studies reported elsewhere (Harington et al., 1975; Bonnichsen, 1978a, 1979; Morlan, 1978, 1980a) have shown that it is possible to distinguish between fresh bone fractures and postpermineralization fractures, and also to make such distinctions regarding other forms of alteration, such as grinding, polishing, and cutting. These studies and others (for example, Farquhar and Badone, 1979; Farquhar et al., 1978) have demonstrated that the artifacts from Old Crow Basin were made when the bones were in a fresh condition, and that the bones are now permineralized rather than simply preserved due to freezing (compare Haynes, 1971: 4; Guthrie, 1980). Other taphonomic considerations show that not all green bone fractures can be attributed to human activity, but that the green fracture of mammoth or mastodon limb bones[1] can be considered, at least hypothetically, to be indicative of artificial bone fracturing (Morlan, 1980a; ch. 3). Additional experiments have shown that the fractured pieces of bone can be flaked by means of many of the same procedures used to flake stone, and that the resulting bone flakes are useful cutting implements (Stanford, Bonnichsen, et al., 1981).

Hundreds of green fractured mammoth limb bone fragments, as well as more than 100 cores and flakes of mammoth bone and ivory, have been found in the Old Crow valley (Morlan, 1980a: Table 9.1; also 1980 and 1981 collections). Only one of these specimens has been directly dated on its collagen fraction: 29,300 ± 2400 B.P. (I-11,050; Harington, 1980a).[2] The others can be attributed to stratigraphic contexts within Unit 2a or 2b on the basis of their states of preservation (for example, staining, degree of permineralization), and this inference assigns them to ages of more than 25,000 years ago. Even if this inference is not correct for every specimen, it is unlikely that any of these mammoth bones is younger than the youngest dates on mammoths in eastern Beringia: 13,500 ± 400 B.P. (QL-1365: N. Ten-Brink, personal communication to J. V. Matthews, Jr.) at the Teklanika Mammoth site in Alaska, and 15,500 ± 130 B.P. (GSC-3053: Morlan and Cinq-Mars, 1982) at Bluefish Cave II in northern Yukon.

When a larger series of vertebrate taxa is considered, a clear pattern emerges from the available radiocarbon dates in the northern Yukon basins (Morlan, 1980a: Table 9.4, Fig. 9.3; Morlan and Cinq-Mars, 1982: Fig. 14). Two dates on extant animals (wapiti and caribou) fall within the Holcene; six dates on *Bison crassicornis* elements, believed to have originated in a channel cut into the upper glaciolacustrine unit, cluster around 12,000 B.P.; and fourteen finite dates are older than 20,000 B.P., with all but one being older than 25,000 B.P. Only three fossils dated thus far from these redeposited contexts have given "greater than" dates. The long gap between 25,000 and 12,000 years ago undoubtedly represents the interval during which the northern Yukon basins were flooded by glacial meltwater, so it is reasonable to infer that the Old Crow valley archaeological and vertebrate paleontological records will be divided into discrete segments that predate and postdate the classical Wisconsinan lakes. This is why it may be permissible in this instance to infer general age categories on the basis of such qualitative, and normally risky, criteria as the degree of staining and permineralization (Harington, 1977: Appendix B).

A more reliable basis for chronological assignments is the stratigraphic context, which permits a more precise assessment of geological, taphonomic, and paleoecological history. Mammoth limb bone fragments broken when fresh have been recovered from Disconformity A at three localities in Old Crow Basin, and a mammoth bone flake was excavated from much deeper deposits believed to represent the foreset beds of a point bar associated with the Disconformity A floodplain (Figure 4.2; Morlan, 1980a: ch. 6). During the 1981 field season, a bipolar mammoth bone core was excavated from an erosional contact thought to represent Disconformity A (Figure 4.3). These finds show that proboscideans were being butchered and their bones broken and flaked by people as early as Early Wisconsinan time, and it is expected that more such materials will be recovered from Mid-Wisconsinan deposits between Disconformity A and the upper glaciolacustrine sediments. Seeming confirmation of the Early Wisconsinan age was provided by the uranium-thorium date of 81,068 ± 7500 B.P. (J. L. Bischoff, personal communication, 1981), which was obtained from a green fractured mammoth limb bone fragment excavated from Disconformity A. A series of such dates is now being prepared.

Ground and polished bones are more difficult to interpret, because we do not have adequate experimental data to guide the interpretation of such specimens. Recent field observations have revealed the significant role of cryoturbation in the production of highly polished facets on bone fragments, and all of the polish on specimens from Old Crow Basin described by Jopling and others (1981: 26-28) could easily have been produced in this way. Nonetheless, by observing the complexity of such alterations and their truncations of and by other features, it is possible to identify some ground and polished pieces that are difficult to explain entirely by reference to natural processes. Such

NOTE: View of outer surface (left) shows multiple flaking at both top and bottom ends, and inner surface (right) exhibits a green bone fracture on the lower right margin.

Figure 4.3   Bipolar Core Made on Mammoth Long Bone Fragment from Disconformity A, Old Crow River Location 94

pieces have been described in detail elsewhere (Bonnichsen, 1979; Morlan, 1980a), and a few examples will be enumerated here with reference to their stratigraphic contexts and possible functions as tools.

A remarkably polished *Bison* sp. ulna (Bonnichsen, 1979: Pl. VIII-22) from a modern bar could have been used as a scraper or fleshing tool. A complexly facetted caribou antler (Harington et al., 1975: 48) from the earliest Holocene terrace deposits in the valley (10 11,000 years ago) may have been used as a pestle or hide grainer. The differential polish on a fragment of tusk from Disconformity A (Morlan, 1980a: Pl. 7.7), and a more extensively polished tusk from deeper deposits (Morlan and Cinq-Mars, 1982: Fig. 6) might illustrate the use of tusk ivory in hide-working functions. These and other polished pieces (Morlan, 1980a: Tables B17, C3) can be construed as artifacts or probable artifacts that served a variety of functions over an unknown span of time. The hypothetical

association between hide-working functions and polished facets needs further study, but it would be quite reasonable to suppose that hide preparation was a major and complex activity in these northern environments.

A final, very important category of archaeological evidence from bones and antlers consists of cuts made by stone tools either during artifact manufacture or during the butchering of an animal. Seven examples are known from the modern banks and bars, three from the earliest terrace deposits, six from Disconformity A, and one from deeper (foreset?) beds (Morlan, 1980a: Table 9.1). Among these pieces are the famous caribou tibia flesher, dated on the basis of its apatite fraction to 27,000 B.P. (Irving and Harington, 1973), and a caribou antler used as a billet for the manufacture of stone tools (Morlan, 1978: Fig. 6).

Several other areas of eastern Beringia have produced altered osseous materials similar to those from the northern Yukon. Broken and flaked mammoth limb bones are known from the mucks in placer mines in the Klondike and Carmacks regions of the central Yukon, and a variety of polished and cut specimens have been recovered from the Klondike and from Alaskan localities near Fairbanks, Lost Chicken, and Jack Wade (see summaries in Bonnichsen, 1979; Porter 1979; Morlan, 1980a; Harington, 1980b; Morlan and Cinq-Mars, 1982). Most of the specimens are thought to represent classical Wisconsinan time on the basis of several radiocarbon dates and the general geological history of the enclosing mucks. Of special interest is a series of butchered caribou skulls from eight eastern Beringian localities, some of which are probably of Upper Pleistocene age (Porter and Hopkins, in press). None of these localities except Jack Wade Creek (Porter, 1979) has been exhaustively studied, and it would be especially useful to reexamine the large collections from placer mines in the Fairbanks area. Even the incomplete data now available, however, show that many of the technological procedures recognized in the northern Yukon were in practice elsewhere in eastern Beringia, and these practices probably continued in many localities through the late Wisconsinan glacial interval, when the northern Yukon basins were under water.

Ever since the discovery of the caribou tibia flesher, the questions raised by the bone, antler, and ivory artifacts from eastern Beringia have so preoccupied the discussion of these collections that the evidence for associated lithic technology has been overlooked in many statements. Other archaeologists have asked repeatedly why there is no evidence for stone artifacts in association with the bones. Such questions need never have been asked given the obvious traces of lithic workmanship preserved on the flesher itself (Irving, 1971: 70; Morlan, 1980a: Pl. 4.30). The absence of stone artifacts in the excavated samples is probably a result of taphonomic factors such as fluvial sorting. Samples troweled and screened from Disconformity A, for example, are always associated with the kinds of lithic fragments that occur in the lag deposits of most streams. These fragments include chert and quartzite pieces with conchoidal fracture, but they are always stream-rolled and obviously rounded, abraded, or frosted; no one would mistake them for artifacts or for the detritus associated with flint-knapping. Although fluvial sorting may seem a facile explanation, a careful consideration of the many complex factors involved in the entrainment and downstream movement of particles in a fluvial environment (Krumbein, 1942; Hanson, 1980) shows that such an explanation is quite reasonable.

The manufacture of stone tools by means of percussion or pressure flaking entails the incidental production of many tiny fragments of stone, in addition to larger flakes. In a recent study of this "microdebitage," Fladmark (1981) has noted that as much as 20 percent by weight of pressure flaking detritus may be less than one millimeter in maximum dimension. Numerically, more than 99.5 percent of hard-hammer percussion detritus falls into this size range. The manufacture of a single stone tool can produce millions of tiny stone flakes with the following generic attributes, according to Fladmark (1981): highly angular forms; transparency or translucency; often larger than mean particle size in sieved samples; usually regular geometric shapes; usually some aspects of conchoidal fracture; and frequent appearance close to the surface plane of the microscopic slide or other container.

Recent microscopic work on sediment samples from the Hungry Creek section in Bonnet Plume Basin has revealed the presence of hundreds of microflakes in fluvial silts and fine sands (Figure 4.4). A detailed discussion of these lithic particles has been presented elsewhere (Hughes et al., 1981). Briefly, the microflakes are composed of chert and quartzite, they measure approximately one millimeter in maximum dimension, and they occur only in an 8.4 m thick zone (Unit 2b), where they are overlain by till of the classical Wisconsinan Hungry Creek glaciation and underlain by varved silts and clays of an older proglacial lake. The microflakes do not resemble any of the particles illustrated by researchers on sand grain textures in natural deposits (for example, Krinsley and Doornkamp, 1973), and they exhibit no evidence of rounding, abrasion, or frosting under a scanning electron microscope. They do, however, exhibit all of the attributes listed by Fladmark (1981) for "microdebitage," and they match perfectly the chert and obsidian detritus experimentally produced for comparison with them.

The attributes of the microflakes and the circumstances of their occurrence have prompted the hypotheses that they were produced incidental to flint-knapping by human occupants in Bonnet Plume Basin, and that they were selectively entrained from eroding archaeological deposits and redeposited in concentrations probably not far removed from their original site(s) of deposition. The radiocarbon date of 36,900 ± 300 B.P. (GSC-2422) directly dates the sample in which the microflakes were first discovered. Their occurrence in a zone extending approximately 5 m below and 3.4 m above this dated level shows that the microflakes span most of the Mid-Wisconsinan record exposed at the Hungry Creek section, but the duration of that portion of the sedimentary sequence is unknown. Unfortunately, there is little likelihood that better archaeological data can be obtained from the Mid-Wisconsinan of Bonnet Plume Basin, because there are very few exposures of that age in the area.

An exposure on Eagle River, northwest of Bonnet Plume Basin, has produced microflakes in such numbers throughout nearly 8 m of sand that their artificial origin seems doubtful, although no geological process has been identified to account for their occurrence there. The sand is interbedded with clays in a setting suggesting repeated

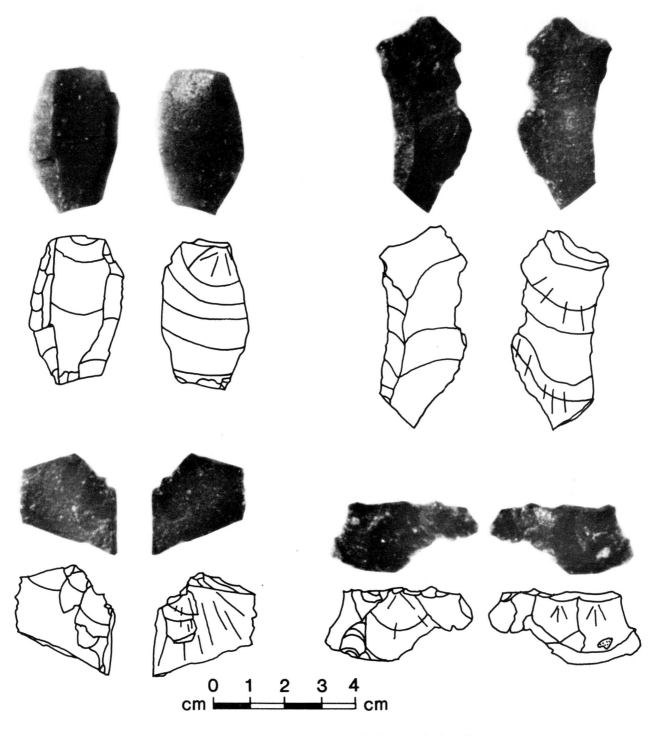

NOTE: Each flake is shown in dorsal (left) and ventral (right) view, and each is rendered both photographically and be sketching with the aid of a drawing tube on a Wild M5 microscope.

Figure 4.4   **Four Microflakes from Hungry Creek Unit 2b, Bonnet Plume Basin**

discharge through the Eagle meltwater channel during the classical Wisconsinan advance represented in Bonnet Plume Basin by the Hungry Creek glaciation. The base of the overlying surface peat has been dated to 9,970 ± 160 B.P. (GSC-3133). A series of samples collected in 1981 should permit both quantitative and qualitative analysis of the microflakes and associated lithic particles throughout the Eagle River sequence. At the present time, they can be construed as indicators of either a rich archaeological deposit upstream from the exposure, or of a geological process of sand grain reduction that has not been previously reported.

These microflake discoveries prompted the reexamination of numerous samples collected and analyzed in previous years. Although most of these samples came from Disconformity A and other contexts where artificially modified bones have been recognized, some of them represent deposits ranging in age from Tertiary to Holocene. No microflakes were seen in samples from very ancient contexts, and the few possible examples from Disconformity A in Old Crow Basin are rounded and exhibit gradation through a series to clearly stream-rolled particles. Nothing like the Hungry Creek or Eagle River pattern has been detected in other basins.

All of this earliest "archaeological evidence" is based on the interpretation of redeposited pieces of stone, bone, antler, and ivory. In most cases, the recognition of these pieces as artifacts, or as byproducts of artifact manufacture, depends upon one or more hypothetical propositions, each of which demands further study. Some archaeologists would apparently dismiss the entire record simply because it has been redeposited (for example, Griffin, 1979: 44). Other writers (such as Binford, 1981: 180; Guthrie, 1980) have noted weaknesses in the interpretive framework with which the record has been presented. We will return to a discussion of these problems after considering recent archaeological finds to final Wisconsinan time.

Final Wisconsinan Evidence

The Bluefish Caves

The Bluefish Caves site is located in the Keele Range, at the western end of a limestone ridge about 65 km southwest of the village of Old Crow. Of three caves discovered thus far, two have been test-excavated by Jacques Cinq-Mars (1979; Morlan and Cinq-Mars, 1982). Caves I and II, oriented north and southwest, respectively, on opposite sides of the ridge, have produced similar stratigraphic sequences in which loess overlies cryofragmented bedrock and is overlain by humus-rich cryoclastic rubble and modern humus and vegetation. Diverse Late Pleistocene fauna have been recovered from the loess in association with evidence of human occupation. A radiocarbon date of 15,500 ± 130 B.P. (GSC-3053) on collagen from a butchered mammoth

scapula from Cave II, and a date of 12,900 ± 100 B.P. (GSC-2881) on horse femur collagen from Cave I, are consistent with stratigraphic and paleoenvironmental data with respect to the general age of the deposits and the likelihood that a complex record of several thousand years can be obtained from the site.

At the present time, the Bluefish Caves site is unique in eastern Beringia. Its importance centers on the excellent state of preservation of Late Pleistocene fauna in association with evidence of human activity. Even if several thousand years are represented by the loess, a large pile of bones outside Cave I shows the contemporaneity of mammoth, horse, bison, sheep, wapiti, and caribou. Other site areas have yielded most of these taxa, as well as moose, Arctic fox, red fox, a canid, a mustelid, and smaller mammals, birds, and fish. The archaeological evidence includes stone artifacts, bone artifacts, spatial patterning of bones, and butchering marks on bones. All such evidence is confined to the loess unit, as are the remains of extinct animals. Overlying units have yielded rather impoverished Holocene fauna and no evidence of human occupation.

Stone artifacts from the loess include an angle burin made on an edge-retouched chert blade, a chert burin spall, and a variety of chert flakes, among which are biface trimming flakes (Cinq-Mars, 1979: Fig. 17; Morlan and Cinq-Mars, 1982: Fig. 9).[3] Chert microflakes have been recovered from sediment samples taken from the loess, and the lithic types represented by these and the larger artifacts are exotic to the cave and its limestone ridge. Also exotic in this context are several small pebbles and a cobble-size hammerstone found near the bone pile outside Cave I.

Tibiae of a caribou and a sheep have been split longitudinally, whittled or scraped with a stone tool, and polished differentially on one end. These may have been used as fleshing tools. The sheep specimen was found in Cave I, whereas the caribou example came from Cave II.

Both cranial and postcranial skeletal elements exhibit cutting, scraping, and piercing marks made by stone tools. Such marks resulted from butchering and defleshing the vertebrate skeletons, and as a group are the most numerous indicators of cultural activity at the site. Nearly all such marks were first recognized during microscopic laboratory examination, since the tiny cuts are readily obscured by the thinnest film of loess or other residue (Morlan and Cinq-Mars, 1982: Fig. 10). The cuts must be carefully distinguished from other marks on the bones, some of which were produced by carnivore gnawing. Evidence of carnivore gnawing appears to be highly correlated with green bone fractures, especially on elements of horse, bison, caribou, and sheep. Hence, the fracture patterns may be difficult to decipher with respect to artificial marrow extraction and possible tool preparation.

Given the location of the Cave I bone pile at the foot of a high bedrock wall that represents the abrupt termination of the limestone ridge (Cinq-Mars, 1979: Fig. 2), it is tempting to suppose that the site functioned as a jump, but it is also possible that the natural amphitheater delineating the front of Cave I served as a surround that could have been used with or without a jump. Ongoing analysis and further excavation may assist in the interpretation of the site.

The Bluefish Caves provide an example of deposits that are rich in paleontological evidence and somewhat cryptic with respect to archaeology. There is absolutely no doubt that people were involved in the processing of animal carcasses (and probably in the deaths of animals) at Bluefish Caves, but the excavations completed thus far have not produced the so-called diagnostic artifacts required by archaeologists to assign cultural-historical labels to their finds. Nonetheless, the site demonstrates that human occupation was ongoing in northeast Beringia during a period characterized by harsh periglacial conditions, with Laurentide ice little more than 100 km to the east and windswept glacial meltwater lakes within sight to the north. The site also shows that the upland environments of the northern Yukon were able to support a large, diverse, ungulate community during full glacial time, and this fact makes it incumbent on paleobotanists to reconstruct a vegetation that meets the requirements of such a community.

Several caves now being investigated in the lower Porcupine drainage to the west of Bluefish are believed to contain Late Pleistocene deposits in which faunal assemblages should be preserved (Dixon et al., 1980), and it will be of outstanding importance to learn whether human activities can be discerned among such remains. As more such localities are discovered and excavated in eastern Beringia, we can expect to elucidate the processes leading to the emergence of later Arctic and boreal environments. We can also hope to assess problems of global importance, such as man's role in late Pleistocene extinction and the nature of cultural adaptations to early Holocene environments.

Dry Creek and Chindadn

Of the sites excavated in Alaska during the past ten years, the most outstanding with respect to possible pre-Clovis evidence, is known as Dry Creek. Located in the Nenana River valley, on the northern foothills of the Alaska Range, Dry Creek is a stratified, multicomponent site that has been extensively studied since its discovery in 1973 (Holmes, 1974; Thorson and Hamilton, 1977; Powers and Hamilton, 1978; Powers et al., n.d.). Component I, dated to 11,000 years ago, contains a variety of cobble and flake tools, including burins, and thin bifacial knives and points, some of which are characterized by triangular or subtriangular outlines and flat retouch. Powers (n.d.) notes that the recovered tool kit "is broadly comparable to Paleo-Indian tool-kits from the Plains of interior North America" (see also Haynes, 1980: 119).

Dry Creek Component II, dated to about 10,000 years ago, consists of a series of artifact clusters, some of which contain microblades, while others do not (Hoffecker, n.d.). The clusters containing microblades are generally similar to other manifestations of the American Paleoarctic tradition as defined by Anderson (1978). This much-discussed tradition is beyond the scope of this chapter (see Anderson, 1980; Dumond, 1980a, 1980b; Morlan and Cinq-Mars, 1982; Workman, 1980), but the absence of the oft-ubiquitous microblades in some of the Dry Creek II clusters raises questions concerning their functional and historical significance in these and other contexts.

For example, the lowest levels of the Village site on the shore of Healy Lake, in the middle Tanana River valley of Alaska, have yielded an assemblage called the Chindadn complex (McKennan and Cook, 1968) dated to between 10,000 and 11,000 years ago. Of all eastern Beringian assemblages presently known, Chindadn is most similar to Dry Creek Component I, except that the former includes microblades along with its variety of bifaces, such as subtriangular knives, small triangular points, and basally thinned, concave-based points. It is possible that the microblades, as well as some of the other artifacts, are mixed due to postdepositional deflation of the rather ∴ in aeolian sediments that comprise the Village site matrix, but some of the Chindadn bifaces are basally thinned to such an extent that they fall within the range of variation of eastern Beringian fluted points (Clark and Clark, 1975: 33; C. Haynes, 1980a, 1982).

Despite these uncertainties, we can see in the Dry Creek I component an example of human occupation in a residual herbaceous or steppe-tundra habitat where bison, caribou, and sheep were still available, although horse and mammoth may already have been extinct (see Ager, 1975: 87-88; Morlan, 1977: 98). The age of Chindadn may indicate that its occupation occurred in shrub tundra, but at a time when herbaceous or steppe tundra still existed in portions of the Alaska Range not far to the south (Ager, 1975). Possibly it was in such contexts that the fluted point complex was formed, but the known sites in eastern Beringia are too late to be considered as true ancestors of the complex, even if Dry Creek I and Chindadn are suggestive of the kind of technology from which the fluted points and associated artifacts could have been derived.

Fluted Points

The past decade has seen a tremendous increase in the recovery of fluted points in eastern Beringia and, significantly, such bifaces continue to be absent, or at least unreported, in western Beringia (Siberia). Most eastern Beringian fluted points are surface finds, and the few buried examples have been recovered from relatively shallow deposits for which chronology is difficult to establish. The Putu complex, excavated by Alexander (1973), for example, produced fluted points, delicate gravers, scrapers, burins, one triangular basally thinned Chindadn-like point, and approximately 140 microblades (Alexander, personal communication, 1977). A radiocarbon date on charcoal is 11,470 ± 1000 B.P. (SI-2382), but other dates on soil samples are much younger (GaK-4939: 6,090 ± 860 B.P.; WSU-1318: 8,450 ± 260 B.P.; Alexander, 1974: 25; personal communication, 1977; see note 2). The sediment covering varies from 45 to 60 cm in thickness, with 85 percent of the artifacts in the lowest 5 cm. The radiocarbon dates are consistent with the stratification, becoming progressively younger toward the surface (Alexander, personal communication, 1981). The refitting of more than 300 flakes on cores and bifaces implies considerable integrity for this assemblage, but the dates imply very slow sedimentation rates that could have precluded adequate separation of the microblades and perhaps other artifacts that might or might not belong with the fluted points.

The Batza Téna obsidian source area on the Koyukuk River has produced several surficial fluted point clusters, and interestingly, despite the co-occurrence of a variety of other bifacial forms, no microblades have been found in these clusters (Clark, 1972; Clark and Clark, 1975, 1980). Other recent finds include Girl's Hill (Gal, 1976) and other localities along the Trans-Alaska pipeline rights-of-way (Cook, 1970, 1977), and several specimens from the uplands bordering Old Crow Basin in northern Yukon (Cinq-Mars, 1978; Morlan and Cinq-Mars, 1982). These join the earlier finds of fluted points in the Utukok and Kugururok River valleys of northwestern Alaska (Thompson, 1948; Solecki, 1951; Humphrey, 1966, 1970) to form a decidedly northern distribution in eastern Beringia, seemingly associated with the Brooks Range and its northern slope and southern foothills.

Obviously, at the present rate of discovery, the number of fluted points known in Alaska and the Yukon will continue to increase rapidly during the coming decade, but there are already enough of them available to exhibit significant technological variations. Only stratified datable sites can resolve such questions as the relative ages of fluted points in Beringia versus those in midcontinental North America and the very important questions concerning possible microblade associations. At the present time, it seems premature to suggest that of two contrasting but contemporary traditions in Beringia, we can derive the fluted point complex from "the one without microblades" (Haynes, 1980a: 119-120).

Discussion

Eastern Beringia, long assumed to be the "gateway" for the first human inhabitants of the New World, has finally produced a primary site – the Bluefish Caves – that contains evidence of human occupation older than the Llano Complex of the south. Many archaeologists have asked why no such site could be found in Alaska or the Yukon, and some of the more conspicuous reasons for the delay are reiterated here. Alaska and the Yukon Territory together comprise nearly 800,000 square miles (circa 2,000,000 km²), of which more than half were not glaciated during the Pleistocene. Hence, an area larger than the states of Texas, Oklahoma, and Kansas combined has the potential to preserve ancient fossil and artifactual remains in undisturbed contexts. Much of the area is remote, and most of it is little disturbed by industrial or agricultural activities. Where the threat of disturbance has prompted intensive archaeological reconnaissance, the resulting discoveries have often been abundant and important (Cook, 1970, 1977; Cinq-Mars, 1973, 1974, 1975). It is still the case, however, that most of the major data points have been created by accidental discoveries or by deliberate, systematic research projects. Then again, there are relatively few data points in this enormous region, although the number is growing rapidly. As of 1973, less than 400 archaeological sites had been recorded in the Yukon Territory (Morlan, 1974); that figure is now approaching 1,000.

The present state of knowledge will not, however, support the reconstruction of a "culture history" of pre-Clovis times north of the ice sheets in North America. The earliest evidence described here is useful only to indicate the presence or absence of humans in the environment and the nature of single technological expressions. Since all of the specimens from the northern Yukon basins and from the muck deposits elsewhere have been redeposited at one or more times in the past, there is no way to know which pieces might belong together historically, or even which animals may have formed living communities. Taphonomic considerations can permit the definition of burial assemblages and reveal the presence of allochthonous elements, but even these analyses cannot always support the reconstruction of primary assemblages that have paleoecological or archaeological validity.

As mentioned above, some archaeologists seem inclined to reject all materials that have undergone secondary deposition (for example, Griffin, 1979: 44), but we cannot really afford that luxury. The identification of artifacts among the bones from Disconformity A shows that we are searching for primary archaeological deposits as much as 15 m below the modern surface in a northern basin where the intervening 15 m of sediments are perennially frozen. Our only access to the deposits is through searching through the exposures along the eroding river banks, and it is possible that the river is not presently eroding a primary archaeological site. Hence, we must continue to refine our interpretations of less than ideal evidence if only to improve our understanding of the range of phenomena that might aid in the recognition of primary materials should we be fortunate enough to encounter them.

Other archaeologists have recently raised some constructive criticisms of the interpretations offered for northern

Yukon fossil bones. For example, Binford (1981: 180) has offered the following comments on the interpretation of green fractured mammoth bones and bone cores and flakes:

> Morlan has reasoned that the bones of elephants are too large to have been modified in this relatively robust manner by carnivores, and that the patterning is too redundant to be the result of accidents of nature. Therefore, he has interpreted these bones as evidence for man's participation in the events represented in the admitted paleontological deposits at Old Crow.
>
> The reader will undoubtedly recognize this as a classic argument from elimination. It might also be recalled that for such an argument to be correct the assumption must be met that all the possible causes have been listed and all but one eliminated. To what degree do you think we are capable of listing all the possible cause [sic] of broken and flaked elephant bones? Given our current ignorance of taphonomic conditions surrounding the burial of elephant bones in differing circumstances, it is impossible to meet the criteria for a valid argument from elimination.

This problem is precisely the reason that the artificial "interpretation" of these fossils was deliberately and clearly phrased as a hypothesis (see Morlan, 1980a: 50) that could be tested with new data and rejected if the data indicated an alternative process or agent in the natural world. Binford continues:

> What is needed is middle-range research aimed at learning about elephant bone taphonomy. This would include actualistic studies of dead elephant carcasses and the behavior of other animals in the presence of elephant bones (the effects of trampling, tossing bones around as is recorded for elephants themselves, and so on). Research might also look at known paleontological assemblages where the presence of man can be ruled out on historical grounds to see if such items occur in assemblages known to be unrelated to human actions.

Binford apparently overlooked the systematic review of such middle-range research that appears in the monograph he cites (Morlan, 1980a: ch. 3), where many suggestions are offered as to the kinds of additional studies that are needed to test the hypotheses linking the green fracture and flaking of mammoth bones with the hand of man. Among these suggested studies were ways of learning about the effects of trampling and the tossing of bones by elephants. In March 1981, an opportunity arose to make such observations when Dennis Stanford was able to present a large group of elephants with a freshly defleshed adult elephant femur. Stanford (personal communication, 1981) observed the elephants at great length while they manipulated the bone on and above the concrete floor of their enclosure. After 24 hours of exposure to the bone, during which the elephants never abandoned it, the bone had been stepped on, tossed, held in the trunk to strike other elephants on the head, kicked, mouthed, and subjected to every other manipulation that elephants can perform on such an object. That the bone was neither broken nor extensively scarred after this extended mistreatment

tells us nothing about the fossil record of Old Crow Basin, but it does tell us that elephant, and presumably mammoth, bones are even more durable than we had suspected, and that the fracture and flaking of such specimens is a "robust" activity indeed.

Likewise, the Ginsberg elephant-butchering experiment (Stanford, Bonnichsen, et al., 1981) did not demonstrate that ancient inhabitants of the northern Yukon butchered mammoths partly with bone flakes made from mammoth bones, but the experiment did teach us that a modern elephant can be partially butchered in this way. The one conclusion that has been drawn from this aspect of the Ginsberg experiment is that artificial bone breaking and flaking is a possible cause for the green fractured and flaked mammoth bones from Old Crow Basin. In fact, this is the only "possible cause" that cannot be eliminated from consideration, whereas all other possible causes can either be eliminated or have not yet been adequately studied.

All references to the Old Crow bone artifacts in the following discussion should be read with their hypothetical status in mind. The interpretation of artificially fractured and flaked mammoth bones from redeposited contexts will always be hypothetical. No matter how much "middle-range research" is completed, the interpretation will always remain a "classic argument from elimination," because someone will always argue that not all possible causes have been considered. From the standpoint of archaeology, this observation does not negate the value of these redeposited materials. In fact, what we need to acknowledge, if we are to gain the most from the fossil and subfossil record of the past, is that there is a wide range of variation in the quality and nature of "evidence" that can contribute to an understanding of human prehistory. Even if a deposit has not been disturbed to the extent of redeposition by fluvial or other processes, an archaeological record can be cryptic and difficult to detect or interpret.

More and more of these cryptic archaeological records are being reported from all parts of the world as archaeologists and paleontologists pay closer attention to "anomalies" in sedimentary deposits. Some of the most outstanding of these are carcasses of mammoths (Chmielewski and Kubiak, 1962; Alekseeva and Volkov, 1969; Tseitlin, 1979: 52-55; Anderson, 1975) and mastodons (Mehl, 1966; Gustafson et al., 1979; Fisher, 1981) where little but fractured bones, butchering marks, peculiar arrangements of anatomical elements, and possible hammerstones signal human intervention in the creation of the deposit. More elaborate but still rather cryptic evidence is seen in deposits incorporating several or many species of animals associated with a few chert microflakes, distinctive fracture patterns, differential polish, and a few nondiagnostic stone tools. Bluefish Caves (Cinq-Mars, 1979) have all of these attributes, and Dutton and Selby in Colorado (Stanford, 1979b) have most of them. The destruction of any one of these assemblages by fluvial erosion and redeposition could produce the kind of record being recovered from the Old Crow River valley. The fact that the remains would then be in secondary contexts would not negate the evidence that would still exist on some of the specimens, although redeposition would make the interpretive problems considerably more difficult; this has certainly been our experience with the Old Crow materials.

The recognition and dating of archaeological materials in Early Wisconsinan sediments in eastern Beringia is inconsistent with the theories and prejudices of some archaeologists, though "predicted" by the speculations of others. For example, most models that link the emergence of fully modern man, as dated in Europe and the Near East, with the colonization of high latitudes (for example, Klein, 1976; Jelinek, 1980) could not have anticipated eastern Beringian human occupations much more than 40,000 years old. The earlier dates from the northern Yukon do not necessarily imply that the first Beringians belonged to a neanderthaloid grade of organization, since no such grade seems clearly definable in the East Asian Pleistocene (Aigner, 1978). No data presently exist to indicate the evolutionary status of the people who made the Old Crow artifacts, and it will be very important to reconcile this early archaeology with the record of human evolution. Regardless of the outcome, the existence of artifacts in eastern Beringian Early Wisconsinan deposits shows that high-latitude adaptations had already been achieved by that time.

Most discussions of the peopling of the New World have devoted at least brief attention to the timing and extent of Bering Land-Bridge exposure. As argued elsewhere (Hopkins, 1979: 35; Morlan and Cinq-Mars, 1982), it is doubtful that Bering Strait was ever a physical barrier to northern adapted peoples, although it could have functioned as a "filter barrier" at many times in the past. A broad land-bridge existed between Alaska and Siberia for at least several millennia around 70,000 years ago (Hopkins, n.d.), and such a bridge could have permitted the eastward movement of people who arrived in the northern Yukon at least by that time.

Many discussions of the peopling of the New World refer to "migrations," a term that seems inappropriate in this context. As Giddings (1954: 88) noted long ago, the arrival of human societies in Alaska and the Yukon was probably the result of gradual shifts in hunting territories, "the sons sometimes hunting beyond the range of their fathers but never really leaving home." Such gradual changes would seem to imply the existence of a land-bridge on which spatially contiguous populations of game animals encouraged the enlargement of the hunting ranges, but there might also have been many ways to discover new hunting opportunities on the other side of a partially or wholly inundated Bering Strait.

A number of writers (for example, Cook, 1975: 132-133) have noted that the regional diversity of eastern Beringian cultures in final Wisconsinan time implies that substantial time-depth must be expected in the total archaeological record there, and others (for example, Bryan, 1978: 316) have made the same observation about other parts of North and South America. In both eastern and western Beringia, the time-depth of the known or suspected archaeological record has more than trebled in recent years (see Mochanov, 1977, 1978, 1980 for western Beringia), but it is not clear how these areas fit together, because the nature of the evidence differs markedly in the two regions. In eastern Beringia, we can merely glimpse the potential for a long record, while in western Beringia, a relatively complete but somewhat shorter sequence can be interpreted in several different ways from the vantage point of Alaska and the Yukon (see Anderson, 1980; Dumond, 1980a, 1980b; Morlan and Cinq-Mars, 1982).

Our longer eastern Beringian record does not necessarily constitute "proof" of the peopling of the "New World," in that physiographically, Alaska and the Yukon can be more sensibly viewed as eastward extensions of Siberia rather than as northwestern North America during some past intervals. This is especially the case during glacial advances, when Laurentide and Cordilleran ice masses coalesced in both early and classical Wisconsinan time (Jackson, 1980b: Fig. 1; Mathews, 1980; Rutter, 1980). It is not known how long such coalescence may have persisted or to what extent it posed a physical or ecological barrier to the movements of plants, animals, and people, and the evidence needed to answer such questions must be recovered primarily from areas south of the glacial limits in North America. It is quite interesting that a number of localities, such as Dutton and Selby in Colorado (Stanford, 1979) and Jarvis-Egeler in Michigan (Fisher, 1981), have recently supplied evidence of the same sort we are finding in the northern Yukon and Alaska, but such similarities do not necessarily imply historical connections. We must expect most "cryptic" archaeological sites to look similar to one another whether or not they are historically related.

It still appears that the earliest historical connections we can perceive between eastern Beringia and midcontinental North America pertain to the fluted points and associated artifacts. In fact, the precise nature of even these connections is uncertain. Various alternatives have been critically examined by Clark and Clark (1975: 34; 1980), with most other authors arguing in favor of a northern origin (Humphrey, 1966, 1970; Haynes, 1980a; Martin, 1973; Morlan, 1977) or a southern origin (Dixon, 1976; Bonnichsen, 1978b; Dumond, 1980b: 991). The apparently rapid spread of the fluted point complex suggests to some writers (for example, Martin, 1973) that previously uninhabited terrain was invaded by its makers, while others

(Stanford, 1978b; Morlan and Cinq-Mars, 1982) suggest that human populations must already have been present to act as carriers and recipients of this tool kit. These stubborn questions can only be resolved with new data, but the pace of new discoveries in the past decade suggests that the answers may soon emerge from ongoing research on the New World Pleistocene.

In this chapter I have adopted the hypothesis that the alterations on fossil bones from the early Wisconsinan floodplain deposits (Disconformity A and deeper), which date to about 80,000 years ago, were the result of human activity. However, there are alternative explanations that do not depend on the presence of man at that early time period. Thus, it cannot be proved or disproved that man was present 80,000 years ago on the basis of present evidence. These alternative hypotheses, which involve the actions of natural forces, do not, however, invalidate the evidence of man's presence based on the C-14 dates of 25-30,000 years obtained on directly dated, definitely man-made artifacts recovered from younger contexts in which they had been redeposited, and these dates are still of a respectable antiquity relative to those from the rest of the New World.

NOTES

1. Since most of the proboscidean limb bones in question are by definition in a fragmentary state, their identification as mammoth or mastodon is usually impossible. The relative abundance of mammoth teeth in Old Crow Basin (Harington, 1977) suggests that most specimens represent mammoths, and further references to the bone fragments will refer to them as mammoth bones, even though some mastodon specimens could be included.

2. All radiocarbon dates are cited in this chapter with 2-sigma errors.

3. Unfortunately, a microblade fragment was found out of context on the weathered floor of a previous year's test pit.

DENNIS STANFORD

5 Pre-Clovis Occupation South of the Ice Sheets

In the past ten years, a number of archaeological investigations have produced evidence suggesting that human populations have been in the New World for a much longer period of time than was previously thought. When all of these sites are carefully scrutinized, however, there appears to be a lack of conclusive supporting evidence. The purpose of this chapter is to present new archaeological data relevant to questions concerning the actual antiquity of human occupation of the continental United States. Specifically, I shall critically discuss new discoveries and the results of several reinvestigations of controversial sites, which may or may not support the hypothesis that the occupation of the New World began more than 12,000 years ago.

The major problem concerning most of these sites is that they do not meet certain criteria that would provide clear evidence of pre-Clovis culture. These criteria are: (1) a clearly defined stratigraphy, (2) reliable and consistent radiometric dates, (3) consonance of data from relevant interdisciplinary studies, and (4) the presence of unquestionable artifacts in an indisputable primary context. In my opinion, none of the currently known archaeological sites found south of the ice sheets, and for which great age is claimed, meets these criteria at this time. I shall discuss some of these localities in an effort to illustrate the nature of the problem and the tenuous data that have been offered as proof of human activity at a very early period (Figure 5.1). Only through evidence found at a site that meets the above criteria will it be possible to gain universal acceptance of the earlier dates, but it is conceivable that we may be able to use limited data that need not come from conventional archaeological sites, which will lend some credence to the hypothesis that occupation occurred at an earlier date than is now generally recognized.

Site Evidence

Colorado: Selby, Dutton, and Lamb Spring

Some of the recent and relatively little published research that has been conducted on possibly very early sites has involved several localities on the High Plains. These sites include the Selby and Dutton sites (Stanford, 1979b; Graham, 1981) and the Lamb Spring site, all in Colorado (Stanford, Wedel, et al., 1981; Rancier et al., 1981).

The Selby site was discovered in the fall of 1975 when a large accumulation of mammoth bones was uncovered by earth-moving equipment in the course of construction of an irrigation pond. A field crew was still working on the final details of the Jones-Miller site (Stanford, 1978a), and fortunately we were in the area when the bone deposit was uncovered. A cursory examination of the locality indicated that the bone bed was below the Rago soil (Knobel, 1947), which is late Wisconsinan in age, indicating that the underlying bone bed was more than 12,000 years old. No stone artifacts had been uncovered, and none of the bones appeared to have been butchered, but it was decided that the bones would be excavated and mapped, and a geologic evaluation would be conducted as rapidly as possible so that the ranch work could be continued. The landowner agreed, and the construction company moved to another job. Shortly after the construction company started their new excavations on the Dutton farm near Idalia, Colorado, more mammoth bones were uncovered. An inspection trip verified the identification of the bones and indicated that the geological situation was nearly identical to that of the Selby site. We decided to salvage any bones that were uncovered during that day's excavation operation. One of the

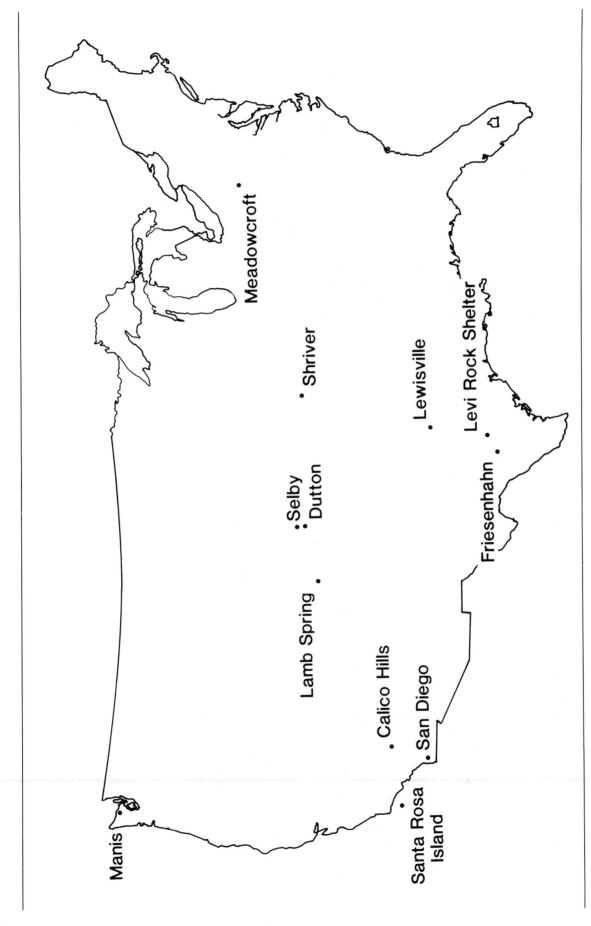

Figure 5.1 Sites Mentioned in Chapter 5

first specimens encountered was a mammoth mandible. The secondary ramus had been broken by several blows. Lying next to it was a mammoth rib that had been split longitudinally and that had a polished transverse facet on one end that made it appear to have been used as a tool.

The crew working at the Selby site found a number of bones that also appeared to have been from butchered animals. With these new data, indicating that the two localities could be important archaeological sites, both ranchers agreed that they would delay their construction activity and allow us to continue research at the localities in the following summer. A National Geographic grant was obtained, and excavations were conducted on these sites during the next three years.

Since the stratigraphy and faunal remains from these two localities are nearly identical, I will briefly summarize the results of both investigations together. The sedimentological sequence and the soils of both sites can be described from the lowest level to the upper as follows:

(1) Peorian loess (estimated age greater than 17,000 years) containing the bones of camelops, equus, and bison; no mammoth remains were found. A single bifacially flaked plano-convex scraper made of dendritic jasper was found in association with a fractured camel bone. Unfortunately, the scraper must be considered intrusive, as it was situated at the bottom of a rodent burrow.

(2) A series of lacustrine unconformities (estimated age between 17,000 and 12,000 years) containing remains of mammuthus, equus, bison, camelops, sloth, peccary, and some smaller mammals. Most bones appeared to have been butchered, and several specimens were found to have differential polish on edges, perhaps the result of their having been used as tools. At the Dutton site, seven very small, thermally altered chert flakes were found in the lacustrine levels. The flakes are of materials not found in the local Arkosic gravels, and they are not rounded by water tumbling, as are the gravels found in these deposits.

(3) A gleysol dated at 11,710 years B.P. (SI 2877) at the Selby site. This unit contained mammoth bones and, at the Dutton site, artifacts of Clovis age were found.

(4) Holocene soils that produced few bones and no artifacts.

Some bones found in all levels bore impact depressions that were thought to be the result of cutting or chopping activities designed to process bone marrow. Many of the diaphyses exhibited flake scars, which could have resulted from the intentional production of bone flakes and cores. A number of these specimens appeared nearly identical when compared with others found at the Old Crow localities in the Yukon (Morlan and Cinq-Mars, 1982; Irving and Harington, 1973; Bonnichsen, 1981), and with others produced experimentally (Stanford, Bonnichsen, et al., 1981).

Some of the putative bone tools had localized high-gloss polish, with rounded edges and step fractures similar to those found on prehistoric bone tools and on ethnographic specimens. Elements most commonly found were tibias

and metapodials of camelops, equus, and bison. A number of large flakes struck from mammoth bones exhibited polish and marks that could be interpreted as wear resulting from use, and in some cases there appeared to be striking platforms, possibly prepared in the production of flakes. The important and controversial issue is whether the "bone tools" are indeed human products, or whether breakage might have resulted from natural agencies, such as feeding by carnivores or trampling by herbivores.

After the discovery of possible bone tools and butchered bone at the Selby and Dutton sites, Waldo R. Wedel brought to my attention the faunal remains from the Lamb Spring site, located in Douglas County, Colorado. This site was discovered by Charles Lamb in 1960 during the excavation of a spring to create a stock pond. He found a large number of mammalian bones and subsequently notified G. Edward Lewis of the U.S. Geological Survey in Denver. Lewis and Glen Scott, a USGS geologist, first investigated the locality and found a number of worked flint flakes and remains of Pleistocene fauna. Since it was possible that artifacts and extinct fauna might be associated, an interdisciplinary investigation of the site was initiated under the direction of Waldo Wedel of the Smithsonian Institution.

Nine sedimentary units that represent different events in the geologic history of the site were identified. Cultural remains were found that span from at least Cody Complex times up to the time of historic utilization of the spring. A level situated below a Cody-age bison kill is of special interest for purposes of this discussion. This unit is a blue-green silty clay with sand and pebble-size particles of feldspar, quartz, muscovite flakes, and granite. Within this unit were found the remains of an extensive bone bed that included bones of mammoth, camel, bison, a cervid, a coyote-sized canid, and one or two birds.

No stone artifacts were found during two seasons of excavation, but a date on mammoth bone collagen of 13,140 ± 1,000 B.P. (M1469) indicated a possible pre-Clovis age for the level. In his report to the National Science Foundation, Wedel (1965) remarked that while he was not positive that the mammoth bones provided evidence of butchering, a number of features, such as the piling of long bones and their fragmentation, might have been the result of human activity.

A back hoe trench was dug at the site during the summer of 1979, and parts of at least three young mammoths were found. The broken mammoth limb bones recovered during this test had interesting radial fractures and impact depressions on the fracture edges. Associated with the mammoth bones was a 33-pound boulder that had clearly not been deposited at the same time as the rest of the sedimentary matrix. One surface of the boulder is heavily scarred in a manner similar to the expectable damage resulting from use as a hammerstone or anvil. The source of the boulder is thought to be the gravels of the South Platte River, nearly two miles away. In the absence of other explanations for the association of the boulder with the bones, it was thought that the boulder might have been brought to the site and used as a bone-processing tool. In replicative studies it was necessary to use boulders of similar size and weight to fracture the long bones of modern elephants that were being butchered (Park, 1978; Hershey, 1979; Stanford, 1979b; Stanford, Wedel, et al., 1981).

After the test trenching was completed, we sought and received a National Geographic grant to conduct more intensive investigations of the Lamb Spring site during the summers of 1980 and 1981. Although the results of these investigations are not yet completed, a brief report of the tentative conclusions can be offered at this time.

Two major geologic unconformities were identified: an upper unconformity that parallels the strike of the local aquifer, the Dawson Arkose, which forms a channel in which Cody-age bison bones were concentrated. A lower unconformity was produced by a channel cut into earlier deposits. It also trends to the southeast and parallels the strike of the aquifer. The bones of mammoths, as well as camelops, equus, bison, and other smaller mammalian species, were found concentrated in this channel and scattered in the banks. At least thirteen individual mammoths were represented by bones found in the course of later excavations. Bones from the earlier investigations indicate that perhaps two dozen animals died in this locality. Possible evidence of butchering was common in the form of impact depressions on the mammoth long bones, as well as on the limb bones of other species. Several bone cores and flakes were found, and there were two piles of bone flakes. One pile contained over twenty specimens from several different mammalian species. The other pile contained one extremely large flake, a core, and several smaller flakes. Most of the mammoth limb bones were incomplete, while many of the more fragile bones were unmodified.

During the 1981 excavations, it was found that the upper Cody-age channel cut down into the mammoth bone bed, causing a mixing of the sediments in the portion of the site where the boulder was found. The boulder recovered during the earlier test excavation may, therefore, have been intrusive. However, a boulder of this size has never been reported from a bison-processing site, and I think there is a high probability that it was associated with the mammoth bones.

Another find of possible significance consists of four flaked chert pebbles. These specimens, found in direct association with the mammoth bones, are crudely flaked. It is not inconceivable that they are artifacts, but I suspect that they are "geofacts." All the specimens are of chert, which is found in pebble form in the Dawson Arkose. Test excavations made in the Dawson Arkose at three localities

near the Lamb Spring site failed to produce similar specimens of natural origin. However, it must be noted that we do not know what effect natural processes such as freeze-thaw cycles or even animal trampling may have on these chert cobbles in a spring environment.

An additional flaked stone specimen was found in the mammoth bone level, and this object is without doubt an artifact. It is made from quartzite, probably obtained from the Dakota formation outcrops located several miles from the site. The specimen was not found *in situ*, although its provenience is known to within a few centimeters, and we therefore cannot be certain of its association.

Two radiocarbon dates on collagen have been obtained from samples of mammoth bone: 13,140 ± 1,000 B.P. (M-1464); and 11,735 ± 95 B.P. (S.I. 4850). If human activity can be demonstrated, this site may represent an early Clovis manifestation. However, excluding the possibly associated boulder, the questionable "flaked" stone tools, and the flaked tool with uncertain provenience, the argument for the presence of hunters utilizing mammoth must rest with the possibility of the evidence for the butchering or flaking of bones.

In an effort to help resolve problems of distinguishing the causes and events that altered bones at Lamb Spring, Dutton, and Selby, an associate, Gary Haynes, has conducted intensive systematic investigations on the condition of recently deposited mammalian bones in undisturbed wilderness areas of northern North America. The results of his research have been reported in *AMQUA* abstracts (Haynes, 1978, 1980b, 1981c), *Ossa* (Haynes, 1981b), *American Antiquity* (Haynes, 1981a), *Arctic* (Haynes, 1983), and *Paleobiology* (Haynes, 1980a). Other papers and reports are in preparation, including analyses of the bones from Selby, Dutton, and Lamb Spring.

Field work has consisted of the study of hunting and feeding behavior of large northern carnivores, such as timber wolves and brown bears, and of the condition and distribution of bison and moose bones resulting from years of predation, disease deaths, and mass catastrophic mortalities. Current field work consists of reconnaissance and survey for concentrations of recent bones potentially analogous to Late Pleistocene deposits, and excavations of water hole deposits heavily used by bison in northern Canada's Wood Buffalo National Park. Field work was also conducted at Isle Royale National Park at Lake Superior, Superior National Forest in Minnesota, Glacier National Park, Montana, Elk Island National Park, Manitoba, and several other parks and preserves in North America. Additional research has been conducted in zoos to study different end-effects of bone modifications by different taxa of carnivores. Laboratory analyses have included Scanning Electron Microscope studies in search of finely distinctive attributes of gnawed, cut, abraded, and weathered bone.

The results of field work include preliminary quantification of the expectable occurrence of spiral fracturing due to gnawing activity by carnivores or trampling and wallowing by large ungulates, and detailed observation of the highly patterned sequences of bone modification due to different species of predators and scavengers. Up to 8 percent of the limb bones of bison and moose in the field study areas have been recorded as spirally fractured, while a much greater proportion of the limb bones of smaller herbivores are spirally fractured by natural agencies. Many fragmented bones display notched edges similar to impact scars left by directed hammerstone blows, damage produced by humans when extracting bone marrow. Bone flaking and localized or differential fracture-edge abrasion and polishing by natural agencies have also been noted on some field specimens. The sequencing and timing of the weathering deterioration of bones have been recorded for numerous microenvironments that might be analogous to those of the Late Pleistocene.

Some of the excavated specimens from Lamb Spring, Dutton, and Selby could plausibly have served as tools, since potential working edges are thought to show damage from abrasion and crushing, while others have been thought to be refuse from butchering or processing activities. However, using the modern observational data as interpretive analogues, G. Haynes is inclined to assign to natural agencies much of the fossil modification such as spiral fracturing, localized abrasion, differential polished edges, dispersal of skeletal parts, and disproportionate bone representation. Such agencies might include such phenomena as gnawing by large carnivores, trampling by megafauna that habitually used the site at the time of deposition, fluvial turbulence or reworking of fossil bones, and deformational pressures within the deposits after burial and fossilization.

It was thought possible that the bone debitage found at the Selby, Dutton, and Lamb Spring sites was the result of human beings processing mammoth limb bones for the extraction of bone marrow and in an effort to obtain bone for making artifacts. It was not known, however, if people could actually accomplish the task and, if so, whether the resulting fractured bone would be analogous to the excavated specimens. In an effort to determine the validity of the hypothesis and to seek the answers to other questions, an experiment was conducted on a deceased zoo elephant (Stanford, Bonnichsen, et al., 1981).

Ginsberg, a 22-year-old African elephant who died in the Franklin Park Zoo in Boston, was used to provide the analogues. The fracturing of limb bones by means of a 12-pound cobble was a difficult task, but finally resulted in an interesting radial fracture after multiple blows. Large sections of the shafts of the broken bones were then flaked, using both hammerstones and antler percussive tools. Plat-

forms were manufactured to help control the fracture direction while producing thin bone flakes to be used for cutting tools. Bone tools, although not as effective as stone tools, were used in butchering the animal. The debitage was remarkably similar, if not identical, when compared with many purported archaeological specimens. The polish that resulted when utilizing these implements was also analogous to that seen on certain questionable excavated specimens.

In some cases it seems possible to differentiate between bones modified by human beings and those changed by natural agencies. However, there appears to be a "grey" area with specimens with overlapping attributes characteristic of both types of modification. Future research may resolve this problem, or at least reduce the number of specimens that fall into this grey area, but at present a clear and simple resolution is not possible.

Texas: Friesenhahn Cave, Levi, and Lewisville

In Texas, a number of sites are often mentioned in the context of pre-Clovis occupations of the New World. The three primary sites that have received widespread publicity are Friesenhahn Cave and Levi Rock Shelter, both located near Austin, and the Lewisville site near Dallas.

Friesenhahn Cave produced several chert flakes and a human molar, together with a large collection of Pleistocene faunal remains (Evans, 1961). It has been suggested that there might be a pre-Clovis occupation of the cave. However, subsequent analysis of the deposits by Graham (1976) has demonstrated two separate periods of sedimentation. The first period occurred between 18-19,000 years ago when the cave was occupied by scimitar cats. After that, the cave was sealed and the modern entrance was first opened between 8,000 and 9,000 years ago. The chert artifacts were found in a talus cone directly below the cave opening and are presumed to have washed into the cave after the formation of the Holocene entrance. They are not believed to be contemporaneous with the remains of Pleistocene fauna. It must also be pointed out that most of the bones of the extinct fauna had been slightly modified by the scimitar cats. It is Graham's contention that this cave was not used by human beings during the time of the deposition of the Pleistocene fauna.

Levi Rock Shelter (Alexander, 1963) has several occupation levels, with two presumed pre-Clovis levels underlying an occupation that has been identified as Clovis. The earliest occupation level is cemented to the back of the cave by a travertine deposit and has practically eroded away. A subsequent (possibly pre-Clovis) occupation occurs in unconsolidated cave fall and detritus. Stone tools in the form of utilized flakes and blades were recovered from these older units. However, the stratigraphy of this site is extremely complex. A tremendous mass of unconsolidated roof fall makes interpretations of the occupation horizons nearly impossible. The cave travertine is currently being formed, and I cannot believe that the break between it and the unaltered cave fill could be designated as an unconformity. It is possible that Levi Rock Shelter has a pre-Clovis occupation, but the stratigraphy and dating need additional clarification.

The Lewisville site, located in Denton County, Texas, was found during River Basin studies by Ted White of the Smithsonian Institution. William Crook and King Harris (1957) made surface collections in the locality between 1951 and 1956, and conducted excavations in 1956. They identified 21 burned areas as hearths and recovered several artifacts, including a Clovis point, a chopper, and several flake tools. The composition of the faunal and floral remains indicated a diversity of ecological conditions in the past, probably the result of several different time horizons being represented.

A number of radiocarbon dates were obtained from carbonized matter found in the hearths. All of the dates were in excess of 37,000 years (Crook and Harris, 1962). Many archaeologists suspected that the artifacts were intrusive and questioned the nature of the burned areas (Heizer and Brooks, 1965). No one, unfortunately, questioned whether or not the dates were correct. The site was inundated by reservoir waters during the 1957 excavation, and there has been controversy since that time. Three basic positions have been taken by prehistorians concerning the Lewisville site: (1) the artifacts were intrusive, the burned areas were of natural origin, and the site was not the result of human occupation; (2) the Clovis point was intrusive and the chopper and flakes were not, the dates are correct, and the site is a 37,000-year-old manifestation of a chopper-tool and flake culture; or (3) the dates are incorrect and the Clovis projectile point is *not* intrusive, and therefore the site is a Clovis Age campsite.

In 1978 a drought in Central Texas brought the level of Lewisville Lake down below the elevation of the hearth area. Archaeologists Larry Banks and Bob Burton of the U.S. Army Corps of Engineers took advantage of this period of low water to investigate the locality. They found two burned features and another flaked stone chopping tool. A complete reinvestigation of Lewisville was deemed necessary because it was found that the flood waters of the lake had not entirely destroyed the site and there was a possibility that the controversy surrounding the original excavation might finally be settled. The site was important if the Clovis point was in fact intrusive, since the artifacts, including the chopper tools, might represent an early technological tradition. Lewisville boasted not only tools, but a possible early date, hearths, and faunal remains that might provide data about the antiquity of human occupation in the New World.

Field research was initiated in the spring of 1979 but was terminated after several weeks when heavy rainfall brought the level of the lake up over the site. However, a drought in the summer of 1980 again brought the water to an unprecedented low level, and excavations were resumed in the fall of 1980. The results of these excavations provided some interesting data that will allow for tentative interpretations of the site.

In the course of the excavations, burned area Number 22 was cross-sectioned, and I feel that there can be little doubt that this feature is of cultural origin. Subsequent analyses of carbonized materials from the hearths indicate that lignite from the underlying Woodbine formation was being burned in the hearths, thus accounting for the early radiocarbon dates.

Additional bone materials were found in the hearths, and other smaller features were located that might be considered post molds. Tiny flakes from alibates, local quartzites, and Edwards' Plateau cherts were also recovered. One of the flakes appears to be of the same material as the original Clovis point.

Stratigraphic studies by John Albanese indicate that an unconformity is present, resulting from erosional destruction of the original occupation surface. Only the bottoms of the hearths and other features remain. This would account for the faunal remains of several different geologic ages and events. The fauna of an earlier age had been deposited in sediments into which the hearths were later dug by Clovis Age peoples who left bones of later fauna within the feature.

The East:
Meadowcroft and Shriver

Another important but controversial site in North America is Meadowcroft Rock Shelter, in southwestern Pennsylvania (Adovasio et al., 1977b; Adovasio et al., 1980). In a deeply stratified sandstone rock shelter, there is a unit known as Stratum IIa. Charcoal obtained from fire pits in the lowest third of this unit produces dates ranging between 12,600 and 19,000 years B.P. A number of small flakes and flake tools and a bifacially flaked projectile point were found, and it has been suggested that these specimens may be more than 16,000 years old. It has been alleged, however, that the charcoal used in dating might have been contaminated by "dead" carbon carried in the ground water (C. V. Haynes 1977, 1980b). Puzzling, too, is the fact that all identified faunal species are recent forms, and no extinct taxa are represented. Recent species do extend back to the Pleistocene in the northeastern United States but the absence of glacial or boreal elements is not easily explainable (Adovasio et al., 1980).

In order to resolve this debate and place Meadowcroft in proper perspective, additional radiocarbon dating should be completed, and testing for radioactive dead carbon in the ground water supply should be undertaken (see Adovasio et al., this volume). Other rock shelters and pollen cores from the area might also offer corroborative data.

The Shriver site in northwestern Missouri is also potentially significant (Reagan et al., 1978). A fluted point associated with end scrapers was found at the site 30-40 cm below ground surface. Attribute analysis suggested that the point is typologically closer to Folsom than Clovis in morphology, although in my opinion it could be related to some of the eastern fluted points, which may be as late as Folsom in age. Below this bed is a Peorian loess level containing burins, end scrapers, tortoise and tabular cores, and unifacial flake tools. Reagan et al. (1978) postulate that the lower level is over 15,000 years old, because of a thermoluminescence determination for the overlying fluted point level is 12,855 ± 1500 B.P. Unfortunately, the validity of dates obtained by this technique may be open to question, and it would be desirable to have verification from other sources.

The West: Texas Street, Calico Hills,
the Channel Islands, and Manis

An intensely controversial locality in southern California, currently being reinvestigated, is Texas Street and related sites in the San Diego area (Carter, 1957, 1980). These localities have produced numerous crudely flaked quartzite "tools" that may date to over 50,000 years B.P. It has been argued that these specimens are not the handiwork of human artisans, but rather are cobbles that have been broken in fluvial transportation to and down the San Diego River. Another explanation for the cause of the manmade appearance of the specimens is that the source of the cobblestones is a loosely cemented conglomerate that caps parts of the upper land surface. As the sites are in an active fault zone, many of these quartzite cobbles have been bipolarly crushed while *in situ*. When they erode out of their primary deposits, they appear identical to manmade flakes, and as they are further transported down the steep embankments, the fragile edges become secondarily flaked.

This scenario could be tested by excavtion of both the conglomerate formation, to demonstrate the exact nature of this observed phenomenon, and of the talus below the capstone. Additional excavation may also produce the natural primary flakes.

Calico Hills, California (Leakey et al., 1968; Simpson, 1978), is another site containing problematical chert objects that have been commonly defined as crude artifacts dating to over 150,000 years old. From an impressionistic viewpoint, I am not convinced of their man-made nature. They are in fact very similar to the specimens recovered from Lamb Spring. However, I am in agreement with Patterson (1980) that there are not yet enough quantitative

data to make a determination of their artificial status. I feel that the case made by Duvall and Venner (1979) against the reality of the artifacts is irrelevant because they compare the Calico Hills specimens to well-developed bifacial technologies from the New World. They could have made a strong case, either pro or con, by comparing these specimens with tools and flakes of lower Paleolithic technologies of Southeast Asia.

A few of the Calico stone objects do resemble artifacts (Bryan, 1978), but given the nature of chert-bearing alluvial deposits, the process by which these "artifacts" were created must be viewed with a certain amount of skepticism. Publication of definitive geological work at the site, sound or supportive dates, descriptions of the so-called hearths, and in-depth lithic analysis will allow for eventual definitive statements.

The Channel Islands of California have also been described as having fire hearths associated with burned bones of Pleistocene fauna dated between 11,000-37,000 years ago (Orr, 1968). It is thought, however, that all of the finds to date are probably situated in a redeposited context (Johnson, personal communication). The weathered bedrock sediments have been oxidized to the same color as burned earth, making it difficult to distinguish hearth features. All of the alluvial sediments on Santa Rosa Island contain abundant charcoal and mammoth bones, and stone tools were also found on erosional surfaces. Additional work is needed to clarify the nature of human occupation of the Channel Islands.

At the Manis Site on the Olympic Peninsula of Washington State, a bone object tentatively identified as the broken tip of a projectile point was found embedded in the rib of an old mastodon that had died in a marsh or bog (Gustafson et al., 1979). Although bone growth around the intrusive object indicated that the wound had been inflicted a number of months before the animal died, the carcass is thought to have been utilized by human beings at the time of its death. Some bones of the skeleton were missing, and the skull had been entirely fragmented. A possible cobble core or chopper was recovered in the bog deposits, together with bones of three bison, a caribou, a duck, and a muskrat. The site is multicomponent. Dates derived from seeds, wood, and other vegetal remains found in the bone-bearing alluvium suggest that the mastodon levels are around 12,000 years old.

If the association of the cobble tool, the presumed projectile point, and the organic material (presumably accurately dated) can be demonstrated, then there is a clearcut case for mastodon utilization by human beings during the terminal Pleistocene of the Northwest Coast. Using the presently available data, it is impossible to attribute the Manis site to any cultural framework or tradition; it may in fact be a Clovis-age site.

Conclusions

We can find fault with the interpretation of all of these sites, and we cannot as yet decisively push back the time of human occupation beyond the 12,000 year B.P. time marker in North America south of the ice sheets. Collec- tively, there appears to be enough evidence to encourage continuation of the search for a pre-Clovis occupation in this area, although perhaps the materials in question are simply "background noise" created naturally during and after the final millenia of the Pleistocene. Only continued research will resolve the problem.

ROY L. CARLSON

6 The Far West

The Far West is that part of North America which Teddy Roosevelt reputedly referred to as "west of the west." In ethnographic terms, it constitutes the nonagricultural and mostly nonceramic parts of western North America – the Northwest Coast, Columbia-Fraser Plateau, the Great Basin, and California. It is the vast and diverse area between the Pacific Ocean and the Rocky Mountains that encompasses the Alaska Panhandle, most of British Columbia, all Washington and Oregon, and most of California, Nevada, and Idaho. This area varies from a narrow, coastal strip backed by high mountains in the north to low hills and coastal plains in the south. Major rivers flowing west connect the coast with the interior plateaux in the northern and central sections, but in the south interior drainage basins with glistening lakes or dried up playas and deserts are typical. The last glaciation rendered all or nearly all of the Alaska Panhandle, British Columbia, and northern Washington uninhabitable because of cold and ice cover, but brought increased precipitation, higher lake levels, and different and more abundant flora and fauna in regions to the south. Man could not have lived in most of the northern section because of cold and glacial cover, but in the south the environment was enhanced, and present-day deserts were oases.

For the purposes of this chapter, Early Man means the earliest human or cultural remains for which there is acceptable archaeological evidence up to about 8,000 B.P. In the process of translating such evidence into meaningful prehistory, certain theoretical principles intervene. While most of these are self-evident, one that needs to be stated explicitly is the principle that preindustrial man will follow the habitat to which his culture is adapted as that habitat shifts location in response to world or regional climatic change. This principle does not mean that man cannot adapt to changed conditions; he can and does, and this is a principle of equal importance. Both are important, as

it is in the throes of environmental change that began with the melting of the last continental glacier that the best evidence for Early Man in the Far West first becomes available.

Our knowledge and comprehension of Early Man in the Far West have been and continue to be beset by those problems that plague archaeological interpretation everywhere. Disputes arise in three areas again and again: artifact recognition; validity of particular dates and dating techniques; and degree or type of association of dated material with man-made materials, or of the latter with particular geomorphic units. In spite of controversies in these areas, there has been considerable progress in Early Man studies in the Far West in the past decade. My intent is to review the research of the 1970s and integrate it with what was previously known or suspected, and to point out where new interpretations have been made or are called for.[1]

Pre-Wisconsinan

Claims for archaeological evidence firmly establishing man's presence in the Far West preceding the last glaciation, the Wisconsinan, more than 70,000 years ago, continue to be made and rejected. The biggest problem is that there is an area of overlap between stone objects flaked naturally and those flaked by man, and a lack of universal agreement as to the boundaries of this overlap. If one extends the boundaries of human flaking rather broadly, all of the proposed artifacts from sites of this period would still fall within this area of overlap. This fact, plus the extremely early dating and lack of cultural context in which these lithics occur, has caused almost all archaeologists except the excavators to reject these objects as definitive evidence of the presence of man at this time period. The best-known site in this category is Calico Hills in San Bernardino County, California.

The Calico Hills site is in an alluvial fan deposit in the foothills of the Calico Mountains near Yermo, California (Simpson, 1978; Simpson et al., 1981). Uranium-thorium dates (Shlemon and Bischoff, 1981) on the subsurface deposits in contact with the flaked stone indicate an age of about 200,000 years; other dates give an age of 80,000 to 125,000 years for development of the surface soils at the site. Excavations into the fan deposits have been both extensive and meticulous, and there is no question of the association of the lithics with the dates. These facts do not compensate for the quality of the flaked stone objects, however, which are crude and irregularly flaked, and interpreted by most archaeologists who have seen them as geofacts. Haynes (1973: 305-310) presents a detailed discussion of natural forces operating at the site that could fracture stone. Selected flaked stone objects, excavated since Haynes's article was written, were exhibited at the Society for American Archaeology meetings in San Diego in 1981, and I again saw them at Calico Hills later that year. They are not convincing evidence for man's presence. There are lithics from the surface of the Calico Hills site, however, that are unequivocally man-made and that will be discussed later.

Early and Mid-Wisconsinan

The Wisconsinan was the last of the major glacial advances in North America. Even though the Mid-Wisconsinan between 63,000 and 23,000 years ago, would probably win first place in a contest for the most favored (by archaeologists) interval for man's entry into North America south of the glaciated regions, archaeological data from this period are meager. In 1977 and 1980, Reeves (1981) reexamined sites in the Mission Valley of San Diego which had previously been promoted as archaeological sites by G. F. Carter. Reeves concluded that there are both naturally spalled stone forms, such as those Carter called the "bipolar blade/core industry," and unifacially flaked, man-made cobbles and flakes. These objects still fall within the area of overlap between natural and human flaking, however, and are not likely to be readily accepted as being of human manufacture. Part of Reeves's argument, however, rests on the absence of any discernible natural percussive force capable of detaching a flake with an eraillure and a pronounced bulb of percussion in the specific environment of the Mission Ridge site. These materials are not directly dated, but Reeves suggests the Mid-Wisconsinan. An irregularly flaked basalt slab from gravel near the Columbia River attributable to the Spokane Flood, which Cressman et al. (1960: Fig. 27) consider an artifact, could belong to the same period.

Other claims for Early or Mid-Wisconsinan man in the Far West have rested until recently on dates obtained from human bones discovered accidentally in California during the 1930s (Berger et al., 1971). Recent redating of two of these finds, Del Mar and Sunnyvale, using uranium

series dating has indicated ages of 11,000 and 8,300 years for these finds instead of the 48,000 and 70,000 years obtained originally using the amino acid racemization technique (Bischoff and Rosenbauer, 1981). A third skull, called Los Angeles Man and dated by C-14, constitutes the best evidence from the Mid-Wisconsinan for Early Man in the Far West. A date of >23,600 years was obtained on the collagen of this darkly mineralized, carbonate-encrusted skull found in 1936, 4 meters below the surface of an ancient river bed and less than 400 meters from mammoth bones reported at the same depths (Berger et al., 1971). While the date and the geological association seem consistent, the circumstances of discovery and the single C-14 date on a sample too small for a finite date will continue to guarantee skepticism about the find. The "Taber Child" from southern Alberta has recently been dated by C-14 to 3,680 ± 420 B.P., refuting earlier claims for its great antiquity.

Claims for carbon dates on hearths associated with tools and dwarf mammoth bones on Santa Rosa Island (Berger, 1978, 1981) at 40,000 years ago await detailed presentation. Earlier claims (Orr, 1968) have not been accepted. Davis et al. (1981) have recently reported a uranium series date of 42,350 ± 3,300 B.P. on a fragment of mammoth tooth found in contact with two sand-blasted flakes at the Basalt Ridge site at China Lake, California. Since redeposition resulting in a fortuitous association of these objects cannot be precluded in this area, this evidence unfortunately cannot be considered definitive.

Late Wisconsinan and Early Post-Glacial

It is only during the Late Wisconsinan, a period beginning some 23,000 years ago, that acceptable archaeological evidence becomes common, and most of it is more recent than 14,000 years ago, the peak of the last glacial maximum. The further into the period of deglaciation between 14,000 and 10,000 years ago, the better the evidence. By 10,000 years ago, several widely distributed basal cultures or cultural traditions can be recognized. There are also several finds from the earlier part of the Late Wisconsinan which are not directly relatable to these traditions. These finds, which will be discussed first, are from Manix Lake, Laguna Beach, and Wilson Butte Cave.

Pleistocene Lake Manix in San Bernardino County, California, has ancient shorelines dated by C-14 at 19,300 ± 400 B.P. (UCLA 121) on tufa, and 20,050 B.P. on Anadonta shells; an earlier phase is more than 47,000 B.P. (Haynes, 1973). Flaked stone artifacts occur around the ancient shorelines and elsewhere in the area, including the surface of the Calico Hills site (Simpson, 1958, 1978). The question has arisen as to whether these lithics constitute an early, primitive industry and relate to the lake levels, or whether they are quarry refuse left behind by more advanced knappers. Glennan (1976: 43-61) has recently studied the Manix Lake collection and applied random sampling collecting techniques in obtaining additional specimens. He concludes:

> The Manix Lake lithic industry probably reflects a workshop activity area and not the cultural remains of a pre-projectile point stage occupation of the Mohave Desert of Southern California.

The industry may still be quite old in view of the heavy patina on the artifacts and the desert pavement in which they lie, but need bear no relationship to the shore lines and their dates.

The Laguna skull with associated long bones was another chance find in the 1930s that was later dated by C-14 (Berger et al., 1971). Collagen from the skull dated 17,150 ± 1470 B.P. (UCLA 1233 A). The long bones were also dated but yielded an insufficient quantity of material for a finite date. However, this date (UCLA 1233 B) was calculated at greater than 14,800 years B.P., which is not inconsistent with the date on the skull. Before undertaking the dating, the researchers did establish that the skull was indeed the one found in 1933 at Laguna Beach by comparing it with photographs taken at the time. In 1968, excavation was undertaken at the point where the bones were thought to have been found. Two shell layers in the vicinity were dated by C-14 to between 8,000 and 9,000 years ago, with the older date on the upper layer. This information only further confused the issue, and the researchers concluded that the excavations produced no information relevant to the presence of the bones.

Wilson Butte Cave in central Idaho contains a series of stratified deposits, of which the earliest containing definite artifactual material is designated stratum C (Gruhn, 1965; Butler, 1968). A single C-14 date of 14,500 ± 500 B.P. was obtained on charcoal from the lower part of Stratum C. The artifactual assemblage associated with this date is unfortunately small and undiagnostic, and consists of two bone object fragments, two flakes, and a crude biface. Camel, horse, and sloth bones were associated with these discoveries. The importance of these finds is that they establish the presence of man and of bifacial technology at this early date. The problem is that it is a single find with a single date on objects that are so general and crude that they are undiagnostic of any known cultural tradition, although they may well eventually prove to be typical of their time period.

With the waning of the last glaciation between 14,000 and 10,000 years ago, sites suddenly become common, and evidence of humans appears throughout the Far West. It no longer becomes necessary to mull over inconclusive data merely to establish their presence or absence. Regional cultural traditions or basal cultures become clearly recognizable, and it seems appropriate to use them to integrate recent research with that accomplished earlier. While it may be argued that once this stage is reached we are no longer discussing Early Man, it must be realized that these traditions did not spring full-blown out of the void,

and that the contents of these traditions are better clues to Early Man than are any earlier data currently at our disposal. The chief task of the archaeologist is, after all, to see which if any historical threads can be traced through the myriad adaptations such cultural traditions would have endured in the face of the changing environments of the period of glacial retreat. There are at least four major basal cultures or cultural traditions in the Far West: the Stemmed Point tradition, the Fluted Point tradition, the Pebble Tool tradition, and the Microblade tradition. These traditions are conceptualized as full cultural traditions and not merely as technological traditions such as Bryan (1980) means, using some of the same terms.

Each of these traditions can be characterized in terms of particular tool types and have been named accordingly. These names do not imply that the content of these traditions is limited to the tool types used to label them. Each of these cultural traditions is conceptualized as a basal culture with components spread over a contiguous geographic area possessed by both a distinctive adaptation or way of life and particular types of tools indicative of a close historical relationship of the local and regional components. These cultures partly overlap in time and space, and some shared tool types are expectable as a result of either acculturation or common ancestry. Not at all clear, however, are the ancestral relationships, if any, of these traditions to each other. Also unclear is the real meaning of differences in tool types, some of which hint at differences in knowledge of weapons systems. For example, bone foreshafts found with Clovis suggest the use of long lances for hunting mammoth (Lahren and Bonnichsen, 1974), but did these hunters also know and use the spear thrower, for which there is evidence in other traditions (but not in Clovis)?

The Stemmed Point Tradition

Stemmed projectile points have been known to be used in the Far West ever since the Lind Coulee site in eastern Washington was excavated in 1951 and 1952 by Richard Daugherty (1956). It was clearly an Early Man site in view of the associations of extinct bison remains with lithics of types unknown from later periods, the geological context in which they were deposited, and the directly associated C-14 dates of 9300 ± 940 B.P. and 8515 ± 460 B.P. (Daugherty, 1956). Although Daugherty pointed out generalized similarities between Lind Coulee and early components in the Great Basin, particularly the Playa industry, the site remained poorly known and enigmatic for many years, partly because the projectile points were stemmed and did not conform to established Early Man types. Stemmed points had been known for a long time, however, from areas to the south around Pleistocene Lake Mohave (Campbell and Campbell, 1937; Amsden, 1937), but their age was subject to considerable debate ranging from estimates of terminal Pleistocene (Antevs, 1937) to 2000-3000 years (Rogers, 1939: 43). Later work at Lake Mohave (Brainerd, 1953) eliminated the necessity of consideration of the younger dating estimates. Such arguments endured, however, and in refuting some on the recency of Lake Mohave material, E. L. Davis (1967: 349) pointedly noted:

> If one reviews cultural sequences in the western Great Basin during the past 10,000 years, it is evident that widespread cultures of a generalized Lake Mohave type underlie them all.

In reviewing the same data, Warren (1967: 182) predicted the existence of "an older, as yet undefined, cultural stratum that is present throughout a large part of western North America." Both researchers considered the Lind Coulee and Lake Mohave materials as related on an early time level. The only C-14 date at that time on Lake Mohave material was 9,640 ± 240 B.P. on shells from one of the lower beaches between 925 feet and 930 feet in elevation (Warren and DeCosta, 1964). Beaches associated with higher lake stands at 937, 943, and 946 feet, where the artifacts had been found (Antevs, 1937: 45; Rogers, 1966), remained undated.

The intervening years have witnessed the accumulation of data from the Oregon and Nevada areas between Lake Mohave and Lind Coulee, and the excavation and dating of a number of sites in the northern end of the distribution, particularly Marmes Rockshelter, the Windust Caves, and Hatwai. More excavations were accomplished in 1972-74 at Lind Coulee itself. Further work on dating the shorelines of Pleistocene Lake Mohave has been undertaken, and surveys and some excavations have continued in much of the desert west. This work suggests that there are two regional variants of this tradition, a northern and a southern (see Figure 6.1).

The northern variant is usually called Lind Coulee or Windust, and the southern Lake Mohave, or in some schemes it is grouped with San Dieguito. Both variants contain long-stemmed, weakly shouldered projectile points, concave-based points, indented stemmed points, chipped stone crescents, well-defined scrapers of ovoid, domed, and keeled types, gravers, and drills (see Figures 6.2-6.5). The unstemmed, indented, or concave-based forms are all small and may actually be the resharpened stems of originally much longer-stemmed points. There is no uniform system of names for these points. The distinctive feature of the southern variant is a type that in some cases may have started out as a long point, but through resharpening ended up as a stubby triangle on a long stem. Tuohy (1969, 1974) has studied these points from Nevada sites and has shown how they are made or sharpened using a series of burin blows. This technique of point manufacture is not typical and possibly not present in the

Lind Coulee sites. The southern variant seems to begin earlier than that farther north, so it seems appropriate to review recent work on it first.

The most recent work at Lake Mohave (Ore and Warren, 1971) provides a number of C-14 dates, a sequence of lacustral events, and concludes that the area was apparently occupied several times by Early Man. They obtained C-14 dates from shell on beaches associated with Rogers's (1966) 33-foot terrace (940 feet elevation), from which he collected artifacts he grouped as belonging to San Dieguito I, II, and III, and C-14 dates on shell from strata that predate the cutting of the outlet channel at the 940-foot elevation. The dates on the beaches are 12,450 ± 160 B.P. (4 feet below the 940-43 feet elevation) and 13,620 ± 100 B.P. (936-38 feet elevation). The dates on the earlier deposits, which predate the channel cutting, are 14,550 ± 140 B.P. and 15,350 ± 240 years ago.

The two younger dates on the beaches could actually date the Lake Mohave occupation, and the older dates limit it on its early end. Beaches at lower elevations gave younger dates of 9,340 ± 140 B.P. and 10,270 ± 160 B.P. The latter is the only date directly associated with artifactual material (nondiagnostic, unfortunately). One C-14 date on tufa from the 940-foot elevation was only 9,960 ± 200 B.P. which, if correct, would indicate water still at that elevation at that recent a time. Tufa dates are normally too young, and this one seems out of phase with others at Lake Mohave and should probably be discounted. The artifacts from the early surveys were not sorted by elevation, so it is not possible to see if there are differences between assemblages from different lake levels. These dates suggest that the materials all belong between 14,500 and 10,000 years ago.

Recent work has also been undertaken in southern Oregon and Nevada. Layton (1972) made obsidian hydration measurements on the projectile points from Cougar Mountain Cave in the Fort Rock Valley of south central Oregon. This site had yielded more early projectile points than any other in the area, but had been excavated by an amateur (Cowles, 1959) without the same level of control used professionally. Layton's (1972) analysis rather clearly demonstrates the succession of point types for this region and is a very significant work. Stemmed points lie at the bottom of the sequence and effectively link those of Lake Mohave to the south with Lind Coulee to the north. Recent work at the nearby Fort Rock and Connley Caves (Bedwell, 1970, 1973) has provided some corroborative C-14 dating. The earliest assemblage is from Square 10, level 10 and lies on the gravel in the bottom of Fort Rock Cave. In this square and level were two projectile points (Figure 6.3), a mano fragment, and eleven casually flaked stone tools. One is a long-stemmed point that has been

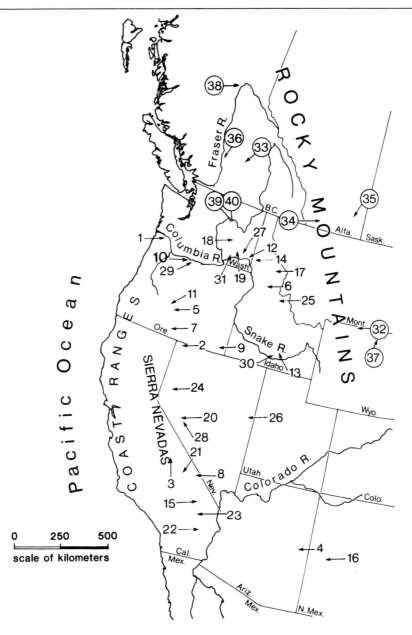

NOTE: Circled numbers indicate sites outside the main area of distribution which are probably related.

Stemmed Point Tradition

1. Astoria
2. Black Rock Desert
3. China Lake
4. Concho
5. Connley
6. Coopers Ferry
7. Cougar Mtn.
8. Death Valley
9. Dirty Shame
10. Five Mile Rapids
11. Fort Rock Cave
12. Gramite Point
13. Haskett
14. Hatwai
15. Lake Mohave

16. Lake San Augustine
17. Lenore
18. Lind Coulee
19. Marmes
20. Mud Lake
21. Panamint Basin
22. Pinto Basin
23. Playa
24. Sadmat
25. Shoup
26. Smith Creek Cave
27. Thorn Thicket
28. Tonopah
29. Wildcat Canyon
30. Wilson Butte Cave
31. Windust Cave

Related Components

32. Big Horn Basin
33. Gore Creek
34. Lake Linette
35. Lindoe
36. Lochnore
37. Medicine Lodge Coulee
38. Stoney Creek
39. 45-OK-58A
40. 45-OK-49

Figure 6.1   Distribution of the Stemmed Point Tradition

a. Pinto Basin lake terrace (Amsden)
b, k, l. Marmes Rockshelter (Daugherty, Fryxell, Rice)
c. Lake Mohave (Amsden)
d. Lake Mohave 940-foot terrace (Rogers)
e. Lake Mohave (Rogers)

f, g, j. Lind Coulee (Daugherty)
h. Salt Spring, Dry Lake, San Bernardino County, California (Rogers)
i. Concho Complex, Arizona (Weber)
m. Lake San Augustine, 8887-foot shoreline (Weber)
n, o. Mud Lake, Nevada (Tuohy)

Figure 6.2   Stemmed and Weakly Shouldered Points of the Stemmed Point Tradition

a   b

0   1   2   3   4   5 cm

NOTE: These two points are associated with charcoal C-14 dated to 13,200 ± 720 B.P. and are the earliest dated projectile points in the Far West. Both have been resharpened and are probably the remnants of much larger points.

Figure 6.3   Points from Bedwell's Excavations at Fort Rock Cave

resharpened almost down to the beginning of the stem, and the other is a small, concave-based specimen. Associated charcoal from the same level gave a date of 13,200 ± 720 B.P. (GAK 1738) (Bedwell, 1973: Table 19). A date on shell from the old lake level, which would have been appropriate for the occupation of Fort Rock Cave, is 13,380 ± 230 B.P. (Bedwell, 1973: 46). The 13,200 ± 720 date is the earliest date on charcoal directly associated with artifacts diagnostic of this tradition. Two levels (20 cm) above this, the date of 10,200 ± 230 B.P. was obtained (GaK 2147). In this period, 11,000-8,000 B.P., the two early point forms continue and are supplemented by more evolved, stemmed, indented base forms, and by Haskett points. Crescents also occur in this later period.

Corroborative evidence for the earliest Fort Rock C-14 date is scant, but there is some. In surface surveys in the China Lake Basin in California, Davis (1978: Table 9) seriated the lithics using weathering as the primary criterion. In this seriation the Lake Mohave points, stemmed ovate points, and crescents were more weathered than both the proto-Clovis and classic Clovis remains, and hence potentially, though not definitively, older. The already-cited shoreline dates on Lake Mohave are close to the early date at Fort Rock, and the artifactual remains are very similar. A stemmed point (Figure 6.2m) has been found at the 8,887-foot shoreline of Pleistocene Lake San Augustine, and a crescent (Figure 6.5c) and stemmed indented base point at the 6960-foot shoreline (Weber, 1981). Fluted point occupations occur at lower elevations around the former lake (Weber, 1980, 1981; Beckett, 1980). In Nevada, Tuohy (1968: 33) notes that Clovis is not associated with the highest levels of Pleistocene Lake Lahontan, but well below. At Smith Creek Cave in eastern Nevada, Bryan (1979:185, 204) discovered fragments of stemmed points in levels C-14-dated between 12,150 ± 120 B.P. (Birm 752, twigs) and 11,680 ± 160 B.P. (Tx-1421, charcoal). All of this evidence suggests that the

Lake Mohave materials predate Clovis in the Great Basin and begin with the last pluvial maximum or shortly thereafter, and that Clovis may overlap with middle portions of the Stemmed Point tradition in this area. A stratified site is very much needed.

Points similar to those from Lake Mohave occur in the Anasazi area of the Southwest, where they are normally considered as early Archaic, postdating the fluted point horizon (Irwin-Williams and Haynes, 1970). There seems to be no real evidence for their time placement, however, and consideration should be given to the possibility that they predate Clovis in that area also.

There has been considerable growth in our knowledge about the internal dimensions and geographic distribution of the northern or Lind Coulee variant of the Stemmed Point tradition in the last decade. Excavated components are now known from the following sites, in addition to Lind Coulee: Marmes Rockshelter, Windust Caves, and Thorn Thicket (Rice, 1972); Wildcat Canyon (Cole, 1968); Hatwai (Ames et al., 1981); small undated assemblages from two sites, 45-OK-58A and 45-OK-49, on the Columbia River in northern Washington (Grabert, 1968); possibly Five Mile Rapids (Cressman et al., 1960); the Dirty Shame Rockshelter in eastern Oregon (Aikens et al., 1977); and Fort Rock Cave (Bedwell, 1973). In central Idaho, the Shoup (Swanson and Sneed, 1966), Lenore (Toups, 1969), Cooper's Ferry (Butler, 1969), and Wilson Butte Cave (Gruhn, 1961) sites have yielded components related to Lind Coulee. Surface finds of Windust Points (a name which has come into usage for the indented stemmed type) have been reported from eastern Oregon (Fagen and Suge, 1973: 68) and from as far west as Astoria, near the Oregon coast (Minor, 1979). There is also evidence of expansion across the Rockies into the western fringes of the Plains.

The Lind Coulee tradition dates between at least 10,810 ± 275 B.P. (WSU363, shell) and 8,700 ± 300 B.P. (W2208, charcoal) on the basis of C-14 dates on stratigraphic unit 1 at Marmes Rockshelter (Rice, 1972).

a. Fossil Spring, San Bernardino County, California (Rogers)
b. Lake Mohave, 940-foot terrace (Rogers)
c, j, n. Marmes Rockshelter (Daugherty, Fryxell, Rice)
d. Stoney Creek, central interior British Columbia (Sewell)
e, g, o. Fort Rock Cave (Bedwell, Cressman)

f, h, i. Lochnore Site (Sanger)
k. Pinto Basin (Amsden)
m. 45-OK-58, Washington (Grabert)
p. Lake Linette, Alberta (Reeves)
q. Paradise River, 50 miles west of Lake Mohave (Amsden)
r. Wildcat Canyon (Cole)

Figure 6.4   Concave-based, Indented-based, and Indented Stemmed Points from Components of the Stemmed Point Tradition

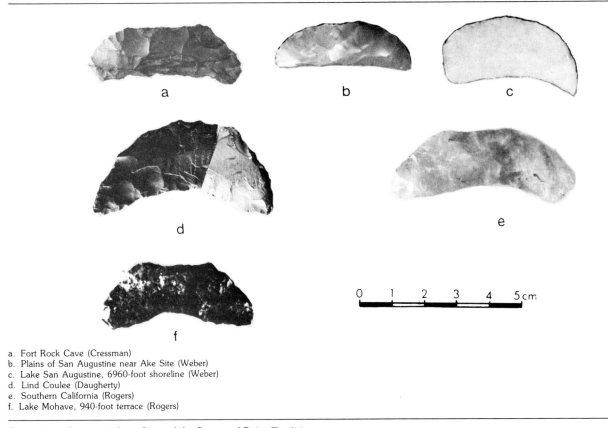

a. Fort Rock Cave (Cressman)
b. Plains of San Augustine near Ake Site (Weber)
c. Lake San Augustine, 6960-foot shoreline (Weber)
d. Lind Coulee (Daugherty)
e. Southern California (Rogers)
f. Lake Mohave, 940-foot terrace (Rogers)

Figure 6.5   Crescents from Sites of the Stemmed Point Tradition

At Hatwai (Ames et al., 1981), C-14 dates on charcoal fall between 10,800 and 9,800 B.P. Moody (1978) analyzed the microstratigraphy, paleoecology, and tephrochronology of the Lind Coulee site based on excavations in the early 1970s and placed the site temporally between 8,600 and 9,000 years ago. She concludes (Moody, 1978: 217):

> The Lind Coulee Site, then, was a spring habitation site near a supply of large herbivores. The site was occupied as part of the economic seasonal rounds of the peoples living in the Columbia Basin 9,000 years ago.

This information alters one of the models of local prehistory which tended to view Lind Coulee as ancestral to, rather than contemporaneous with, the Windust phase (see Warren, 1968; Rice, 1972).

David Rice (1972) analyzed the material from the Marmes Rockshelter and related sites excavated in the mid-1960s, and defined the Windust phase on the basis of similarities among ten components in the drainages of the Columbia and Snake rivers. He notes the resemblances with early assemblages from Fort Rock, Connley, and Cougar Mountain Cave in south central Oregon. He also demonstrates an evolving system of related projectile point forms which contrasts with models in which each type is considered to represent a different group of hunters. This work, plus that of Layton (1972), have rather effectively destroyed the model of simple leaf-shaped "Cascade" points as the earliest type in this region. This type group is present but becomes more common in later cultures.

In British Columbia, Lind Coulee material is not well documented, although it is present. The Lochnore Complex (Sanger, 1968, 1970) may eventually prove to be derived in part from this cultural tradition. The Lochnore Creek site, the type site for the Lochnore Complex, is large, over 700 feet above the Fraser River, and contains evidence of a number of occupations, including some with multiple excavations for housepits (Sanger, 1966). Three stratigraphic zones were identified, although Zones II and III were from different parts of the site and were not superimposed. No C-14 dates were obtained on either of these older zones. Sanger (1970: 43) queries the stratigraphic position of those points (Pl. V a, l,m,n) that resemble Windust types. Farther north, in surface collections from the Stoney Creek site near Burns Lake, I have seen a few points that could be lost in the Windust phase assemblage, but they are not among the most diagnostic forms. Choquette (1982) has also discovered Lind Coulee points on ancient terraces around glacial Lake Kutenai.

The earliest material so far dated in the interior plateau country of British Columbia is a partial (no skull) human skeleton from a mud slide deposit below Mazama ash at

Gore Creek in the Thompson river drainage. The skeleton is C-14 dated at 8,250 ± 115 B.P. (S 1737) (Cormie, 1981: 124). Unpublished carbon isotope studies on the bones by Brian Chisholm of Simon Fraser University indicate that the individual in question did not subsist on anadromous fish or marine fauna, but on terrestrial resources. This finding is significant in that if one assumes that the individual in question was representative of the population present 8,000-8,500 years ago in the Thompson drainage, then that subsistence must have been based on hunting and not fishing, and that the pattern of reliance on salmon had not yet spread inland from the lower reaches of the Fraser system. Unfortunately, no artifacts were recovered, so it is not possible to tie this skeleton in definitely with a specific cultural tradition such as Lind Coulee.

Human skeletal material is present in the early levels of Marmes Rockshelter and in the early floodplain deposits outside the shelter (Fryxell et al., 1968; Krantz, 1969; Rice, 1972). Some of these remains had been cremated, and Krantz has suggested cannibalism as the most probable explanation of their condition. The skeletons are clearly *Homo sapiens sapiens* and not some ancestral type.

There has been considerable expansion of knowledge of the eastern extent of this tradition across the Rockies. In northwest Wyoming, at the Medicine Lodge Creek and Southsider Cave sites, Frison (1978: 40) reports points similar to those of the Lind Coulee-Windust series in levels radiocarbon-dated between 9700 and 8500 B.P. Types called "Lovell Constricted" and "Pryor Stemmed," and what Frison calls "unnamed mountain oriented complexes" could probably be grouped with the Lind Coulee tradition. To the north, in southern Alberta, Reeves (1975) has noted Lind Coulee similarities with the basement complex in the Waterton Lakes locality, and nearby at the Lindoe site, Bryan (1980) found C-14 dates of 9710 ± 190 B.P. and 9900 ± 120 B.P. on charcoal and bison bones associated with a long-stemmed point of similar type. Such occurrences may represent seasonal forays onto the Plains for bison or other big game.

In addition to better dating and expanded knowledge of its geographic distribution, there is now increased understanding of the internal dimensions of Lind Coulee culture. While it has been necessary methodologically to emphasize projectile point types and styles in delineating this cultural tradition – since in attempting to draw boundaries between different cultural traditions, comparisons must be made using artifacts which at least theoretically are capable of transcending cultures – this emphasis should not obscure the fact that there are other artifacts present in the better sampled components. These include: bolas stones, bone needles, barbed bone harpoon heads, atlatl hooks, shell beads and pendants, antler bevel faces, and various scrapers and choppers in addition to chipped stone crescents (Daugherty, 1956; Rice, 1972). Rice's study

(1972: Fig. 44) rather clearly shows hunting as the most important activity pattern reflected in Windust phase artifacts, and Moody (1978) has shown the seasonal nature of big-game hunting in regard to bison. Both these works are major contributions to our knowledge of the culture content of this area prior to the advent of salmon exploitation. At Marmes, elk, antelope, and a number of smaller mammals were found; river mussels and fish (no salmonids) were also taken. Lind Coulee yielded most of the same species as well as bison. On the Plains at Medicine Lodge Creek (Frison, 1978: 343-349), much the same faunal assemblage is found – elk, deer, mountain sheep, smaller mammals, and fish. The settlement pattern was seasonal nomadism based on hunting. The shell beads in the Windust phase are Olivella, and are indicative of trade or other contact with the coast.

There is possibly a third variant of the Stemmed Point Tradition typified by Haskett points, which have a distribution from the Fort Rock Valley in eastern Oregon (Bedwell, 1973), east through the Snake River Plain in Idaho, and out onto the Plains (Butler, 1968: 65). In Idaho they are C-14 dated on associated charcoal to 9,860 ± 300 B.P. and 10,000 ± 300 B.P. This variant seems to grade into the Plano horizon of Plains hunters.

Various proposals have been put forward concerning the origins of the Stemmed Point tradition. All of them have some merit, but none have yet experienced wide acceptance. Dikov (1977, 1979) derives this tradition from the Ushki Lake sites in Kamchatka, where stemmed points (Figure 6.6) occur in the earliest component (Ushki VII), dated by C-14 at 14,300 ± 200 B.P. I have examined some of the points from this component and photographs of others. Some of these points have expanding stems, more like North American types of younger periods, whereas others fall into the range of Windust materials. They are indicative of similar ways of hafting projectile heads, however, and a few are not so different in form as to rule out the possibility of a historical relationship. The Russian archaeologists are very critical of the time placement of the Ushki VII component, however, and have suggested that the burial with which the points were associated was intrusive. Dikov rejects that interpretation and indicates that points were found both with the burial and elsewhere in the layer. This debate will not be resolved until more sites with components like Ushki VII are found, excavated, and dated. The Ushki VII points do constitute a possible Siberian ancestor for the Stemmed Point tradition. Similar points are also reported from Hokkaido at about 13,000 B.P. (Aikens and Higuchi, 1982: Fig. 2.24). New World origins for stemmed points have been proposed by other researchers (for example, MacNeish, 1971; Davis, 1978). The relationship of the stemmed-point complexes of the Plains (Scottsbluff, Alberta, and the like) and those of the Far West has never been satisfactorily explored.

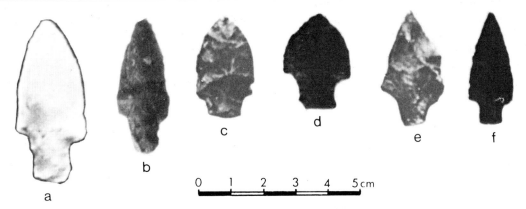

NOTE: a and b are similar to points of the Stemmed Point tradition, but the full range of types is different.

Figure 6.6   Stemmed Points from Dikov's Excavations, Ushki VII, Kamchatka

In the upriver areas of the Columbia and Snake, and possibly the Fraser, cultures belonging to the Stemmed Point tradition persisted until changed into cultures relying as much or more on the salmonids as on mammalian fauna. In the Great Basin, this tradition was associated with the pluvial lakes and disappeared with the demise of that environmental system. With increasing aridity in the post-Pleistocene, the bearers of this culture may have spread north and west following their retreating environmental system into better watered areas of California and Oregon. Given this proviso, the distribution of the Stemmed Point tradition correlates best with the northern group of Macro-Penutian languages (Penutian, Sahaptin and Klamath-Modoc, Chinook, Kalapuya, and possibly Tsimshian), and the peoples speaking these languages are perhaps the descendants of the bearers of this early culture. The Kutenai, linguistic affiliation unknown, should probably be placed with this group. Far to the south in Belize, the basement archaeological phase, estimated to be older than 9,500 years, is also typified by stemmed and concave-based points (MacNeish et al., 1980). The southern group of Macro-Penutian languages is found there, and one wonders if this proposed correlation of early stemmed points and this language phylum may eventually be extended to that area. Although distributional correlations between 10,000-year-old artifact types and 200-year-old language phyla should be pointed out, inferences based on such correlations can be pushed too far. The widespread distribution of stemmed points in younger periods suggests that they represent an advance in hafting technology adopted by diverse peoples. As such, correlations of the type proposed above could only have validity during the early period, the period of initial settlement, if then.

The Fluted Point Tradition

The Fluted Point tradition is the most widespread of the early cultural traditions in North America. There are many variants of this basal culture, but the best known are Clovis and Folsom. Clovis seems to be continentwide in distribution, but is best documented in the Southwest and Plains, where it occurs in dated, excavated contexts between 11,000 and 12,000 B.P. Folsom is confined almost entirely to the Plains and is usually dated between 10,000 and 11,000 B.P. Other variants of this culture are indicated by somewhat different fluted points, such as the Borax Lake fluted (Harrington, 1949), the Arctic Fluted (Alexander, 1973), the Peace River Fluted (Fladmark, 1980; Spurling, 1980; Gryba, 1981), and various eastern styles (MacDonald, 1968; Bonnichsen, 1981). The enigmatic Sandia variant, which seems to stretch from Alberta to Texas (Wormington, 1957), is sometimes placed at the beginning of the Fluted Point tradition. This tradition is present throughout the Far West south of the glaciated regions on the basis of surface finds of points, most of which are Clovis, but has been found in only one excavated, dated, primary context, and that is at the Wasden site (Miller and Dort, 1978; Butler, 1978) in eastern Idaho, almost on the Plains. With the exception of this site, Hester's (1973: 63) formulation, that sites of the Fluted Point Tradition lack a firm temporal span and cultural association in the Great Basin, can be extended to the entire Far West (see Figure 6.7).

There have been several recent surface finds of fluted points within the previously known area of distribution. The most western fluted point known is a Clovis point from near Olympia, Washington (Figure 6.8) reported by Osborne (1956). Recent finds of Clovis points in the Northwest are from the central Columbia basin in eastern Washington (Moody, 1978: 32), from the headwaters of the MacKenzie River (Alley, 1975), from the Mitchell site on the Snake River near its confluence with the Columbia (Dale Croes, personal communication), and several fragments from the Alvord Basin in eastern Oregon (Pettigrew, 1975). Davis and Shutler (1969) have previously given the distribution

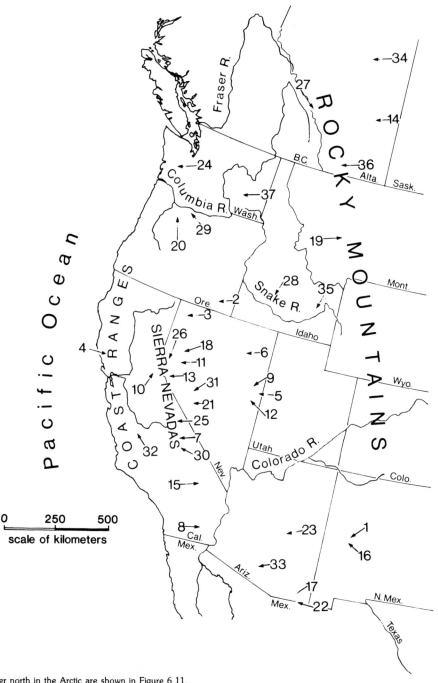

NOTE: Site location further north in the Arctic are shown in Figure 6.11.

1. Ake	14. Johnston Locality	27. Sibbald
2. Alford Basin	15. Lake Mohave	28. Simon
3. Black Rock Desert	16. Lake San Augustine	29. The Dalles
4. Borax Lake	17. Lehner	30. Tiefort Basin
5. Caliente	18. Lovelock	31. Tonopah
6. Carlin	19. MacHaffie	32. Tulare Lake
7. China Lake	20. MacKenzie R.	33. Ventana Cave
8. Cuyamaca Mts.	21. Mud Lake	34. Vilna
9. Dry Lake Valley	22. Naco	35. Wasden
10. Ebbett's Pass	23. New River	36. Waterton Lakes
11. Fallon	24. Olympia	37. Winchester Waste Way
12. Groom	25. Panamint Dry Lake	
13. Huntoon Valley	26. Reno	

Figure 6.7   Distribution of Fluted Points in the Far West and Part of the Southwest

a, d, k, l. Lake Minnewanka, southwest Alberta (Reeves)
      b. Southern California (Rogers)
  c, e. Putu Site, Alaska (Alexander)
      f. Lake Mohave (Rogers)
      g. Tonopah, Nevada (Tuohy)

  h. Reno, Nevada (Davis, Shutler)
  i. Fallon, Nevada (Davis, Shutler)
  j. Olympia, Washington (Osborne)
 m. Harvey Site, Nevada (Tuohy)

Figure 6.8   Fluted Points from the Far West and Adjacent Areas

of fluted points in Nevada and California, and both Tuohy (1974) and Davis (1978) have published on more recent work there. Tuohy (1974: 97) notes:

> Clovis Points in Nevada tend to be found near extinct sluggish streams feeding pluvial lakes or on intermediate or low strand lines of those lakes, ideal watering places for large and small game.

The question of whether stemmed points or fluted points appeared earlier in the Far West remains open. Most researchers consider Clovis and the Lake Mohave variant as either coeval in time or the latter as earlier (Campbell, 1949; Tuohy, 1968: 151-152; Hester, 1973: 61-62; Tuohy, 1974; Davis, 1978).

In the Far West, the closest known association between Clovis points and elephant is in the China Lake Basin of California (Davis, 1978). This locality is one of a number of basins that contained pluvial lakes during the Wisconsinan, but which are now part of the Mohave Desert. Davis has meticulously plotted the bones and artifacts that occur in surface scatters near the ancient shorelines of the lake, and placed stratigraphic tests at various points. These surface scatters clearly document the presence of fluted points, early stemmed Lake Mohave points, crescents, single-shouldered, fluted "Clovis knives," which in another day would have been called "Sandia points," and other lithics, along with mammoth, camel, horse, and other animals all associated with this ancient lake (Davis, 1978). Useful C-14 dates are so far lacking, as is stratigraphic information that could potentially either validate or contradict the sequence Davis proposes on the basis of differential weathering and typology. Davis sees local evolution in the pluvial lake grasslands of both the early stemmed and fluted projectile point types from earlier, cruder Siberian prototypes, the development of a mammoth-hunting specialization in this biome typified by Clovis points, and the spread of this culture onto the Plains and eastward as mammoth-hunting became a way of life and the grasslands followed the retreating forests as the glaciers waned.

Excavations at the Wasden site in eastern Idaho have provided the only direct association of elephant remains, fluted points, and C-14 dates in the entire Far West. Excavations in 1971 yielded fragments of three fluted points, classified as Folsom, associated with elephant, bison, camel, and pronghorn remains. Three C-14 dates on collagen from the elephant bones are 12,850 $\pm$ 150 B.P., 12,250 $\pm$ 200 B.P., and 10,920 $\pm$ 150 B.P. (Butler, 1978: 60; Miller and Dort, 1978). The dates are surprising, as they are within the Clovis range, whereas the associated points are Folsom. In addition, elephant is normally associated with Clovis, and not with Folsom. Only further work may resolve these seeming inconsistencies.

The disappearance of the Fluted Point tradition is as fascinating as its origin. Where did it go? Clovis seems to have disappeared along with the mammoth and to have evolved in part into Folsom, which persisted later by hunting bison. Other variants, particularly in eastern North America, may be more equivalent temporally to Folsom than to Clovis. The Fluted Point tradition is far too widespread to correlate in toto with any ethnographic language phylum. However, if one looks to areas where fluted points should have persisted the longest, which are the newly deglaciated grasslands along the southern margins of the glaciated areas, the Macro-Algonquian phylum offers a possible correlation. Only two languages of this phylum are known from the Far West, Yurok and Wiyot in far northwestern California, where they have obviously been isolated from their sister languages for a long period of time.

The Pebble Tool Tradition

The Pebble Tool tradition was initially defined as composed of Mousteroid and Upper Paleolithic elements derived from the Pacific coastal zone of Siberia, as lacking bifaces, as dating to the height of the Wisconsinan glaciation, and as widespread in the New World (Borden, 1969: 9). The Pasika complex from the South Yale site near the mouth of the Fraser Canyon in British Columbia was the type complex for this construct. During the 1970s several new sites in the same general area (Gaston and Grabert, 1975) were found. In 1979 I modified this construct, limited its distribution to southern British Columbia and western Washington and Oregon, restricted its precedence to local cultures, and divided it into tentative early (without bifaces) and late (with bifaces) segments (Carlson, 1979: 222). Although there may or may not be a pan-American pebble tool tradition, there is such a tradition in the Pacific Northwest. Its earliest dates and the range of its culture content (other than pebble tools) are what are in question, not its existence. Unlike the other traditions so far described, this basal culture was initially coastal and rivermouth in distribution, and is conceived as an adaptation to the postglacial forested environment and to salmon exploitation. It was distributed from at least the central coast of British Columbia south to the Strait of Georgia, the lower Fraser, and Puget Sound, and then south to the lower Columbia. It may also be present in the Queen Charlotte Islands (see Figure 6.9).

The existence of the early Pebble Tool tradition, with lithics consisting solely of unifacial pebble tools and utilized flakes, has always been controversial, and recent work on assemblages from the type site at South Yale has now invalidated its claim to great antiquity (Haley, 1982). The South Yale site (Mitchell, 1965; Borden, 1968) consists of a series of terraces well above the present flood level of the Fraser river. Pebble tools and large flakes are practically ubiquitous in the deposits (Mitchell, 1965), and the few more advanced tool types have been attributed to intru-

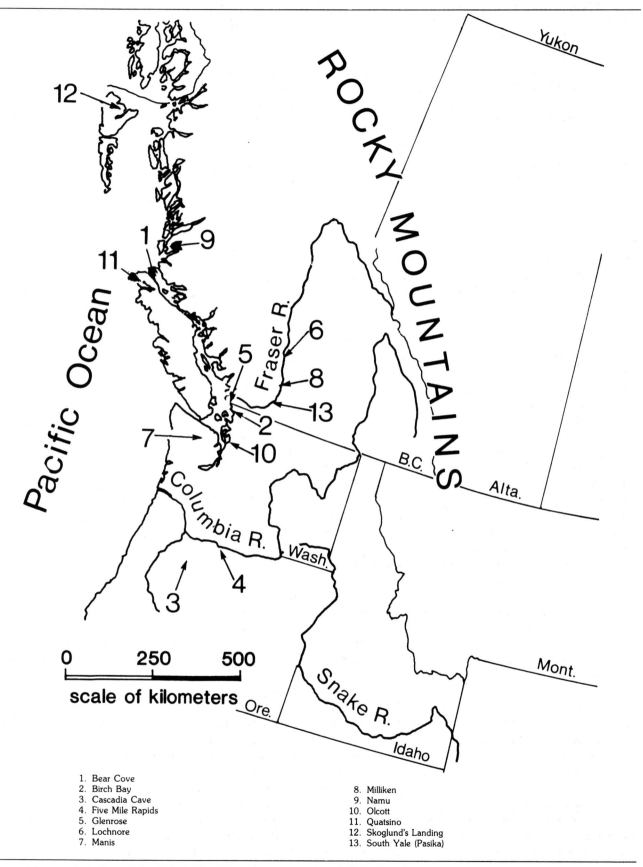

1. Bear Cove
2. Birch Bay
3. Cascadia Cave
4. Five Mile Rapids
5. Glenrose
6. Lochnore
7. Manis

8. Milliken
9. Namu
10. Olcott
11. Quatsino
12. Skoglund's Landing
13. South Yale (Pasika)

Figure 6.9   Distribution of the Pebble Tool Tradition Earlier than 8,000 Years Ago

sion (Borden, 1975: 56-58). The basis for the early time placement of about 12,000 B.P. was the simple technology combined with preliminary geological work, which identified the deposits as kame terraces left behind by the retreating glacier. A C-14 date of 5240 ± 100 B.P. (I8208) was relegated by Borden (1975: 58) to forest fire activity in postdepositional times. Two additional C-14 dates obtained by Haley are, however, in the same time range (4000-6000 B.P.), indicating strongly that the previous date is correct and that South Yale and similar components all belong to the *later* Pebble Tool tradition. Pebble tools persist up to the time of Christ in this region, and sites such as South Yale could be the result of special activities rather than representative of an ancient, crude technology. None of these sites are satisfactorily dated except the early component at the Manis Mastodon site, and while it is certainly ancient, it is hardly typical.

In 1977 a mastodon skeleton with the tip of a bone point embedded in a rib bone was excavated at the Manis site near Sequim in western Washington (Gustafson et al., 1979). Healing had taken place around the point tip, and there was no indication that the animal had died of this wound. The only associated stone artifact was a crudely flaked cobble spall. Organic material from the alluvium gave two C-14 dates of about 12,000 B.P. for this animal. In younger periods the use of bone projectile heads and the absence of chipped stone points and bifaces are typical in this region, particularly on the outer coast. It is possible that this pattern may have already been present 12,000 years ago and been typical of the early Pebble Tool tradition, but more evidence is needed. It is somewhat difficult to consider mastodon as typical fare for Early Man in this area, even at this early period of time. Perhaps – but again, perhaps the fact that the Manis mastodon got away at least once and was only finally butchered in old age was more typical. Elephant remains dating to about 21,000 B.P. are known from this same part of coastal Washington and British Columbia but lack associated cultural remains. Whatever the beginning date for the Pebble Tool tradition, the proliferation of its hallmark, the unifacial pebble chopper, along the lower Fraser and vicinity seems most likely a reflection of adaptation to coastal forests and the working of wood for dugouts and houses rather than the chopping of elephant carcasses. With the late Pebble Tool tradition, evidence for dependence on the salmon resource finally becomes available.

The later Pebble Tool tradition rests on a much firmer foundation of archaeological fact than does the earlier. Until recently, the tendency has been to lump all the early assemblages with bifaces into one tradition, namely the Old Cordilleran (Butler, 1961) or the Protowestern (Borden, 1975). Such a grouping obscures the difference between the earliest coastal and interior plateau cultures. The 1970s witnessed excavations at three important sites whose earliest components fall into this tradition: Glenrose (Mat-

son, 1976), near the mouth of the Fraser; Bear Cove (C. Carlson, 1979), on the northeast end of Vancouver Island; and Namu (Hester and Nelson, 1978; Carlson, 1979), on the central coast of British Columbia near the mouth of Burke Channel. These components contain leaf-shaped unstemmed points, pebble tools, and various scraper and graver types consistent with the definition of this culture. Glenrose I dates by radiocarbon to between 8500 and 5500 B.P. (Matson, 1976: 17). Bear Cove I (C. Carlson, 1979: 183) begins about 8020 ± 110 B.P. (WSU-2141) and terminates before 4180 ± 90 B.P. Namu I (R. Carlson, 1979: 214) dates between 9720 ± 140 B.P. (WAT 452) and 4540 ± 140 B.P. (GaK 2716) and can be subdivided further by a series of eight stratigraphically consistent C-14 dates falling between these two extremes. Additional sites discovered during the 1970s consist of a series of beach assemblages on northern Vancouver Island (Carlson and Hobler, 1976), and similar assemblages further north (Apland, 1977). Other early components of this tradition from excavations before 1970 include the following: Milliken and Mazama components at the Milliken site (Borden, 1968); all the materials in northwest Washington designated as Olcott (Butler, 1961; Grabert, 1979); the earliest component in Cascadia Cave (Newman, 1966); and the Early Stage at Five Mile Rapids (Cressman et al., 1960), although there is some evidence of an interface with the Lind Coulee tradition in the earliest levels (see Figure 6.9). Unifacial pebble tools and simple unstemmed leaf-shaped points (Figure 6.10) in association are the hallmarks of this tradition. Stemmed points and microblades are absent except in interfaces with the other early traditions and in younger components where further acculturation has taken place.

The excavations at Namu provided a large enough sample of flaked stone debitage to lay to rest the idea of "Mousteroid" affinities of early coastal flaked stone industries. There are typical Levallois flakes and prepared cores in the early assemblages, but it is clear that these are part of a pebble reduction technique of stoneworking that need bear no historical relationship to Old World Mousterian industries whatsoever.

Faunal remains vary from site to site, partly because of the varying ecology and partly because of preservation. The best empirical evidence for salmon exploitation is still the thousands of salmon vertebrae from Five Mile Rapids dating to 7675 ± 100 B.P. and earlier (Cressman et al., 1960: 23-24), although the location of the site and of others such as Milliken at the mouth of the Fraser Canyon argue strongly for salmon utilization between 9,000 and 10,000 years ago. The recent excavations at Namu (Carlson, 1979) demonstrated that all the faunal material from the "black matrix" analyzed by Conover (1978) dates between 5000 and 6000 B.P., and that no bone from earlier levels has been preserved. One can only suspect that the fauna of that period, which included salmon and other fish and marine mammals, as well as terrestrial

NOTE: These artifacts all date between 10,000 and 8,000 years ago except those from the Lochnore Complex (g, l, m), which may be younger.

a, b, d, j. Milliken Site (Borden)
c, e, f, h, i. Namu Site (Carlson)
g, l, m. Lochnore Site (Sanger)
k. Five Mile Rapids Site (Cressman)
n. Bear Cove (C. Carlson)

Figure 6.10 Points and Other Bifaces from Components of the Pebble Tool Tradition

animals, are also typical of the earlier part of the deposit. At Bear Cove, the situation on preservation is similar, with fauna found only in the upper levels of the lower component and dating older than 4,000 but younger than 8,000 years ago (C. Carlson, 1979); a high percentage of sea mammal bones characterize this component. At Glenrose (Matson, 1976), some shellfish lenses were found within the early component. There were also salmon and other fish, small mammals, and a considerable number of elk bones.

Like the two traditions already discussed, the origins of the Pebble Tool tradition are obscure. There are two models that seek to explain the origins of this basal culture. The first is a relict population model (Borden, 1975: 60):

> After arriving at an early period, groups of the ancient and tenaciously persisting Asian pebble tool tradition managed to survive the Vashon Glaciation in an isolated marginal situation somewhere in the western Pacific Northwest area uninfluenced by people of more advanced lithic technologies.

The second model would see the earliest of these peoples arriving coastwise in the immediate postglacial. There are similar cultures in Siberia at the same time period (8,000-11,000 B.P.), but very little from intervening areas. Although the coast has long been mentioned as a possible corridor for early migrants (MacGowan, 1950; Heusser, 1960), it was never given serious consideration until Fladmark (1975, 1978) marshaled all the evidence for the feasibility of this route. Hopkins has brought together the most recent assessment of glacial and sea-level conditions relevant to this problem, and notes that the Koryak and Kamchatkan coasts and the Alaskan and British Columbian coasts were deglaciated early, and that peoples with the requisite technology and coastal adaptation could have reached Puget Sound from Beringia as early as 12,000 B.P. (Hopkins, 1979: 17).

The coastal fringe from the Strait of Juan de Fuca northward is totally unknown archaeologically between 13,000 and 10,000 B.P. There is a small assemblage of crude pebble tools and flakes from a raised beach deposit in the Queen Charlottes at the Skoglund's Landing site (Fladmark, 1970: 44) and other small undated pebble tool assemblages from the Aleutians that could conceivably fall within this time period and link the more southerly coastal assemblages with those of the Old World. Pebble tools have a respectable antiquity in Asia, although in Far Eastern Siberia they seem to be most common in late sites. In Asia, the components most similar to the Pebble Tool tradition are Ushki, in Kamchatka, in Layer VI (10,760 ± 110, 10,360 ± 350 B.P.), and the Siberdik culture of the Upper Kolyma (Siberdik 8480 ± 200; Kongo 9470 ± 530) (Dikov, 1979: 289). Salmon utilization first appears at Ushki in this component, and pebble tools and leaf-shaped, unstemmed points are typical. A coastal movement of people with a culture related to that at Ushki is not out of the question, but is far from being demonstrated.

The fate of this early basal culture is unlike that of either the two cultural traditions described earlier. Unlike the pluvial lakes, which were drying up, and the mammoth, which was becoming extinct, the subsistence system linked with the Pebble Tool tradition continued to expand. The reverse of Kroeber's (1939) developmental model seems to be the case. This culture likely originated as coastal, later became river mouth, and even later, but only in part, riverine, as it accompanied the spread of lake-spawning species of salmon further and further up the rivers into the interior as part of the postglacial environmental adjustment. Components of the Cascade phase (Leonhardy and Rice, 1970; Rice, 1972) in sites up the Columbia and Snake Rivers in which salmon is first known likely represent an interface with the Lind Coulee tradition. Further downstream at Five Mile Rapids, this interface seems to have occurred earlier. Rice (1972: 164) suggests that the small assemblage of about a dozen artifacts of the Initial Early Stage at Five Mile Rapids is actually a Windust phase component, and Cressman (1978: 134) seems to agree with him. With the Full Early Stage dated at about 8,000 B.P., full acculturation between the two is found, and this acculturation is logically time-transgressive up the Columbia and Snake. The situation on the Fraser is similar. Sanger's (1970: 126-127) upriver Lochnore Complex contains all of the artifactual complexes associated with the Pebble Tool tradition and a few points similar to Windust types. Additional surface finds (Stryd and Hills, 1972: Fig. 3b, c, e, s) grade into this series.

There are salmon vertebrae from below the Mazama ash at the Drynoch Slide site in the Thompson River canyon, a tributary of the Fraser. This occurrence indicates that these fish were ascending the river before 6,700 B.P., the date of the Mazama eruption. If one again assumes that the Gore Creek skeleton dating to 8,200 B.P. is representative of a population not dependent on salmon, then one might predict the penetration of the Pebble Tool tradition into this region between those two dates. The underlying assumption is, of course, that the Pebble Tool tradition does represent a salmon-based subsistence pattern, although one that was not necessarily as intensive or as heavily dependent on this genus as that of the ethnographic occupants of this same region. Most artifacts used in fishing ethnographically were made of perishable materials, so artifact assemblages of stone tools are really not a guide to this subsistence pattern in a functional sense. The Pebble Tool tradition correlates best with the distribution of speakers of Salish and Wakashan languages, who still take salmon in this same area.

The Microblade Tradition

Since Nelson's (1937: 267-272) first comparison of core and blade industries in Asia and Alaska, there has been an ongoing accumultaion of facts about types and distributions of blades and cores coupled with a proliferation of type names and technological traditions based usually on core preparation techniques. My inclination has been to lump them all togehter (Carlson, 1979) as a single basal Microblade tradition on the basis that technological divergence is a natural function of distance through time and space. Microblade technology is distributed from Siberia and Beringia south into the Yukon, British Columbia, and Washington. In the Pacific Northwest, microblades were first recognized on the basis of specimens excavated from the Whalen site near the mouth of the Fraser, and from the Natalkuz Lake site in the northern Plateau (Borden, 1950, 1952). These blades were made by the reduction of obsidian nodules with little platform preparation. The next technique to be recognized was that in which quartz crystals (Carlson, 1960) were used as cores for microblades. Sanger (1967, 1970) reported blades from early but undated contexts along the Fraser in the northern Plateau.

In 1968 Ackerman reported microblades of both quartz and obsidian in contexts seeming to date from 10,180 ± 800 B.P. (WSU 412) at Ground Hog Bay in Alaska, which brought the industry into the "Early Man" field on the Northwest Coast. Additional early finds had been made in Alaska, and in 1969 Borden (1969: Fig. 1) published a distribution study of the then known microblade assemblages and noted their time transgressive distribution from north to south and west to east between approximately 11,000 B.P. (Healy Lake, Alaska), and A.D. 350 (Whalen site, N.W. Washington). This general model still holds, but a number of additional sites have provided information as a result of work in the 1970s (see Figure 6.11).

Further excavations were undertaken at the Ground Hog Bay 2 site in 1971 and 1973 (Ackerman, 1974) which resulted in some modification of the original sequence; microblades there now date between 4155 ± 95 (I-7056) and 8880 ± 125 (I-7057) B.P. and are associated with bifaces, pebble choppers, and a macroblade industry. Cores were made from obsidian nodules, chert, or argillite and involved minimal platform preparation. Another early site with microblades in the Alexander Archipelago, Hidden Falls, has recently been reported by Davis (1979). Here the early component contained microblades, scrapers, pebble choppers, and various flakes in a deposit dated at its base to 9870 ± 75 B.P.

At Namu, excavation in 1969-70 resulted in the identification of a microblade-bearing component at the base of the deposits dated at 9140 ± 100 B.P. (Luebbers, 1978). Further work at the site in 1977 and 1978 (Carlson, 1979) pushed back the sequence to 9720 ± 140 B.P. Microblades occur in levels dated between 9,000 and 9,700 B.P., but are of greater frequency in levels dating between 8,000 and 5,000 B.P. Most microblades are of obsidian, but there are a few of andesite from the earlier levels. No complete cores were found, as once they were exhausted

they were further reduced by bipolar percussion to produce microflakes. Nevertheless, replication studies by Flenniken (1980, 1981) have shown the cores to be conical to subconical, with a flake scar platform. The earliest assemblages from Namu, Ground Hog Bay, and Hidden Falls are very similar in total content.

The earliest known microblade assemblage in the Queen Charlottes is below a microblade component dated at 7400 B.P. (Fladmark, 1970). Assemblages from two excavated sites, Lawn Point and Kasta, are known, and from surface finds at other sites (Hobler, 1978). Basalt was employed as the raw material for microblades. Platforms are simple flake scars or natural surfaces. The closest comparable assemblage is from Anangula in the Aleutians, dated at 8400 B.P. (Aigner, 1976). Unlike the early assemblages on the mainland, there are no bifaces from the Queen Charlotte and Anangula sites. The earliest phase at Ugashik on the north side of the Alaska Peninsula was discovered in 1974 and dated between 8995 ± 295 B.P. and 7675 ± 260 B.P. (Henn, 1978: 36). Typical artifacts included wedge-shaped microblade cores and other types, leaf-shaped unstemmed points, and transverse and dihedral burins. Microblades have also been reported in early contexts in Bluefish Cave (Cinq-Mars, 1979). To the south, microblades become progressively younger and in part represent interfaces with the Pebble Tool tradition. Actually, the concept of a separate Pebble Tool tradition is based partly on the absence of microblades in early assemblages in southern British Columbia, Washington, and Oregon. The earliest known microblades in southern British Columbia occur below the Mazama ash at the Drynoch Slide site in the Thompson canyon and are dated by C-14 on associated charcoal to 7530 ± 270 B.P. (GSC 530) (Sanger, 1967: 189). Points made on microblades have been found in this region but seem to be younger than this date (Sanger, 1966: Plate V). On the southern British Columbian coast, microblades occur first in the Mayne phase (5,000-3,000 B.P.) (Carlson, 1970).

Microblade technology should be viewed as simply another way of making cutting and piercing tools. There are no indications that these small blades, presumably used as insets in wooden or bone hafts, were any more efficient than the flaked stone points and knives that served the same use in other cultures. Recent finds of small quartz flakes, hafted as knives, from waterlogged deposits dating to about 2,500 years ago (Flenniken, 1980) are probably analogous to how some microblades were used.

It is with the Microblade tradition that one glimpses the closest ties of any early New World culture with any of Asia. This tradition likely represents the culture of the final inhabitants of Beringia prior to the submergence of the landbridge, an event that Hopkins (1979) places between 13,000 and 10,000 B.P. Whether it also represents at that time a subsistence pattern resting on river and coastal exploitation remains to be determined, but this certainly

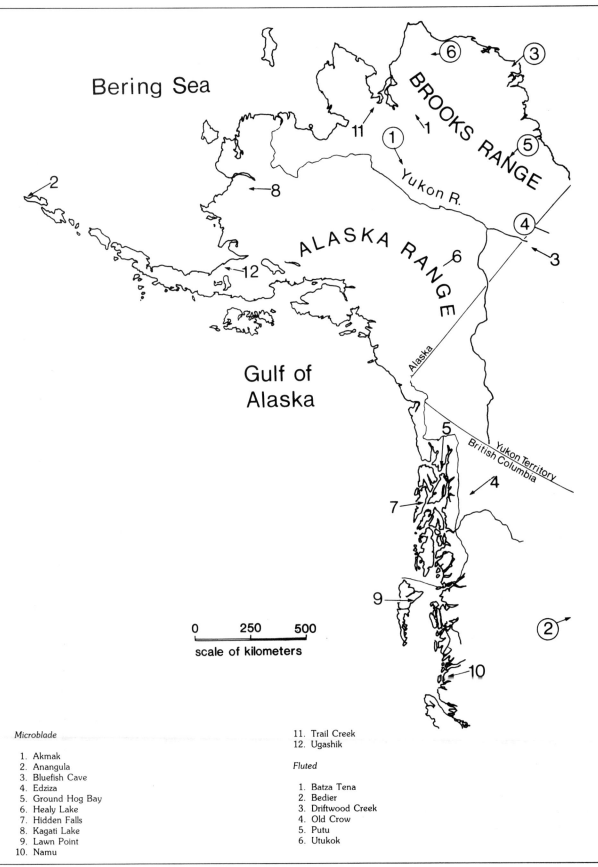

Bering Sea

BROOKS RANGE

Yukon R.

ALASKA RANGE

Alaska

Gulf of
Alaska

Yukon Territory
British Columbia

0   250   500

scale of kilometers

Microblade

1. Akmak
2. Anangula
3. Bluefish Cave
4. Edziza
5. Ground Hog Bay
6. Healy Lake
7. Hidden Falls
8. Kagati Lake
9. Lawn Point
10. Namu

11. Trail Creek
12. Ugashik

Fluted

1. Batza Tena
2. Bedier
3. Driftwood Creek
4. Old Crow
5. Putu
6. Utukok

Figure 6.11   Distribution of the Microblade Tradition Before 8,000 Years Ago and Locations of Fluted Point Sites in the Arctic

seems to be the case later, between 8,000 and 10,000 B.P., in Kamchatka, south coastal Alaska, and British Columbia – that is, near both sides of what had become Bering Strait. Turner has made detailed metrical comparisons of the human teeth from Namu with those of other New World aborigines (see Turner, this volume, and Turner and Bird, 1981, for other comparisons). The Namu teeth are so similar to those of prehistoric Kodiak Islanders from the coast to the north as to suggest a close genetic linkage between the two populations. Although these teeth date to later time periods (4,500-2,000 B.P. for the Namu material), the similarities could be the result of earlier coastwise population movements. There are no really early coastal skeletal remains on which to make comparable comparisons.

There is technological divergence within the Microblade tradition, but how much of this is related to the properties of difference sizes and kinds of stone remains uncertain. Smith (1974: 348-369) notes three types of microblade cores – wedge-shaped, nodular with varied platform preparation, and flake cores – and their simultaneous occurrence in Asia. The most specialized of these are wedge-shaped cores. Flenniken (1981) has recently studied this type of core from the Dyuktai culture of Siberia, which dates between 35,000 and 11,400 years ago. In Siberia, the wedge-shaped core is used as an index artifact for separating Late Paleolithic from Mesolithic complexes. Ushki VII at 14,300 B.P., has "underdeveloped" wedge-shaped cores, and Dikov (1979: 89) contrasts these with Verkholenskaya Gora, Dyuktai, and preceramic Japan, where wedge-shaped cores are already present. By Ushki VI, at 10,360 B.P., wedge-shaped cores were common, and these continue into the final Paleolithic of the area (Dikov, 1979). Later cultures (Sumnagin, Maltan) have prismatic and conic core forms. In North America, wedge-shaped cores are known only from the Arctic and from Mt. Edziza in N.W. British Columbia (Smith, 1974). Northwest Coast and Plateau cores are more similar to the generalized nodular type, which could include the prismatic and conical forms (see Figure 6.12).

The interface with the Pebble Tool tradition has been mentioned previously. There is also an interface between the Microblade tradition and the Fluted Point tradition. In the Arctic in Alaska, microblades and fluted points have been found at several sites (Clark, 1973: 35, referencing Holmes; Alexander, 1973). In the Peace River Country, there are both sites with fluted points and others with microblades, but their temporal order is unknown (Spurling, 1980). Larger samples that contain both cores and blades, in addition to more specific associational information, are desirable, but these occurrences may represent the meeting of Asian and New World traditions.

An alternative hypothesis is that fluted points actually derive from the Beringian microblade tradition (West, 1981). The distribution of the microblade tradition correlates best with the distribution of Tlingit, Haida, and Athabascan, and this tradition likely represents the ancestors of peoples speaking these languages, although it is not all unlikely that the ancestors of the Eskimo and Aleut were also the bearers of microblade technology.

Conclusions

Earliest man in the Far West is just as elusive as ever. Exactly when humans arrived and the route they took as either coastal foragers or interior hunters or both remain unknown. Between 13,000 and 10,000 B.P. there is evidence for the presence of four early, different basal cultures. By 13,000 B.P., peoples of one of these early basal cultures, the Stemmed Point tradition, occupied a niche as hunters and foragers around the pluvial lakes, which then stretched from interior Oregon to southern California. Another of these cultures, specializing in fluted points, was in this same area and, as E. L. Davis has suggested, may have diverged from this presumably more generalized and conservative Stemmed Point tradition in pursuit of both mammoth meat and machismo, and in the course of hunting mammoth expanded geographically across the continent to the east and north. The Fluted Point tradition disappears from the archaeological record of the Far West except for a short stint in eastern Idaho as mammoth gave way to bison.

By 10,000 B.P., the stemmed point hunters had expanded eastward across the Rockies and northward into the drainages of the Columbia and Snake Rivers. They came into contact with another culture, one that used pebble tools and leaf-shaped points, relied on coastal and river resources, and was spreading up the rivers following the salmon runs. Whether this culture was newly arrived from the far North or had been in the coastal areas south of the glaciated regions all along, and with the retreat of the ice sheet had begun to expand northward as well as eastward, remains unknown. The bearers of this Pebble Tool tradition in turn encountered new people spreading from the north into previously glaciated areas, people who used microblades for cutting and piercing tools and who were adept at both coastal and interior subsistence pursuits. The bearers of these traditions were responsible for settling almost all of the Far West.

The methodology employed in this chapter has been to assess the archaeological facts in the Far West and to develop a scenario that takes into account the information currently available and organizes it into a consistent picture of the events and processes of the past. Such scenarios are called cultural-historical models. The model that has been presented here is one of four early basal cultures, each different in content and each adapted to a somewhat different ecological niche. Through time, these cultures expanded or contracted in response to environmental change and to interaction with each other through processes of

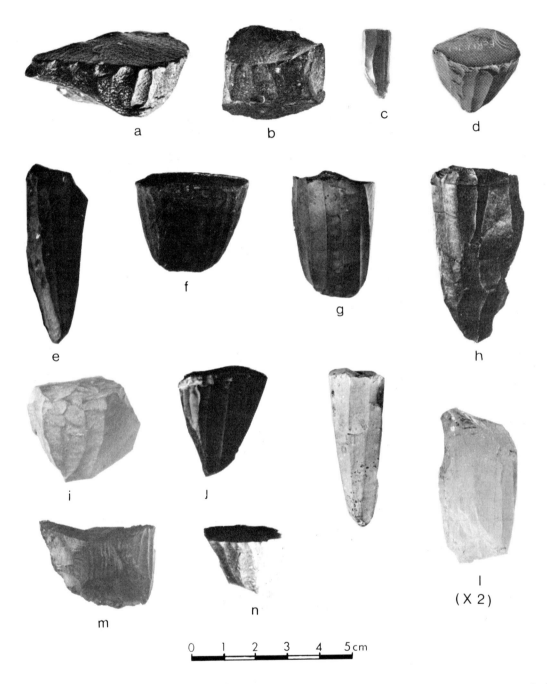

a.   Beach assemblage near Namu (Carlson)
b, c.   Namu (Carlson)
d.   Fraser River near Lillooet (Stryd and Hills)
e, f.   Queen Charlotte Islands (Fladmark)
g, h, k.   Kagati Lake – Kuskokwim River (Ackerman)
i, m.   Ugashik Narrows, Alaska; m is wedge-shaped (Henn, Dumond)
j.   Ust Kayum, Siberia
l.   Cattle Point, Washington (Carlson)
n.   Ground Hog Bay, (Ackerman)

Figure 6.12   Microblade Cores from Various Sites in the Pacific Northwest, Alaska, and Siberia

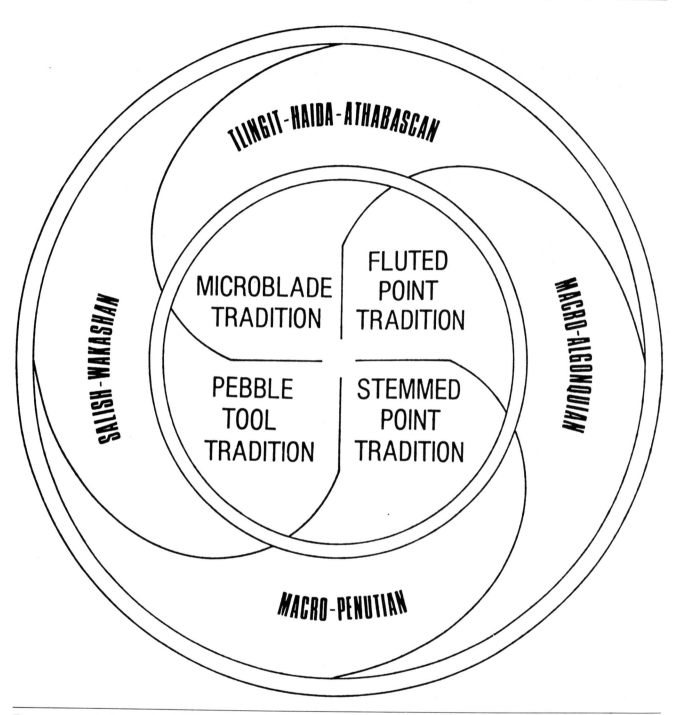

MICROBLADE TRADITION

FLUTED POINT TRADITION

PEBBLE TOOL TRADITION

STEMMED POINT TRADITION

TLINGIT-HAIDA-ATHABASCAN

SALISH-WAKASHAN

MACRO-ALGONQUIAN

MACRO-PENUTIAN

Figure 6.13 Early Period Basal Cultures of the Far West (inner circle), and Their Provisional Historic Period Ethnolinguistic Correlates (outer circle)

adaptation, diffusion, and acculturation, until such time that their technology and way of life were no longer clearly distinctive, and they were no longer recognizable as archaeological entities on the basis of the same criteria used to define them originally. This statement does not mean that the peoples who were the bearers of these cultural tradi-

tions became extinct; quite the contrary. Through population growth, they continued to spread into unoccupied territory, where some of their descendants are still found today.

Models also permit further predictions to be made. One such prediction is that these basal cultures represent the ancestors of speakers of four of the main phyla of Indian languages still spoken in North America (see Figure 6.13). The phyla used are those proposed by Voegelin and Voegelin (1966), plus Salish and Wakashan, which have sometimes been grouped together in a phylum called Mosan. While linguists themselves argue over the validity of these phylotic groupings, whether they are or are not valid is not crucial to the prediction of their relationships to the archaeological remains. If these phyla are each composed of languages that interacted over such a long period of time that they became similar enough to be suggestive of "genetic" relationships, that is all that is required. It should be kept in mind, however, that in inexact sciences such as archaeology and linguistics, models can change as research provides new and different data. Someday the archaeologist will be able to plug in his retroscope, punch in his hypotheses, and obtain probability readings and simulated models based on all relevant available data.

Early Man, then, becomes both early and late if the earliest peoples for which there is definitive evidence are also the ancestors of the Indians living here at the time of Cook, Mackenzie, Lewis and Clark, and the other early explorers. A further prediction is that given the extent and geographic positions of these basal cultures, other than possibly the Aleut-Eskimo of the Far North, the Microblade tradition represents the last incursion of people from the Old World via Bering Strait, and that the ancestors of everybody else in both North and South America were already here.

NOTE

1. A grant from the President's Research Grant Committee, Simon Fraser University, enabled me to examine a number of collections of early material in North America institutions, and an exchange scholarship between the Academy of Sciences of the USSR and the Social Science and Humanities Research Council of Canada allowed me to study Siberian collections in the USSR. I am indebted to R. D. Daugherty, R. Ackerman, and their staff at Washington State University for assistance in examining Lind Coulee, Marmes, Ground Hog Bay, and Kagati Lake artifacts. D. Dumond and his staff at the Museum of Anthropology, University of Oregon, assisted in the examination of materials from Fort Rock Cave, Wildcat Canyon, Five Mile Rapids, and other sites in Oregon, and the Ugashik material from Alaska. B. Reeves, University of Calgary, made available the artifacts from Lake Minnewanka and Waterton Lakes, and A. Bryan, University of Alberta, the Lindoe material. D. Pokotylo, University of British Columbia, arranged for the loan of the Sewell Collection from interior British Columbia and G. Keddie, Provincial Museum of British Columbia, provided additional information on surface collections. R. Tyson and K. Hedges, San Diego Museum of Man, made arrangements for me to examine Lake Mohave and San Dieguito material, and C. Warren, University of Nevada at Las Vegas, assisted in this examination and later provided a tour of Pleistocene Lake Mohave. R. H. Weber, New Mexico Institute of Mining and Technology at Socorro, kindly provided information on Pleistocene Lake San Agustine and permitted me to examine archaeological materials from his work there. R. Vasilievsky, Institute of History, Philology, and Philosophy at Novosibirsk, and interpretor Olga Pavlova provided every possible assistance in the study of collections there. R. Simpson gave us a personally conducted tour of the Calico Hills excavations. N. Dikov arranged for the exhibit of the Ushki artifacts at the Pacific Science Congress in Khabarovsk. H. Alexander assisted in my examination of his Putu material. Don Tuohy of the Nevada State Museum made available the artifacts from early sites in Nevada and assisted in their examination. Without the cooperation and active assistance of these institutions and individuals, this chapter would not have been possible. Most of the illustrations of artifacts are from photographs I have taken myself, but a few are from published sources. The excavator or collector of the artifacts is listed in the figure captions, and the reader may refer to them or to their publications for further information.

7 Eastern North America

Despite the past decade of intensive research on the question of Early Man's entry into eastern North America, the boundary of our hard evidence has remained steadfast at the Clovis penetration about 12,000 years ago. If anything, that frontier has become more evident than it was a decade ago. The search for a pre-Clovis population east of the Mississippi has taken on the importance of a quest to many prehistorians, to some almost a search for the Holy Grail. Like most quests, however, it occasionally requires the suspension of logic and the acceptance of arguments on faith alone.

The site that stands at the center of the controversy of pre-Clovis man in the east is the Meadowcroft Rock Shelter, in the Cross Creek Valley of southwestern Pennsylvania. The shelter was excavated by a team led by Adovasio between 1973 and 1977. The critical level that is so controversial is Substratum IIa. Above the middle of Stratum II there is no problem in any quarter about the radiocarbon dates. Dates of 10,850 ± 870 B.C. and 14,225 ± 975 B.C. occur below a heavy rockfall in the lower part of IIa, followed by a major gap, and then dates of 17,150 ± 810 B.C. and 17,650 ± 2400 B.C. In a series of papers (Adovasio et al. b, 1975, 1977a, 1977b, 1978; Adovasio et al. d, 1980; Adovasio et al. e, in press), the team presented the case that the site was occupied in the twentieth millennium B. P.

Dincauze (1981: 3) has recently summarized the controversy that has built up as the evidence, which is still short of a final report, was presented. She states:

> The skeptics' position has been most publicly defended by C. Vance Haynes, who has published critiques of the evidence and interpretations of lower Stratum IIa. Others have joined the fray (Mead, 1980) and the debate rages in less public forums. The published critiques can be summarized under five issues: (1) the absence of the expected extinct Pleistocene fauna in lower IIa, (2) the presence of hardwood forest species macrofossils in IIa, (3) the absence of stratigraphic unconformities matching the radiocarbon gaps in IIa, (4) the absence of diagnostic Early Archaic and Eastern Clovis Paleo-Indian

artifacts or occupations in the sequence, and 5) the possibility of systematic contamination of the organic samples from lower IIa.

The radiocarbon dates for Stratum IIa at Meadowcroft are, in my view, the most pivotal to the controversy surrounding the site and have engendered debate that is difficult for anyone but directors of dating laboratories to evaluate. Haynes (1980b) has centered his argument on the fact that the sample material is from black charcoal lenses or "mungs" that consist of organic carbon that has not been defined chemically. The samples are thus, according to Haynes, "mixtures of finely divided carbon and carbonaceous matter with fine-grained sediments and a significant percentage of soluble organic matter." Stratum IIa samples contain large percentages of soluble humates. As Haynes points out, in most cases humates come from overlying soils and, therefore, are younger than the charcoal that absorbs them. If the humates orginate in ancient buried soils, peats or coal deposits, then they affect the charcoal toward older dates.

Humic acids can derive from sample decay as well, so that samples can contain humic acids that are older, younger, and/or contemporary with the samples, in variable portions. Precipitated humic acid from Stratum IIa dated 26,150 ± 800 B.C., while the residue, which may still not have been treated long enough, dated only 14,225 ± 97 B.C. Haynes (1980b: 584) states: "The results show the soluble organic content to be older than the residual carbon, an unusual circumstance that is compatible with a model of groundwater leaching carbonaceous deposits." And he concludes: "These results clearly indicate that not only is the soluble component significantly older than the residue, but it is also larger." He further points out that there are old carbonate materials in the bedrock that are soluble in groundwater, and that level IIa is in the damp bottom of the deposit most affected by fluctuations in the water table during the Pleistocene/Holocene transition and most open to contamination from the bedrock in which the cave is situated. He states (1980b: 585): "The shale underlying the shelter fill very likely has a significant organic content and may, in fact, be the source of most of the carbon in the 'mung' of Stratum I." This is hotly denied, but not disproven, by Adovasio et al. d (1980: 580).

Haynes outlines tests that would resolve the problem of contaminants to the satisfaction of most critics, but this solution is thwarted by the fact that the samples recovered are considered to be too small for this procedure. The only hope of resolving the dilemma is offered by the milligram samples potential of the atomic accelerator technique. Until that time, the onus is on the excavators to define the exact nature of the samples and prove that they are not contaminated. From the limited tests done to date at Haynes's suggestion, he extrapolates that the real age of the site is something less than 13,000 years (1980b: 586).

A less likely candidate for a pre-Clovis find is the Timlin site near Cobbleskill, New York, first reported in the late 1960s, but which surfaced again in a number of journals and symposia collections in the late 1970s. A long debate with rebuttals from both sides was waged in *Current Anthropology* in 1977 (Raemsch and Vernon, 1977) and 1978 (Cole and Godfrey, 1977; Cole et al., 1978), until the editor called it to a halt. At that point neither side had conceded any ground. The original proponents were harshly criticized for their lack of understanding of Pleistocene geology, lithic technology, the archaeological sequence of the region, concepts of typology, and so on. If any conclusion was achieved by the debate, it was the need to involve a more experienced archaeologist who could examine the existing material and conduct new field work. This challenge was taken up by Bryan et al. (1980: 52). Their excavations "discounted prior claims of a mid-Wisconsinan dating for a distinctive lithic industry recovered from the site in previous excavations; but found clear evidence for the direct association of definitely man-made lithic artifacts with fluvial gravel deposits of earliest postglacial age." They also report: "A radiocarbon assay of 16,040 ± 170 years B.P. was recovered from the surface of a sandy clay lens just beneath the fluvial gravel in the highest terrace (T2) of West Creek."

The unresolved problem appears to be that the radiocarbon date of just over 16,000 years ago is in a stratum that underlies the fluvial gravels containing the artifacts. While the date does establish the maximum date of the artifacts, it does nothing to establish the actual, or even minimum, dates. The acceptable artifacts may be Archaic, as others have argued. Work continued during the 1980 season at Timlin Location 2, but until new data are published, there is still nothing to confirm that this site is pre-Clovis. It may, in fact, turn out to be only Archaic.

Bonnichsen et al. (1980) have reported lithics from river gravels in the Munsungun Lake area of Maine that are very similar in description to the presumed early forms from the Timlin locality. A detailed study of both the lithics and their stratigraphic context is planned, which should throw significant new light on all such finds in the east.

Somewhat outside the survey area, but of great significance to it, are two sites just to the west of the Mississippi River in Missouri. The first is the Kimswick site (Anonymous, 1979), where a fluted point was found in direct association with an American mastodon. Excavations in 1979 indicated a distinct stratigraphic separation of Paleoindian and Archaic horizons and the possibility of multiple Clovis or pre-Clovis occupation (Graham et al., 1981).

The second site that must be at least mentioned here is the Shriver site in northwest Missouri (Reagan et al., 1978: 1272). Flake tools were found there underlying a fluted point assemblage in a locus distinctly separate from that of the fluted point assemblage. Thermoluminescence dating of the stone tools from the fluted point component yielded dates of 10,640 ± 1000 and 14,805 ± 1500 B.P. The underlying tool assemblage consisting of flake tools thought to be struck from prepared cores are believed, on the basis of geologic correlation, lithic analysis, and cultural stratigraphy, to be at least 15,000 years old.

Fluted Point Industries

In contrast to the lack of conclusive results in the search for pre-Clovis finds in the east in the 1970s, that decade was particularly productive in terms of producing new Clovis and related fluted point sites. Systematic surveys that characterized many areas of eastern North America, particularly the northeast sector, combined checking find reports with field searches oriented to strategies worked out from paleoenvironmental models of the region for the last 10-12,000 years.

Great Lakes Area

Ontario

No area exemplifies these developments better than does Ontario. In 1970, not a single fluted point site was known in that province. Through the systematic field programs of Stork, Dellar, and Roosa, a series of fluted point sites were located. Virtually all of the sites are on or near the Lake Algonquin Strandline.

The Parkhill site on the Algonquin beach ridge was excavated in the mid-1970s and reported on by Roosa (1977) and Deller (1976). The site is a large camp, the surface of which has been cultivated, but which yielded preserved subsoil features. Unfortunately, there was no datable material recovered from the site. The artifact collection contains over 80 fluted bifaces and 44 channel flakes. Small points had been made on the channel flakes, as has been noted at other sites. Although there are now two published reports on the site, they deal only with the fluted bifaces.

With the exception of a reference to one end-scraper, no other tool types are even mentioned. A preoccupation with the minutiae of fluting technology precludes a balanced overview of this assemblage.

Further to the north and east along the Lake Algonquin shoreline, Storck (1979) has found and excavated three Paleoindian sites. These finds resulted from a thorough survey of the old strandline over several years in the early 1970s. The Banting site, near Alliston, Ontario, produced fluted points from two localities. Plowing had disturbed most of the features, and there are no radiocarbon dates for the site. Although the collection is small (about 150 pieces), a full range of tool types was recovered including drills, beaked scrapers, bladelike flakes, biface knives, a variety of scrapers, and reworked flakes. The nearby, multicomponent Hussey site contains fluted points as well as Plano, Archaic, and possibly Woodland occupations.

The Fisher site, on the Algonquin terrace near Stayner, Ontario, overlooks a barrier bar of Lake Algonquin. Three occupation areas produced what is described as a large number of fluted points in various stages of manufacture. Unfortunately, no counts are given, but a variety of other tools are referenced. Two other areas on a lower terrace produced a large number of cores, preforms, and debitage, but no fluted points. Storck postulates that the five areas of artifact concentration may represent different activity areas of a large base camp that was simultaneously occupied. All three sites produced points that Storck claims are very similar to those from the Parkhill site in form and material. Roosa (1977) goes further in suggesting that many of the Algonquin shoreline sites with fluted points of this material are part of what he calls the Parkhill Complex. Both agree that perhaps a single band ranged along the old strandlines on the eastern side of the Huron basin. Surface finds of fluted points to the south further suggest to Roosa that another band ranged the Erie Basin, that the Barnes site in Michigan may represent another Parkhill Complex band, and that another band on the eastern edge of the Lake Michigan basin was responsible for the Dobblaar site.

Although it appears that Roosa is trying to overstructure the scant data available into a series of tightly linked complexes, the fluted point sites on the Lake Algonquin shoreline in Ontario do in fact present a unique opportunity to test hypotheses about band size and itinerary that would not be possible without such postulated linkages between sites. The next decade may bring some new insights into the problem of band size and range if work continues unabated in this region of the Great Lakes.

Michigan

The Barnes site in the lower peninsula of Michigan has been known for decades. Excavation of the site was undertaken in 1974 (Voss, 1977). Twelve features were excavated, of which only two appear as credible Paleoindian ones. Nine projectile point fragments were found in the excavations, along with five bifaces and the same number of end-scrapers, two other scrapers, and three utilized flakes. Although 102 channel flakes are reported, it would appear that this is a misidentification of biface trimming flakes, as it is not conceivable to me that there would be that many channel flakes in such a small collection.

In southeastern Michigan, the Jarvis-Egeler site (Fisher, 1981) produced evidence that has been interpreted as human/mastodon interaction analogous to the evidence from the Yukon Refugium Project (Morlan, 1980b). That is, no stone tools have been found to date, but the arrangement and condition of the mastodon bones suggest that they were made into temporary tools that were used directly in further butchering of the carcass, as Stanford, Bonnichsen, et al. (1981) have replicated in the Ginsberg experiment. The Jarvis-Egeler mastodon, a mature male, came from a peat layer immediately above a grey marl, at a depth of circa 2.5 m below present ground surfaces. The date on wood fragments from silt and clay deposits inside the tusk cavity is $10,359 \pm 100$ B.P., while underneath the remains is a date of $12,845 \pm 165$ B.P. Cut-marks on the epiphysis of many bones are interpreted as butcher-marks. Although the dates are not earlier than many other sites in the east, it will be most significant if further work at this site demonstrates that the mastodon was killed by man.

St. Lawrence Area

Quebec and the Maritime Provinces

Despite the success in finding fluted point sites in Ontario, such has not been the case in Quebec. It appears that the incursion of Lake Champlain and standing ice to the north virtually precluded human occupation during the period in which fluted points were in vogue. New Brunswick has reported single fluted point finds, but no sites have been located or tested. A site near Souris on Prince Edward Island that had produced several late Paleoindian basally thinned points was investigated in 1978 by Keenlyside (personal communication, 1980), but only later material was encountered in test excavations in the find areas.

New England

Maine

In Maine a large early fluted point site was recently found in the northwest part of the state (Gramley and Rutledge, 1981). The Vail site is located on a fossil channel of the Magalloway River. The collection contains between 4,000 and 5,000 stone tools. Artifact-to-debitage ratios are a low 1:1.5. The source of raw material outcrops between fifteen and eighteen miles from the site. Only flakes have been found at the quarry locations. A full range of tool forms were found at more than a dozen loci. There is evidence of only one cultural phase, which appears to be virtually identical to that at the Debert site in Nova Scotia. Like the latter, the frequencies of tool forms at Vail show end-scrapers and *pièces esquillées* to be the most abundant, with utilized flakes, fluted bifaces, and side-scrapers next in frequency, followed by gravers and unfluted knives as rarer items. Fluted drills and limaces were relatively frequent (see Figures 7.1-7.4 for examples of Vail site artifacts). Despite the close similarity of tool forms between the two sites, there were no shared materials according to a comparative study conducted by Gramley (personal communication, 1981).

Of particular significance were the radiocarbon dates obtained on a single sample from an intact hearth feature in association with artifacts. The first half of the sample was dated by the Smithsonian Laboratory at 10,300 ± 90 B.P. (S.L. 4617). This date seemed acceptable in relation to the Debert dates, which averaged 10,600 B.P. on similar material. The other half of the sample was sent to Beta Analytic labs in Coral Gables, where a date of 11,120 ± 180 B.P. was obtained. The humic acid pretreatment on the second part reduced the sample by a larger factor than did the Smithsonian pretreatment. Both labs counted the samples for three days. Gramley explains the difference in terms of humic acid contamination of a greater magnitude than laboratories had previously suspected. Most Paleoindian C-14 samples are of minimal size to begin with, and any drastic reduction by pretreatment is always a concern.

The suggestion is raised again that other dates on Early Man, from the acidic soils of the northeast in particular, may have been seriously contaminated by the addition of younger humates from the groundwaters. The possibility, although far from proven at this stage, has profound implications for the whole question of the origin and relationships of eastern fluted point assemblages to those in other areas. Part of the problem of the slow acceptance of the term "Clovis" in the east was due to the fact that the dates on early fluted points in the east were closer to those of Folsom in the west. The anomalously early date of 12,500 B.P. on the fluted point from Dutchess Quarry Cave that has troubled many scholars, may be partially explained by its position inside a cave where groundwater contamination by humic acids might be much less than they would be on an open site with forest cover.

Another recently discovered fluted point site in Maine is at Munsungun Lake, locality 154-14 (Bonnichsen et al., 1980). Another locality, 154-7, has produced Plano points. Site 154-14 covers an area greater than 3,000 square meters. Three localities have tested, one of which produced six fluted point fragments and channel flakes. Other

tools occur, but pedoturbation has been identified as a major factor in mixing less diagnostic specimens. Although Bonnichsen concludes that this was a lithic workshop, he feels that the rough preforms were prepared elsewhere and brought to the site. A variety of lithic materials outcrop locally in the Munsungun formation. It is hypothesized that the sites were occupied when water flowed through an ancient spillway as stagnant ice melted from the New England glaciers.

Massachusetts

The only significant new find was a site near Hadley, Massachusetts (Curran and Dincauze, 1977: 334) that produced an assemblage of clearly identifiable Paleoindian affiliation, including the midsection of a large fluted point, an unfluted biface with a prepared striking platform base, two large ovoid bifaces, two channel flakes, an ear-shaped side-scraper, one unspurred and one spurred thumbnail scraper, and several flake gravers. Unfortunately, this site had been destroyed by ploughing, although it is possible that some features may extend below the plough zone.

The most significant fluted point site in the state, and one of the largest in the northeast, the Bull Brook site had been destroyed by gravel extraction. A significant new analysis of the site was undertaken during the review period by John Grimes (1979). Approximately 5,000 tools, plus floral and faunal remains, which are thought to represent only about 40 percent of the total removed from the site, have been catalogued from scattered collections. The analysis, which is still underway, is attempting to reconstruct the assemblage according to discrete living floors, and the first map of the 45 find spots has been published (Grimes, 1979: 125). It graphically portrays the large circular configuration of the living floors, which may indicate simultaneous occupation of numerous components at once in an overall patterned arrangement, presumably one that was also maintained over a series of visits to the site.

New Hampshire

Another important fluted point site in southwest New Hampshire is the Whipple site, investigated by Curran (Curran and Dincauze, 1977). Although little has been published on the site, finds included fluted points, gravers, and spurred end-scrapers. Between 20 and 25 fragmented projectile points have been found to date. The points have deeply concave bases similar to those from Vail and Debert. Small quantities of charcoal have been recovered, but no dates have been run as yet. Small pieces of calcined bone have been tentatively identified as caribou or deer.

Connecticut

In Connecticut, the 6LF21 site (Moeller, 1980) has yielded an important radiocarbon date on a fluted point assemblage at 10,190 ± 300 (W-3931). One burned wood

NOTE: Top row, from left: six limaces or slug-shaped unifaces, a *pièce esquillée*, a *pièce esquillée* based on a denticulate; middle row, from left: graver on the proximal end of a trianguloid end-scraper, graver with two flaked points, graver with points made by snapping, two denticulates (possibly saws) made by snapping; bottom row, from left: three trianguloid end-scrapers, side-scraper convergent at its distal end.

Figure 7.1   Flaked Stone Tools Representing the Principal Classes at the Vail Site

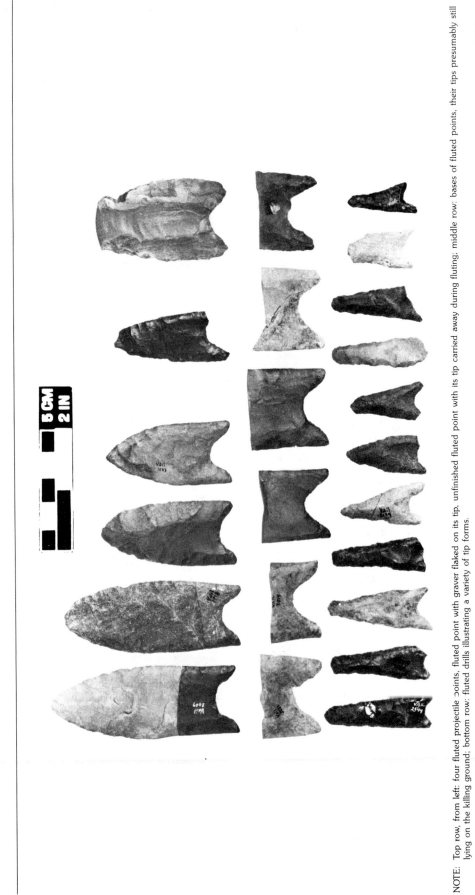

NOTE: Top row, from left: four fluted projectile points, fluted point with graver flaked on its tip, unfinished fluted point with its tip carried away during fluting; middle row: bases of fluted points, their tips presumably still lying on the killing ground; bottom row: fluted drills illustrating a variety of tip forms.

Figure 7.2   Fluted Projectile Points and Drills Excavated by the Maine State Museum in 1980 from the Vail Site

NOTE: The bases (fitted together with the tips shown in the upper row) were unearthed in excavation at the habitation. All told, four complete fluted projectile points and tips of six others were found at the killing ground.

Figure 7.3   Fluted Projectile Points Discovered upon the Killing Ground Approximately 250 m West of the Vail Paleoindian Habitation Site

sample from a hearth was identified as red oak, and another as either juniper or white cedar. About 80 artifacts were recovered that included an unfinished fluted point and four miniature fluted points, along with drills, gravers, spoke shaves, knives and a variety of scrapers. Artifact-to-debitage ratios approach 1:9, which conforms to the fact that the source of the chert employed at the site was nearby.

The Paleoindian layer at the site was deeply buried, an unusual feature in most eastern fluted point sites located to date. Moeller claims the site has only a single Paleoindian locality, but it would appear from reading the report that there is reason to believe that other buried loci exist at the site and that his interpretations on settlement patterns are somewhat premature. Because the fluted point

NOTE: Artifact photos courtesy of R. M. Gramly

Figure 7.4   Reverse Side of Artifacts Listed in Figure 7.3

component is well isolated from later components, and since the site has yielded datable material from intact features, more work at this site should be encouraged.

New York

In New York State, no major sites have been located in the past decade, but several known ones were reinvestigated. Dutchess Quarry Cave, which looms so large in the eastern Paleoindian picture because of its date of circa 12,500 B.P., was the most productive. An electrical resistivity survey located three new caves with archaeological deposits along the ridge that contains the original site (Kopper et al., 1980). Dutchess Cave No. 8, only 12 meters from the original cave, contained five strata, all of which produced evidence of occupation, including fragments of charcoal and animal bone. Corner-notched and side-notched points were found, as well as three fluted points, two from Stratum III and one from the upper part of Stratum V. Faunal remains were well preserved and included the cracked left radius of a caribou from 3b, reinforcing the original association between fluted point and caribou in Cave 1. Also reported for the Paleoindian and Archaic levels at Cave 8 were large bird and fish remains.

A radiocarbon date from Stratum III yielded a disappointing date of 5880 ± 340 B.P., which the excavators interpret as evidence of mixing in Stratum III, although Stratum V, with its fluted point, is securely in place below the breccia.

Pennsylvania

In Pennsylvania, the Shawnee-Minisink site provided one of the most significant fluted point finds of the decade. The site, on a terrace of the Delaware River, near Stroudsburg, produced a stratified deposit containing Woodland, Archaic, and Paleoindian components, the last of which was isolated from other components by up to five feet of sterile sediments. In all, 74 Paleoindian artifacts, including one classic Clovis point, have been published, and thousands of utilized flakes and debitage items are mentioned (McNett et al., 1977: 295). In addition to the usual classes of scrapers, bifaces, and cores were rough stone implements, including five hammerstones and an anvil.

Two radiocarbon dates for the Clovis occupation produced dates of 10,590 ± 300 B.P. and 10,750 ± 600 B.P. The first dated sample came from a hearth, which also yielded wild hawthorne pits and tiny fragments of fish bones of an unidentifiable species (McNett et al., 1977: 284). Later work at the site has not yet been reported.

New Jersey

In New Jersey, the Plenge site was one of the most significant fluted point sites investigated in the past decade. Kraft (1973), who excavated at the site in 1972, considers it one of the largest Paleoindian occupation sites in the east. The site commands a view that would provide Paleohunters with a strategic vantage over game movements in the valley. Kraft suggests that it was also favorably located for fishing and the collection of fresh water mussels (Kraft, 1977: 269).

Unfortunately, almost all of the Paleoindian remains at the Plenge site are within the cultivated areas, and excavations have been devoid of undisturbed features or datable charcoal. Remote sensing for buried features would appear to be warranted at this site as well, in order to date this major occupation site.

Virginia

In a series of papers, Gardner (1974, 1976, 1979) has defined the Flint Run Complex based on a jasper industry from the Thunderbird site and the surrounding area in Virgina. He defines an Early (Clovis), Middle, and Late (Dalton) phase that are revealed in the stratigraphy for the first time in the east. Almost 3,000 years are covered by this tradition. The most significant change in the shift from unnotched to notched points occurred about 10,000 B.P., which Gardner links to the introduction of the spear-thrower in the east. Otherwise, he maintains that the Paleoindian and Early Archaic periods represent a cultural continuum (Gardner, 1977: 258).

Five functionally distinct sites are isolated, namely:

(1) the quarry;
(2) quarry reduction stations;
(3) quarry-related base camp;
(4) periodically revisited food procurement sites; and
(5) sporadically visited hunting sites.

The Thunderbird site typifies the base camp, a multiple-purpose activity camp where jasper was reduced to its final forms, and includes generalized processing and maintenance tools, numerous preforms, and trimming flakes. Gardner sees spatial separations between hunting-kit fabrication areas and generalized living areas that take account of such lifestyle factors as exposure to sunlight and wind, and accessibility to local food resources. The last two types of sites are characterized by a variety of points from revisits, and broken and discarded points from the hunt. The stratified Fifty site exemplifies the fourth type of site. The last type of site is found in upland areas.

Gardner concludes that the Flint Run Complex provides a different view of Paleoindians than as highly mobile big-game hunters. He sees the population as mobile within a prescribed territory, with eventual return to a central base. He envisages all of the eastern Paleoindian sites as fitting into this model (Gardner, 1977: 262).

Although detailed descriptions of projectile points have been provided and careful comparisons made with other collections such as Shoop and Williamson, very little has been presented on the rest of the industry, which makes the sites of the Flint Run Complex of somewhat limited use in comparison with other sites. Another feature of great interest that is only mentioned is the occurrence of post moulds defining a structure of oval pattern approximately 10 by 24 feet in size. This would appear to be the best evidence for a Paleoindian dwelling structure anywhere in the east.

Up to this point, this review has dealt with sites in states and provinces along the Great Lakes/St. Lawrence or Atlantic coastlines. Many of these sites are near major waterways which, taken collectively, suggest that the Paleoindians of the fluted point period made significant use of waterways as natural barriers or traps for their prey, and perhaps also for transportation, both on frozen waterways and probably by watercraft. Their exploitation of fish is also indicated by several recent finds.

It is notable that no fluted point sites of significance have been reported from the southeast. Several sites in Florida, without fluted points but of the right time period, have been reported and deserve comment for the unique contributions they make to the study of Early Man in eastern North America.

Florida

It is in southern Florida, however, that the most interesting finds of the 1970s have been reported. A number of the sink holes in the limestone areas of southeast Florida, near Venice, appear to have been used during low sea-level periods at the end of the Pleistocene by human populations, as well as watering holes for animals.

> We speculate that since the peninsular fresh water hydrostatic head is related to the sea level, at lower sea levels many present surface rivers would leave a series of sink holes which could then become foci for intensive human utilization [Cockrell and Murphy, 1978: 2].

At Warm Mineral Springs, on a ledge 13 meters below the present water level, a human burial has been recovered and radiocarbon dated to 10,310 B.P. (Cockrell and Murphy, 1978). With the burial was found a worked shell hook of a spearthrower. The burial and artifacts were dry deposited and later submerged. Recently, human remains were found below the 3 m ledge at Warm Mineral Springs in the same grey-green clay stratum as a basically articulated ground sloth and portions of a sabertooth cat, as well as a number of extant species. Dates on associated wood are expected to be greater than 11,000 B.P. (Cockrell and Murphy, 1978: 6).

Not far away at Little Salt Springs, Paleoindian remains have been found on the lower reentrant. The collapsed shell of an extinct giant land tortoise (*Geochelone crassiscutata*) was found with a sharply pointed wooden stake between the carapace and plastron. The stake has been dated at 12,030 B.P. Several of the longbones and parts of the carapace have been carbonized, and numerous fragments of fire-hardened clay were found under the tortoise remains. Clausen concludes that the animal was killed with the stake and cooked in its own shell. Other faunal remains from the reentrant surface include mammoth, mastodon, and extinct bison.

The potential of the Florida sink holes for interpreting the Paleoindian period in eastern North America is almost beyond imagination. The thousands of sink holes throughout the state have the potential to yield well-preserved human remains, including brain tissue, as well as a wide range of associated fauna and perishable artifacts. All of these items are lacking from northeastern sites. The complementarity of the evidence from the two regions is striking. Nevertheless, the unusual technical requirements for sink hole archaeology will limit severely the degree to which this kind of recovery of data is practiced.

Late Paleoindian

The late Paleoindian picture has received less specific attention than the prefluted and fluted point periods. In the south, Dalton provides the transition from the fluted point to the notched point tradition, as do the Flint Run sites. In addition, most of the well-reported Dalton sites are west of the Mississippi River and fall into another review area. Further north, most of the late Paleoindian evidence comes from the Great Lakes/St. Lawrence drainage. Again, the association of sites with shorelines and waterways is remarkable and suggests a late Paleoindian adaptation to newly drained lake shores, with what Fitting (1975) calls "a pioneer vegetation and high browse potential." Unfortunately, most sites reported contain no floral or faunal remains nor C-14 dates to add to this picture.

In general, the Great Lakes/St. Lawrence intrusion of late Paleoindians appears to be from the west, with close affinities to the Agate Basin, Cody (Eden-Scottsbluff), and Firstview Complexes in that area (Storck, 1979). At the western end of our review area, the Lakehead Complex is represented by more than a half dozen sites in an almost continuous lithic scatter for over 20 km around Thunder Bay on the Lake Minong shoreline, thought to date from 10,500-9,500 B.P. No faunal or floral remains have been found in association with the abundant lithics, but caribou is generally thought to be the dominant quarry. At the opposite end of the Great Lakes/St. Lawrence waterway, Plano points have been reported from two sites in the Gaspé Peninsula (Benmouyal, 1976), one of which was a stratified site yielding considerable lithic material but no dates. Recent finds of late Paleoindian in the Munsugun Lake area of Maine by Bonnichsen promise a new Paleoecological tie-in for the extreme northeast. Somewhat less typical Plano forms have been found as far to the southeast as the Plenge site in New Jersey (Kraft, 1977) and throughout western New York (Ritchie and Funk, 1973).

There is some evidence from the Strait of Belle Isle region of Labrador that the Maritime Archaic may have developed out of late Paleoindian complexes in that area (McGhee and Tuck, 1975). Wright (1972) has suggested a similar origin of Shield Archaic from late Paleoindian across much of the eastern Canadian Shield. Indeed, the continuity model for a gradual transition from Paleoindian to Archaic seems to be gaining ground throughout the northeast.

Conclusion

As stated at the beginning of this chapter, the outstanding problem in eastern North America, as it is over the rest of North America south of the Yukon-Bering Refugium, is the lack of unequivocal evidence for pre-Clovis populations. In the decade since this type of evaluation was last

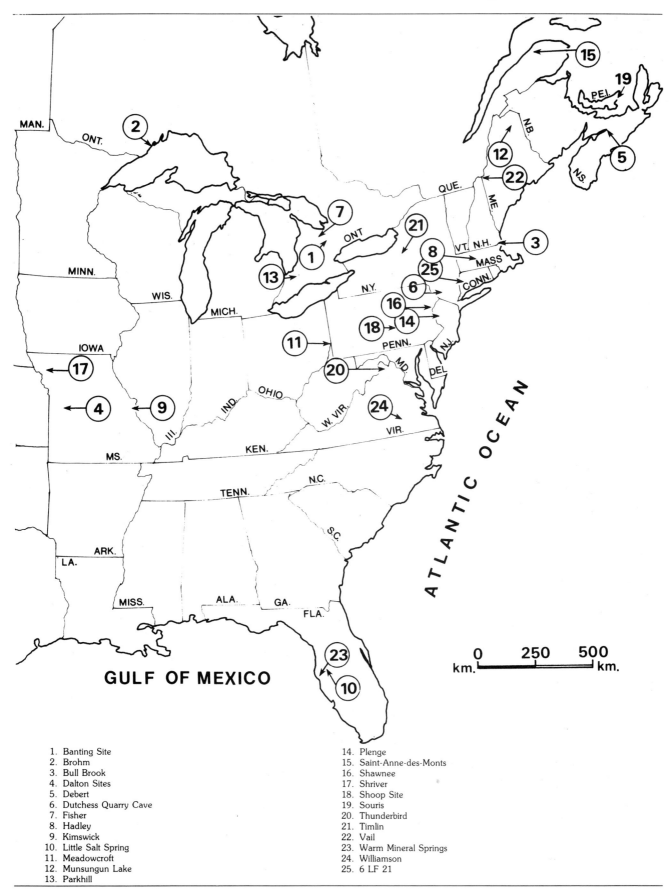

Figure 7.5   Site Map of Eastern North America

1. Banting Site
2. Brohm
3. Bull Brook
4. Dalton Sites
5. Debert
6. Dutchess Quarry Cave
7. Fisher
8. Hadley
9. Kimswick
10. Little Salt Spring
11. Meadowcroft
12. Munsungun Lake
13. Parkhill
14. Plenge
15. Saint-Anne-des-Monts
16. Shawnee
17. Shriver
18. Shoop Site
19. Souris
20. Thunderbird
21. Timlin
22. Vail
23. Warm Mineral Springs
24. Williamson
25. 6 LF 21

done, no great strides have been made, although a great deal of effort has been expended on the search (Figure 7.5). I do not for a moment suggest that the search for pre-Clovis remains should be abandoned or even slackened, but at the same time I would advocate that the standards for scientific validation of claims in this are not be compromised with polemics as we have witnessed over the past decade.

The critical question that demands immediate attention is that of humic acid contamination of C-14 dates, since there is growing evidence that current lab pretreatments are inadequate and that we are confounded by dates that may in some cases be too old, and in other cases too young to allow an accurate reconstruction of the prehistoric framework. The development of accelerator dating of microgram samples over the next decade should at least allow us to solve most of our chronological problems in the east as well as elsewhere in the New World.

GEORGE C. FRISON

8 The Western Plains and Mountain Region

By the latter part of the 1950s, Paleoindian studies were well summarized by Wormington's (1957) landmark work, which is still the most referenced work used by students of the Paleoindian. The decade of the 1960s witnessed an even greater emphasis on the study of the Paleoindian. Efforts were directed toward establishing a more reliable chronology based on stratigraphy, projectile point typology, and radiocarbon dates. Several years of work at the Hell Gap site (Irwin-Williams et al., 1973) were productive along these lines, although adequate publication of results is still pending. Geological, paleontological, and other related studies aimed directly at the Paleoindian problem also expanded during this time period (see, for example, Haynes, 1968, 1969b, 1970; Martin and Wright, 1967).

It was almost a general consensus of opinion at the beginning of the 1970s that this decade would witness the solution to the problem of the origins and the peopling of the New World. The chronologies established in the 1960s have withstood the test of time reasonably well, even though more data are still needed to establish more satisfactorily the validity and chronological position of certain projectile point types that may be diagnostics of actual cultural complexes. However, the peopling of the New World is still far from being solved.

Paleoindian data collection and analysis have continued steadily throughout the past decade. Continual experimentation with new interpretive methods, reanalysis of older data, reinvestigation of older sites, and the discovery and investigation of many new sites have significantly increased our knowledge of Paleoindian cultural systematics. The following discussion presents this investigator's view of the last decade of studies in the plains and mountains of western North America. A strong provincial bias toward the Northwestern Plains is readily admitted based on an intense, long-term research commitment to this area and an unfamiliarity with adjacent areas.

Methodological Trends in Paleoindian Studies

The decade of the 1970s witnessed a continual demand for greater rigidity and care in data recovery and analysis. Data recovery methods have been innovative for the purpose of extracting the maximum in terms of interpretive potential. Culture-bearing deposits are being examined more carefully and have been proven to yield more and more information. Increased mechanization has become important; there is no longer the need to hesitate in the removal of large volumes of overburden or in the digging of long, deep exploration trenches. Large volumes of matrix can be subjected to intense scrutiny by water-screening and flotation methods, and the power to provide the necessary water volume and pressure can be provided at almost any site location. This situation is in contrast with the not-too-distant past when most archaeological recovery methods relied almost entirely on human effort. Power equipment has proven indispensable to Paleoindian archaeologists in areas such as the high plains, where cultural strata may lie deeply buried under thick alluvial, colluvial, or aeolian deposits. It is up to the investigator, however, to understand the limitations of the use of power equipment in archaeological sites.

Paleoecological Studies

During the past decade, an increasing emphasis on Quaternary studies has significantly aided the Paleoindian archaeologist. As more accurate reconstructions of paleoenvironments are realized, more accurate interpretations of past human subsistence strategies become possible. Areas of relatively great topographic relief and low precipitation, as characterized by the western high plains and mountains, may offer the greatest visibility for archaeological sites, but there is also the highest probability of loss through geological activity. Consequently, it is rare for all or even a large percentage of original occupational surfaces in Paleoindian sites to be preserved intact. In addition, a large share of Paleoindian sites on the high plains are related to large animal procurement events that took advantage of topographic features, particularly arroyos, to enhance the chances of success. Since Paleoindian times, numerous "cut and fill" events have almost always altered the original topography so that only remnants are present. From these remnants, the general character of the original topography must be determined if accurate assessments of animal procurement methods and related human activities are to be realized. The Olsen-Chubbuck site (Wheat, 1972), the Colby site (Frison, 1976b), the Hudson-Meng site (Agenbroad, 1978), and the Agate Basin site (Frison and Stanford, 1982) are all examples of arroyo traps, and the reconstruction of the paleolandforms involved was necessary for accurate interpretations of animal procurement methods. The same is true of animal procurement sites that utilized certain types of sand dunes for trapping purposes (Albanese, 1974).

Studies in soil genesis are closely allied with those of geology and demonstrate a high potential to aid in paleo-ecological reconstructions (Reider, 1980). Pollen preservation in high plains Paleoindian sites has not proven reliable enough for accurate reconstructions of past plant communities (Beiswenger, 1974, 1981). Hence, most reliable pollen studies rely on core samples taken from high altitude ponds and are of limited value (see Wright, 1978). Opal phytolith studies are still in the developmental stages but offer the promise of future value (see, for example, Lewis, 1978). Mollusks are usually restricted to certain ecological situations, and their potential as paleoecological indicators has probably not yet been fully realized (see, for example, Wu and Jones, 1978).

Faunal Analysis and Taphonomy

Faunal remains have always been an integral part of Paleoindian studies because of an interest in extinct animal species and the strong possibilities of learning more of past human economic activities. Interest in noncultural small mammals in Paleoindian sites is also growing because many of these were restricted to very limited environments and their presence could be an aid in paleoecological reconstructions (see, for example, Semken, 1980). Humans, carnivores, and scavengers all leave diagnostic evidence of their modification of bone, and the investigator needs to know if a bone in its present form resulted from human butchering or processing, or from carnivore or other animal activity. Certain kinds of bone tools are difficult to identify; the worn edge of a bone may have resulted from human use, rodent chewing, or some other noncultural event. An accurate assessment of the number and kinds of animals brought to a site by the human group tells much of animal procurement and the amount of food products acquired. The potential for past cultural interpretations from faunal materials is high and has not yet been fully exploited.

Paleoindian sites, particularly those on the high plains, are commonly associated with large bone beds resulting from the procurement of large numbers of animals. Accurate age determinations of the animals in these situations can tell the investigators the time of year and whether or not the remains resulted from a single kill or were from animals taken over periods of time. In addition, sex determination would reveal the population structure. All of this added increments of knowledge useful to the investigator in site interpretations. Another product of faunal analysis has been an increased interest in bison taxonomy (see for example, Wilson, 1978).

Paleontological methods proved adequate for aging the animals (see Reher, 1974; Frison et al., 1976), but the nature of the sampling processes of animal populations as are manifest in archaeological sites is not well understood. Consequently, the science of taphonomy has become a byword in Paleoindian studies. The concepts of taphonomy have been presented by Efremov (1940), Voorhies (1969), and more recently by Olson (1980) and Behrensmeyer and Hill (1980). The area of study covered by taphonomy includes all events between the biocoenose and the thanatocoenose. It also includes the study of the entombing sediments. Its implications for Paleoindian studies are many, and the methodology is still very much in its developing stages, but taphonomy provides the unifying body of principles necessary for faunal analysts to achieve the necessary systematic approach.

Lithic Technology

A host of studies in the last decade have centered around the manufacture and use of flaked stone tools and weaponry. As a result, archaeologists better understand the selection of raw stone flaking materials, the processes of their reduction into usable artifacts, and their subsequent use in economic activities. Many functional studies of tool and weaponry use have been the result (see, for example, Hayden, 1979). The journals *Lithic Technology* and *Flintknappers Exchange* emerged in response to the need for lithic technologists to share their information. These efforts have become more than replications of artifacts; instead, they have contributed heavily toward a better understanding of the cultural systematics involved.

The Use of Hypothetical Models

Studies of modern hunters and gatherers provide hypothetical models that may be of value in reconstructions of Paleoindian cultural systems. The inherent dangers in the use of ethnographic analogy are recognized, but investigators are also aware that viable band-level societies demonstrate patterned behavior and that Paleoindian band-level groups had to behave accordingly. The seasonality evident in large animal kills strongly suggests an element of patterned behavior, and the study of present-day hunters and gatherers may be useful in the development of subsistence strategies where the archaeological evidence is nearly always incomplete.

Paleoindian Cultural Complexes

The Clovis Cultural Complex

The origins of Clovis seem as dim as ever. There is still no acceptable stratigraphic evidence that offers any reasonable cultural complex out of which Clovis could have developed. Davis (1978) offers the possibility that an ancestral Clovis horizon is present in the interior California lakes area, and that it may have developed there and subsequently spread to other areas. The hypothesis is based on differential artifact weathering. Lacking either stratigraphic evidence or actual dates for support, the idea is intriguing, but there is still insufficient proof for its universal acceptance.

As a cultural complex, Clovis is little better understood than a decade ago. However, the advances in the understanding of stone technology during the last decade have had a positive effect on Clovis, as well as on all Paleoindian studies. The flint-knapping work by Crabtree (1971) and Bradley (1974), along with somewhat more theoretical approaches such as that by Knudson (1973), have brought chipped stone tool and weaponry manufacture into a new and different perspective. Their interpretive value can now be used more effectively in cultural reconstructions rather than for the mere replication of artifacts.

Cylindrical ivory and bone objects with tapered and cross-checked ends from Clovis components are still questionable with regard to function (see Lahren and Bonnichsen, 1974). It is the writer's personal opinion that one of these, from an *in situ* Clovis component at the Agate Basin site in eastern Wyoming (Frison and Zeimens, 1980: 235), is a projectile point and not a foreshaft. However, one can easily draw other conclusions from the Anzick site specimens.

Ideas on mammoth hunting have proliferated somewhat, speculative as they must be (see Saunders, 1977). Much of this has resulted from reanalysis and more recent studies of the Lehner site, along with studies of modern elephants and elephant behavior. This argument will probably continue because of the weak likelihood that decisive evidence will appear. One realtively large mammoth site has appeared that provides few conclusive data with regard to actual mammoth procurement, but that does provide a hypothetical model for cold weather meat storage. Known as the Colby site (Frison, 1976b), it yielded a small projectile point assemblage with attributes that are slightly outside what is normally considered Clovis (Figure 8.1). The technology, however, is unmistakably Clovis, as is the time period involved.

Intermediate cultural complexes between Clovis and Folsom are as yet unclear. The Goshen Complex has been proposed for the period of 10,800-11,000 B.P. at the Hell Gap locality for lanceolate unfluted projectile points (Irwin-Williams et al., 1973), but more data are badly needed. Significant numbers of fluted projectile points that do not fit the typological configurations of either Folsom or Clovis are known from discrete surface areas of the Bighorn Mountains (Figure 8.2a-e). These could be intermediate forms between Clovis and Folsom, but stratigraphic and/or reliably dated, *in situ* components are needed before anything other than the present conjecture is possible.

The Folsom Cultural Complex

New data on Folsom have proliferated in the past few years: the Adair-Steadman site; the Lake Theo site; the Hanson site; and the Folsom component at the Agate Basin site in particular have added much to our knowledge of the cultural systematics of the Folsom Complex (see Tunnell, 1977; Harrison and Killen, 1978; Frison and Bradley, 1980, 1981; Frison and Zeimens, 1980; Frison and Stanford, 1982). Of importance also is the final publication of the results of the Lindenmeier investigations during the 1930s (Wilmsen and Roberts, 1978). Folsom lithic technology is better understood along with bone and antler technology and weaponry. The economic orientations of Folsom seem now to be better explained by hunting and gathering, and by utilization of a broad spectrum of plant and animal resources that extended into many ecological zones. The known geographic spread of Folsom is expanded by the Moe site in North Dakota (Schneider, 1975), and by the Fowler-Parrish site (Agogino and Parrish, 1971) in eastern Colorado. A Folsom level at the stratified Carter/Kerr-McGee site in the Powder River Basin, dated at 10,400 $\pm$ 600 years B.P. (RL917), demonstrated the use of the arroyo trap for bison procurement (Frison, 1977) and also yielded a limited tool assemblage.

Folsom stone tool assemblages are strongly suggestive of expert craftsmen. Decorative work on bone at Lindenmeier (Wilmsen and Roberts, 1978) and Agate Basin (Frison and Stanford, 1982) further argues for this, and the tool assemblages indicate similar decorative work on hide and wood. The use of bone and antler for projectile points (Frison and Zeimens, 1980), and the deep grooving of elk antler to produce what is believed to be a fluting tool (Frison and Bradley, 1981), suggest a well-developed bone and antler technology that is still poorly represented in archaeological sites.

The true status of the Midland cultural complex is still unresolved. Unfluted Folsom projectile points, as well as

Figure 8.1   Projectile Points from the Colby Site

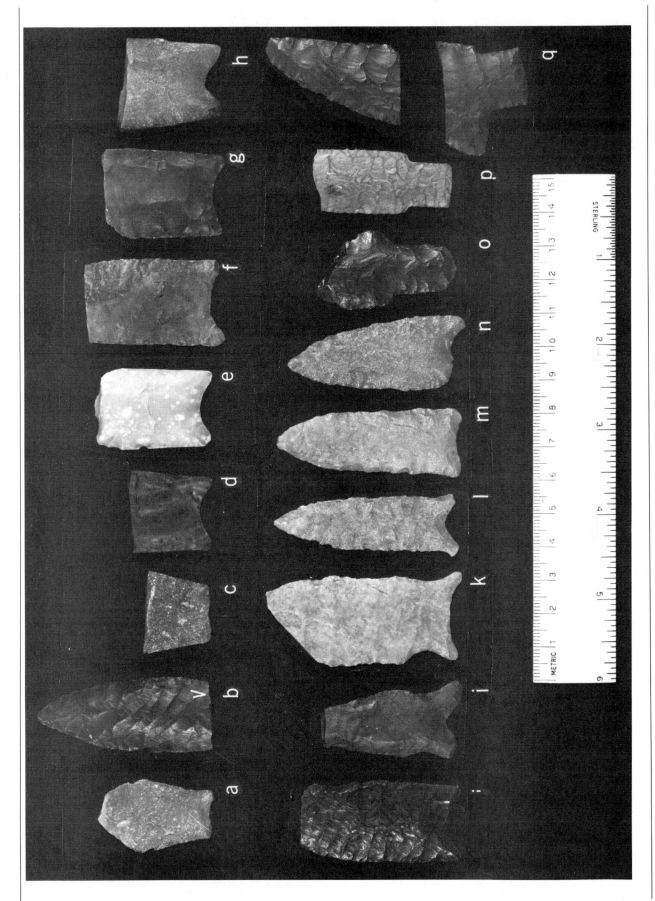

Figure 8.2 Fluted Points from the Bighorn Mountains (a-e), the Betty Greene Site (f), and the Medicine Lodge Creek Site (g-q)

113

pseudo-Folsom points that are simply outline forms imposed on thin, flat flakes with no interrupting flake scars, occur along with fluted points in Folsom sites. The Hanson site demonstrates a wide range of fluted (Figure 8.3a-e) and unfluted variants (Figure 8.3g-j). In addition, the Folsom component at the Agate Basin site produced well-fluted preforms that appear deliberately broken and/or discarded, while functional projectile points were poorly made or of the pseudo-Folsom variant made on a thin blade to give a superficial appearance of fluting (Bradley, 1982). For example, at the Agate Basin site, bone points, a pseudo-Folsom point, and a poorly made fluted point (Figure 8.3f) resembling a miniature Clovis point demonstrate evidence of actual use as weapons for killing bison, while apparently successfully fluted preforms were lost, discarded, or deliberately broken. Whether or not Midland is a separate cultural complex or part of Folsom on the Northwestern Plains will be determined only by the recovery of more materials in proper context.

Agate Basin and Plainview

The ultimate fate of the Folsom cultural complex, with its distinctively fluted points, remains unsolved. On the Northern and Northwestern Plains, the next known cultural complex is Agate Basin; further south, it is Plainview. The writer feels much more comfortable claiming a possible direct relationship between Plainview and Folsom than Agate Basin and Folsom based on technology alone. On the other hand, the Agate Basin site has dated, stratigraphic evidence of Agate Basin immediately above Folsom with no apparent change in site activities and no significant changes in tool assemblages. The fluted Folsom points may have simply been replaced by the Agate Basin. The Agate Basin point type from the type site (Figure 8.4) is now better understood since the publication of the final report (Frison and Stanford, 1982). Agate Basin has been a problem in Paleoindian studies because of the use of the term "Agate Basin-like" used to describe projectile points that resemble the Agate Basin type in outline form but that are usually several thousand years later in date.

Further south, knowledge of the Plainview Complex has been greatly enhanced by the investigations conducted under the Lubbock Lake project (see, for example, Black, 1974; Johnson, 1977; Johnson and Holliday, 1980).

Hell Gap

Since its discovery and final confirmation as a cultural complex at the Hell Gap site during the 1960s, there have been two major Hell Gap sites that have increased our knowledge of Paleoindian bison procurement and the Hell Gap Complex itself. The Casper site in Wyoming (Frison, 1974) was a bison trap in a parabolic sand dune, and the Jones-Miller site in Colorado (Stanford, 1978a) may have been accomplished by the use of some sort of an artificial

structure. Both provided large extinct bison (Reher, n.d.) and samples of projectile points and tools. The Casper site provided a reliable late date for the camel in North America and, along with the Clovis level at the Carter/Kerr-McGee site, some hypothetical ideas on Paleoindian camel procurement (Frison et al., 1978).

Hell Gap levels are present at the Agate Basin site, providing stratigraphic evidence of Agate Basin-Hell Gap relationships. Technologically, there seems to be no difficulty in deriving Hell Gap directly out of Agate Basin. In fact, the shouldered Hell Gap projectile point as it is manifest at the Casper site (Figure 8.5) is seen developing in the Agate Basin assemblage (Figure 8.4a).

The tool assemblages, at least in bison procurement situations, are practically identical, but there is no evidence at the Casper, Jones-Miller, or Hell Gap sites of the "Hell Gap knife" described earlier (Irwin-Williams et al., 1973: 48). However, there were four distinctive, elongate chipped artifacts from the Hell Gap component at the Carter/Kerr-McGee site at Gillette, Wyoming that are vaguely similar to this but that lack the single shoulder of the Hell Gap site specimens.

Alberta, Cody, Firstview, and Kersey Complexes

The Hudson-Meng site (Agenbroad, 1978) has greatly increased our comprehension of the Alberta complex, both in material culture and in bison procurement. The site is a large bison procurement manifestation with many unanswered questions and possibilities for studying actual bison procurement techniques. If the radiocarbon dates from the site are correct, there may be an overlap in time between Hell Gap and Alberta, but any actual relationships are not yet clear.

Recent work at the Horner site has revealed a separate cultural component that, if not Alberta, is apparently Alberta-related. Dated at about 10,060 years ± 220 B.P. (I-10,900), it is in the form of a bison kill. The operation may have incorporated an artificial structure, and certainly involved a late fall or early winter time of year. Preliminary studies reveal large bison comparable in size to those from the Casper site. Although the date compares well to the oldest from the Hudson-Meng site, the projectile points are somewhat smaller (Figure 8.6f-i). Also included in the assemblage are a number of very small projectile points. Some are larger points that were reworked (Figure 8.6a,b), while others are not (Figure 8.6c-e). One suggestion is the use of the bone bed as a secondary attraction for the procurement of carnivores and scavengers.

The single Alberta component is present under nearly two meters of alluvium, in contrast to the nearby bone bed dug several decades earlier by Princeton University and the Smithsonian Institution, which was nearly at the surface. The relationships between the two components are unclear. What is suggested is that the earlier work was in

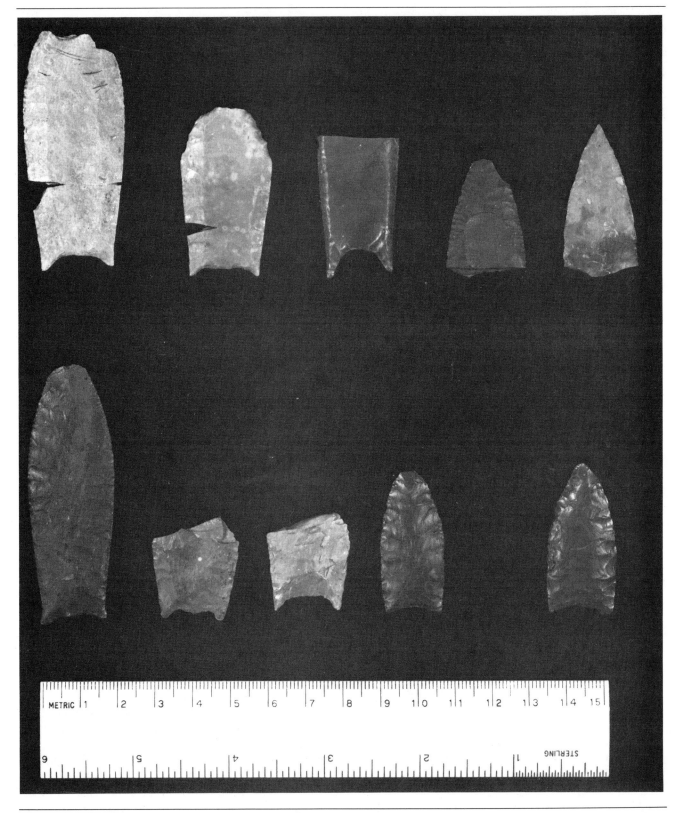

Figure 8.3   Projectile Points from the Hanson Site

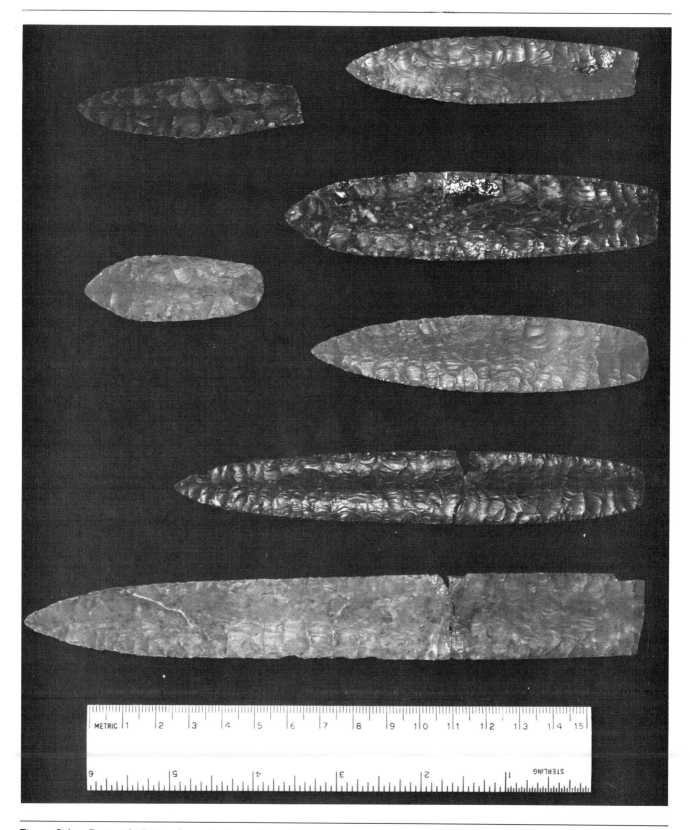

Figure 8.4   Projectile Points from the Agate Basin Site

Figure 8.5   Projectile Points from the Casper Site

a mixed component, judging from the projectile point assemblage. If the dates of the earlier work are correct, they represent the Cody Complex, but the projectile point assemblage contains the true Cody Complex (Eden-Scottsbluff) (Figure 8.7f-j), and also a number of the Alberta-like materials that are similar to the projectile points represented in the recently excavated bone bed. The differences in projectile point manufacture technology in the final product are readily observable. Several items of interest include Cody knives that were found in both the Alberta (Figure 8.7a) and Cody components (Figure 8.7b-d) at Horner. A Cody knife was also found at Hudson-Meng. Also discovered in the mixed component at the Horner site were broken bifaces that are wide and extremely thin (Figure 8.7e) and that appear different from the projectile points. They are believed to belong to the Cody Complex, since nothing similar was recovered in the adjacent Alberta bone bed area. There seems little difficulty in

deriving the Cody Complex directly from the Alberta Complex. The Cody Complex component at Horner is also believed to have been a bison kill utilizing a corral or other artificial structure.

A remnant of an extensive Cody Complex bone bed was found at the Carter/Kerr-McGee site with a wide range of projectile point styles (Figure 8.6j-o). Unlike the Horner site, the Carter/Kerr-McGee site is believed to be a butchering area alongside an arroyo trap.

The Firstview and Kersey Complexes of the Central and Southern Plains are considered by Wheat to be the time equivalent of Alberta and Cody Complex materials in the Northern and Northwestern Plains. The validity of this Firstview concept is further argued by Johnson and Holliday (1980), based on their work associated with the Lubbock Lake project, where Firstview is stratigraphically above Plainview. A significant contribution to Late Paleoindian studies is Wheat's (1979) analysis of the Jurgens site along

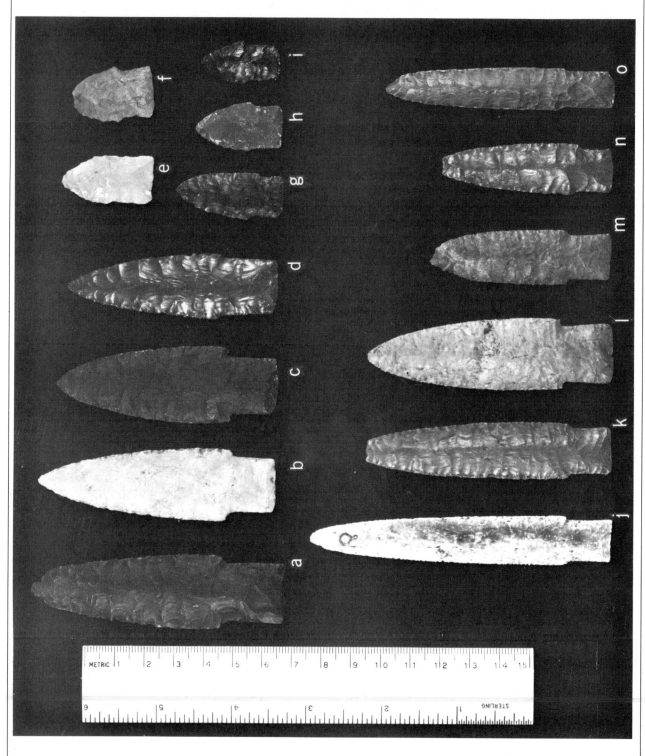

Figure 8.6 Projectile Points from the Alberta Component at the Horner Site (a-i) and the Cody Component at the Carter/Kerr-McGee Site (j-o)

Figure 8.7 Cody Knives from the Alberta Component (a) and the Cody Component (b-d) at the Horner Site, and Biface Fragment (e) and Projectile Points (b-j) from the Cody Component at the Horner Site

the South Platte River just east of Greeley, Colorado. Wheat's analysis argues for four aspects of Late Paleoindian animal procurement processing and utilization. He also coins the term "Kersey Complex" for regional development of the Firstview and Milnesand Complexes of the Southern and Central Great Plains. According to Wheat, the placing of stems on lanceolate projectile points occurs on both Firstview and Kersey points, but only on broken pieces and by reworking. However, Milnesand points were not stemmed when salvaged, but maintained the lanceolate shape. These ideas will undoubtedly evoke many future arguments.

From Folsom through Cody Complex, there was a considerable amount of movement of exotic stone flaking materials. The societal mechanisms responsible are poorly understood. Knife River flint is a prime example. It was moved over distances of several hundred miles beginning in Folsom times and continuing at least through Cody Complex times, after which stone flaking materials in Paleoindian sites appear to be more local. The procurement, distribution, and use of all raw stone flaking materials during Paleoindian times need intensive study.

Terminal Paleoindian Complexes

Little, if anything, has occurred to clear up the confusion of the Late Paleoindian groups characterized mainly by projectile points with diagonal flaking patterns. The James Allen site and projectile point type (Figure 8.8f,g) were associated with bison procurement, but other sites have not appeared that can claim a close association with this complex. Angostura, Fredrick, Meserve, and Lusk cultural complexes are still not well known with regard to their geographic spread, economic orientations, dates of occurrence, and internal and external relationships. A site claimed to be of Meserve-Dalton affiliation, presently under investigation in western Nebraska, may reduce the confusion in this area of study when fully investigated (see Myers, 1979). A reevaluation and further investigation of the Ray Long site (Hughes, 1949; Wheeler, n.d.) might be of considerable value along these lines.

The Foothill/Mountain Paleoindian Groups

These are probably the least understood of all Paleoindian manifestations. Husted's (1969) concept of an ecological barrier between mountains and plains still appears to have some merit. Mummy Cave (Wedel et al., 1968) and Medicine Lodge Creek (Frison, 1976a) provide records of cultural groups back to around 9,000 B.P. in the former and 10,000 B.P. in the latter. Recognizable and separable only by projectile point styles at this time, the complete chronology is still to be resolved.

At about 10,000 B.P. at Medicine Lodge Creek, the projectile points (Figure 8.2g) are lanceolate and concave-based, and the flaking patterns are transverse. Similar pro-

jectile points (Figure 8.2h) were found at Bush Shelter, a stratified site in the southern Bighorn Mountains of central Wyoming with a date of 9,000 ± 240 years B.P. (RL-1407). Split base or expanding base styles follow at around 9,500 to 9,600 years ago at Medicine Lodge Creek, still with transverse flaking (Figure 8.2m-p). Immediately afterward is a stemmed style with rounded base (Figure 8.2k) that has a vague resemblance to Alberta. After this is a projectile point style with a concave base (Figure 8.2l), but this may be nothing more than a variant of the slightly earlier styles with expanding bases.

The Cody Complex is present at the Medicine Lodge Creek site, as is manifest by both projectile points (Figure 8.2j) and a Cody knife (Figure 8.2i). Above the Cody materials is a series of levels containing lanceolate projectile point styles with diagonal flaking patterns and straight-to-concave bases (Figure 8.8k-p). Above this is a level containing projectile points reminiscent of what Husted (1969) named as the Lovell Constricted type (Figure 8.2g,h).

Pryor Stemmed (Husted, 1969) is now best known as a cultural complex (Frison, 1980). It is presently restricted to the Bighorn and Pryor mountains, although more recent evidence suggests a much wider distribution. Settlement patterns favor caves and rockshelters in deep canyons and areas around sandy buttes from the base of the mountains to near the timberline. Two Pryor Stemmed levels were present at the Medicine Lodge Creek site. The projectile points range from lanceolate (Figure 8.8a) to stemmed styles (Figure 8.8b-e). They are manufactured with lenticular cross-sections, but with a later bi-beveling that is apparently progressive in nature and may continue until the point is weakened and breakage occurs, or sometimes until the width is nearly the same as the thickness.

The last Paleoindian level at Medicine Lodge Creek is dated at 8,000 years B.P. and contains a single stemmed projectile point (Figure 8.8h). After this is an abrupt change to the side-notched projectile point types of the Early Plains Archaic.

Mummy Cave (Wedel et al., 1968; McCracken, 1978) produced a number of Paleoindian levels. Around 9,200 years ago, one of these levels produced a diagonally flaked point with concave base, and slight restrictions with edge-grinding above the base (Figure 8.10k). Slightly later, the projectile point style is lanceolate with lateral edges that expand distally and are heavily ground (Figure 8.10h-j). A similar point was recovered at Medicine Lodge Creek (Figure 8.8j) but in an area of mixed Paleoindian levels. After this, and continuing until about 8,000 B.P., there are a number of Paleoindian levels with lanceolate projectile point styles revealing straight-to-concave bases and grinding on the lateral edges (Figure 8.10a-g).

Several other stratified sites have produced late Paleoindian materials. Southsider Cave, on the western slopes

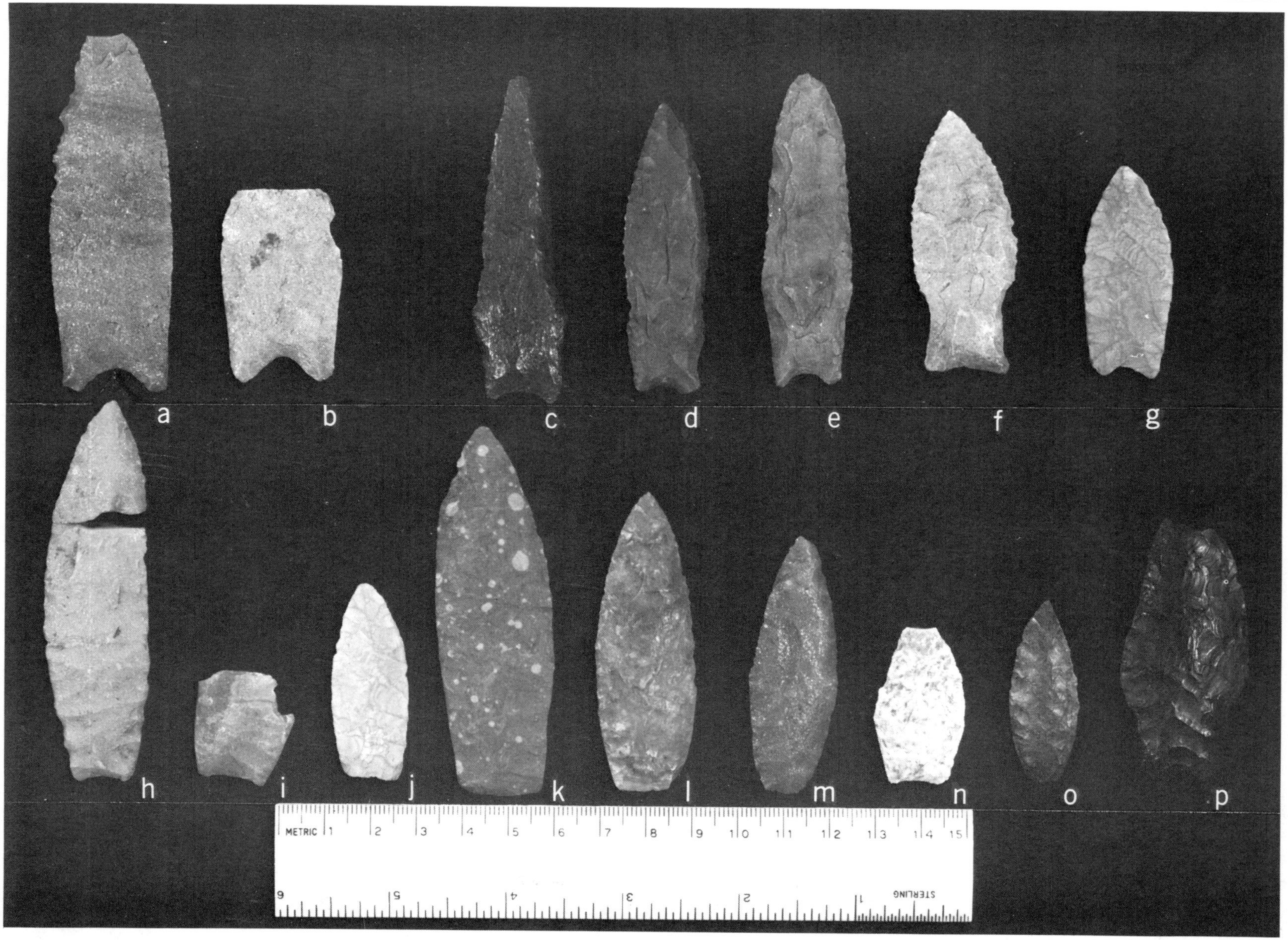

Figure 8.8 Prior Stemmed Projectile Points from Schiffer Cave (a, d), Paint Rock V Site (b), Site No. 48J0303 (e), and a Surface Find (c), as well as Projectile Points from the James Allen Site (f, g), the Medicine Lodge Creek Site (h, j, 1-p), and Southsider Cave (i, k)

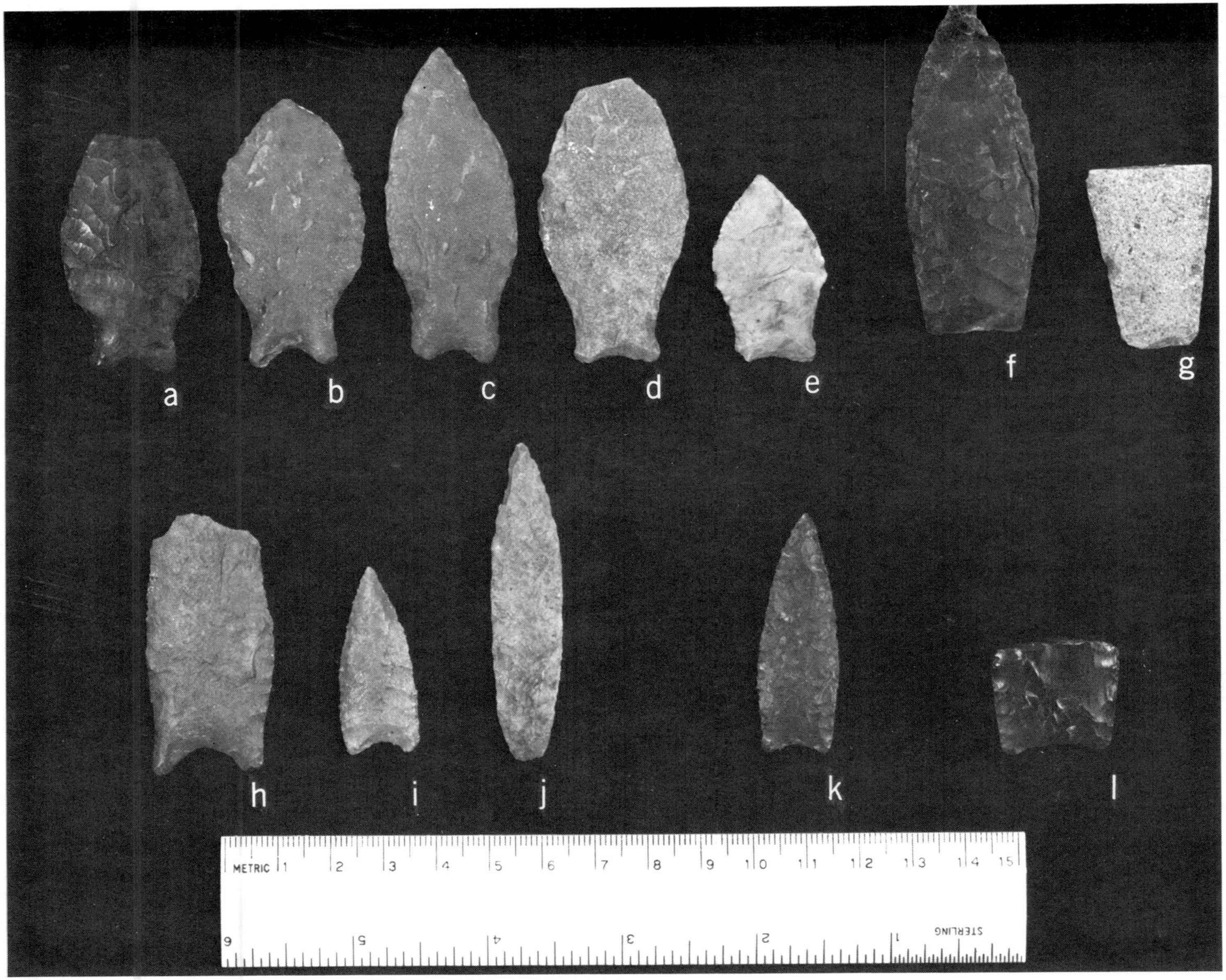

Figure 8.9 Projectile Points from the Lookingbill Site (a-g), Bush Shelter (h), and Southsider Cave (i-l)

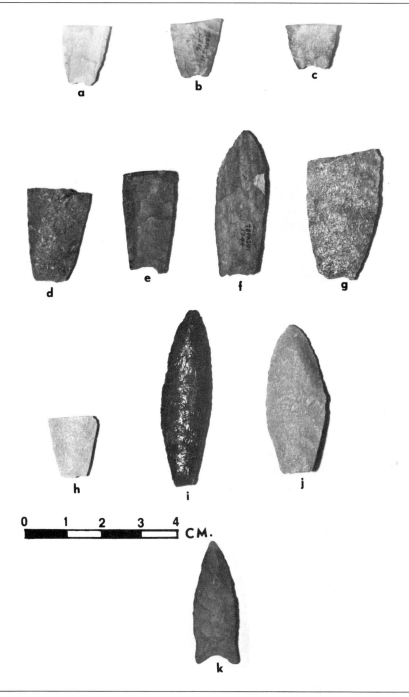

Figure 8.10 Projectile Points from Mummy Cave

of the Bighorn Mountains (Frison, 1978: 39), has a date of 9,360 ± 230 B.P. (RL-665), with a projectile point (Figure 8.9k) that is similar to one (Figure 8.2l) with a similar date from Medicine Lodge Creek. A projectile point (Figure 8.9l) that could not be definitely associated with a radiocarbon date is reminiscent of the oldest Mummy Cave specimen (Figure 8.10k). At 8,500 ± 210 B.P. (RL-666) is a long, narrow, lanceolate projectile point (Figure 8.9j) with a rounded, heavily ground base. Other

rockshelter sites have produced similar materials (Figure 8.8i,k), but dated levels are lacking. At Southsider Cave, in stratified sequence, are projectile points dated at around 4,000 years B.P. possessing many attributes of Paleoindian materials and that might easily be taken as such if not found in context (Figure 8.9i).

The Lusk Complex was described (Irwin-Williams et al., 1973) from materials recovered at the Betty Greene site near Lusk, Wyoming (Greene, 1967). A recent visit to the Betty

Greene site revealed cultural materials eroding from a definite cultural level, including a projectile point base (Figure 8.2f). The site needs more work and a reevaluation of the lithic technology involved. The site appears to contain a lithic manufacturing area, and a better understanding of the projectile point manufacture strategy may aid in better placing the Lusk Complex within the late Paleoindian sequence.

The stratified Lookingbill site in the southern Absaroka Mountains at an elevation of 8,200 feet (Frison, 1978: 44) has recently produced Paleoindian components that are as yet undated. The oldest associated with extinct bison contains projectile points (Figure 8.9a) that appear closer in technology to the Haskett type (Butler, 1965). This is not surprising, considering that the Lookingbill site is close to the Continental Divide and could easily have cultural affliations with the west. Surface finds of similar projectile points are common to the area and may be a regional variant of Hell Gap.

Directly above the Haskett level is an unconformity, and directly above the unconformity (and directly below a series of stratified Early Plains Archaic levels with the distinctive, large, side-notched projectile points) is a terminal Paleoindian component containing a distinctive projectile point style (Figure 8.9d-g). Another (Figure 8.9c) is reworked, and another (Figure 8.9b) may be a slightly different style, or more likely one that was not completed. The bases are concave, relatively thick and, along with the lower portion of the lateral edges, heavily ground. These are frequent surface finds in the higher altitudes of the Absaroka Mountains and are thought to be of late Paleoindian age rather than Archaic, as has also been suggested. Their suggested age is around 8,000 years B.P., and a radiocarbon date on an Early Plains Archaic level immediately overlying is forthcoming.

Also important in the understanding of the Paleoindian occupation of western North America is the Myers-Hindman site (Lahren, 1976). The stratified deposits and the assemblages present expand the knowledge of Paleoindian occupation into the mountains and river valleys away from the Plains.

There is a definite sharp break in terms of projectile point types about 8,000 years ago when notching suddenly dominates archaeological assemblages. It is considered by some investigators to be the result of human population movement. Other investigators regard this as the result of a technological change among the same residents, since there appears to be no discernible changes in population size or economic orientations. However, the plains have been an area of quick and drastic changes in animal populations due to the fact that small changes in yearly precipitation resulted in significant increases and decreases in animal carrying capacities. As a result, the human groups were often forced to move or change economic orientations, or both, quite suddenly.

Conclusions

The last decade has witnessed a continual increase in the Paleoindian data base. Chronologies are better known – still incomplete, but well enough developed to allow more time to be spent on the development of valid subsistence and settlement models. The technological aspects of flint technology, bone technology, and tool use are better known. The multidisciplinary approach is recognized as vital because accurate reconstructions of Paleoindian ecological conditions are necessary in order to better understand the critical relationship between the Paleoindians and their environment. Clovis origins are still in doubt, and the transition from Paleoindian to Altithermal cultures is not yet well understood in terms of population movements or technological changes in resident populations.

The continued investigations in older sites such as Agate Basin and Horner, and the discovery of new stratified sites such as Medicine Lodge Creek and Carter/Kerr-McGee give the impression that the Paleoindians in western North America were systematic in their economic and settlement strategies. They were definitely not wandering continually over the area taking advantage of the economic resources they happened to encounter; to the contrary, their movements were systematic and predictable.

There have been no spectacular breakthroughs in Paleoindian studies in the past decade. Instead, there has been a continual building and improvement on the methodologies developed earlier. This is encouraging, and if Paleoindian studies are allowed to continue in the next decade as in the past one, we can afford to be rather optimistic.

RICHARD S. MacNEISH

9 Mesoamerica

In Mesoamerica, finds of Early Man before the time of the final extinction of the Pleistocene megafauna, about 9,000 to 10,000 years ago, are not numerous, and most of them were discovered during the last twenty years. Nevertheless, there are hints that here also, Early Man went through a series of technological stages that are related to or are the same as those that seemed to exist for the rest of the New World (MacNeish, 1976) (Figure 9.1).

The earliest stage – elsewhere characterized by chopping/chopper tools – is still almost unknown, and hypothetically it should date before 30,000 or 40,000 years ago. It has been suggested by Epstein (1969) that some of his earliest finds from the San Isidro site in Nuevo Leon may belong to this earliest stage, and perhaps they do. However, they are not in excavated contexts, nor have they been dated. Epstein also suggests that these finds are related to my poorly documented Diablo complex of Tamaulipas, which included a few artifacts in high terrace gravels indicative of some antiquity (MacNeish, 1958). However, I would like to point out the fact that the majority of the Diablo artifacts are unifaces — types characteristic of the second stages — and, further, that high terrace gravels are probably less than 30,000-40,000 years old. Mirambell (1973) has also suggested that some of the basalt and andesite artifacts from various tests on the slopes above Tlapacoya are older (33,500) than those dated at 20,000 years ago and may be of this stage. Unfortunately, there is no documentation of this speculation.

Perhaps more reliably representative of this hypothetical first stage are the El Bosque remains from Nicaragua (Gruhn, 1978). Here at least one pebble- or flake-chopper and some worked bone from good context were associated with bones of extinct sloth (Eremotherium and Megalonychidae), mastodon (Stego mastodon), and horse (Amerhippus). Dating these finds, however, presents some problems, as the radiocarbon estimates range from 18,100 ± 500 to more than 35,000 years ago (Espinoza, 1976).

Only time and more research will tell just how reliable these finds are and if they really do represent this first stage.

Our second hypothetical stage seems to be represented by some fairly reliable data from 15,000 to 40,000 years ago. It is characterized by bone tools and a unifacial industry and is best evidenced in good dated context at Valsequillo, which was excavated by Cynthia Irwin-Willams many years ago (Irwin-Williams, 1967). She found thirteen unifacial artifacts, such as points, burins, side-scrapers, wedges, end-scrapers and spokeshave-like objects, in association with extinct animals at five locations – El Horno, Mirador, Tecacanco, lower Hueyatlaco, and Caulapan. Further, shell near the flake artifact at Caulapan dated to 21,850 ± 850 B.P. (W1895). Also, Juan Armenta (1978), working in the same area but often at other locations, found more unifacial chopper stone artifacts, as well as many bone tools and pieces of worked bone of extinct animals. C-14 dates on these remains range from 23,940 ± 1,000 B.P. (W1911) to more than 35,000 years ago. Although the context of these is not as good as that of the Irwin-Williams material, there is no denying the fact that this cultural complex existed at that time.

Further, this stage II-type of artifact occurs at a number of other early sites in other parts of Mexico, including, in my opinion, the Diablo complex of Tamaulipas that was mentioned above. The most publicized of these is Tlapacoya, with its dates of 21,700 ± 500 B.P. (L449) and 24,000 ± 4,000 B.P. (A794) (Mirambell, 1973). Unfortunately, there were few artifacts found in these early complexes, mainly andesite flakes. In fact, one of the most publicized of these artifacts was an obsidian blade that was actually found in the backfill, not in situ. Again, although the final description of these finds has yet to be put into print, there was an indisputable association of man's unifacial tools with the bones of extinct animals such as the mammoth, mastodon, horse, and others.

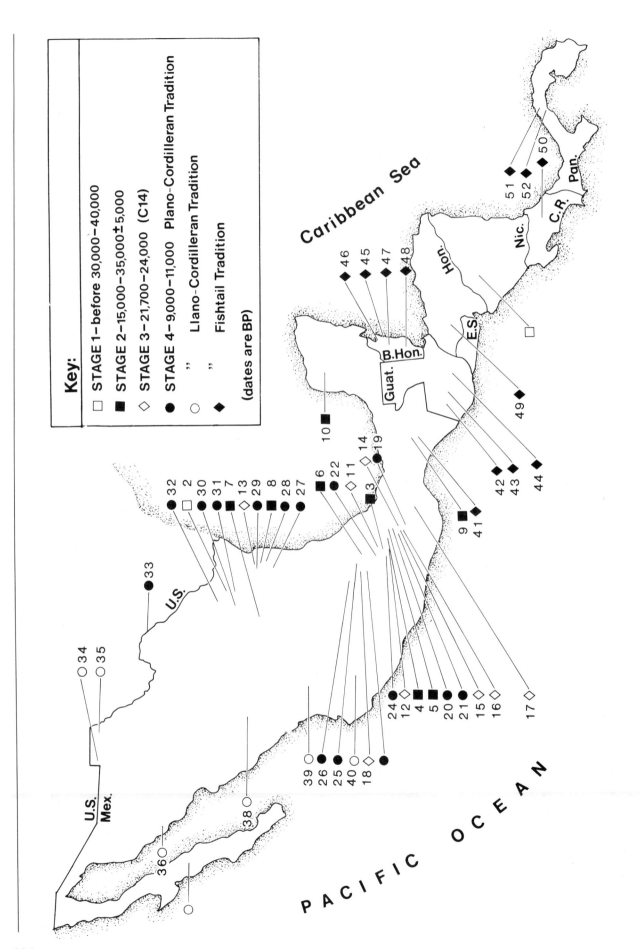

Key:

STAGE 1 – before 30,000 – 40,000   □

STAGE 2 – 15,000 – 35,000 ± 5,000   ■

STAGE 3 – 21,700 – 24,000 (C14)   ◇

STAGE 4 – 9,000 – 11,000   Plano-Cordilleran Tradition   ●

       "   Llano-Cordilleran Tradition   ○

       "   Fishtail Tradition   ◆

(dates are BP)

Figure 9.1   Early Man Sites in Central America

KEY TO MAP

Stage 1: Chopping-chopper tool complex – before 30,000-40,000 B.P.
(1) El Bosque, Nicaragua (C-14 range from 22,640 to more than 35,000); (2) Doubtfully earliest San Isidro, Nueva Leon, Mexico – no date.
Stage 2: Uniface and bone tool complex (15,000-35,000 ± 5,000)
(3) Caulapan, Valsequillo, Puebla (C-14 to 21,850 B.P.); (4) Irwin's sites – El Horno, Mirador, Tecacanco, Valsequillo, Puebla (n.d.); (5) Armenta sites – Valsequillo, Puebla (C-14 range from 23,940 to more than 35,000 B.P.); (6) Tlapacoya, Mexico D.F. (C-14 to 21,700 and 24,000); (7) possibly El Cedral, Matehuula, San Luis Potosi (21,980 and 31,850); (8) possibly Diablo complex – Tamaulipas (n.d.); (9) possibly earliest Santa Marta, Chiapas (n.d.); (10) possibly lowest Loltun Cave, Yucatan (n.d.).
Stage 3: Burins, blades, well-made end-scrapers, bifacial leaf points (11,000 to 15,000 ± 1,000 B.P.)
(11) 4 excavated to 50 early Ajuereado components, Coxcatlan, Puebla (n.d.); (12) IE-Hueyatlaco, Valsequillo, Puebla (n.d.); (13) earliest La Perra layer 6 at Tmc 174, Tamaulipas (n.d.); (14) Ts500, Tehucan, Puebla (n.d.); (15) Ts39, Tehuacan, Puebla (n.d.); (16) Ts391, Tehuacan, Puebla (n.d.); (17) Zone F. Cueva Blanca, Mitla, Oaxaca (before 9050 B.C.); (18) worked bone, Tequixquiac Valley of Mexico (n.d.).
Stage 4: Specialized bifacial projectile points – 9,000-11,000 B.P.
Planoid-Cordilleran tradition
(19) 4 excavated Tc50 late Ajuereado components, Coxcatlan, Peubla (n.d.); (20) layer six of El Riego Cave (Tc35), Tehuacan, Puebla (n.d.); (21) 7 surface components (Ts383, 380, 372, 343, 204, 368, 255) from the Tehuacan Valley, Puebla (n.d.); (22) Valsequillo, Puebla (9,150 B.P.); (23) Plano point surface find, Tlaxcala (n.d.); (24) Tlapacoya II, Mexico, DF (9,250 B.P.); (25) Iztapan, Mexico, DF (9,920 B.P.); (26) lower levels, San Nicolas Cave, Queretaro (n.d.); (27) surface site 305, Tamaulipas (n.d.); (28) layers 4 and 5, La Perra Cave Tmc 174, Tamaulipas (n.d.); (29) layer 4 and 5, Diablo Cave (Tmc81), Tamaulipas (9,270 B.P.); (30) possibly San Isidro, Nuevo Leon (n.d.); (31) La Cazada, Nuevo Leon (9,940 B.P.); (32) Plano surface find, Nuevo Leon (n.d.); (33) Devil's Mouth Cave, Texas (8,780 B.P.).
Llano-Cordilleran tradition
(34) Clovis point, Rancho Colerado, Chihuahua; (35) Folsomoid Pt., Camaleyucan, Chihuahua (n.d.); (36) Clovis point, Guaymas, Sonora (n.d.); (37) Clovis point, San Juaquin, Baja, California (n.d.); (38) Fluted point, Rancho Weicker, Durango (n.d.); (39) Clovis point, San Sebastian, Jalisco; (40) Clovis point, San Marcos, Jalisco.
Fishtail tradition
(41) Los Grifos Cave, Chiapas (8,500-10,000 B.P.); (42) Tapieles, Guatemala (C-14 range 8,810-11,170 B.P.); (43) Chajbal fluted point, Chajbal, Guatemala (n.d.); (44) San Raphael fishtail point, Guatemala City (n.d.); (45) 3 sites – 190, 191, 192 – Ladiesville, Belize (n.d.); (46) lowest layer, site 35, Sand Hill, Belize (n.d.); (47) Site 100, Melinda, Belize (n.d.); (48) Site 158, Dry Creek, Belize (n.d.); (49) Esperanza site, Lb-20 – Esperanza, Honduras (n.d.); (50) Turrialba site (9-FG-t) – Costa Rica (n.d.); (51) Madden Lake sites – Panama (n.d.); (52) Panama Canal Channel site – Panama (n.d.).

Figure 9.1 (Continued)

It might be added that there are two other possible examples of this stage that have not been reported, either. One includes the lower levels of the Santa Marta cave of Chiapas. Again, there were but a few unifacial tools and no date, but the stratigraphy was clear and these levels lay under strata that dated to 9,000 years ago. Once the lower levels of this cave are dug again with the same techniques that I used in my initial testings (MacNeish and Peterson, 1962), I'm sure we will have a more adequately documented example of stage II. Somewhat similar are the lower levels of Loltun Cave in Yucatan, where Umberto Gonzales has found unifacial tools in association with bones of the extinct horse, mammoth, and other animals.

Thus, stage II does exist. Although Haynes (1969b) and Stanford (Humphrey and Stanford, 1979) have their doubts, they cannot ignore the facts and "Martinize" (Martin, 1973) these finds out of existence. While none of these finds have yielded large inventories, and though the stage is ill defined, there are a number of sites which, upon excavation, will give us better samples of artifacts and ecofacts so that the whole matter may be settled shortly to everyone's satisfaction.

In my scheme of things, the final two Early Man stages are characterized by specialized bifacial projectile points as well as other tools. The first of these is not well documented and might date between 10,000 and 15 or 20,000 years ago and should be characterized by blades, burins, and leaf-shaped points. Earliest Ajuereado of the Tehuacan Valley of Puebla (MacNeish et al., 1967), perhaps some Lerma components of Tamaulipas (MacNeish, 1958), Unit 1E of

Hueyatlaco of Puebla (Irwin-Williams, 1967), and perhaps the next to earliest levels of Santa Marta Cave (Garcia et al., 1976) may be examples of this stage.

One salient feature of stage III is the presence of bifacial leaf-shaped Lerma points, although obviously this type is not very distinctive and lasts way beyond this time period. It is not known whether future research will find other point types, such as fluted Clovis-like (Haynes, 1970), Meadowcroft-like (Adovasio et al. b, 1975), or Fells Cave-like (Bird, 1946), but the fact remains that in this stage the first bifacial points do appear and may well reflect not only new lithic manufacturing techniques but also new ways of hunting. Other bifacial tools also occur in this hypothetical stage III which also reflect these new lithic techniques.

Perhaps more significant for this stage in terms of lithic manufacturing techniques is the seeming initiation of the blade-burin technique of manufacture. Here is a whole field yet to be adequately studied where implications are not well understood. Obviously, one implication is that the burins appear to reflect a new kind of bone industry, but the details of this are still unknown. Second, the well-made, snub-nosed end-scrapers and blade-scrapers of this stage probably imply new skin-working techniques. However, because of the limited number of finds and the lack of in-depth study of what we have found, we are in fact certain of very little about the culture of this stage, including whether there was a highland-lowland cultural dichotomy at this time, as our Belizean and some Guatemalan sites suggest (MacNeish et al., 1980). Nevertheless, the ever-increasing finds of hypothetical stage IV, with its numerous regional traditions of projectile points, suggest that some sort of regional adaptation had commenced during stage III.

In fact, it is only with our final hypothetical stage IV that we have even a semblance of an adequate set of artifacts from a number of sites that allows us to hypothesize about regional traditions. On a general level, this final preceramic stage had many more specialized bifacial projectile points – Clovis, Plainview, Golondrina, Lerma, Fells Cave, and so forth – as well as a number of other tools, such as mullers and milling stones, which show that these peoples had other subsistence options besides big-game hunting, and that they may have had specialized adaptations to various ecozones or environmental zones.

In spite of these generalities, working out the details of the traditions in Mexico at this time is still very difficult at this stage of our research. In 1966 I thought there was only one tradition – Cordilleran (MacNeish et al., 1967). By 1974, I thought there were two, an eastern – Planoid Cordilleran – and a western – Llanoid Cordilleran – and now with our work in Belize, I see a third – the Fishtail Point tradition (MacNeish et al., 1980). Who knows what tomorrow will bring? In fact, all I can do now is describe, and in part repeat, what I have said before.

In terms of representatives of the easterly tradition, the best-documented example is the late Ajuereado Complex of the Tehuacan Valley of east central Mexico, and although no C-14 dates are directly associated with it, bracketing dates suggest that it existed roughly from 12,000 to 9,000 years ago (MacNeish et al., 1967). Although indigenous Lerma points (named after one of the major sites in Tamaulipas) predominate in this latter part of the phase, Flacco and Plainview points that were probably derived from northeast of Mexico have also been found. Crude blades, burins, gravers, spokeshaves, and a host of special end-scraper types were used, and the hunting of herd animals by the lance-ambushing technique, rabbit (or other animal) drives, and the collecting of small animals were the predominant subsistence activities, in that order, in all seasons, in all environments (MacNeish, 1975). Proportions of deer bones, as compared with horse and antelope, increase in the floor layers, suggesting new hunting strategies, such as stalking individual large animals using atlatl-propelled darts equipped with barbed foreshafts. Mortars, grinding stones, and mullers appear in association with spring seeds, agave, and opuntia leaves, and the presence of fall fruits suggests seed-collecting, leaf-cutting, and fruit-picking subsistence activities. The leg bones of some of the smaller animals are broken in a manner that suggests the use of traps (MacNeish, 1975). All these late additions strongly suggest that these groups had new sup-

plementary subsistence options that could be seasonally and environmentally adaptive.

The materials from the nearby Valsequillo region, dated at just before 9,150 years ago (Irwin-Williams, 1967). A concave-based, stemmed point found along with laurel-leaf points among numerous horse and antelope bones suggests that a process similar to that of Ajuereado was unfolding. The data from the Valley of Mexico, also meager, are from two sites: the Iztapan Mammoth Kill, dated at about 9,250 years ago (Aveleyra and Maldonado-Koerdell, 1953) and Tlapacoya II, a campsite dated at 9,920 years ago (Mirambell, 1973). Both sites seem related to the Valsequillo region and indicate similar developments. Although household tools including an obsidian blade, gouge, semilunar knife, and end-of-blade scraper were found at Iztapan, it was obviously a kill site and not a camp. Further, the occurrence of Lerma-type leaf-points (in the same animals as at Agate Basin) and a trianguloid point of the Plano tradition of the United States, suggests multiple hunting techniques, the former being used for lance-ambushing and the latter for dart-stalking. These remains, obviously related to those from just across the lake at Tlapacoya, may belong to a different seasonal subsistence pattern, for while Lerma points, blades, and semilunar knives still occur at Tlapacoya, choppers, grinding stones, and mortars are found in association not only with extinct megafauna, like horse and tapir, but also with deer and rabbit bones (Mirambell, 1973).

Also possibly related is a fluted point from Tlaxcala (Garcia, 1973). Some of the earliest remains from Texcal Cave near Puebla might be of this stage (Mall, 1977), but again, better archaeological contexts are needed.

There is some evidence that this Plano-Cordilleran tradition, documented for central Mexico, extended as far north as the Rio Grande in northeast Mexico. Although the evidence is poor, a related complex of Lerma points, blades, burins, choppers, and snub-nosed scrapers was found in the lowest levels of San Nicolas Cave, near San Juan del Rio in Queretaro, associated with large and small extinct and modern mammalian remains (MacNeish et al., 1967).

Somewhat better evidence comes from the Lerma phase of Tamaulipas, dated at 9,270 years ago (MacNeish, 1958). Here, extinct beaver and deer bones were associated with Lerma points that perhaps were fastened to lances and other chipped stone tools. Both a triangular Plano-type point that perhaps tipped an atlatl dart, and one of the pebble hammerstones that might well have functioned as a pestle, may indicate supplementary subsistence options. North of Tamaulipas, toward the Rio Grande, although the ecological data are less secure, there are hints from sites like San Isidro, La Calzada, and Devil's Mouth that the

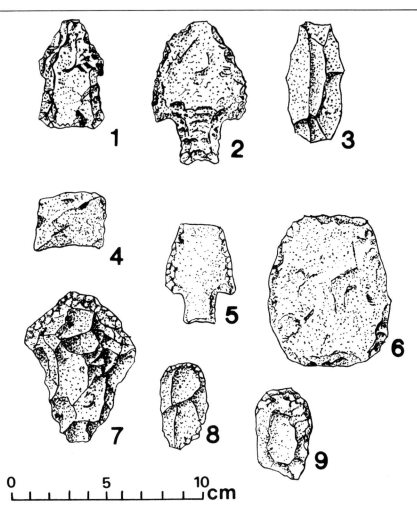

NOTE: The complex also includes pointed blades, crude blades, laterally used flakes, crude bifaces, and anvil end-scrapers.

1. El Inga-like point (Pp la)
2. Madden Lake-like point (Pp 16)
3. Crude blade unworked striking platform (N 1)
4. Plainview-like point (Pp 2)
5. Madden Lake-like point (Pp 16)
6. Fine ovoid biface (B o)
7. Small stemmed end-scraper (Z 52)
8. End of blade scraper (ES 13)
9. Small snub-nosed end-scraper (ES 1)

Figure 9.2 Lowe-ha Complex Artifacts—7,500 to 9,000 B.C.

Planoid Cordilleran gave way to Plano and other specialized complexes (Figures 9.2-9.6) (Epstein, 1969).

Most of the more northeasterly Mexican sites in latest Pleistocene times form a unit, although they seem to have been increasingly influenced by the many specialized contemporary complexes in the central United States, such as Plainview, Agate Basin, Scottsbluff, and Eden, all of which might be called Plano.

How far south this Planoid Cordilleran complex or tradition extended is unknown, but some of the dates – 8,100 B.C., 8,780 B.C., 8,960 B.C., and 9,050 B.C.– from Cueva Blanca in Oaxaca seem to be as early as those in the complexes just mentioned (Flannery, 1969). However, the projectile points and many of the other artifacts – like those from Texcal Cave, phase I – seem related to our El Riego remains from Tehuacan, which we believe date from roughly 7,000 to 5,000 B.C. in radiocarbon time. Quite frankly, the reporting of the Oaxaca material is only in a preliminary stage, and other remains to the south are most inadequate. Hence, we cannot solve the dilemma. It might

(text continued on p. 135)

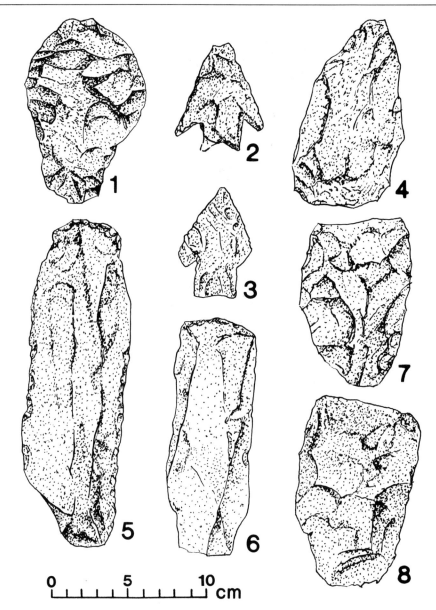

NOTE: The complex also includes sole-shaped end-scrapers, coup de poing-like bifaces, and large ovoid end-scrapers

1. Snow shoe-shaped end-scraper (E 53a)
2.-3. Pedernales-like points (Pp 3)
4. Thick crude biface (B 2)
5. Macroblade end and side retouched (N 4)
6. Macroblade end retouched (N 4)
7. Gouge (ES 5a)
8. Petaloid adze-gouges (ES 5)

Figure 9.3   Sand Hill Complex Artifacts – 5,500 to 7,500 B.C.

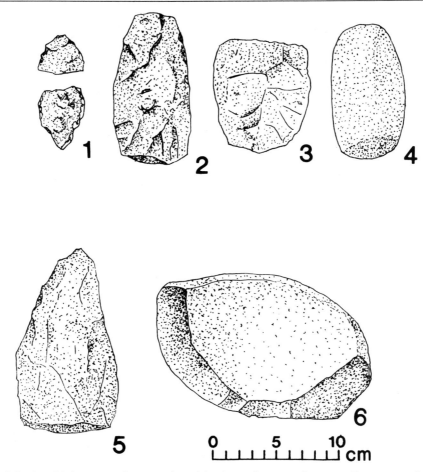

NOTE: The complex also includes discoidal choppers, crude scraper planes, bifaced cone-choppers, milling stones, Tecomate stone bowls, and oblong stone dishes.

1. San Nicolas-like point (Pp 4)
2. Thick crude biface (B 2)
3. Petaloid adze-gouge (E 53)
4. Sharp conical pestle (G 16)
5. Triangular coup de poing-like biface (B 7)
6. Hemispherical stone bowl

Figure 9.4   Belize Complex Artifacts – 4,200 to 5,500 B.C.

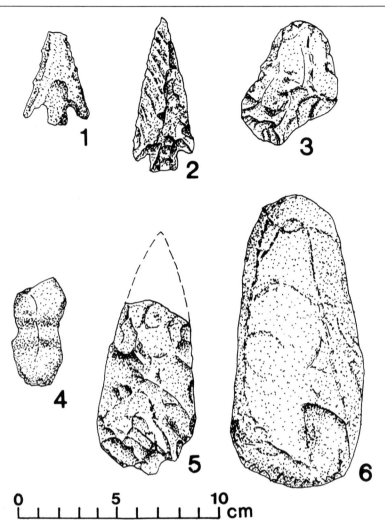

NOTE: The complex also includes small discoidal choppers, discoidal scraper planes, triangular coup de poings, and large ovoid bifaces.

1.-2. Shumla-like points (Pp 5)
   3. Triangular end-scraper (ES 7)
   4. Pebble net sinker (G 18)
   5. Finely chipped biface knife (B 8)
   6. Hamenslow pestle (G 7)

Figure 9.5   Melinda Complex Artifacts – 3,300 to 4,200 B.C.

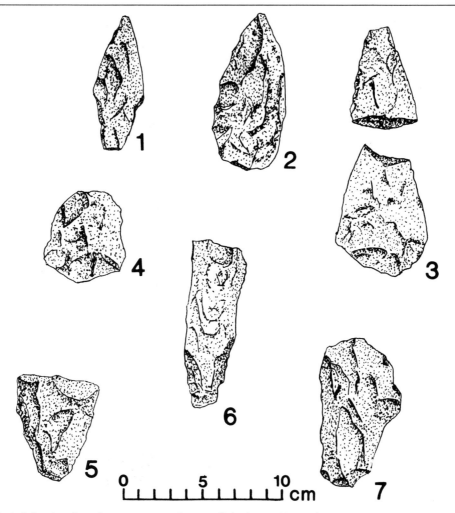

NOTE: The complex also includes triangular end-scrapers, scraper planes, anvil abraders, metates, and manos.

1. Progreso stemmed point (Pp 7)
2. Leaf point (Pp 6)
3. Finely chopped ovoid biface (B 8)
4. Small discoidal scraper plane or end-scraper (E 8)
5. Adze tranchet (ES 10)
6. Long keeled end-scraper (ES 11)
7. Triangular scraper plane (ES 9)

Figure 9.6   Progreso Complex Artifacts – 2,500 to 3,300 B.C.

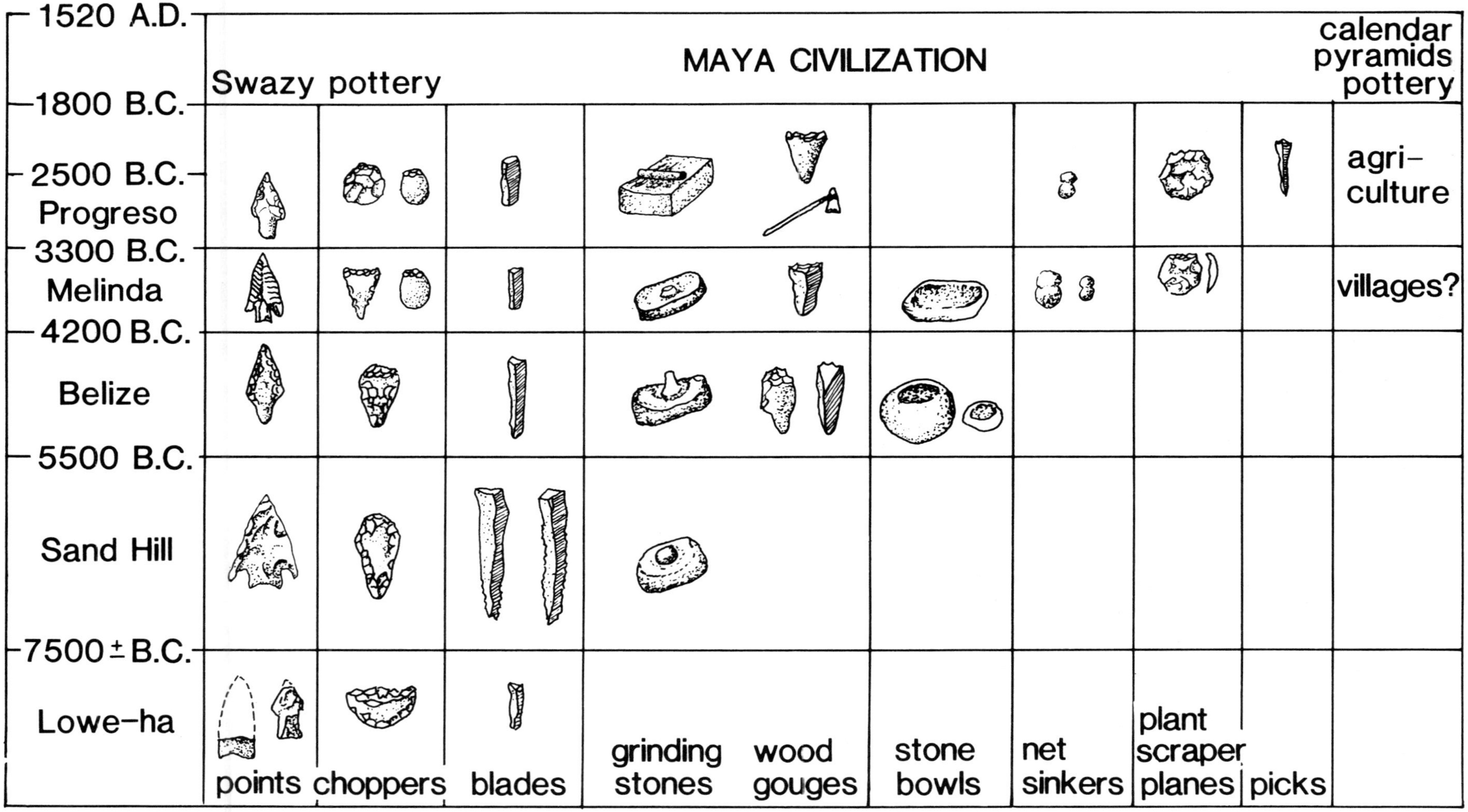

Figure 9.7 — Tentative Belizean Pre-Ceramic Archaeological Sequence

MAYA CIVILIZATION

	calendar pyramids pottery	agri-culture	villages?

Date	points	choppers	blades	grinding stones	wood gouges	stone bowls	net sinkers	plant scraper planes	picks
1520 A.D.									
1800 B.C. — Swazy pottery									
2500 B.C. Progreso	●	●	●	●	●		●	●	●
3300 B.C. Melinda	●	●	●	●	●	●	●	●	
4200 B.C. Belize	●	●	●	●	●	●			
5500 B.C. Sand Hill	●	●	●	●					
7500 ± B.C. Lowe-ha	●	●	●					●	

Figure 9.7 Tentative Belizean Pre-Ceramic Archaeological Sequence

134

mean that our dates for Tehuacan, in Puebla, Mexico and more northerly regions for this Planoid Cordilleran tradition are just too conservative, or that the Archaic started earlier in Oaxaca. Again, we plainly need more adequate materials, as well as more reported analysis of materials.

Equally difficult to document is the Early Man tradition in northwest and southwest Mexico, but Clovis points found at a number of surface sites in northwest Mexico, a fluted point in association with about fourteen Lerma points, blades, burins, and other artifacts found at Los Tapiales in Guatemala dated at 10,710 years ago (Gruhn et al., 1977), hint that the basic Cordilleran Complex of western Mexico and the Pacific drainage area of Guatemala was undergoing a similar set of influences from the north. In this case, however, the source of the influence seems to have been the Folsom and/or Clovis (Llano) complexes of the western United States. Perhaps this should be called Llanoid Cordilleran. Exact definition of this latter hypothetical tradition must await more thorough excavation with better samples and artifacts. Thus, the best is yet to come from people digging in the northwest of Mesoamerica (Figure 9.7).

The southern border of both these Cordilleran traditions must be somewhere in Guatemala and southern Mexico, for our third tradition that is literally just coming out of the ground seems to occur in Central America. Early finds by Bullen (Bullen and Plowdan, 1963) in Honduras hinted that such traditions existed, as he found surface sites with fluted fishtail points. Also, in Panama, the find of Madden Lake (Bird and Cooke, 1978) indicated that this new tradition existed there, and Brown's (1980) recent finds in Guatemala showed that something similar existed there. So far, good contexts and exact dates are missing. In Belize, our Lowe-ha Complex promises to better define the tradition (MacNeish et al., 1980), but what we have now are mainly materials from surface collections (Hester et al., 1981) and a couple of dozen artifacts from tests. Let me mention briefly what we have found so far: fishtail- and Plainviewlike points, snub-nosed end-scrapers, fine bifacial knives, half-moon choppers, pointed choppers, and side-scrapers, both big and little. In fact, the complex is all so new and so ill defined that it is best to say no more.

Thus I close, reiterating how poorly we know Early Man in Mesoamerica, but emphasizing that we do know that he was there. Our hopes for the future are running high. In fact, one of these days we may even be able to describe Early Man and his culture during each time period in Mesoamerica.

ALAN L. BRYAN

10 South America

Twelve years ago, Gordon Willey (1971) proposed a set of hypotheses concerning Early Man in South America. After he had reviewed the available archaeological evidence (most of which had been surface collected or obtained from other undated contexts), Willey hypothesized that there was a basic early Flake Tool tradition composed of unifacially retouched scrapers, knives, beaked tools, and burins made on percussion flakes but lacking any carefully shaped bifacial implements. This flake tradition had arrived with the first immigrants into South America sometime before 12,000 years ago and had gradually spread throughout the continent. Either developing from this early flake tradition, or possibly due to new influences arriving from the north, a Chopper tradition composed of heavy crude bifacial "choppers" was innovated. Subsequently, a Biface tradition featuring somewhat better finished large bifaces either developed locally or possibly was introduced by new immigrants bringing with them a somewhat more advanced technological skill. Most likely all of these early technological traditions, involving only artifacts made by percussion flaking, were utilized to fashion wooden and bone tools.

About 12,000 years ago new immigrants arrived, presumably related to the North America Llano mammoth hunters, who in turn were ultimately related to the Levalloiso-Mousterian tradition of the Old World. A new technology was introduced for manufacturing bifacially flaked lanceolate projectile points, which Willey termed the Old South American Hunting tradition. A diagnostic artifact of this tradition was the "fishtail" fluted projectile point. Another aspect of this Old Hunting tradition, characterized by a leaf-shaped lanceolate type of point, appeared later, perhaps as a result of indirect stimulus from people who made the fishtail type, or perhaps directly out of the earlier Biface tradition.

About 9,000 years ago, the Andean Hunting-Collecting tradition, based on hunting deer and camelids and collecting vegetable foods, had developed throughout much of

the Andean cordilleras. This broadened subsistence base, akin to the North American Archaic stage, witnessed greater differentiation as people adapted more closely to regional environments. Eventually, after 6,000 years ago, some of these Andean regional cultures started living in permanent villages based on localized maritime and plant resources, while in other areas, including Patagonia and the Pampas, land hunting continued to be the major basis of subsistence.

Meanwhile, north of the Pampas, an East Brazilian Upland tradition, little affected by the contemporary Andean Hunting-Collecting tradition, developed directly out of the old Flake tradition. In this region, flake tools continued to be used primarily for making wooden and bone tools, including projectile points for hunting deer and large rodents, but the diet was probably based largely on plant and land-snail collecting. The coastal Sambaqui tradition probably developed from the Brazilian Upland tradition as an adaptation to available maritime resources.

Willey's tentative sketch of early South American prehistory involves certain assumptions, in addition to a thorough review of the archaeological evidence. The primary assumption is, of course, that people have moved to South America ultimately from Northeast Asia via North and Central America. A related assumption is that South American stone tool types and technological traditions that appear to be similar to better-known types and traditions in North America (and in Eurasia) are probably derived from the north, either by diffusion or being introduced directly by new immigrant groups. These two correlated assumptions have been employed in one form or another by all synthesizers of early South American prehistory. Willey, as did Krieger (1964), assumed from the evidence that there was a pre- (bifacially flaked stone) projectile point stage of technological development in South America. Both Krieger and Willey recognized that this early technological stage was not a time period and could persist into late times in some areas. Although most synthesizers, using various terms with somewhat different connotations, also recognize from the evidence that there must have been a technological stage in America before the development of bifacial projectile points, some, most notably Martin (1973) and Lynch (1974), have argued that the available evidence does not warrant acceptance of this assumption. They feel that assemblages lacking bifacially flaked projectile points can be explained by inadequate sampling, specialized activities including quarrying, or local environmental restrictions, including the lack of flakable stone. They assume instead that the earliest colonists into the continent brought with them a specialized big-game hunting economy characterized by carefully flaked bifacial projectile points, presumably derived from the Clovis fluted point tradition of North America. This is a good scientific model as it is falsifiable by new evidence, which we now have.

Willey differs from all other synthesizers in that he clearly distinguishes a unifacial Flake tradition as the earliest basic technological stage preceding those stages which include bifaces. Everyone else, myself included (Bryan, 1973: 253), has assumed that bifacial flaking, although perhaps in a rudimentary form, was part of the material cultural repertoire of the earliest colonists to enter South America. Willey reached his unorthodox conclusion only from his broad continental perspective and particularly after analyzing the abundant evidence from eastern South American assemblages, which frequently lack bifacial flaking altogether and which only occasionally include carefully shaped bifacial projectile points.

During the last decade a significant body of new evidence has been reported from early radiocarbon-dated stratigraphic contexts in many parts of South America. It is no longer necessary to use undated assemblages in constructing a synthesis of the early prehistory of South America, as Krieger (1964), Willey (1971), and others had to do. A review of all the available radiocarbon-dated evidence has led me to accept Willey's insightful outline of early South American prehistory, with certain important modifications.

Since I last published (Bryan, 1973) on the general problem of Early Man in South America, I was forcefully made aware of the significance of the Isthmus of Panama to the question of the peopling of South America. I had always realized that all preceramic peoples must have somehow squeezed through this narrow neck of land in order to expand throughout the southern continent, but it was only after visiting, in the company of Professor J. M. Cruxent, an extensive area north of Panama City (straddling the Continental Divide about 300-350 m above sea-level) containing abundant sources of high-quality yellow chert that I realized that this region may hold the critical key for opening the door and revealing the early prehistory of South America.

Cruxent showed us several quarry workshop localities

extending for miles around a place known as Agua Bueno. Thousands of flakes and cores of this beautiful chert littered all of the hills and had accumulated in the stream valleys. Although I had visited many extensive quarry workshop areas in various parts of North, South, and Central America, the flaking detritus obtained from this area was significantly different from anything I had ever seen before because of the notable absence of evidence for bifacial shaping. Among the thousands of flakes, blades, and cores, there were no whole or broken bifacial preforms such as those that characterize other quarry workshop sites I had seen throughout the Americas. Cruxent had been digging deep test trenches in the lower river terraces, and he reportedly had found no evidence anywhere of bifacial artifacts such as he had found on the Rio Pedregal terraces of northern Venezuela. He had realized the potential significance of this comparison and was trying to find charcoal in his deep tests for dating purposes. In the day that my wife, Ruth Gruhn, and I had available, we persuaded Cruxent to move out of the valley, which had been subject to very rapid rates of erosion and deposition since the clearing of the tropical forest vegetation, and up onto a high bench containing a shallow swale, in which deposits would accumulate more slowly and tend to retard erosion. We succeeded in finding charcoal in direct association with quarry detritus at a depth of less than a meter. Subsequent analysis yielded a date of 5785 ± 50 years B.P. (SI-3852), obviously not early enough to be directly relevant to the problem at hand.

Elsewhere in Panama there are carefully controlled stratigraphic excavations with radiocarbon dates ranging back to 6,560 B.P. (Ranere, 1976) that have yielded essentially unifacial percussion flaked stone assemblages completely lacking bifacial projectile points, bifacial knives, blades, or drills. Ranere has shown experimentally that the rough stone tools evidently were used to process wood, bone, and shell. With the exception of the well-known scatter of fluted "fishtail" points at Madden Lake (Bird and Cooke, 1978), a few miles north of Agua Bueno, the only bifacially flaked stone artifacts known from Panama are several crude "celt-like wedges" evidently fashioned for working wood (Ranere, 1976: Fig.8), and a few cores with flakes removed bidirectionally, recovered from the lowest levels of two rock shelters in western Panama.

Back in the area of the Panama Canal, projectile points were fashioned from the excellent local chert, but they were made on blades or bladelike flakes that are usually naturally pointed without retouch. Only the stem may be unifacially retouched to fit a haft. Coincidentally, these points are quite similar in technology and shape to the North African Aterian tanged points.

Interestingly, although Madden Lake is not far from the area yielding the abundant yellow chert, evidently none of the fluted points are made of this excellent material (Bird and Cooke, 1978: Table 1). Combined with the lack of evidence for fluted points elsewhere in Panama, this fact supports the frequently expressed opinion that the fluted point makers moved rapidly through the region. To speculate, perhaps one reason they did so was that they were in hostile territory already occupied by other cultural groups. Junius Bird (personal communication, 1980) would interpret the available evidence from Panama as indicating that the earlier hunters passed through the area quickly on their search for large game animals, while their successors, more intensively adapted to the tropical forest environment, eventually dropped the art of bifacial flaking in favor of projectile points made of wood, bone, or sharp elongated flakes. On the face of it, this generally accepted hypothesis appears to be a reasonable explanation of the available excavated evidence from Panama.

I believe, however, that the evidence from eastern Brazil, where I have also worked, supports the alternative model suggested by Willey, that an early flake tradition was brought by the first colonists of South America. Occasionally they may have made a rough biface, but they did not emphasize bifacial technology and were unaware of the knapping techniques necessary to thin a biface (Bryan and Gruhn, 1978; Bryan, n.d.). I reasoned that any cultural group that expanded their hunting and collecting territory slowly in a normal manner would have taken full advantage of the readily flakable chert nodules easily visible along any watercourse penetrating the forested hills north of where Panama City is now located. As we saw no evidence of bifacial shaping in this extensively quarried region, I concluded that no one who knew the technique of fashioning bifacial preforms for reduction to thin bifacial tools ever used these quarry workshops. In other words, I hypothesized that the first people who gradually expanded through the isthmus carried with them a simple Flake and Core Tool tradition that constituted the only archaeologically visible technology until the later group of migrants who made fluted fishtail points. Meanwhile, the original Flake and Core tradition, which always lacked bifacially thinned artifacts, persisted locally in modified form into late ceramic times. Unquestionably, the bulk of flaking detritus at Agua Bueno was deposited in the last few thousand years.

Acceptance of such an unorthodox hypothesis would have several ramifications. First of all, it would explain the apparently anomalous technology at Agua Bueno. Second, Willey's alternative hypothesis, that the "bifacial chopper" and the subsequent biface traditions may have been introduced into South America by new immigrants, would be nullified. Both of these sequent traditions must have developed indigenously in South America from the early flake tradition, as Willey has alternatively proposed. Willey's assumption that new immigrants after 12,000 B.P. brought with them a new pressure-flaking technology for thinning bifacial projectile points is not negated by the Panamanian evidence, although it is obviously imperative to date a site like Madden Lake. If fishtail fluted points are significantly later than 12,000 years old in Panama, both Willey's

hypothesis, that new immigrants with fishtail fluted points introduced bifacially flaked stone projectile points to the continent, and the Martin/Lynch hypothesis, that the Fluted Point tradition represents the earliest South Americans, would be refuted.

Rather, an alternative hypothesis first presented by Rouse (1976) would be supported. Rouse concluded that the radiocarbon-dated evidence for the Fishtail Point tradition in South America suggests that it originated in southern South America about 11,000 years ago and spread northward, where it is dated 9,000 B.P. at El Inga, Ecuador. Madden Lake could well represent an even later northward penetration of the Fishtail Point tradition. Mayer-Oakes (1983) has recently proposed, from a detailed typological analysis of all of the projectile points collected at El Inga, that the art of fluting may well have developed independently in highland Ecuador. If this hypothesis is substantiated stratigraphically, Rouse's model of northward movement would be supported, and fluting could be seen as an additional part of the Fishtail Point tradition.

The alternative model, based on the assumption that the art of fluting had a single origin in North America because it is not found anywhere in the Old World, and was subsequently introduced to South America by immigrant hunters (compare Gruhn et al., 1977: 259-263; Ranere, 1980), would be negated. Although I am generally a proponent of the model of independent invention of South American projectile point traditions, I think that the lack of fluted points in the Old World and the presence of fluted points in the North American tradition, at least as far south as Guatemala, suggests that the North American Fluted Point tradition did penetrate, at least by the process of diffusion, through Panama and down the Andes at the same time that the South American Fishtail Point tradition was diffusing northward. Fishtail fluted points in lower Central America and northwestern South America therefore represent a fusion of the two point styles. Clearly, more field work is necessary to clarify this complex situation.

Ranere's (1980) model of Paleoindian population expansion (represented by fluted points) through Central America is quite relevant to the entire problem; Ranere is careful to state that his model refers only to specialized big-game hunters who presumably moved through the Isthmus between about 12,000 and 10,000 years ago, and not necessarily to the earliest people who entered this strategic passageway to South America. Nevertheless, certain of his arguments helped to formulate my model for the initial penetration of people through the Isthmus of Panama. His major premise is that "an expanding population successfully adapted to a particular ecosystem will spread to the geographic limits of that ecosystem before entering another" (Ranere, 1980: 44). He also presents evidence that, although during the Late Pleistocene each altitudinal ecosystem in mountainous Central America evidently was lowered by a maximum of about 900 m, below about 300 m above present sea-level the vegetation would have been little different than it would be now in the absence of human disturbance. In other words, anyone adapted to the relatively open savannas found at high altitudes in Central America would have eventually been forced to adapt to the steamy tropical forests of northeastern Panama before they were able to readapt themselves to any South American savannalands. Evidently, the Isthmus of Panama, where the Continental Divide falls near or below 300 m above present sea-level for significant stretches, was always an important geographical filter that would have slowed the progress of any people not already adapted to the tropical forest ecosystem. Similarly, farther north the continental divide through the Nicaraguan lowlands does not rise above 300 m for considerable stretches. Espinosa (1982) has cogently argued that Nicaragua also must have been a significant geographical filter for early migrants.

Leaving the always knotty questions concerning the origin of fluted points, which seem so difficult to resolve, we shall now return to the question of what stone technology the first people had who lived in Panama. Clearly, the technological anomaly presented by the lack of bifacial preforms at the Agua Bueno quarry should be pursued by continuing the effort to obtain earlier radiocarbon dates. Typology is useful for generating working hypotheses, as Krieger, Willey, and Mayer-Oakes have done, but such hypotheses must always be substantiated by dates obtained from controlled excavations. Such a project would have considerable theoretical significance to general anthropological theory involving the age-old question of whether or not significant independent inventions can occur. Obviously, I disagree with Tom Lynch (1967: 79),who found it "inconceivable" for bifacially flaked stone projectile points to have evolved in South America independent from North American projectile point traditions. Lynch's assumption will be challenged here on the basis of the archaeological evidence.

Partial resolution of this vital question of the independent development of projectile point traditions is available from northern Venezuela, where a broken El Jobo point was found in the pubic cavity of a young, partially butchered mastodon at Taima-taima (Bryan et al., 1978; Ochsenius and Gruhn, n.d.). The stratigraphic context is clear, and the kill is securely dated between 12,000 and 14,000 years ago by 18 stratigraphically consistent radiocarbon dates on various materials obtained from the stratum containing the slain animal. In fact, Taima-taima is, to my knowledge, the best dated Paleoindian kill site anywhere in the Americas. More of the site remains to be excavated by anyone who wishes to confirm our conclusions.

The major significance of this evidence is that the El Jobo hunters were using nearly cylindrical willow leaf projectile points to hunt mastodons in Venezuela at least a millen-

nium before Clovis hunters are generally thought to have been killing mammoths in North America. In order for Clovis fluted points to have stimulated the development of El Jobo cylindrical points, the Fluted Point tradition would have had to pass through Panama before 13,000 years ago. Clearly, this conclusion is at odds with all of the evidence.

As soon as the 13,000-year dating for Taima-taima had been confirmed, staunch diffusionists began to argue that El Jobo must somehow have received its stimulus from willow leaf-shaped points in North America, perhaps from those at Hueyatlaco, Mexico, which might be older than Taima-taima (Irwin-Williams, 1967). Technologically, the Taima-taima points are quite different from any dated assemblages anywhere in North America, or South America for that matter, although certainly the later Lauricocha and Ayampitín varieties could have been derived from an El Jobo stimulus. Furthermore, as stressed above, there are no willow leaf-shaped points known from Panama. In fact, the geographical gap between known distributions of willow leaf-shaped points in North and South America seems to be quite significant – sufficient, I suspect, to refute the hypothesis of a Pan-Cordilleran willow leaf-shaped point tradition that I once espoused (Bryan, 1965). The evidence also refutes Willey's hypothesis that willow leaf-shaped lanceolate points were later than and probably stimulated by the introduction of a new technology for making fishtail fluted points by hunters who entered South America about 12,000 years ago. At least a millennium earlier, Willey's Old Hunting tradition was already well established in northern Venezuela, evidently from strictly local stimuli, including the availability of large game animals. Rouse and Cruxent (1963) long ago hypothesized that the technological stages of development, including heavy bifacial "choppers" and later better-finished large bifaces, could have developed into El Jobo projectile points in the region. Their still viable hypothesis remains to be tested by excavations in stratified sites.

The most significant of the relatively abundant evidence now available from radiocarbon-dated stratigraphic contexts in various parts of South America will be reviewed below. This evidence has led to a modified version of Willey's model after critically challenging several working hypotheses derived from generally accepted assumptions that had in turn been extrapolated from the current understanding of North American prehistory. If these exotic assumptions are abandoned and the evidence from South America is examined largely on its own merits, a different set of working hypotheses emerges. In 1973, I concluded from a review of the early archaeological sites throughout the continent that the technological diversity that was evident in various parts of South America by

11,000 B.P. implied that the first people must have entered the continent at a significantly earlier time (Bryan, 1973). The much more abundant dated evidence now available, not all of which I have time to mention, has confirmed that this was a viable working hypothesis.

Another working hypothesis I used in 1973 was that the earliest people arrived, not as specialized big-game hunters, but rather as generalized hunters and gatherers carrying a basic tool kit composed of pebble tools, core tools, flake tools, and thick bifaces with which they were well equipped technologically to innovate many kinds of wood, bone, and stone tools in the several highly variable natural areas they ultimately occupied (Bryan, 1973: 253). As discussed above, I would now delete bifaces from this list and stress that pebble tools are really only one simple kind of core tool. Although these early people may well have carried with them carefully made tools of bone, wood, and fiber, their archaeologically visible tool kit normally consists only of artifacts made from simple cores and flakes. Also important in constructing a model of the early peopling of South America is the premise that the earliest occupants of any environmental region would occupy all parts of that region before expanding into a different environmental region, because they first had to teach themselves by means of observation and experimentation the local ecological rules that were essential for survival in the new ecosystem. Thus the initial expansion of hunting territory into the several ecologically diverse environments of South America must have been a slow process.

With these premises and hypotheses in mind, I would suggest the following model for visualizing early South American prehistory. Sometime before 20,000 years ago people first expanded their hunting and gathering territory through Panama and eventually into the several significantly different environments clustered in northwestern South America. Some stayed in the tropical forests of northwestern coastal Colombia, while others moved eastward across the narrow cordilleras into environmentally similar country where they retained their ancient unifacial Flake and Core Tool tradition for working wood and bone, eventually expanding throughout lowland South America.

Other groups moved northeastward along the Caribbean Coast into more arid thorn forest environments, where they encountered herds of large herbivores. Burned megafaunal bones associated with bones intentionally grooved before permineralization were excavated at Muaco, near Taimataima, and dated at 14,730 and 16,870 B.P. (Rouse and Cruxent, 1963: 36). To take better advantage of the presence of these bulky animals for food, these people gradually developed more efficient hunting techniques, including the substitution of cylindrical bone and wooden projectile points by heavier stone points of similar shape suitable for insertion into socketed hafts. Later, some of

these big-game hunters, with their newly developed economic adaptation, probably expanded their hunting territory southward across the Venezuelan Andes and onto the llanos, where more herds of herbivores were grazing. Further expansion of hunting territory would have taken them southward down the eastern flanks of the Andes, traversing the Montaña and its intermittent grasslands, and eventually reaching northwestern Argentina, where very similar cylindrical stone points have been found on the surface of one locality (Alberto Rex Gonzalez, personal communication, 1970).

Meanwhile, some of the original people adapted themselves to the high-altitude open savannas, where simple flake and core tools were left at El Abra Rockshelter 2 near Bogotá before 12,500 B.P. (Hurt et al., 1976). The persistence of this simple flake industry for almost two millennia constitutes evidence that after people with a simple Flake and Core Tool tradition had expanded from the torrid coast into the frigid highlands, some of them stayed and adapted themselves to the new economic possibilities, while others undoubtedly moved further eastward into the lowlands. People were killing mastodons, horses and deer in the suburbs of Bogotá at the Tibitó kill site, which has been dated at 11,740 ± 110 B.P. The associated assemblage consists of many unifacial flakes (several retouched by percussion), cores, and a few simple bone tools. Gonzalo Correal Urrego (personal communication, 1981, 1983) believes that the mastodon hunters were using wooden or bone projectile points. However, by 11,000 B.P., hunters in the Sabana de Bogotá were using pressure-flaked projectile points and knives (Van der Hammen and Correal, 1978).

In environmentally more variable mountain valleys farther south, sloths, proboscideans, and horses (but more often deer and camelids) were hunted, and abundant plant foods were gathered during the prolonged growing season. We know that people were living in Pikimachay Cave near Ayacucho in southern highland Peru, using unifacial flake tools and ground bone projectile points, unquestionably by 14,000 B.P., and probably several millennia earlier (MacNeish, 1979, 1981). Eventually, the descendants of these people expanded into the Pacific Coast deserts along water courses, where some eventually developed large-stemmed Paiján points, the makers of which buried two of their numbers in a layer dated to 10,200 B.P. (Chauchat and Dricot, 1979).

Others moved on into the relatively lush environments of central Chile, where they encountered abundant large herds of herbivores by 11,000 B.P. at Tagua-Tagua (Montané, 1968). We now have evidence that people were successfully hunting mastodons further south in central Chile before 12,000 years ago with simple sharp stones, one large percussion flaked biface, a scraper mounted on a wooden haft, many pieces of cut, grooved, and scraped wood, and two grooved bolas stones at the Monte Verde wet site, where a possible house structure has recently been excavated near the butchered remains of at least four mastodons (Dillehay, 1981).

By 12,500 B.P., people were already living in Patagonia, where simple flake tools have been found in the lower levels of Los Toldos 3 Cave (Cardich, 1978). By 11,000 B.P. at Los Toldos, bifacially flaked stone projectile points appeared, as well as farther south in Fell's Cave and Palli Aike, where fishtail points were used to hunt horses and guanacos (Bird, 1938, 1970). It is not clear what stimulated the development of the Fishtail Point tradition in southernmost South America, but there is no evidence that it was anything other than a local development.

The La Moderna site in Buenos Aires Province on the Argentine pampas contains simple flake tools associated with two genera of glyptodonts, the bones of which have been dated at more than 10,000 years old (Palanca and Politis, 1979). At Arroyo Seco site 2, also in Buenos Aires Province, Fidalgo et al. (1983) have recently reported on a unifacial flake, flake blade, and core-scraper assemblage associated with *Megatherium*, *Mylodon*, *Macrauchenia*, *Equus*, and *Hippidion*. The age of several human burials relative to the age of the megafauna has not definitely been determined.

Recent excavations in the flood plain terrace of the Rio Uruguay near Salto Grande, Uruguay, revealed bifacially pressure-flaked artifacts, including projectile points, in deep levels dated earlier than 10,000 B.P. Wesley Hurt (Weber, 1981, and personal communication, 1982) reports a subsequent decrease in the use of pressure flaked tools. On higher terraces he collected a presumably older and technologically different complex composed of large, minimally retouched quartzite blades, many with an intentionally hooked form, which had been removed from polyhedral quartzite cores. Still in the Rio Uruguay Basin but farther north in Rio Grande do Sul, thick discoidal bifaces, blades and other unifacial tools were recovered with a *Glossotherium* sloth skull that yielded a date of 12,770 ± 220 B.P. (Bombin and Bryan, 1978). Two thin bifacial tools were recovered from the Arroio Touro Passo in a stratum containing a large faunal assemblage, mostly of extinct taxa, and a radiocarbon date on wood of 11,010 ± 190 B.P.

As recognized by Willey, the East Brazilian Upland tradition evidently was quite remote from what was going on in the Andes. In general, it is a story of the persistence of a simple unifacial Flake and Core Tool tradition until very late times; however, there is an important exception to this generalization. Bifacially flaked projectile points with contracting stems (tanged or pedunculated points) appear at several sites from Rio Grande do Sul to Minas Gerais at least by 10,000 B.P. At the Alice Boër site, near Rio Claro

in the State of São Paulo, tanged points occur in stratigraphic contexts above assemblages containing steeply retouched unifacial flake tools, burins, and the occasional biface (Beltrão, 1974; Bryan and Beltrão, 1978). The deepest tanged point is associated with a date of 14,200 ± 1150 B.P. Thermoluminescence dates of 10,000 B.P. on burnt chert from a higher level tend to support the radiocarbon date (Beltrão et al., 1983). Eventually this Tanged Point tradition was found over much of lowland South America. The evidence suggests that the Tanged Point tradition was developed indigenously by southern Brazilian hunters of deer, armadillos, large rodents, rheas, and the occasional tapir.

In the state of Goiás, near Brasilia, Schmitz (1983) has reported on an early Paranaíba phase, abundantly dated between 10,700 and 6,700 B.P., characterized by a unifacial blade industry with careful steep retouch to shape "limaces," one bifacially flaked artifact, plus bone projectile points used for hunting deer, rodents, tapir, and birds, including rheas. In the following phase, land mollusks and palm nuts become more important in the diet than mammals and birds, and the unifacial artifacts become much less carefully flaked.

Relevant work in the semi-arid northeast Brazilian highlands was begun more than a century ago by Wilhelm Lund, who reported the association of man with extinct animals from one of the many caves he had excavated for Pleistocene megafauna remains at Lagoa Santa, near Belo Horizonte in Minas Gerais State (compare Paula Couto, 1950: 461-488; Bryan, 1978: 320; Bryan and Gruhn, 1978). In modern times, Hurt (1964; Hurt and Blasi, 1969) recovered from Cerca Grande No. 6 rockshelter a simple flaked stone industry that also included bifacial tanged projectile points associated with several radiocarbon dates back to 9,720 B.P. But confirmation of Lund's claim of association of man with extinct animals has been found only recently. Andreé Prous (1983) has recovered an unidentified megafaunal bone worked by man in the nearby Santana cave that has yielded dates back to 11,960 B.P. Worked (cut and chopped) megafauna bones have also been identified from other undated sites in the area (Bryan, 1978: 318; Prous, 1983). Nearby, the large rockshelter of Lapa Vermelha yielded a simple flake and core industry associated with *Glossotherium* bones and dates of 9,580 ± 200 and 10,200 ± 220 B.P. (Laming-Emperaire et al., 1975). Exotic quartz crystal flakes were recovered from levels dated between 11,680 and 15,300 B.P. A retouched quartz scraper came from above a level dated 22,410 B.P. (Prous, 1983).

Farther north in Minas Gerais, near Montes Claros, the small solution cavern of Lapa Pequena yielded an abundant assemblage of artifacts but no evidence of extinct animals or bifacial flaking. The assemblage is most similar to the second phase from Goias, although the radiocarbon dates are somewhat earlier – between 7,500 and 8,200 B.P. Flaked stone artifacts include simple utilized flakes and core scrapers associated with bone projectile points and human skeletal remains from a well-stratified sequence of occupation floors containing extensive ash deposits (Bryan and Gruhn, 1978). Evidently the people who lived in the Lapa Pequena cave subsisted mainly on palm nuts and giant land snails, to judge by their abundant remains and numerous "quebra cocos." Very few mammal bones were recovered, and most of these had been shaped into artifacts.

Most recently, Guidon (1983) has reported on a very important series of stratified sequences of occupation floors from several rockshelters near São Raimundo Nonato farther north in the state of Piauí. Several sites have yielded a unifacially flaked stone industry containing end- and side-scrapers and utilized flakes associated with charcoal dates between 7,000 and 10,000 years, while the lower levels of two sites have yielded dates older than 12,000 years on hearths associated with retouched and unretouched flakes. The shelter called Toca do Sitio do Meio has yielded a "typical limace" and many unretouched flakes associated with a date of 12,200 ± 600 B.P. In 1978, several flakes were found at deeper levels dated 13,900 ± 300 and 14,300 ± 400. A fragment of a pictograph spalled from the wall of Boqueirão da Pedra Furada was found associated with several lithic artifacts recovered from a level dated 17,000 ± 400 B.P. Excavations in 1982 yielded quartz and quartzite flake and pebble tools from lower levels dated 26,300 ± 600 and 26,400 ± 400 B.P. (Guidon, 1983). These early dates on a quartz flake industry confirm the early dated context at Lapa Vermelha. Further verification of these early dates promises to establish the caves of eastern Brazil as one of the most important areas yielding early occupation localities in the Americas.

It is important to note that none of the São Raimundo occupation floors has as yet yielded any remains of extinct megafauna, nor any projectile points made of either stone or bone (unfortunately, bone is not preserved in levels dated 17,000 B.P. and older). Nevertheless, the spectacular naturalistic rock art depicts spear throwers and speared animals (Guidon, 1983). Tentative conclusions to be drawn therefrom are (1) that early people used wooden projectile points, as did most Amazonian Indians until recently (although they may have had good flakable stone available for flake scrapers and perhaps knives), and (2) that Pleistocene megafauna, for whatever reason, were not a significant factor in the economy. In other words, not all early Americans passed through a recognizable "Paleoindian" stage of big-game hunting. Whether or not people became "Paleoindian big-game hunters" depended on whether Pleistocene megafauna were locally available

and/or whether it was to their advantage to develop special stone-flaking techniques for hunting these animals. The implications of this evidence may well be relevant to the "Early Man problem" in North America.

One great characteristic of the simple northeast Brazilian Highland Flake and Core tradition is its extremely long persistence with minimal evidence for technological change until the addition of ceramics. Despite the simple recoverable material culture, this vast region is rapidly becoming known as containing some of the most impressive cave art in the Americas, with both geometric and realistic designs, often in polychrome. We may only guess at how much finely crafted material culture composed of perishable materials has been lost to the elements.

To recapitulate, sometime before 20,000 years ago, people entered South America with a generalized hunting, fishing, and gathering economy and a basic unifacial flaked-stone technology designed for working wood, fiber, bone, skin, shell, and feather tools and ornaments. Gradually, people expanded their hunting territories and eventually adapted themselves to all of the environmentally variable major ecosystems of the continent, a process that would have taken many millennia.

In heavily forested environments, to which they were adapted upon initial entry, people tended to retain their basic generalized economy and simple stone technology. Those groups who adapted themselves to coastal maritime environmental resources also tended to retain the old technology. But in more open environments, where herds of large herbivores were living, people adapted their basic stone technology in order to exploit the available resources. In some areas people were successful in hunting large game without the use of bifacially flaked stone projectile points. Eventually, hunters living in three widely separated parts of the continent developed their unifacial flake technology to produce bifacially flaked stone projectile points. There is no evidence that external stimuli precipitated these three original developments. The three major projectile point traditions that were innovated in South America and diffused widely during the "Paleoindian" stage as forms and techniques for efficiently hafting bifacially flaked-stone projectile points can conveniently be termed (on the basis of form): (a) cylindrical willow leaf-shaped (Figure 10.1; examples – El Jobo, Lauricocha, Ayampitín); (b) fishtail (Figure 10.2; examples – Fell's Cave, Los Toldos, El Inga, Madden Lake); and (c) tanged (Figure 10.3; examples – Alice Boër, Cerca Grande) (see Figure 10.4). Although the evidence is not clear, other projectile point traditions (for example, Paiján) that developed in the Andean region appear to have been derived directly from these early traditions or indirectly by stimulus diffusion. In many areas of the continent, bone and wooden projectile points continued to be used throughout time for hunting and fishing. The bolas, probably a very ancient weapon brought to

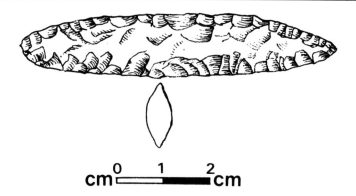

Figure 10.1 El Jobo Point from Rio Pedregal, Venezuela

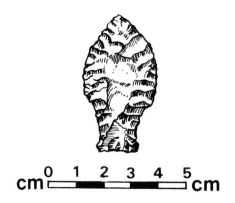

Figure 10.2 Fishtail Point from Fell's Cave, Chile

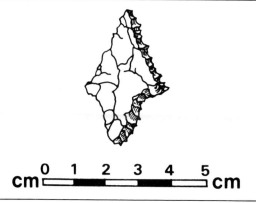

Figure 10.3 Tanged Point from Level 10 (dated 14,200 B.P.) at Alice Boër Site, Brazil

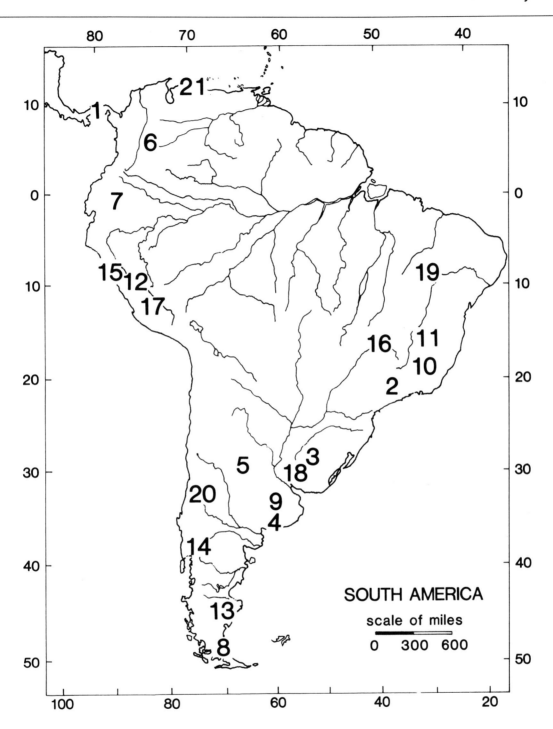

Figure 10.4   Site Map of South America

America by the original colonists, evidently was used 12,000 or more years ago at Monte Verde for hunting large as well as small animals and birds. It is important to realize that stone tools were shaped by pecking and grinding that long ago in South America. For whatever purpose, well-shaped ground stone discs were found in the 11,000-year-old levels at Fell's Cave (Bird, 1970). In North America such tools would be labeled "Archaic" (that is, Post-Paleoindian).

Without any intention of arbitrarily imposing an alien model on the South American data, North American concepts and terminology can be useful for comparative purposes and clarification simply because most American archaeologists are familiar with these concepts. The "Archaic" (or "Proto-Archaic") economic stage or organization, with a generalized hunting, gathering, and fishing economy, was always present in South America, although in certain places between about 14,000 and 10,000 years ago a "Paleo-indian" stage appeared that was characterized by greater emphasis on hunting locally available large game animals with more effective bifacially flaked stone projectile points.

From a continental perspective, the two economic stages were for a time contemporaneous; the "Archaic" persisted without the local innovation of bifacial stone projectile points from earliest times up to the time of innovation of domesticated plants, or up to European contact in some places, while the "Paleoindian" stage appeared in other areas only briefly, and died along with the herds of large game animals that the hunters helped to annihilate. The more specialized technological (projectile point) traditions persisted later in those areas (for example, Patagonia) where large game animals continued to be available for efficient hunting with bifacially flaked stone projectile points.

The most important implication of the early dated occupation and kill sites being found in South America is that much earlier sites remain to be discovered and verified in North America. North American archaeologists need a hemispherical perspective in order to focus their research more effectively on the unresolved problems concerning the early peopling of North America.

CHRISTY G. TURNER II

11 Dental Evidence for the Peopling of the Americas

Dental morphology is proving to be a significant resource for aiding the reconstruction of human population history, particularly when 5,000 to 10,000 or more years are involved.[1] This is because of (1) the substantial evolutionary stability of the numerous crown and root traits (3 shown in Figure 11.1); whose (2) intergroup differences or similarities signal past degrees of relationship; (3) tooth hardness, which enhances the probability of long-term preservation; and (4) the high genetic component in trait occurrence and expression, which minimizes many environmental effects, sex dimorphism, and age influences that reduce the usefulness of osteological remains.

The problem of the peopling of the Americas appears to be a relatively simple one from a dental anthropological viewpoint. The pattern that prehistoric New World dental variation exhibits is a partitioning into three fairly clear geographic clusters: Arctic coast (Aleut-Eskimo), Alaska interior-Northwest Coast (mainly Na-Dene-speaking Indians), and all the rest of North and South America (Indian). These three groups can be recognized in both univariate (Table 11.1) and multivariate (Table 11.2) comparisons. Since very little dental evolution can be demonstrated as having occurred since the time of Paleoindian arrival (Turner and Bird, 1981), the Aleut-Eskimo, Na-Dene, and Indian dental differences are probably best looked upon as due to original differences in their respective Old World ancestral populations. This is not to say that the three groups could not have arisen some other way. Figure 11.2 illustrates four reasonable possibilities based on the information in Tables 11.1 and 11.2.

Figure 11.2 does not include two other possible origin models, namely that all three groups diverged from one original New World population, or that the Eskimo and Na-Dene are commonly derived, a suggestion recently put forth by Szathmary and Ossenberg (1978) on osteological and serological grounds. The former model can be ruled out because of the many genetic differences between Aleut-Eskimos and Indians (Laughlin, 1963, 1966, and elsewhere), and because wherever I have been able to assess New World dental evolution, either synchronically or diachronically, it can be shown that not enough time has elapsed for the many significant differences between Aleut-Eskimo and Indian teeth.[2] Unquestionably, these two groups represent two separate migrations to the New World, a conclusion in accord with the majority archaeological view (Griffin, 1979) and other physical anthropological evidence (Stewart, 1973). The Na-Dene and Eskimo could not have had a common ancestor within the New World, since the Na-Dene are not significantly more like Eskimos than like Indians, according to both univariate and multivariate dental analyses (Table 11.3). Furthermore, Na-Dene dental characters are generally intermediate in frequency between Aleut-Eskimo and Indian, a quality that might only have arisen if strong parallel selection had occurred, for which there is no evidence. Elsewhere (Turner, 1981), I have identified some of the methodological problems in the Szathmary and Ossenberg analysis, other than those pointed out by Cook, Dumond, Harper, Salzano, and others in the CA treatment published with their study. Thus the peopling of the New World, as assessed by all existing odontological data, reduces to the four possibilities in Figure 11.2.

All three New World dental groups possess crown and root trait frequencies similar to those of North Asians, whose dental characteristics I have termed Sinodonty (Turner, 1979a). Sinodonty consists of trait intensification and addition, in contrast with the simplified or retained Sundadont condition present in Southeast Asia (Figure

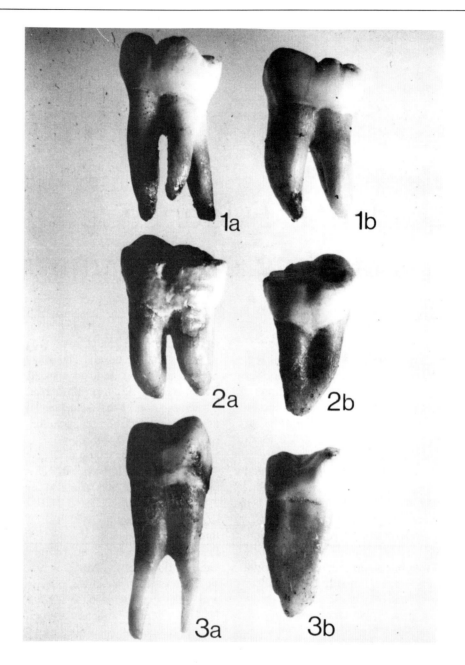

(1a) Three-rooted lower first molar; (1b) Two-rooted lower first molar; (2a) Two-rooted lower second molar; (2b) One-rooted lower second molar; (3a) Two-rooted upper-first premolar; (3b) One-rooted upper-first premolar.

Figure 11.1   Dental Crown and Root Polymorphisms Employed in This Study

11.3). All Paleoindians (Minnesota Lady, Midland, Tepexpan, Lagoa Santa, Cerro Sota, Palli Aike, and others), Archaic (California, Saskatchewan, Quebec, Alabama, Tehuacan, Cuicuilco, and others), later prehistoric Indians (Table 11.2), and Aleut-Eskimos, represented by more than 4,000 personally studied individuals, possess the Sinodont pattern. This means that in the Americas incisor shoveling, double-shoveling, 1-rooted upper first premolars, and

3-rooted lower first molars, among other traits, are relatively common. Relatively uncommon are Carabelli's cusp, Y-grooved lower second molars, and so forth (Table 11.1).

Since Sinodonty occurs only in North Asia and the Americas (ignoring recent Chinese, Japanese, and Mongol migrations), a Siberian origin and Bering Land-Bridge route, proposed on many other bases (Hopkins, 1979; Griffin, 1979; Laughlin et al., 1979; Wormington, 1957),

Table 11.1: Frequency Means and Ranges of Subsample Means for Key Dental Traits of Aleut-Eskimo, Na-Dene, and Indian Groups (individual counts, sexes pooled)

Trait	Expression dichotomy*	%	Aleut-Eskimo**	Na-Dene	Indian	A−E + N−D	A−E + I	N−D + I
Winging I1	1/1−3	x̄	29.1	35.9	46.3	1.6	16.6	4.8
		R	8.3−36.5	31.9−40.9	30.4−72.7	ns		
		n	51/175	47/131	292/630			
Shovel I1	3−6/0−6	x̄	79.3	82.9	91.2	0.5	18.2	6.1
		R	71.8−83.8	74.3−93.1	86.8−100.0	ns		
		n	115/145	73/88	743/815			
Double-shovel I1	+/0,+; or 2−6/0−6	x̄	52.3	54.5	71.3	0.1	18.4	10.4
		R	26.6−66.1	45.4−60.7	50.9−100.0	ns		
		n	68/130	48/88	512/718			
Tuberculum dentale I2	+/0,+; or 1−5/0−5	x̄	39.8	39.5	36.1	0.0	0.8	0.5
		R	20.3−66.7	25.0−45.2	20.6−53.7	ns	ns	ns
		n	70/176	45/114	318/880			
Interruption groove I2	+/0,+	x̄	66.1	61.1	50.4	0.8	15.0	5.2
		R	60.6−77.8	41.2−83.3	43.1−61.9	ns		
		n	121/183	80/131	452/896			
Cusp 5 M1	1−5/0−5	x̄	17.9	24.8	17.6	3.9	0.0	7.0
		R	9.3−33.3	17.9−29.2	5.7−32.5	ns		
		n	49/274	66/266	178/1010			
Hypocone M2	2−5/0−5	x̄	75.9	86.4	87.9	11.5	28.4	0.5
		R	58.4−85.3	68.2−93.1	72.8−95.0			ns
		n	243/320	279/323	1002/1140			
Carabelli M1	2−6/0−6	x̄	14.8	24.5	33.2	8.6	37.7	7.7
		R	6.1−24.2	19.0−27.3	21.3−60.0			
		n	43/291	68/277	372/1121			
Enamel extension M1	1−3/0−3	x̄	72.7	68.0	63.6	2.7	14.7	3.3
		R	68.8−76.0	62.3−75.5	54.2−72.1	ns		ns
		n	389/535	347/510	978/1538			
Parastyle M3	+/0,+	x̄	3.9	3.4	4.5	0.1	0.1	0.6
		R	1.1−7.5	0.0−5.5	2.0−10.5	ns	ns	ns
		n	10/253	8/237	32/706			
1-root P1	1/1−3	x̄	94.4	92.6	85.3	1.5	30.4	18.5
		R	91.9−96.3	90.5−95.2	75.4−96.1	ns		
		n	522/553	500/540	1077/1263			
3-root M2	3/1−3	x̄	35.4	45.9	58.3	9.5	60.3	17.9
		R	29.0−47.3	40.4−64.8	42.9−68.7			
		n	146/412	192/418	564/968			
Peg M3 (<7 mm dia.)	+/0,+	x̄	8.2	2.4	3.8	12.8	12.2	1.5
		R	4.0−13.7	0.9−7.0	0.0−6.9			ns
		n	36/437	9/369	37/976			
Occurrence M3	LR+/L & or R−	x̄	87.7	90.0	89.0	1.6	0.6	0.4
		R	85.4−90.9	85.0−96.1	75.5−97.0	ns	ns	ns
		n	520/593	489/543	880/989			
Lingual cusp number P2	2−3/0−3	x̄	46.8	45.7	43.6	0.0	0.7	0.3
		R	37.3−52.9	34.6−70.0	75.5−97.0	ns	ns	ns
		n	95/203	79/173	431/989			
Y groove pattern M2	Y/Y,+,X	x̄	18.4	9.9	9.9	10.8	20.5	0.0
		R	15.7−20.2	7.9−13.3	0.0−13.1			ns
		n	70/380	35/353	124/1258			
Cusp 6 M1̄	1−5/0−5	x̄	47.7	49.8	54.0	0.2	3.5	1.3
		R	44.4−51.7	42.2−54.8	39.4−66.2	ns	ns	ns
		n	134/281	115/231	544/1008			

(continued)

Table 11.1 (Continued)

Trait	Expression dichotomy*	%	Aleut-Eskimo**	Na-Dene	Indian	A – E + N – D	A – E + I	N – D + I
4-cusp M$\overline{2}$	4/4 – 6	x̄	6.0	4.4	9.5	0.8	3.9	9.0
		R	2.8 – 11.0	2.1 – 6.0	4.9 – 15.9	ns		
		n	19/319	15/342	113/1192			
Deflecting wrinkle M$\overline{1}$	1 – 3/0 – 3	x̄	67.8	54.2	73.7	5.4	2.2	20.3
		R	61.8 – 76.6	44.4 – 63.6	60.3 – 87.5		ns	
		n	101/149	71/131	511/693			
Protostylid M$\overline{1}$	1 – 7/0 – 7	x̄	23.0	34.8	45.0	11.1	54.9	10.7
		R	18.8 – 25.8	31.2 – 41.9	31.7 – 58.3			
		n	80/347	109/313	582/1292			
Cusp 7 M$\overline{1}$	1 – 4/0 – 4	x̄	12.9	7.0	9.8	6.8	3.1	2.5
		R	9.2 – 14.9	6.3 – 10.4	3.5 – 17.0		ns	ns
		n	48/371	23/329	135/1378			
3-root M$\overline{1}$	3/1 – 3	x̄	36.7	15.0	6.7	66.2	295.6	35.9
		R	19.8 – 42.2	10.4 – 25.0	0.0 – 10.5			
		n	190/517	83/552	108/1620			
1-root M$\overline{2}$	1/1 – 3	x̄	33.3	40.8	32.4	6.2	0.1	11.1
		R	29.7 – 36.2	32.1 – 45.3	25.3 – 76.5		ns	
		n	172/517	204/500	420/1295			

*Scaling and observation procedures are in Turner (1979 b).
**Includes Kodiak.
ns denotes not significant at the 0.05 probability level

Table 11.2: Mean Measure of Distance (based on 23 dental crown and root traits)

	Esk	Al	Kod	N Ma	C Ma	Gulf	Atha	Arch	Iroq	Mary	Ark	N M	N Az	C Az	Cal	Equa
Esk		.108	.068	.058	.073	.092	.111	.129	.165	.209	.206	.125	.195	.172	.247	.213
Al	.108		.055	.058	.069	.105	.045	.085	.137	.156	.160	.131	.157	.116	.172	.179
Kod	.068	.055		.012*	.007*	.019	.043	.042	.063	.095	.079	.055	.075	.078	.076	.069
N Ma	.058	.058	.012*		.003*	.013*	.026*	.024	.054	.067	.074	.029	.062	.058	.075	.081
C Ma	.073	.069	.007*	.003*		.015*	.031*	.051	.075	.065	.104	.022*	.061	.088	.095	.100
Gulf	.092	.105	.019	.013*	.015*		.029*	.037	.039	.055	.061	.018	.018	.061	.055	.053
Atha	.111	.045	.043	.026*	.031*	.029*		.039	.033	.042	.060	.018*	.049	.041	.082	.069
Arch	.129	.085	.042	.024	.051	.037	.039		.016*	.077	.038	.047	.038	.033	.058	.081
Iroq	.165	.137	.063	.054	.075	.039	.033	.016*		.039	.021	.031	.034	.038	.032	.059
Mary	.209	.156	.095	.067	.065	.055	.042	.077	.039		.025	.028	.037	.042	.041	.032
Ark	.206	.160	.079	.074	.104	.061	.060	.038	.021	.025		.049	.034	.028	.015	.030
N M	.125	.131	.055	.029	.022*	.018	.018*	.047	.031	.028	.049		.017	.041	.065	.070
N Az	.195	.157	.075	.062	.061	.018	.049	.038	.034	.037	.034	.017		.032	.035	.050
C Az	.172	.116	.078	.058	.088	.061	.041	.033	.038	.042	.028	.041	.032		.052	.064
Cal	.247	.172	.076	.075	.095	.055	.082	.058	.032	.041	.015	.065	.035	.052		.033
Equa	.213	.179	.069	.081	.100	.053	.069	.081	.059	.032	.030	.070	.050	.064	.032	

*MMD is not significant

corresponds perfectly with the dental evidence. Certainly there is nothing novel in this finding. However, what the dental evidence does suggest that is original is the possibility of not just two migrations (Paleoindian and ancestral Aleut-Eskimo), but three, as previously noted.

At present it is unclear if the three migration model or one of the others in Figure 11.2 best fits other sorts of human history information. It is clear, however, that multiple migration hypotheses erected to explain cultural variation south of Canada (ignoring the recent arrival of

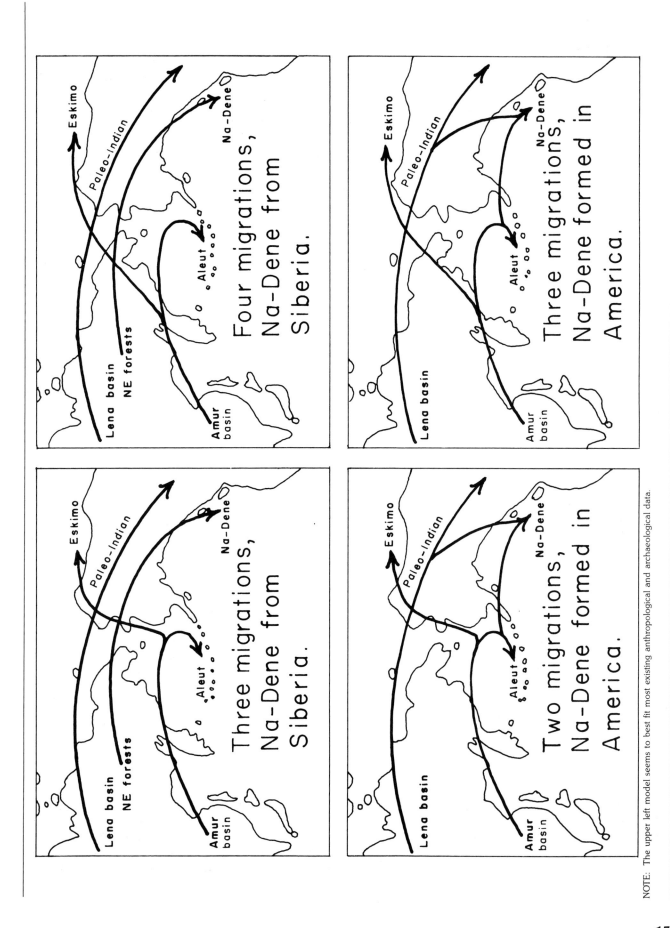

NOTE: The upper left model seems to best fit most existing anthropological and archaeological data.

Figure 11.2 Four Possible Sources of Dental Variation in the Americas

Table 11.3: Summary Statistics Comparing Aleut-Eskimo, Na-Dene, and Indian Teeth

Statistics	Aleut-Eskimo + Na-Dene	Aleut-Eskimo + Indian	Na-Dene + Indian
Univariate			
Number of traits with significant differences	11/23	14/23	13/23
Percent of traits with significant differences	47.8	60.9	56.5
Sum of chi square values for 23 comparisons	162.7	638.0	175.6
Multivariate			
Mean measure of distance (all significant values)	.02953	.08799	.03185
Standard deviation	.00281	.00151	.00188
Effective divergence	.03958	.09959	.02793
Maximum value	.99046	.99393	.99349
Standard effective divergence	.03996	.10020	.02811
Significance (23 degrees of freedom)	166.081	588.975	171.064

Group Composition:

Aleut-Eskimo = Eastern and western Aleut, Kodiak, Point Hope, Point Barrow, Mackenzie Delta, Southhampton I., Smith Sound

Na-Dene = Yukon River, Apache, Northern Maritime, Central Maritime, Gulf of Georgia and Puget Sound, Intermountain, B.C.

Indian = Archaic Saskatchewan, Archaic Quebec, Canadian Iroquois, Maryland, Arkansas, New Mexico, Northern Arizona (and southern Utah), Central Arizona, Northern and Southern California, Ecuador

Navajo and Apache in the Southwest) have absolutely no support in my dental findings. Except for the Na-Dene-speakers, and perhaps other adjacent groups, all remaining North and South American Indians are very likely descended from the original Paleoindian population. Dental samples from Peru, Ecuador, Chile, Panama, Mexico, and throughout the United States and eastern Canada (not all shown in Table 11.2) show very little intergroup difference. There is in fact more dental variation between Aleuts and Eskimos, generally accepted genetic and linguistic relatives, than in the entire Indian population of North and South America. This can be appreciated in Figures 11.3-11.5.

Correlating Odontological and Archaeological Interpretations

Dumond (1977, 1980) has suggested that the early 7,000 to possibly 10,000-year-old stone tool remains from interior and coastal Alaska, those termed Paleoarctic tradition (microblades, wedge-shaped cores, bifaces, and so forth), were left by the ancestors of modern Eskimos and Aleuts. Both Paleoarctic and its eastern Siberian counterpart, Diuktai culture, lack unambiguous evidence of fluted spear points, a situation, along with earlier dates for Clovis to the south, that led Dumond (1977: 155) to propose that the Paleoindians arrived before the Wisconsinan glacial maximum, and prior to Paleoarctic people who "represent tundra-dwelling Eskaleut hunters." Dumond recognizes that this reconstruction involves a good deal of classificatory lumping, and that other reconstructions are possible.

Odontologically, I see a somewhat different scenario based on the evidence at hand. Because of the apparent dental distinctiveness of the Na-Dene group, and the fact that they occupy today almost the entire area wherein Paleoarctic remains have been found, it would be more parsimonious to correlate Paleoarctic tradition with the Na-Dene than with the Aleut-Eskimo. The latter's cranial and genetic traits evidence a stronger affinity with North Asians than with Na-Dene or Indians (that is, a high degree of facial flatness, more frequent mandibular tori, a high frequency of 3-rooted lower first molars, presence of B allele, no Diego, no albumin Naskapi, and so forth). Taken together, the degree of Mongolization in the New World may in fact signal the order of arrival: least and first, Paleoindian; more and second, Na-Dene; most and last, Aleut-Eskimo.

When the Gulf of Alaska region is considered, a serious problem arises with the Paleoarctic/Aleut-Eskimo correlation. Kodiak Islanders (Uyak site, all levels), usually looked upon as Eskimo, and in Dumond's view developing along with the Aleuts from the Ocean Bay tradition (Clark, 1979), are dentally more like Na-Dene than like the Aleut or Eskimo (Table 11.2, Figures 11.3 and 11.4). Given the dissimilarity between the Aleut and Na-Dene, say, relative to that between California and Ecuador, or California and Arkansas, groups that must have been separated for as long or longer, we find that there is no odontological support for the assumption that the prehistoric Kodiak was Eskimo rather than Na-Dene. If the Kodiak cannot be shown to align with the Eskimo more than with the Na-Dene, then that island's fairly well-established archaeological sequence cannot be used to justify a Paleoarctic tradition and Aleut-Eskimo biological correlation. Similarly, the early and later teeth from Namu, British Columbia (Carlson, 1979), are

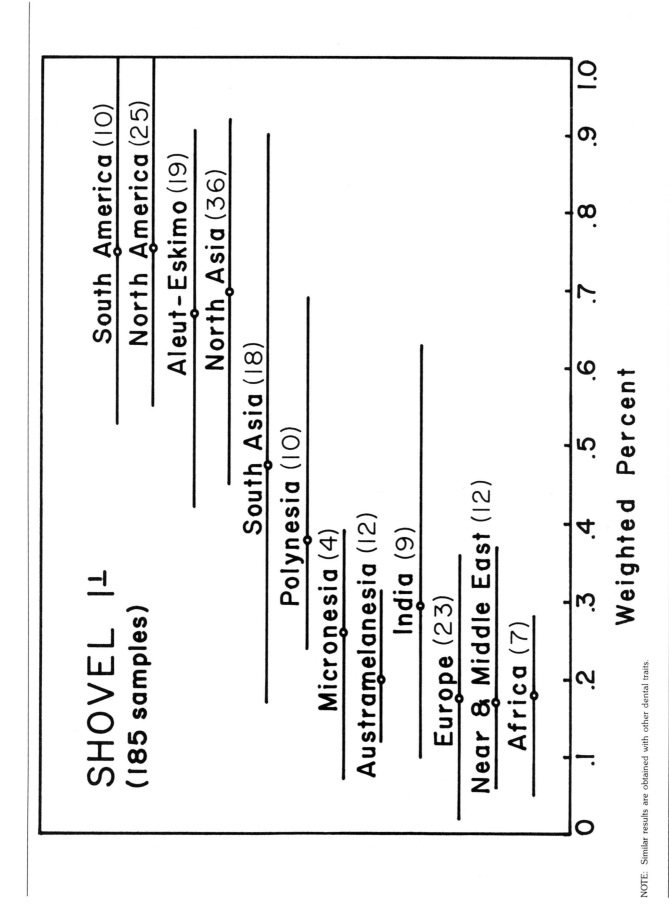

NOTE: Similar results are obtained with other dental traits.

Figure 11.3 Upper Central Incisor Shoveling Based on 185 Literature Reports (means and ranges of means)

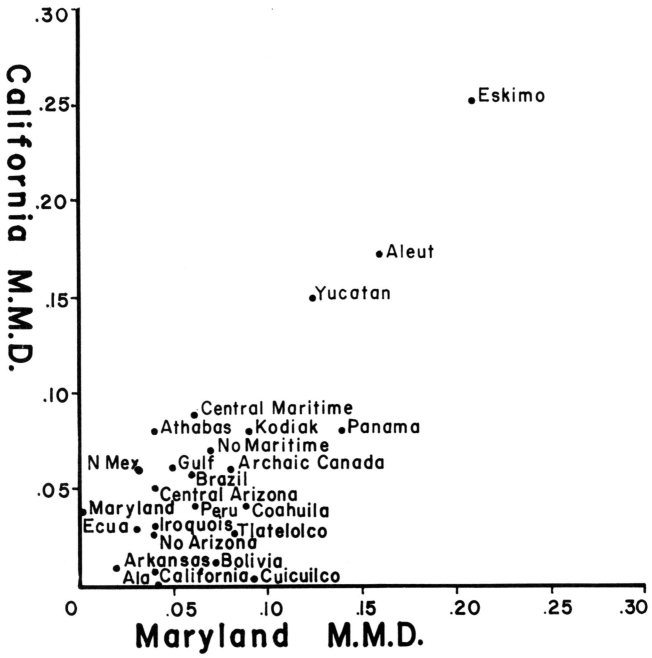

NOTE: The dissimilarity of Aleut-Eskimo to Indian is clearly exhibited, and the tendency for the Na-Dene group to cluster with Indians but toward Aleut-Eskimo can be seen.

Figure 11.4 Mean Measures of Distance Plotted Relative to California and Maryland

statistically indistinguishable from other and later teeth in the same area and in Kodiak. This can be appreciated in the following mean measures of distance between Namu and: Indian, .043; Northern and Central Maritime, .041; Kodiak, .005; Eskimo, .100; and Aleut, .037. Although a small sample, the Namu teeth are critically important in their suggestions both for population stability and distribution in the Northwest Coast to the Kodiak area.

The point of all this is that Na-Dene dental distinctiveness, apparent stability, and probable distribution cannot readily be accounted for by Dumond's two-migration population-culture correlations. We agree that Aleut-Eskimo and Indian are distinctive, must represent two migrations, and somehow represent different ancient adaptations. But there is an intervening population, the Na-Dene, who today, and apparently for a considerable time

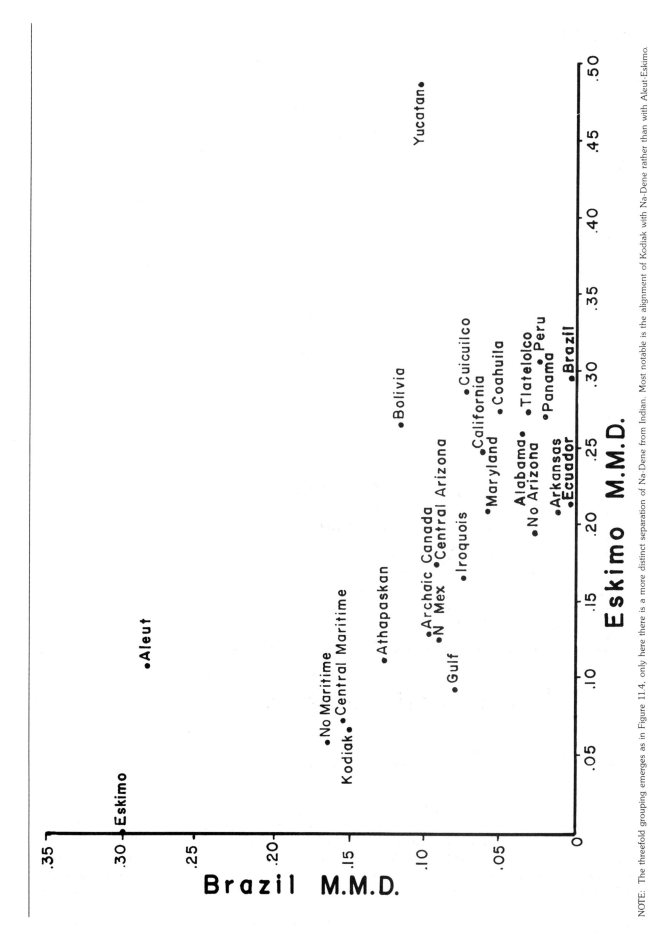

NOTE: The threefold grouping emerges as in Figure 11.4, only here there is a more distinct separation of Na-Dene from Indian. Most notable is the alignment of Kodiak with Na-Dene rather than with Aleut-Eskimo.

Figure 11.5 Mean Measures of Distance Plotted Relative to the Two Most Extreme Distance Values (excluding Brazil, which is based on a much smaller sample size than California)

now, have occupied the Paleoarctic tradition area, and must somehow be integrated into reconstructions of the Late Pleistocene populations of North America.

In 1969 I proposed the three-migration model as a means to explain New World variation in the frequency of three-rooted lower first molars (Turner, 1971). In 1979, with many more data on this and 30 other traits, I still found the three-migration model to explain New World dental variation satisfactorily (Turner, 1979a). The culture history scenario I envisioned from these dental data can be briefly restated as follows: big-game-hunting, Clovis (Diuktai-like) culture-bearing, spear-using Paleoindians reached eastern Beringia before 15,000 years ago (Irving et al., 1977), exiting Siberia via the Lena basin. Upon deglaciation, commencing 16,000 years ago, these Paleoindians moved southward from Alaska as boreal forest replaced the big-game-supporting Beringian Arctic steppe habitat. The human void in eastern Beringia permitted ancestral Na-Dene-speakers, a smaller-game-hunting bow-and-arrow-using Northeast Siberian riverine and boreal forest folk, to cross into Alaska between 14,000 and 12,000 years ago – just before Bering Strait became a serious barrier to overland travel (Hopkins, 1979). Their entry is possibly signaled by arrow points and other forest-efficient artifact types like those discovered at Healy Lake (Cook, 1969), Dry Creek (Powers, 1978), Ground Hog Bay (Ackerman, 1974, 1980a), Ugashik (Dumond et al., 1976), and elsewhere. Ancestral Aleut-Eskimo first appeared in Alaska 8,500 years ago on Anangula Island, the southern terminus of the Bering Land-Bridge. Like Laughlin (1980 and elsewhere), I can see in my own dental data support for the possibility that ancestral Aleut-Eskimo, or at least ancestral Aleut, entered Alaska by way of the now-submerged southern coast of the Bering Land-Bridge. They may well have been on the coast before the Na-Dene crossed into Alaska. It follows from this model that there can be no archaeological record of the Aleut-Eskimo antedating the present day sea-level, which would give the appearance that they were the last migration from Siberia to Alaska. There are a few dental clues that ancestral Aleut-Eskimo could have originated within or near the Amur basin, from which they reached the Sea of Okhotsk before 16,000 years ago. Here they began to evolve their maritime lifeway in the midst of the sea-mammal populations crowding the southern Okhotsk Sea due to the severe ice conditions to the north.

Similarly, Ackerman (1979) apparently senses three population-culture pulses accompanying environmental changes throughout Beringia in late Pleistocene times: (1) "Siberian interior, upland, lake, and riverine folk" arrive in New World first (Paleoindian); (2) "estuarine fisher folk" along the Beringian coast develop a maritime orientation as Beringia floods (Aleut-Eskimo); and (3) the "Beringian interior hunters" move into today's Alaskan interior as Beringia floods (Na-Dene).

The Dental Situation in Eurasia

The odontological bases for the selection of the three-origin region (Lena basin, Amur basin, Northeast Siberian forests) are straightforward. American Indian teeth, while Sinodont, do shift slightly in some features toward the European condition. This suggests that their origin was somewhat closer to European influence than was that of the ancestral Aleut-Eskimo, whose teeth are quite unlike those of Europeans. Na-Dene teeth are intermediate in many trait frequencies between those of Indian and Aleut-Eskimo, a condition that one would expect for occupants between the Lena and Amur basins – that is, within the Diuktai culture area. While all three New World dental groups are Sinodonts and therefore closely related, I prefer that they commence their divergence by isolation in Siberia because of the very small amount of divergence that can be demonstrated after Paleoindian arrival (Table 11.2). Testing the validity of this scenario obviously depends on information from Siberia. To that end I have begun study of Siberian dentitions and have worked out the correlations between Soviet dental anthropologist A. A. Zubov's observation procedures and mine. This will make possible in the near future highly accurate use of his many ethnographic odontological observations throughout the USSR (Zubov and Kaldiva, 1979, and elsewhere). I will conclude with a few preliminary interpretations on past (1980-81) observations of teeth from more than 1,000 crania from various locations in the Soviet Union.

The teeth of the seven Upper Paleolithic Cro-Magnon individuals from Sunghir and Kostienki are much like those of modern Europeans and quite unlike the teeth of prehistoric Americans. However, if such people had been in minor contact with Upper Paleolithic Lena basin Sinodonts, the latter could well have shifted to the condition of Paleoindian (and later Indian) teeth.

The unerupted permanent teeth of the older of the two Upper Paleolithic Mal'ta children from near Lake Baikal also exhibit a European quality (no incisor shoveling or double-shoveling, no deflecting wrinkle, protostylid, or cusp 6 of the lower first molar, and moderate Carabelli expression of the upper first molar).[3] This was an unexpected finding that probably eliminates the Mal'ta people as candidates for the ancestors of the Paleoindians.

Samples of other, more recent teeth from the Soviet central steppe region, coupled with the Sunghir, Kostienki, and Upper Paleolithic Samarkand teeth from Uzbekestan suggest that an Archaic Caucasoid (Europeoid in Soviet terms) population ranged widely from the Atlantic coast of Europe to at least the western shores of Lake Baikal in Upper Paleolithic times. Such a distribution would be in keeping with a Lena basin origin hypothesis for Paleoindians, whose Sinodont affinity is clear but with a minute Caucasoid quality compared with Aleut-Eskimo, Mongol, Chinese, and Japanese – all full-blown Sinodonts. If we can trust the dental impressions of the 18,000-year-old Upper Cave cranial casts, Sinodonty can be said to have been present in North China by that time.

Although no ancient or clear-cut prehistoric crania were available from the Amur region, historic Amur teeth are more like those of Aleut-Eskimo than like those of Indians. Pooling a series of 104 Goldi, Ulchi, Negedal, and Orochi crania, preliminary analysis of 13 crown and root traits gave the following mean measures of distance, all significant: Amur/Aleut-Eskimo, .0599; Amur/Na-Dene, .0370; Amur/Indian, .0908. Interestingly, the Amur/Na-Dene distance is slightly less than the Amur/Aleut one, a situation not wholly unexpected if the Na-Dene had been the last to leave Siberia. However, no literal interpretation of these values should be made since they are based on a relatively small and pooled series, not all traits have been included due to lack of time, and the Goldi series almost certainly has some Chinese admixture judging from historic accounts.

In sum, New World dental morphology as it is presently known shows much less variation than that of eastern Asia. All prehistoric Americans have a strong odontological affinity with North Asians. The markedly low amount of inter-Indian group dental variation is consistent with hypotheses of relatively late entry into the New World by a relatively small number of individuals. Two quite distinct migrations can be recognized in New World dental variation – Paleoindian and ancestral Aleut-Eskimo. It is possible that a third migration of ancestral Na-Dene-speakers reached Alaska just before Bering Strait flooded the final overland link between Siberia and Alaska. Once Alaska's coasts and interior were occupied and moated by Bering Strait, it is doubtful that the Holocene population of Siberia added much to the New World gene pool. However, this has to remain an open odontological question until there is a description of Ipiutak dental morphology and until a skeletal series is uncovered from a Norton culture site.

NOTES

1. Support for this five-year study has been provided by the National Geographic Society, Arizona State University Research Committee and Department of Anthropology, Wenner-Gren Foundation, International Research and Exchanges Board, National Academy of Science, and the USSR Academy of Science. Data processing has been assisted by Linda Nuss. Institutions and individuals that have made this research possible include: U.S. Museum of Natural History, J. L. Angle, D. Ubelaker, T. D. Stewart, B. Meggars, C. Evans, L. Machada; American Museum, H. Shapiro, I. Tattersall, P. Ward, J. Bird; Peabody Museum, W. W. Howells, E. Trinkaus; National Museum of Man, J. S. Cybulski, D. W. Clark; University of Toronto, F. J. Melbye; University of Manitoba, W. D. Wade; Simon Fraser University, R. Carlson; University of Minnesota, E. Johnson; Southern Methodist University, E. Fry; University of Arkansas, A. McCartney, M. Hoffman, J. Rose; Lowie Museum, F. Norick; Field Museum, G. Cole; University of Connecticut, W. S. Laughlin; San Diego Museum of Man, R. Tyson; Los Angeles County Museum, C. Rozaire; Forsyth Dental Center, C.F.A. Moorrees; University of Colorado, D. Breternitz; University of Arizona, W. Birkby; Provincial Museum of British Columbia, S. G. Boehm; University of Alabama, K. R. Turner; Museum of Anthropology, Mexico City, M. E. Salas; Burke Memorial Museum of Washington State, D. Swindler; USSR Institute of Ethnography, Yu. V. Bromley, A. A. Zubov, V. P. Chtetzov, E. E. Gokhman, S. A. Arutinov, A. Kozintsev, V. Alexeev; Zoology Museum, Copenhagen, T. Hatting; University of Oregon, D. Dumond. This is the twelfth paper in the Peopling of the Pacific and Adjoining Areas series. It is a preliminary report on a larger study of New World dental anthropology.

2. Dental variation in the Americas can be interpreted as having arisen completely or mainly in North Asia. The marked difference between Aleut-Eskimo and Indian suggests more time for their divergence than can be demonstrated for occupation of the New World. However, the substantial difference between Aleut and Eskimo could mean that they too began to diverge in Siberia rather than in Alaska. The Na-Dene could have formed in North America as a result of mixing between ancestral Aleut-Eskimo and Paleoindian, or in Siberia in a similar way.

3. With regard to my finding of the Mal'ta dental morphology to be more European than Asian or American, a similar relation occurs for the Mal'ta stone tools. H. M. Wormington reported on October 31, 1981, during a graduate anthropology seminar at Arizona State University on cultural and biological relations between Asia and the Americas in Late Pleistocene and Early Holocene times that her study of the Mal'ta stone tools showed no resemblances to those of the Paleoindians. Instead, the Mal'ta materials evidenced much stronger similarities with finds from Europe.

12 New Dating Techniques

Radiocarbon dating coupled with stratigraphic analysis, has shown that anatomically modern humans emerged in the Early Wisconsinan, with their roots lying even further in the past. Some of the earliest traces lie in Africa, with subsequent appearances in the other continents. As yet unresolved is the exact space-time framework of their spread around the world. Since Africa, Europe, and Asia are closely connected geographically, migrations into these continents were not as impeded as those into the Americas, Australia, or the Pacific. For the latter, ocean-level changes played a major role, which is especially true of Early Man's path to North America via Eastern Siberia.

Just as archaeological studies are reaching further into the past, so are new improvements expected in the physical methods that permit more precise and quantitative assessments of anatomically modern humans worldwide in both their physical and cultural aspects. This chapter specifically discusses recent advancements in scientific dating methods and their potential in current anthropological research.

Radiocarbon Dating with Accelerators or Small Counters

The invention of radiocarbon dating by Libby (1952) revolutionized prehistoric research because events could now be dated on an absolute time scale and, consequently, related to each other both chronologically and geographically. The reason for this lies in the fact that at any given time, plants worldwide experience the same concentration of radiocarbon. After its formation in the stratosphere from cosmic ray-produced neutrons and nitrogen, radiocarbon is oxidized to carbon dioxide, which is mixed rapidly into the tropospheric air. Plants then utilize this well-mixed atmospheric carbon dioxide via photosynthesis to build living tissue, which remains slightly radioactive as long as the plant lives. After the death of a plant, or any organism feeding on plants, radiocarbon decays with the speed of its half-life, 5730 ± 30 years.

Radiocarbon dating was verified by measuring samples of historically known age and improved in accuracy by the introduction of tree-ring calibrated dating. The latter became necessary inasmuch as sensitive modern counting equipment pointed to secular variations in the production rate of radiocarbon. The measurement of ^{14}C in dendrochronologically dated wood provided the necessary corrections, so that today most of the Neolithic can be particularly well assessed by radiocarbon dating.

Sample selection for dating remains, however, of critical importance. Charcoal or wood-based dates have been found to be superior to those obtained from shell or tufa. This is due to our exact knowledge of what the radiocarbon content of the terrestrial biosphere was or is today. Shells and tufa originate from water bodies whose isotopic composition is not well known, except for the ocean, which is much more predictable than lakes or rivers. Other sample materials such as bone have been found to give reliable radiocarbon dates if the protein portion of the tissue is dated (Berger et al., 1964). In the end, the quality of a radiocarbon date depends on the quality of the archaeological association between the sample material used and the feature in question. Sample size is also important, inasmuch as a full counter will give the smallest statistical error. However, often only very small samples may be available due to natural circumstances or the importance of a rare and valuable specimen. Consequently, it has long been desirable to date small samples accurately.

AUTHOR'S NOTE: This is publication No. 2267 of the Institute of Geophysics and Planetary Physics, UCLA.

Since the first publication on the prospect of direct radiocarbon dating with a cyclotron (Muller, 1977) and the immediately subsequent studies by Nelson et al. (1977) and Bennett et al. (1977), the promise of quick radiocarbon dates performed on milligram samples has been very appealing. However, the difficulties encountered in developing a routine analytical methodology have been considerable. This has been due not only to technical obstacles, but also to the considerable costs involved. A radiocarbon laboratory employing radioactive counting methods can be set up, depending on complexity, for several tens of thousands of dollars. But an accelerator dating facility may cost about $1 million until it is fully operational. Therefore, accelerator-derived dates are still very scarce. It is not known at this point when accelerator-based dates will be routinely available at reasonable cost. There are groups at work in a number of countries trying to perfect the analytical base, yet it is difficult at the moment to predict who will be first operationally.

Inasmuch as accelerator dates may reach further into the past (theoretically to about 100,000 years), contamination becomes the premiere issue (Berger, 1979). However, chemical methods exist to prepare small, isotopically clean samples. For example, amino acids found in bone can be specifically selected by chromatography for precise dates. Moreover, more than one date can be run on the same skeleton in order to provide greater certainty. This direct dating approach avoids difficulties encountered by field associations of dubious nature. Finally, the small sample size on the order of 10-100 mg makes this method a prime candidate for the analysis of scarce fossil material.

Another method for reducing sample size has been the design of small radiation counters. We are now using a 200 ml CO_2 proportional counter with three energy channels. This unit needs only 100 mg of carbon for filling and competes effectively for smaller archaeological samples thought to be only appropriate for accelerator dating. Typically, a 1,000 minute counting run (approximately one week) reduces the statistical counting error of a 1-sigma standard deviation to about 1 percent.

This accuracy is at present far greater than that obtainable by accelerator methods. However, the measurement time required by a small proportional counter is also vastly greater. In essence, when only a few very small samples need to be dated, a counter of the type described above will be very satisfactory. Many samples mean either an accelerator-dater or several small systems. Insofar as a small counting system costs only 1.5 percent of an accelerator installed, the economics are obvious. Yet an accelerator may also be used to perform other tasks, such as $^{13}C/^{12}C$ measurements, which counters cannot do. Moreover, when suitably tuned they also permit other isotopic measurements. Simply stated, accelerators have greater measurement potential than small proportional counters. Never-

theless, a small proportional counter could solve the question of the antiquity of the Turin Shroud or the age of scarce Early-Man-in-America bone materials.

Amino Acid Racemization Dating

This method permits the dating of small bone or shell samples at a relatively small cost on a par with or even less than radiocarbon dates. Of primary importance is a precise knowledge of the temperature and environment in which a given sample acquired its racemization. Such effects can be significantly controlled by the appropriate excavation strategy.

If, for example, human and animal bones are found together in good stratigraphic context or in closed deposits, both can be analyzed for their stereochemical composition of certain amino acids, such as aspartic acid or isoleucine. Often the quantity of animal bones exceeds that of human remains, so the animal bones can be sacrificed and dated by radiocarbon, which permits a precise calculation of their racemization rate. If the racemization behavior of animal and human bones is the same, the calculated racemization rate can be used to determine accurately the age of the human fossils (Bada et al. b, 1974).

In coastal areas of the Pacific, occasionally human remains are found in association with shells. Since amino acid racemization dating often has a greater range than radiocarbon dating, a similar approach to the example above can be taken. Thus shells of the same species are dated in the upper stratigraphy by radiocarbon. Subsequently, their racemization rate is used to date indirectly the human material associated with the same, but older, shell species below it. This method has particular application in the island groups of the Western Pacific close to the Asian mainland.

Recently, a major discordance was shown to exist between aspartic acid racemization and uranium series dates for the Del Mar and Sunnyvale Early Man fossils in California (Bischoff and Rosenbauer, 1981). Del Mar had been dated by racemization to 48,000 years ago (Bada et al. a, 1974), and Sunnyvale to 70,000 years (Bada and Helfman, 1975). In conjunction with internal concordance between ^{230}Th and ^{231}Pa dating, Bischoff and Rosenbauer calculated recently that Del Mar is circa 11,000 and Sunnyvale 8300-9000 years old. The answer to this dating dilemma lies in the direct radiocarbon dating of collagen from these fossils, which may be possible using the small sample ^{14}C system described before.

Uranium Series Dating

In archaeology and geology, the radioactive decay systems of uranium and thorium have been used in a variety of modes for age determinations exceeding the limits of radiocarbon dating (Broecker, 1965). The most suitable materials are well-preserved specimens of biological hard tissues such as corals, mollusks, or bones.

Corals have proven to be especially useful, in that they experience less contamination due to their tight biological structure. Mollusks may not always remain a completely closed system, resulting in leading or in enrichment by secondary uranium early in the diagenetic history of the fossils (Kaufman and Broecker, 1965; Valentine and Veeh, 1969). Similar concerns apply to bone-based dates, which means that only very firm primary bone is suitable for uranium series dating (Bischoff and Rosenbauer, 1981).

Just as dates have been determined in California for fossils or marine terraces (Veeh and Valentine, 1967; Valentine and Veeh, 1969; Ku and Kern, 1974; Kern, 1977), similar measurements in the Western Pacific geographic region are possible. If deposits of shells are found in caves, as is often the case, the exchange of radioisotopes may be minimal. Therefore, such sites can offer suitable dating materials related to Early Man dating beyond 40-50,000 years.

Generally, concordance between ^{230}Th and ^{231}Pa dates is taken as an additional assurance that the ages calculated are indeed correct. Any serious perturbation of the radioactively and chemically different ^{238}U → ^{230}Th and ^{235}U → ^{231}Pa decay systems will result in discordant ages and thus signal a warning.

Recently, considerable disagreement was observed between aspartic acid racemization and ^{230}U/^{230}Th and ^{235}U/^{231}Pa dates, as outlined in the previous section of this chapter. The reason remains uncertain.

Fission Track Dating

Only in very few instances have fission track ages been utilized in archaeology (Fleischer, 1975). The classic application of Fleischer et al. (1965) holds considerable prom-

ise for other archaeological applications in the volcanic regions of the world. Thus, the entire circum-Pacific area is a prime candidate for the fission track exploration of volcanic ash layers. These in turn have affected the human ecology of the past (Sheets and Grayson, 1979). While the technique of fission track analysis is not very expensive, it offers significant advantages in certain situations. For example, very recent potassium-argon dates may possess relatively large errors. Equivalent fission track dates based on mineral concentrates may in fact have significantly smaller statistical errors and therefore may be more valuable to the anthropologist. Moreover, occasionally K/A dates can be subject to petrological conditions, producing erroneous dates if argon has leaked either into or out of the system. Inasmuch as fission track dates have no upper limit, they can be used to date fossils no longer within the analytical range of radiocarbon, racemization, or uranium series dating. In addition, fission track dates are not temperature-dependent, so that heating by volcanic ash falls will not be as prohibiting as in the case of racemization dates. Unfortunately, the direct dating of calcite found in bones by fission track methods has not been successful (MacDougall and Price, 1974), so that this approach remains confined to stratigraphy.

Summary

This overview presents a current status report on the potential and the limitations of several dating methods useful in establishing frameworks for dating Early Man and his environment. Smaller radiocarbon samples for dating are becoming feasible. Racemization and uranium series dating have both found wider application, though with some perplexing questions still remaining, and fission track dating continues to have substantial potential in paleoanthropology.

J. M. ADOVASIO, J. DONAHUE, K. CUSHMAN,
R. C. CARLISLE, R. STUCKENRATH, J. D. GUNN, and W. C. JOHNSON

13 Evidence from Meadowcroft Rockshelter[1]

Few topics in archaeology have engendered so much debate, concern, and undeniable long-term appeal as the story of the first Americans. Virtually none of the participants in this complex, highly interdisciplinary study would deny that human beings first passed from Asia to the western hemisphere across the Bering Land-Bridge that joined Siberia and Alaska at several times (50,000-40,000 years ago, and again from 25,000 to 14,000 years ago) during the Wisconsinan glaciation (Haag, 1962; Fagan, 1980: 119). Beyond this agreement, however, there is little consensus. Researchers have differed widely with each other on the Asiatic sources for the incipient American populations, the timing of the "migration(s)," and the possible route(s) that these early hunters may have taken in their dispersion throughout the Americas (Turner, this volume). Much discussion also has focused on the nature of the artifactual tool kits (Dragoo, 1980), as the tools often provide the only tangible link with the present.

To date, some of the most promising (but elusive) data on the first Americans have come from Yukon Territory sites such as Old Crow, where the first of a growing number of redeposited, fossilized bones believed to have been altered by human agency were discovered in 1966. The original radiocarbon dates for this material produced results between 25,000 and 29,000 years ago (Morlan, 1978), and claims of even greater human antiquity in the area have recently been offered (Morlan, this volume).

Much farther south, Richard S. MacNeish's investigations at Pikimachay (Flea Cave) and Jayamachay (Pepper Cave) in the Ayacucho Valley of Peru have yielded both lithic artifacts and the bones of extinct fauna. In 1969, four stone tools of volcanic tuff and a few flakes (one of which was

a green, nonindigenous stone) were discovered in Basal Zone k at Pikimachay. Radiocarbon dating of a ground sloth vertebra from overlying Zone j produced a date of 19,600 ± 3000 years (MacNeish, 1971).

The Old Crow and Pikimachay data (to which much other information could be added) are important for what is in retrospect a comparatively modest suggestion that man was resident in and widely dispersed throughout the western hemisphere by approximately 15,000-20,000 years ago. It is therefore not illogical to think that human groups of similar age might also be found in the eastern part of the United States. Here, sites of somewhat later fluted projectile point-using Paleoindian groups, though not numerous in contrast to sites of succeeding periods, are far from absent. Debert, in Nova Scotia (MacDonald, 1968), on the northeastern fringe of the Paleoindian sites, is among the best known and dates to circa 8600 years B.C. Dutchess Quarry Cave in Orange County, New York, gives the best evidence for the contemporaneity of fluted projectile point-using human populations and woodland caribou (*Rangifer* sp.) at 10,580 ± 370 B.C. (Griffin, 1978).

These Paleoindian sites and others, such as the Vail site (Gramly and Rutledge, 1981), are convincing evidence for the presence of man in northeastern North America by circa 10,000 B.C. or slightly later. So far, however, only Meadowcroft Rockshelter in Pennsylvania has provided tangible, well-dated indications of aboriginal human occupation for the critical period prior to this time.

Meadowcroft Rockshelter (36WH297) is a stratified, multicomponent site located 48.27 air km (78.84 km via road) southwest of Pittsburgh and 4.02 surface km northwest of Avella in Washington County, Pennsylvania (Figure

AUTHORS' NOTE: The authors wish to stress that this report is an overview of a segment of the work done at Meadowcroft. It is expected that a portion of the data presented in this chapter will be modified by further analyses of the Meadowcroft data base.

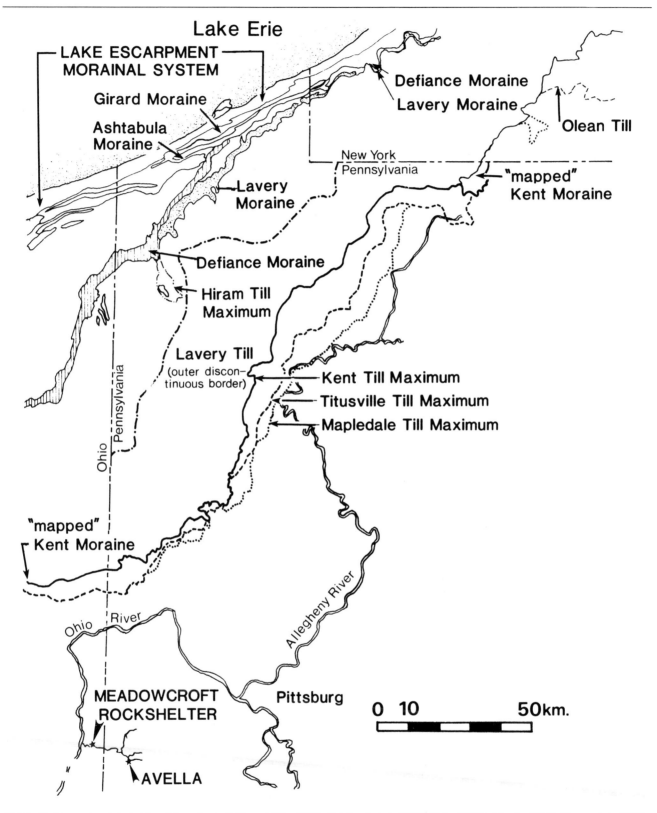

NOTE: Glacial mapping abstracted from information in Calkin and Miller (1977); Goldthwait et al. (1967); Muller (1963); Schooler (1974); Shepps et al. (1959); Tesmer (1975); White et al. (1969). This is a revised version of that presented in Johnson (1981).

Figure 13.1 Location of Meadowcraft Rockshelter on Cross Creek in the Upper Ohio Valley of Southwestern Pennsylvania (depicted in relation to Pleistocene glacial deposits in northwestern Pennsylvania and adjacent states)

13.1). The site is situated on the north bank of Cross Creek, a small tributary of the Ohio River, which lies 12.16 km to the west. The exact location of the site is 40°17'12"N, 80°29'0"W.

Meadowcroft Rockshelter is oriented roughly east-west; it has a southern exposure and stands approximately 15.06 m above Cross Creek and 259.90 m above sea-level. The area protected by the extant overhang is approximately 62 m², while the overhang itself is some 13 m above the modern surface of the site. Water is available from Cross Creek, and springs are abundant in the immediate vicinity of the shelter. Prevailing winds are west to east across the mouth of the shelter, providing nearly constant ventilation.

Meadowcroft is in the unglaciated portion of the Appalachian or Allegheny Plateau, west of the Valley and Ridge Province of the Appalachian Mountains and on the northwest margin of the Appalachian Basin. The surface rocks of this region are layered sedimentary rocks of Middle to Upper Pennsylvanian age (Casselman Formation). Predominant lithologies are shale, quartz sandstone, limestone, and coal in decreasing order of abundance. Deformation is very mild, with a regional dip of 3-5° to the southeast.

The topography near Meadowcroft is maturely dissected. More than 50 percent of the Cross Creek watershed is in valley slopes. Maximum elevations in the Cross Creek drainage are generally above 396 m.

The main stem of Cross Creek flows for approximately 31.3 km, and the maximum north-south width of the watershed is approximately 15 km. The Cross Creek drainage pattern is northwestward to westward toward the West Virginia-Ohio Border and the Ohio River.

Present topography near Meadowcroft is the result of Late Pleistocene precipitation and runoff that promoted extensive downcutting. The area is unaffected by glacial ice; the terminal Wisconsinan till (Figure 13.1) extends south only to northern Beaver County, Pennsylvania, approximately 48.5 km north of the site.

Two terrace levels are discerned along Cross Creek and can be related to Pleistocene history. A discontinuous, largely dissected pre-Wisconsinan terrace occurs between 304.2 and 320 m. A second, continuous Wisconsinan age terrace at 247.88-253.98 m above present sea-level is also recognized regionally (Wagner et al., 1970). The 247.88-253.98 m terrace at Meadowcroft correlates with a 213-221 m terrace on the Ohio River at its junction with Cross Creek between Follansbee and Wellsburg, West Virginia. A still lower 204 m terrace on the Ohio also can be followed up Cross Creek but dies out before reaching Meadowcroft (Beynon, in press). The 204 m terrace appears to be Late Wisconsinan in age (circa 21,000 B.P.), while the 213-221 m terrace may be of Mid-Wisconsinan age (circa 40,000 B.P.). These tentative ascriptions are presently under detailed investigation and may be revised in the future.

Artifactual deposits at Meadowcroft Rockshelter are located in colluvial sediments emplaced by rock fall, grain-by-grain attrition from the overhanging sandstone cliff, and by sheet wash from the upland surface. The only clear indication of postdepositional movement is deformation caused by large rockfalls that have pushed through sediments at points of impact.

At the time of initial human occupation of the rockshelter, Cross Creek was probably 5-10 m higher than at present and thus somewhat closer and slightly more accessible to the habitation locus. As noted elsewhere (Adovasio et al. d, 1980), the reconstruction of the aboriginal condition of Cross Creek is based on the analysis of backhoe trenches on the south bank of Cross Creek directly across the valley from the rockshelter. Another trench was manually excavated from the present lip of the Meadowcroft colluvial pile to the modern stream level. Stream-deposited materials in both the backhoe trenches and in their hand-excavated counterparts across the stream occurred *no higher* than 10 m above the present stream level for at least the past 21-22,000 years. The radiocarbon chronology indicates that the colluvial sediments emplaced at Meadowcroft were being deposited by at least Late Wisconsinan time.

Excavation Procedures

The excavation procedures employed at Meadowcroft Rockshelter are detailed in other publications (Adovasio et al., 1975, 1977a, 1977b, 1978; Adovasio et al. c, 1978, 1979-1980a, 1979-1980b; Adovasio and Johnson, 1981; Adovasio, 1981). During the 466 working days of the 1973-1978 projects, approximately 60.5 m² of surface area inside the drip line and ca. 46.6 m² outside the drip line were excavated (Figure 13.2). Over 230 m³ of fill were removed. Nearly all of the excavation was conducted with trowels or smaller instruments. As many visiting archaeologists have noted, absolute vertical and horizontal controls over the enormous artifactual and "ecofactual" assemblage recovered from the site are as rigid as the current state of the art of archaeological excavation will allow.

Site Geology

Meadowcroft Rockshelter is formed beneath a cliff of Morgantown-Connellsville sandstone, a thick fluvial or channel sandstone within the Casselman Formation (Flint, 1955) of the Pennsylvanian period (Figure 13.3). The cliff above the rockshelter is 22 m high (Figure 13.4) and was deposited as two superimposed pointbar or sandbar sequences. The Morgantown-Connellsville reaches its maximum thickness in thhe Cross Creek Valley at the rockshelter site.

The rock unit immediately underlying the Morgantown-Connellsville sandstone consists of shale, a less resistant lithology that permitted the development of a reentrant or

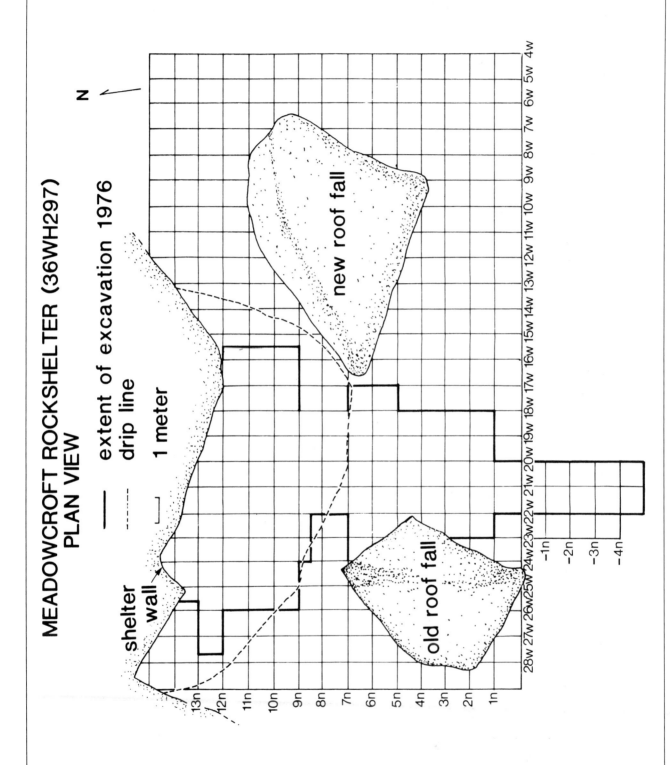

Figure 13.2 Plan View of Meadowcroft Rockshelter (dark lines indicate limits of excavation)

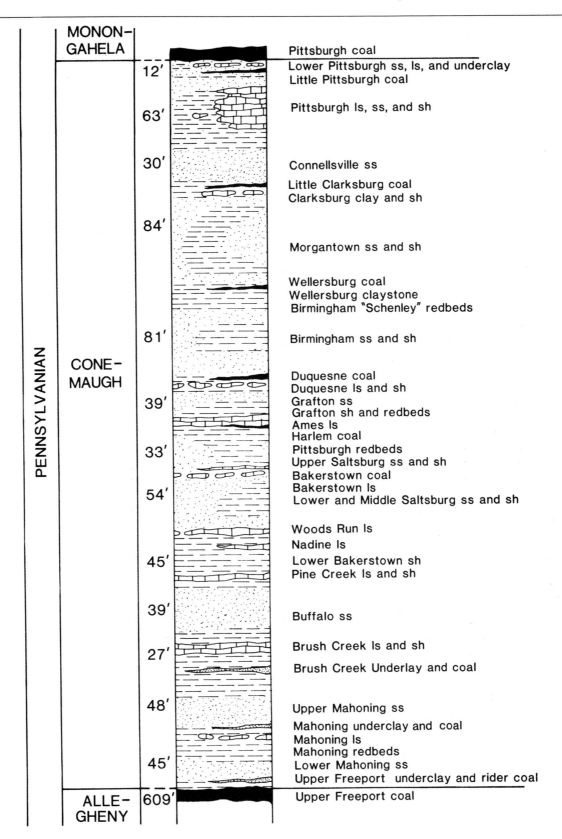

NOTE: The Casselman Formation includes all units from the Crafton shale and redbeds to the Lower Pittsburgh sandstone, limestone, and underclay. In the area of Meadowcroft Rockshelter, the Connellsville and Morgantown sandstones are combined as one unit.

Figure 13.3 Generalized Stratigraphic Section for the Conemaugh (Pennsylvania) Rocks in Southwestern Pennsylvania

MEADOWCROFT ROCKSHELTER
(36WH297)

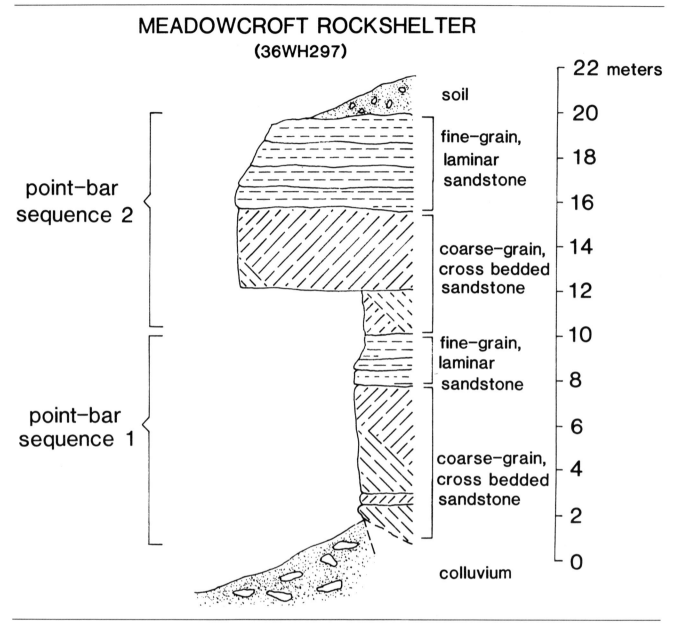

Figure 13.4 Diagrammatic Sketch of Morgantown-Connellsmille Sandstone at Meadowcroft Rockshelter Showing Change in Sedimentary Structure and Grain Size Through the Two Point-Bar Sequences

rockshelter beneath the sandstone cliff. The ceiling of this reentrant is gradually migrating upward and cliffward as erosion occurs on the rockshelter ceiling and the cliff face. Within the excavations, the sequential recession of the drip line marking the cliff edge position can be seen plainly and traced from its maximum extent to its present position (Figure 13.5).

Eleven natural strata have been distinguished in the Meadowcroft Rockshelter deposits. These have been assigned numerical designators beginning with the earliest stratum (I) and proceeding to the latest (XI). A composite profile of the stratigraphy is presented in Figure 13.5, while

a photograph of the eastern face of the excavation appears in Figure 13.6. Details of the composition and characteristics of the sequent Meadowcroft strata are available in other publications on the site (Adovasio et al. b, 1977a; Adovasio et al. d, 1980; Donahue et al., 1978).

Weathering and downslope movement of boulder- to clay-sized sediment grains, both from the upland surface and the sandstone cliff, produced a colluvial pile of sediments at Meadowcroft with a thickness in excess of 3 m. A distinct drip line shows that sediment was not transported after falling from the cliff and upland region. Moreover, there is no evidence of stream or lake deposits.

If the sediments had been reworked by stream or lake currents, a finer stratification could be expected, and any indication of a drip line would have been erased. Rock fall, grain-by-grain attrition, and sheet wash supply sediments to the Meadowcroft colluvial pile. Stratification observed in the excavation profiles consists essentially of thick, poorly sorted units. Sandstone blocks that have fallen from the Morgantown-Connellsville cliff are scattered throughout the sediment, occasionally in large concentrations indicative of major roof-fall episodes.

Size analyses are now complete for a long series of microstrata from the east face of the excavation, and these provide a good picture of changes in sedimentation from the top of Stratum IIb upward to Stratum XI. From upper Stratum IIb (circa 1820 ± 90 B.C.) through Stratum V (circa A.D. 285 ± 65) times, attrition was a dominant sediment source. During Stratum VI times, with dislodgment of the New Roof Fall, rockfall became a more important sediment source, as reflected by an increase in mean grain size and a shift to more poorly sorted sediments. Finally, from Stratum VII (circa A.D. 660 ± 60) through Stratum XI times (circa A.D. 1775 ± 50), attrition and (especially) sheet wash were important sediment sources. After the time of the New Roof Fall (circa A.D. 300-600), a reentrant opened on the east side of the rockshelter and allowed access to sheet wash from the upland surface. Attrition was the primary source of sediment at the beginning of the Meadowcroft depositional sequence. The construction of paleotopographic maps for the site (Donahue et al., 1979) reveals a very similar picture. A hummocky terrain existed prior to the Old Roof Fall (circa 10,000 B.C.). A pronounced change in topography took place after the New Roof Fall in which a sheet wash cone rapidly took shape behind the New Roof Fall on the eastern margin of the site.

It appears likely that the rockshelter configuration at any particular time exerted a dominating control over both sedimentation rate and source. The role of paleoclimatic fluctuations in determining or influencing rates of rockshelter sedimentation is masked (though not obscured) by the conditions noted previously. It would be illogical to think that paleoclimatic changes *governed* the rate of sedimentation within the rockshelter. Rather, it appears that the overall configuration of the site, as reflected in the extent and character of the overhand, has affected sedimentation more than any other single factor.

Cultural Features

The most common cultural features encountered at Meadowcroft Rockshelter are firepits, ash and charcoal lenses, large burned areas or firefloors, refuse/storage pits, concentrations of lithics, ceramics, and bone that suggest the presence of specialized activity areas, roasting pits, and the internment of one human and one dog. The frequency of these features is shown in Table 13.1; the data here differ from many previously published tabulations of feature type and frequency at the site, as the table includes data from the 1977 and 1978 excavations. Further, the criteria for specific categories of features have been altered somewhat from previous tabulations. The four features listed from Stratum I are all from the surface of that stratum *inside* the drip line of the site.

The frequency of cultural features throughout the Meadowcroft deposits is a reflection of the changing intensity of human occupation at the rockshelter and of changing depositional conditions within the site. Cultural features are most numerous *before* the cataclysmic New Roof Fall episode associated with Stratum VI and trail off markedly thereafter. The New Roof Fall collapsed over the epicenter of the Archaic-period occupation at Meadowcroft, forcing all later occupants to utilize the western and west central portions of the site. The eastern segment of the site was essentially unused after circa A.D. 600, as this was a locus for rapid sheet wash deposition.

Radiocarbon Chronology

In all, 100 Meadowcroft samples were submitted for radiocarbon assay to the Radiation Biology Laboratory of the Smithsonian Institution. In all but two cases the charcoal was derived from firepits, firefloors, or charcoal lenses within the deposits. The exceptions represent portions of completely carbonized simple plaited basketry fragments (Adovasio et al. b, 1977a). To date, 69 of the samples have been processed; 22 samples were too small to count. The results of the other assays are presented in absolute stratigraphic order in Table 13.2

As indicated in Table 13.2, the initial occupation of the rockshelter is positively ascribable to the fifteenth millennium B.C., while the latest radiocarbon assay on purely aboriginal materials is A.D. 1265 ± 80. The deepest microstrata within Stratum IIa have produced two radiocarbon dates in excess of 17,000 B.C., suggesting an even earlier initial occupation. Cross-dated lithics and ceramic remains from Strata VII-XI indicate continuing occupation or utilization of the rockshelter through the Historic period, as attested to by both the radiocarbon date of A.D. 1775 ± 50 and historical information (Carlisle, in press).

The radiocarbon sequence is remarkably consistent with the observed stratigraphy. Currently, Meadowcroft represents the longest human occupational sequence in eastern North America and one of the longest and most thoroughly documented in this hemisphere. The Meadowcroft Stratum IIa dates and associated stratigraphy have great significance for understanding the prehistory of the Upper Ohio Valley and the northeastern United States, as well as for the problem of the timing of the peopling of North America across the Bering Land-Bridge.

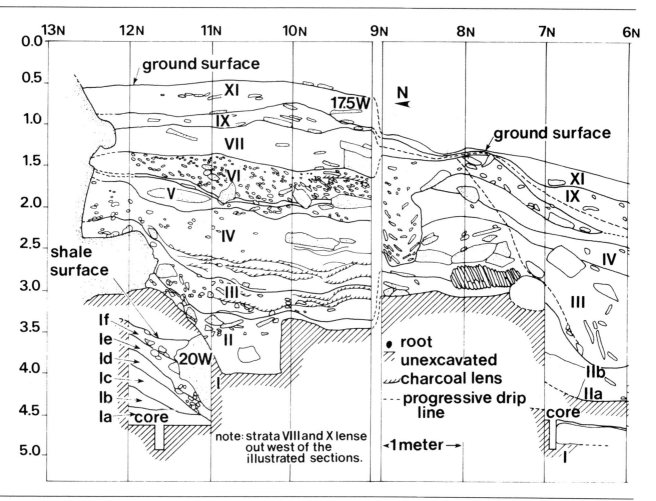

Figure 13.5   Composite North-South Profile from Meadowcroft Rockshelter (note drip line position)

Stratum IIa is the deepest and oldest culture-bearing depositional unit at Meadowcroft Rockshelter. This unit lies conformably beneath and is uniformly separated by a roof-spalling event from Stratum IIb in all excavated units at the rockshelter both inside and outside the extant drip line. Stratum IIa consists essentially of sand-sized and finer material derived principally through grain-by-grain erosion from the roof and walls of the rockshelter. For analytical and discussion purposes, Stratum IIa is subdivided into three subunits of unequal thickness that are simply labeled upper, middle, and lower Stratum IIa. Each of these units is bracketed by major roof-spalling episodes, and each is well-dated by radiocarbon assay (Table 13.3).

Upper Stratum IIa has a terminal date of 6060 ± 110 B.C. from the uppermost living or occupation floor within this subunit and a date of 7165 ± 115 B.C. from a slightly deeper occupational surface within the unit. At the base of upper Stratum IIa is a substantial roof-spalling episode that marks the boundary between this subunit and middle Stratum IIa.

While the top of the roof-spalling event that separates upper from middle Stratum IIa is undated, an assay of 9350 ± 700 B.C. is available from directly beneath the roof spall-

ing event at the top of middle Stratum IIa. Hence, for all intents and purposes, upper Stratum IIa dates from 9000 to 6000 B.C. and is of Holocene age.

Middle Stratum IIa, sealed from upper Stratum IIa by a roof-spalling episode, is also terminated by a roof-spalling eposide. Directly beneath the latter roof spall is a date of 10,850 ± 870 B.C. Middle Stratum IIa is therefore bracketed by dates ranging from 9000 to 11,000 B.C.; it is of terminal Pleistocene age.

Lower Stratum IIa, which lies beneath the roof-spalling episode that separates this unit from middle Stratum IIa, has seven additional radiocarbon dates ranging from 11,290 ± 1010 B.C. to 17,650 ± 2400 B.C. The eighteenth millennium B.C. date constitutes the deepest date from the rockshelter that is associated with materials of *indisputable* human manufacture and also marks the onset of human utilization of this locality.

The maximum excavated depth of Stratum IIa varies between 70 and 90 cm in different portions of the rockshelter. At the interface of lower Stratum IIa and underlyng Stratum I are several lenses of charcoal that have produced radiocarbon dates in the twentieth and twenty-ninth millennia B.C. range. These dates are *not* associated with any cultural

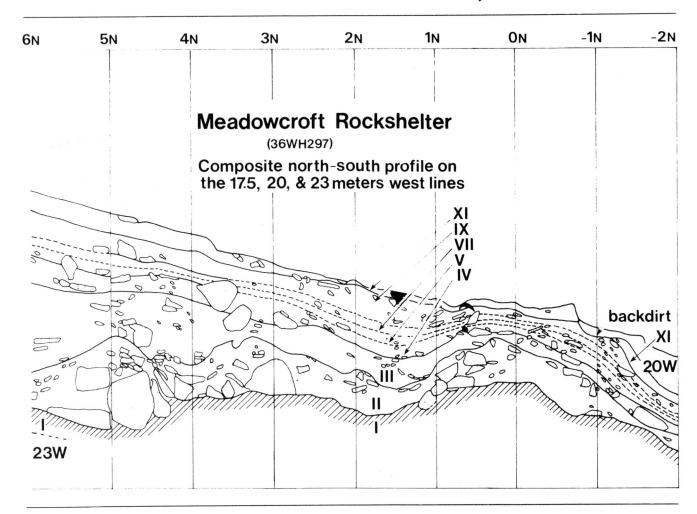

materials. Furthermore, they are separated from the deepest occupational floors within Stratum IIa by a considerable thickness of sterile deposits (Adovasio et al. d,1980: 588-589).

Virtually no questions have been raised about the post-10,000 B.C. Meadowcroft dates or their cultural associations. The earlier suite of dates, collected by the same researchers using the same field techniques and analyzed by the same radiocarbon laboratory, however, have not been accepted so readily in some quarters (C. Haynes, 1977, 1980b; Mead, 1980; Dincauze, 1981). Perhaps this is not too surprising, as a well-established "school" of archaeological thought exists whose now dwindling number of proponents firmly and sometimes dogmatically adhere to the notion that human beings did not enter the New World from Asia prior to the end of the Wisconsinan glaciation. The "late entrance" school of thought has a lengthy history in the development of American archaeology. The criteria by which putatively early archaeological sites are judged and evaluated are and must be rigorous. In this, proponents of the "late entry" hypothesis have long guarded the temple doors; some have

done so as "devil's advocates" (C. Haynes, 1977: 165), while other seemingly have accepted their position as a matter of faith.

The ensuing dialogue between "early" and "late" entry advocates has not been without its salutary aspects. Conservatism of thought in this respect has insured that virtually every site held up as evidence of "early entry" has received critical examination by a relatively circumscribed number of professionals. Under what is inevitably a withering barrage of skeptical inquiry, few sites in the New World have withstood the tests to the satisfaction of all. This is as much a comment on the fragility and sparsity of the physical evidence as it is on the manner in which that evidence has been extracted from the ground and assessed in the laboratory. It was for these reasons that the excavations at Meadowcroft proceeded with excruciating care and exactitude. Nowhere is this more evident than in the radiometric dating of the site. No other site of its age and cultural complexity in the eastern United States has the luxury of so many radiocarbon dates as does Meadowcroft. Although the excavation and sampling techniques have not been questioned by even the most strident of Meadow-

Figure 13.6 Photography of the Eastern Face of the Excavations at Meadowcroft (the interior of the rockshelter is to the left, while Cross Creek is to the right)

croft's critics, there have been suggestions that the radiocarbon dates from the oldest levels at the site, specifically middle and lower Stratum IIa (Figure 13.5), have been rendered too old by virtue of contamination via the injection of "dead" carbon in the form of coal particles or so-called organic solubles (C. Haynes, 1977, 1980b). For reasons fully explained in other publications, however, evidence for particulate (Adovasio et al. b, 1978) and nonparticulate (Adovasio et al. a, 1981; Adovasio et al. d, 1980) contamination of the Stratum IIa samples is nil.

Dincauze (1981) has generated observations and queries which in essence raise anew the "question" of the age of the Stratum IIa deposits at Meadowcroft Rockshelter. While her summary of the collective Meadowcroft reports is broadly acceptable, certain points require explanation. All of these matters will be treated in far greater detail in the final Meadowcroft/Cross Creek volume. The publication of that work is approximately one year away, however, and summary comments are therefore warranted.

In her commentary, Dincauze implies that the Stratum IIa radiocarbon dates cannot by themselves resolve the age of the deposit, since they cannot be shown conclusively to be uncontaminated. No additional sources of contamina-

tion other than "groundwater" via "obscure" mechanisms or "ways impervious to the state-of-the-art laboratory protocols" (Dincauze, 1981: 4) are suggested, however. Our observation of a distinct drip line preserved in the Meadowcroft sediments from the top to the bottom of the deposits is important for this criticism. "Outside" this line, the percentage of carbonates is very low to nonexistent, while to the "inside," the proportion of carbonates is much higher. If extensive subsurface groundwater movement was a factor in potential contamination, the carbonates inside the drip line would have been leached out, and there would be no observable drip line based on carbonate frequencies. The fact that such a situation has not occurred negates the possibility of extensive groundwater mechanisms operating at the site. There is therefore no demonstrable evidence either for particulate or nonparticulate contamination of any of the Stratum IIa radiocarbon samples at Meadowcroft. Similarly, Dincauze's questions about the organic samples within Stratum I are not germane, as they reflect a misreading of previous work. There is *no* datable carbon in Stratum I. The samples, as we have noted (Adovasio et al. d, 1980: 589), derive from the interface of Stratum I and Stratum II and have been so described.

Table 13.1: Frequency of Cultural Features at Meadowcroft Rockshelter by Stratum

Stratum (Field Designation)	Firepits	Refuse/Storage Pits	Roasting Pits	Firefloors	Ash/Charcoal Lenses	Burials	Specialized Activity Area	Total
XI (F3) (F8)	4					1 (dog)		5
X (F25)	1							1
IX (F9)	2							2
VIII (F12)	1							1
VII (F13)	9				1	1 (human)	1	12
VI (F63) (F129)	9		1		2			12
V-IX (F4) (outside drip line)	5	1		2	2			10
V (F14)	20	1	1	2	6		4	34
IV (F16)	35	9	3	13	15		3	78
III (F18)	26	2		8	17		1	54
IIb (F46)	6	3		6	8		2	25
IIa (F46)	26	5	1	1	1		4	38
I (F85) (F99)	3						1	4
TOTAL	147	21	5	33	52	2	16	276

NOTE: F numbers denote sequent feature numbers assigned during excavation.
Stratum numbers are expressed by Roman numerals.

These materials *were* deposited within the last 30,000 years (Dincauze, 1981: 4), but apparently not by humans. The samples appear to us to have nothing to do with the integrity of the other Stratum IIa dates.

Dincauze correctly points out that there is nothing in the stratigraphy of the site that in and of itself argues for a Pleistocene ascription to the lower and middle Stratum IIa deposits. However, there is also nothing in the stratigraphy that argues against just such an ascription. As we have stated and restated in other publications (Adovasio et al. b, 1978: 636), there are eleven major strata at Meadowcroft that vary greatly in thickness, composition, and in some cases, color. Each stratum reflects somewhat different depositional circumstances, and each derives from somewhat different sources or combinations of sources. While none of the strata with associated artifactual materials is of fluvial origin, each represents accumulation from one of a very limited or fixed set of nonfluvial sources. These include attrition of individual sand grains from the roof and walls of the shelter, roof spalling, sheet wash of gravel through clay-sized material from the western edge of the site, and sheet wash of gravel through clay-sized material from the eastern edge of the site. None of these potential sediment sources is in any way dependent on climatic parameters for their operation. While to some extent climate does affect the rate of sedimentation from these sources, the sources themselves will provide sediments indefinitely if certain basic conditions are met. This means that there is no depositional hiatus in the deposits, because nothing can cause attrition or rock spalling from the roof and walls of the rockshelter to cease. Cold, heat, moisture, aridity, or any combination of these factors does not alter the fact that attrition and rock spalling occur. Under these circumstances there can be neither a depositional hiatus nor the formation of a paleosol. The familiarity of C. Haynes (1980b) and Dincauze (1981) with fluvial sedimentation regimes and the relationship of these regimes to Pleistocene/Holocene climatic fluctuations notwithstanding, the simple fact is that these fluctuations cannot and do not operate in the same way in closed-site depositional contexts. Deposition in closed-site contexts will be continuous if the source area remain continuously available.

Two other sediment source mechanisms that collectively fall under the heading "sheet wash" will operate continuously if there is an entrant in the rockshelter roof to provide access for these materials and if there is rainfall and downslope water movement to bring these materials into the site. Unlike attrition and roof spalling, which have operated since the creation of the Meadowcroft reentrant, there has not always been an entrant for sheet wash sediments into the site. Before the Old Roof Fall (circa 10,000 B.C.), there was no access for sheet wash-derived

Table 13.2: Radiocarbon Chronology from Meadowcroft Rockshelter as of March 1979
(all dates uncorrected and in absolute stratigraphic order)

Stratum (Field Designation)	Provenience/ Description	Lab Designation	Date		Cultural Period
XI (F-3)	Charcoal from firepit/ middle 1/3 of unit	SI-3013	A.D. 1775 ± 50		Late Woodland/ Historic
X (F-25)	Charcoal from firepits	Too small to process			Late Woodland
IX (F-9)	Charcoal from firepit/ upper 1/3 of unit	SI-2363	A.D. 1265 ± 80		Late Woodland
VIII (F-12)	Charcoal from firepit	SI-3023	A.D. 1320 ± 100		Late Woodland
VII (F-13)	Charcoal from firepit/ middle 1/3 of unit	SI-2047 SI-3026	A.D. 1025 ± 65 A.D. 660 ± 60		Late Woodland Late Woodland
VI (F-63)	Charcoal from firepits and lenses	Too small to process			Middle/Early Woodland
V (F-14)	Charcoal from firepit/ upper 1/3 of unit	SI-3024 SI-3027 SI-3022 SI-2362 SI-2487	A.D. 285 ± 65 A.D. 160 ± 60 A.D. 70 ± 65 125 ± 125 205 ± 65	B.C. B.C.	Middle/Early Woodland
IV (F-16)	Charcoal from firepit/ upper 1/3 of unit	SI-2051 SI-1674 SI-2359 SI-3031	340 ± 90 375 ± 75 535 ± 350 705 ± 705	B.C. B.C. B.C. B.C.	
	Charcoal from firepit/ middle 1/3 of unit	SI-1665	865 ± 75	B.C.	Early Woodland/ Transitional
	Charcoal from firepit/ middle 1/3 of unit	SI-1668	870 ± 75	B.C.	
	Charcoal from firepit/ firefloors/lower 1/3 of unit	SI-1660 SI-2049	980 ± 75 1100 ± 80	B.C. B.C.	
III (F-18)	Charcoal from firepit/ upper 1/3 of unit	SI-2066 SI-1664 SI-2053 SI-3030 SI-2046	980 ± 75 1115 ± 80 1140 ± 115 1150 ± 90 1165 ± 70	B.C. B.C. B.C. B.C. B.C.	Transitional (Broadspear Tradition)/ Archaic
	Charcoal from firepit/ middle 1/3 of unit	SI-1679	1305 ± 115	B.C.	
	Charcoal from firepit/ firefloors, lower 1/3 of unit	Too small to process			
IIb (F-46 Upper)	Charcoal from firepit/ upper 1/3 of unit	SI-1681	1260 ± 95	B.C.	
	Carbonated basketry fragment/upper 1/3 of unit	SI-1680	1820 ± 90	B.C.	
	Charcoal from firepit/ middle 1/3 of unit	SI-2063 SI-2058 SI-2054 SI-2356 SI-1685 SI-2358	2000 ± 240 2020 ± 85 2054 ± 85 2356 ± 500 2870 ± 85 4340 ± 355	B.C. B.C. B.C. B.C. B.C. B.C.	Archaic
	Charcoal from firepit/ lower 1/3 of unit	SI-2055	4720 ± 140	B.C.	
	Charcoal from firepit/ lower 1/3 of unit	SI-2056	3350 ± 130	B.C.	
	Charcoal from firepit/ firefloors/lower 1/3 of unit	Too small to process			

Table 13.2 (continued)

Stratum (Field Designation)	Provenience/ Description	Lab Designation	Date	Cultural Period
IIa (F-46 Lower)	Charcoal from firepits/[A] upper ⅓ of unit	SI-2064	6060 ± 110 B.C.	
		SI-2061	7165 ± 115 B.C.	
	Charcoal from firepit/ firefloor/middle ⅓ of unit	SI-2491	9350 ± 700 B.C.	
	Charcoal from firepit/ lower ⅓ of unit	SI-2489	10,850 ± 870 B.C.	Paleoindian
		SI-2065[B]	11,290 ± 1010 B.C.	
		SI-2488	11,320 ± 340 B.C.	
		SI-1872[B]	12,975 ± 620 B.C.	
		SI-1686	13,170 ± 165 B.C.	
		SI-2354	14,225 ± 975 B.C.	
	Charcoal concentration deepest level within unit	SI-2062	17,150 ± 810 B.C.	Paleoindian?
	Carbonized fragment of cut bark-like material possible basketry fragment/deepest level within unit	SI-2060	17,650 ± 2400 B.C.	
I (F-85) (Omega Unit)	Charcoal from lenses at interface of Strata I/IIa	SI-2121	19,430 ± 800 B.C.	No cultural associations
		SI-1687	28,760 ± 1140 B.C.	

a. *Provenience originally listed incorrectly in Adovasio et al. b (1975)*
b. *Data originally listed incorrectly in Adovasio et al. b (1975)*

sediments from either the western or eastern margins of the site. For the period from 17,000 to 10,000 B.C., attrition and roof spalling alone provided sediments to the Meadowcroft colluvial pile. Only after the circa 10,000 B.C. Old Roof Fall did the western entrant for sheet wash become operational. Not until the period A.D. 300-600 did the much more massive eastern entrant caused by the New Roof Fall come into existence. Prior to 10,000 B.C., *only* grain-by-grain attrition of sand and limited roof spalling contributed sediments to the Meadowcroft colluvial pile. When the roof and walls had been subjected to this mechanism for an extended period, they became unstable, and this allowed heavier spalling and roof flock detachment. Put another way, the sediments of lower and middle Stratum IIa, those deposited *before* the Old Roof Fall and associated collapse, accrued very slowly. Attrition samples have been collected year-round from Meadowcroft for a five-year period, and the analysis of these data suggests that while cold coupled with increased moisture *may* slightly increase the release of individual grains of sand, it certainly does not drastically alter the sedimentation rate from this source.

As far as sediments derived from sheet wash are concerned, the critical variables (as noted above) are rainfall and downslope movement of water, coupled with the existence of an entrant for these sediments. The first entrant created by the Old Roof Fall on the western edge of the site represents a relatively small collapse through which on-

ly limited amounts of sediment were introduced into the deposits via sheet wash. Nonetheless, the occurrence of this roof fall and the entrant that it created increased sedimentation at the site markedly. Upper Stratum IIa accumulated much more quickly than did lower Stratum IIa. The reason is simple: Sheet wash, even of brief duration, introduces more material into a site in one "normal" episode than do centuries of attrition. This fact is epitomized by the sedimentation rate in evidence after the colossal New Roof Fall that effectively opened the formerly protected eastern portion of the site to massive sheet wash. It appears that the sedimentation rate and source at Meadowcroft are not and have not been controlled solely or even primarily by climate per se, but rather by the changing configurations of the rockshelter through time. While rockfall variation *within* the deposits may well be controlled to some extent by climatic factors, this is certainly not the most important variable in the sedimentary history of the site. Thus, during most of early Stratum IIa times (during which a continuous overhang protected the rockshelter), attrition was the main sediment source within the excavated portion of the site. This is reflected in the comparatively well-sorted, sand-sized sediments that accumulated at a relatively slow rate.

The release of the Old Roof Fall, and especially the dislodgment of the New Roof Fall, opened the site to finer grained sheet wash deposits from the western and eastern margins of the site, respectively. Depositional rates in-

Table 13.3: Radiocarbon Chronology from Strata I and IIa at Meadowcroft Rockshelter as of March 1979

Stratum (Field Designation)	Provenience/ Description	Lab Designation	Date	Cultural Period
IIa (F-46)	Charcoal from firepit/ upper ⅓ of unit	SI-2064	6060 ± 110 B.C.	
		SI-2061	7165 ± 115 B.C.	
	Charcoal from firepit/ firefloor middle ⅓ of unit	SI-2491	9350 ± 700 B.C.	
	Charcoal from firepits/ lower ⅓ of unit	SI-2489	10,850 ± 870 B.C.	
		SI-2065[B]	11,290 ± 1010 B.C.	
		SI-2488	11,320 ± 340 B.C.	
		SI-1872[B]	12,975 ± 620 B.C.	
		SI-1686	13,170 ± 165 B.C.	
		SI-2354	14,225 ± 975 B.C.	
	Charcoal concentration deepest level within unit	SI-2062	17,150 ± 810 B.C.	
	Carbonized fragment of cut barklike material, possible basketry fragment deepest level within unit	SI-2060	17,650 ± 2400 B.C.	
I/IIb Interface	Charcoal from lenses at the interface	SI-2121	19,430 ± 800 B.C.	No cultural associations
		SI-1687	28,760 ± 1140 B.C.	
I (F85) (Omega Unit)	No samples	No dates		No cultural associations

a. *Provenience originally listed incorrectly in Adovasio et al. b (1975)*
b. *Data originally listed incorrectly in Adovasio et al. b (1975)*

creased markedly thereafter. Once again, it appears that the type and rate of sedimentation were influenced primarily by changes in the configuration of the rockshelter through time.

Thus paleoclimatic conditions, especially temperature and rainfall patterns, played a part in the sedimentological dynamics of the Meadowcroft colluvial pile. The long-term effects of these factors, however, have been overshadowed by the consequences of relatively sudden and profound alterations in the morphology of the rockshelter overhang, specifically the major spalling episodes referred to as the Old and New Roof Falls.

It is certainly true that there have been changes in sedimentation rate through time (Table 13.4). A calculation of this rate (.015 mm per year) published in 1977 (Adovasio et al. b, 1977a: 26) was offered as an average rate of sedimentation through a 16,000-year span. It was reckoned on the basis of the initial and terminal radiocarbon dates and the maximum thickness of the deposits as then known. There was never any suggestion that this figure represented a constant rate throughout the history of the deposits, as has been suggested (Dincauze, 1981: 4).

Electron microscopy of quartz grains was undertaken to demonstrate that subsurface water movement is more pronounced outside the drip line than it is inside this demarcation. This analysis has supported the carbonate data and argues against extensive groundwater movement within the drip line of the site. These data provide no "gross contradic-

tions" (Dincauze, 1981: 4) above and beyond the fact that the samples from outside the drip line are (as expected) different from those inside.

Of particular note is the fact that the floral and faunal records from the site indeed do *not* clarify or render any definitive statement on the antiquity of the lower and middle Stratum IIa deposits, as they are of essentially modern rather than Pleistocene aspect. An appraisal of the sedimentology indicates that sediment accumulation in lower Stratum IIa was, as Dincauze (1981: 4) has put it, "exquisitely slow." That this rate was slow does not, however, prove or disprove anything about the age of the site.

Further argument probably will not alter any firmly skeptical impressions about Meadowcroft's antiquity. Comments and criticisms about the site (C. Haynes, 1980b; Dincauze, 1981; MacDonald, this volume) are recognizably profitable when constructively expressed. However, misreadings of previously published data and the apparent proclivity of some within the archaeological profession to interpret the evidence in a rigid perspective, one that simply dismisses out-of-hand the possibility of pre-Clovis occupations in the New World, are unwarranted.

The excavation of Meadowcroft has not been predicated on "proving" the existence of prefluted projectile point (that is, pre-Clovis) populations in the New World. The project has not suffered from an addiction to finding the "first" or the "oldest." Rather, it has attempted to provide, within the

Table 13.4: Macrofloral Remains Identified from Meadowcroft Rockshelter Stratum IIa

Stratum (Field Designation)	Depth in Stratum	Taxa	Common Name	Element(s) Identified
IIa (F-46)	60-70 cm	*Juglans* sp.	walnut	nutshell, charcoal
		Celtis sp.	hackberry	charcoal
		Quercus sp.	oak	fruits, charcoal
		Carpinus sp.	hornbeam	charcoal
		Platanus sp.	sycamore	fruit
		Acer sp.	maple	fruit
		Prunus sp.	black cherry	fruit pit
		Carya sp.	hickory	charcoal
		Tsuga sp.	hemlock	charcoal
	70- 80 cm	*Juglans* sp.	walnut	nutshell
		Quercus sp.	oak	wood, charcoal
		Tsuga sp.	hemlock	wood
		Nyssa sp.	blackgum	fruitstone
		Prunus sp.	black cherry	fruit pit
	80- 90 cm	*Juglans* sp.	walnut	nutshell, charcoal
		Carya sp.	hickory	nutshell
		Quercus sp.	oak	fruit
		Fagus sp.	beech	charcoal
		Nyssa sp.	blackgum	fruit stone
	90-100 cm	*Juglans* sp.	walnut	nutshell
		Quercus sp.	oak	wood, fruit
		Carya sp.	hickory	charcoal
		Carpinus sp.	hornbeam	nutlet
	100-110 cm	*Juglans* sp.	walnut	nutshell
	140-150 cm	*Pinus* sp.	pine	charcoal

limits of modern technology and with extremely generous funding, as complete a data recovery from Meadowcroft itself and from the surrounding Cross Creek drainage as the state of the archaeological art will permit.

Artifactual Remains

Lithic (stone), bone, wood, shell, basketry, cordage, and ceramic materials have been recovered from Meadowcroft. These materials are confined to Stratum IIa and above. Summary comments are warranted on the middle and lower Stratum IIa cultural assemblages.

The earliest flaked stone assemblage from Meadowcroft is associated with the deepest occupational floors within basal Stratum II, designated as middle and lower Stratum IIa. This assemblage presently includes 13 tools and 104 pieces of flaking debitage recovered during the 1973-1976 excavations, and an additional 300+ specimens recovered in 1976-1978. These 400 or so items are directly associated with the radiocarbon-dated fire features from middle and lower Stratum IIa and presently represent not only the earliest securely dated collection of lithic tools in eastern North America but also one of the earliest reliably dated assemblages recovered anywhere in the western hemisphere. All of these artifacts are from units sealed beneath the rockfall associated with the onset of the deposition of middle Stratum IIa. Representative artifacts and flaking debitage excavated from middle and lower Stratum IIa dur-

ing the 1973-1975 excavations are illustrated in Figures 13.7 and 13.8 (pertinent technical details are available in Adovasio et al. b, 1977a, 1977b; Adovasio et al. c, 1979-1980a, 1979-1980b).

The lithic assemblage from the 1976 excavation season includes some 30 items found on a single occupation floor directly beneath the rockfall that marks the middle and upper Stratum IIa interface. These artifacts potentially represent the terminal Pleistocene occupation at the shelter. This group of tools includes the first definite projectile point from the deeper levels at the site. A sample of these materials is illustrated in Figures 13.8, 13.9 and 13.10 (pertinent technical details are again available in Adovasio et al. b, 1977a, 1977b; Adovasio et al. c, 1979-1980a, 1979-1980b).

The lithic assemblages from the remaining strata include diagnostic and well-dated projectile points of the Early, Middle, and Late Archaic, as well as the Transitional period and the Early, Middle, and Late Woodland. Associated with these points are a variety of unifaces, bifaces, drills, gravers, denticulates, cobble choppers, and varying quantities of flaking debitage. With the exception of the limestone cobble choppers, most of the flaked stone tools and lithic debitage are cherts, "flints," chalcedonies, or jaspers from an astonishingly wide range of quarries. Only 10 percent of the material is of local origin (that is, Washington County). The Stratum IIa assemblage is largely composed of ex-

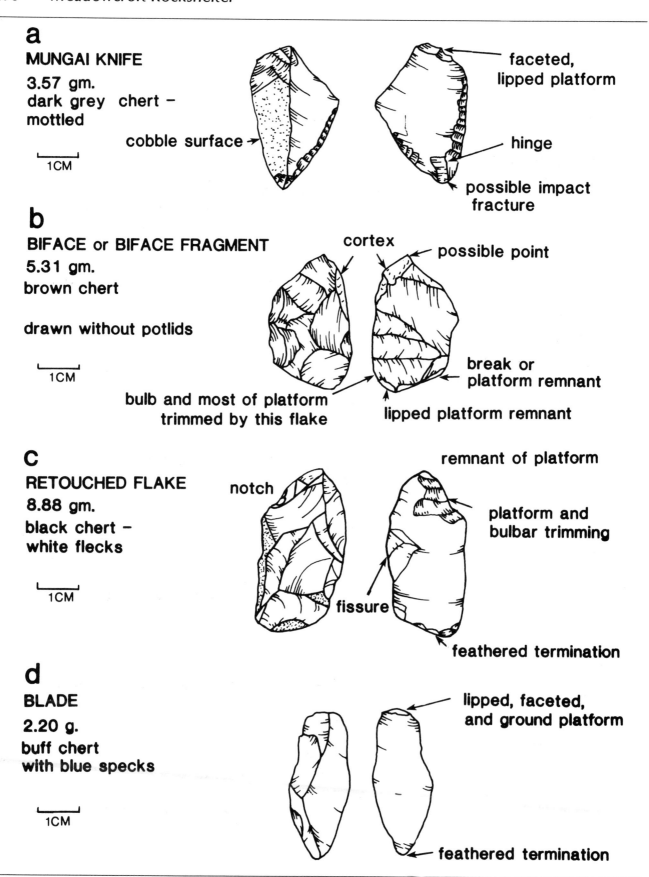

a

MUNGAI KNIFE

3.57 gm.
dark grey chert –
mottled

1CM

cobble surface →

faceted,
lipped platform

hinge

possible impact
fracture

b

BIFACE or BIFACE FRAGMENT

5.31 gm.
brown chert

drawn without potlids

1CM

cortex

possible point

break or
platform remnant

lipped platform remnant

bulb and most of platform
trimmed by this flake

c

RETOUCHED FLAKE

8.88 gm.
black chert –
white flecks

1CM

notch

fissure

remnant of platform

platform and
bulbar trimming

feathered termination

d

BLADE

2.20 g.
buff chert
with blue specks

1CM

lipped, faceted,
and ground platform

feathered termination

Figure 13.7 Artifacts from the Deepest Occupational Floors in Lower Stratum IIa at Meadowcroft Rockshelter

e
BLADE
1.30 g.
grey chert with
reddish rust patina

1CM

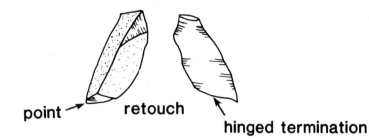

point retouch

hinged termination

f
BLADE
1.30 g.
grey chert with
reddish rust patina

1CM

lipped, flat platform

feathered termination

g
BLADE
.98 g.
dark grey
mottled chert

1CM

hinge

slight lip,
ground platform

patina

hinged termination

h
BLADE
.77 g.
brown chert

1CM

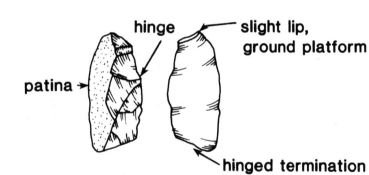

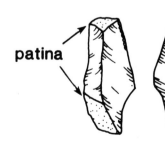

patina

ground, lipped platform

feathered termination

(continued)

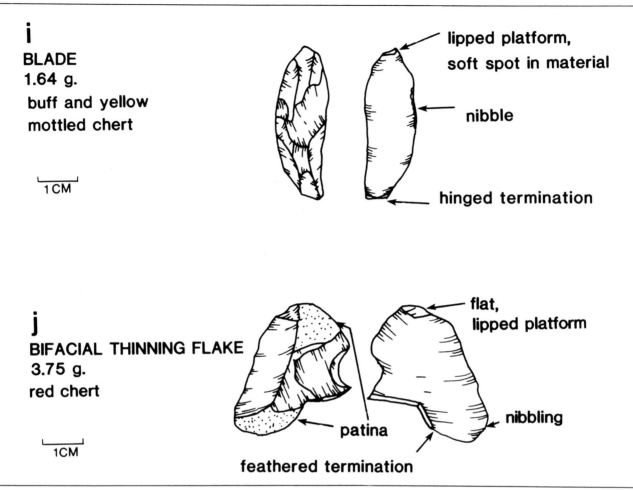

i

BLADE
1.64 g.
buff and yellow
mottled chert

1 CM

lipped platform,
soft spot in material

nibble

hinged termination

j

BIFACIAL THINNING FLAKE
3.75 g.
red chert

1 CM

flat,
lipped platform

nibbling

patina

feathered termination

Figure 13.7 (Continued)

otic materials, notably Flint Ridge flint. There is little evidence of extensive lithic tool manufacture at the site, except for the linestone choppers. Virtually all of the flaking debitage consists of minute resharpening flakes, although some decortication and bifacial thinning flakes do occur.

Most of the nonlithic artifactual assemblage is confined to Stratum IIb and above. Carbonized simple plaited basketry fragments are found in Stratum IIb. Crude, grit-tempered ceramics with associated dates of 870 ± 75 B.C. and 865 ± 80 B.C. are present in Stratum IV. Again, there is little evidence of extensive *in situ* manufacture of any nonlithic tools.

Human and Vertebrate Faunal Remains

Human remains from Meadowcroft Rockshelter are realtively rare and include only one possible interment and 32 isolated occurrences of individual bones, bone fragments, and teeth. All human remains, with two exceptions, are confined to Stratum IIb or above. The two exceptions include the distal one-third of a small middle phalanx and a weathered fragment of an occipital bone, both of which are ascribable to lower Stratum IIa. Both specimens derive from the same occupation surface, and both are directly associated with firepits that have produced radiocarbon dates of 11,320 ± 340 B.C. and 11,290 ± 1010 B.C. Presently, these two specimens constitute the earliest securely dated human osteological remains from the northeast.

Vertebrate faunal remains (studied by J. E. Guilday and P. W. Parmalee) constitute the single most commonly encountered set of inclusions in the rockshelter. Over 115,166 bones or fragments were individually examined. Remains of at least 5,634 individual vertebrates, representing 151 taxa, were identified: 149 to the species level – 66 birds, 44 mammals, 26 reptiles, 8 fish, and 5 amphibian species are present (compare Adovasio et al. c, 1979-1980b: 108-109). Over 90 percent of the remains are from disintegrated digestive pellets regurgitated by raptorial birds, primarily owls, that formerly roosted on the cliff face of

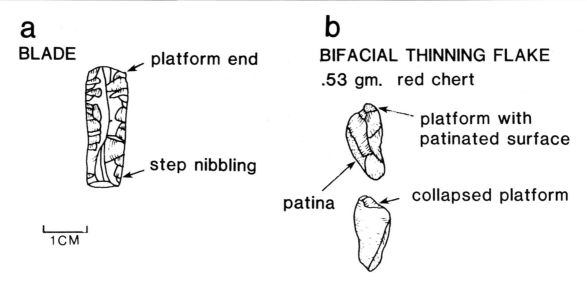

a

BLADE

platform end

step nibbling

1CM

b

BIFACIAL THINNING FLAKE
.53 gm. red chert

platform with patinated surface

patina

collapsed platform

Meadowcroft Rockshelter – stratum 2a

NOTE: a. Blade located on floor directly beneath the circa 10,000 B.C. rock-spalling event associated with the Old Roof Fall; b. Bifacial thinning flake from deep occupational floor.

Figure 13.8   Artifacts from Lower and Middle Stratum IIa at Meadowcroft Rockshelter

the rockshelter during the time that the deposits were building. Southern flying squirrel, the extinct passenger pigeon, and toad *(Glaucomys volans, Ectopistes migratorius, Bufo* sp.) account for 68 percent of all the identified vertebrates. Some idea of raptor activity at the site can be gathered from the fact that 44 percent of all the individual vertebrates from the site constitute but a single species, the mouse-sized southern flying squirrel – at least 2,503 individuals. Approximately 7 percent of the bone collection is probably attributable to Indian activity.

The Indian refuse component is dominated by white-tailed deer *(Odocoileus virginianus).* Butchering marks were noted on elk, turkey, ruffed grouse, and hooded merganser bones *(Cervus elaphus, Meleagris gallopavo, Bonasa umbellus, Lophodytes cucullatus).* Deer and turkey bone awls, deer bone beamer fragments, and three partial turtle *(Terrapene carolina)* carapace cups were recovered.

Bone preservation at all levels within the present drip line of the rockshelter is good, but remains of large and medium-sized vertebrates have been reduced to bone fragments or isolated teeth. In all, 23 percent of all fragments are charred, a figure that increases to 93 percent outside the drip line. No charring patterns were noted. All species were involved in what appears to have been the result of a random, accidental burning of fragments in the aboriginal hearth substrata; they were not necessarily burned as a result of aboriginal food preparation techniques.

A clear picture of a temperate "Carolinian Zone" fauna characteristic of the oak-dominant forest of southwestern Pennsylvania in early Historic times is presented from ear-

ly Historic levels to as far back as 9350 ± 700 B.C. At least 21 species, 14 percent of the identified taxa, no longer occur at or near the site. Fifteen of these are absent due to human-induced ecological changes, and six reptiles, whose ranges now lie somewhat south or west of the site and whose presence suggests warmer, milder conditions in at least the mid-levels of the deposit, are no longer resident in the area.

Faunal remains from older levels of the rockshelter and beyond the present drip line are too poorly preserved to furnish explicit environmental conclusions. The remains include white-tailed deer, passenger pigeon, southern flying squirrel, and chipmunk *(Tamias stiatus).* These four species ranged in Historic times marginally into Canadian Zone situations, but are more characteristic of the modern Carolinian fauna of the area. However, taken in conjunction with the botanical evidence, also temperate in nature, they suggest temperate conditions as far back as 17,150 ± 110 years B.C. This conclusion is at variance with other studies that suggest boreal woodlands and associated boreal vertebrates in the eastern periglacial prior to circa 11,000 years B.P.

Invertebrate Faunal Remains

A modest assemblage of invertebrate faunal remains was recovered from Meadowcroft Rockshelter, including terrestrial and aquatic snails, as well as naiads, crayfish, and insects. With the notable exception of naiads, which *were* extensively exploited during Strata IV and V times, invertebrates do not seem to have contributed extensively to the diet of the sequent Meadowcroft populations. A

Meadowcroft Rockshelter – stratum 2a

a
MUNGAI KNIFE

11.41 gm.

black, fine grained chert
with translucent bands

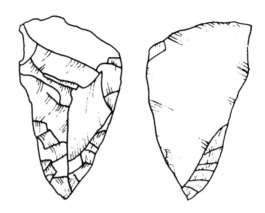

1 CM

b
MICROENGRAVER

1 CM

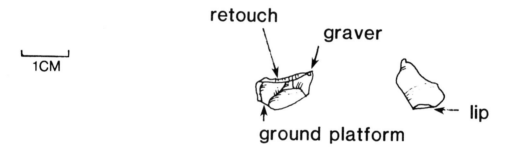

retouch

graver

ground platform

lip

c
MICROENGRAVER

1 CM

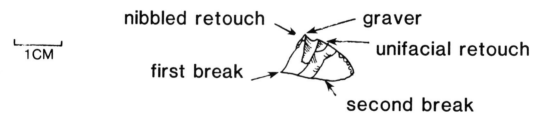

nibbled retouch

graver

unifacial retouch

first break

second break

NOTE: All specimens were located on the same occupational floor directly beneath the circa 10,000 B.C. rock-spalling event association with the Old Roof Fall.

Figure 13.9 Artifacts from Surface of Middle Stratum IIa at Meadowcroft Rockshelter

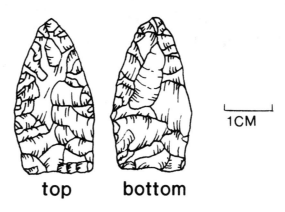

Meadowcroft Rockshelter (36WH297)

BIFACE from stratum 2a
46 cm occupation floor, FS 4471

1CM

top   bottom

Terminology for bifaces found in situ
and cross section of BIFACE 4471.

top left   top right
bottom left   bottom right
occupation floor

NOTE: This specimen was located on the same occupational floor as the items illustrated in Figure 13.8a and Figure 13.9.

Figure 13.10   Lanceolate Projectile Point, Surface of Middle Stratum IIa at Meadowcroft Rockshelter

detailed study of the climatic implications of the Meadowcroft molluscan assemblage is in preparation (Lord, in press).

Floral Remains

Floral remains constitute the second most abundant class of material recovered from Meadowcroft Rockshelter. These remains include everything from moderately large sections of tree trunks and limbs, with and without bark, to minute seeds and seed coats, fruits, charcoal, and small amounts of pollen. Intensive scrutiny of the floral material indicates that some vegetal remains have been recovered from all occupational levels, including Stratum IIa. The Meadowcroft floral materials therefore span approximately 16,000 years (Volman, 1981: 4).

Paleoenvironmental reconstructions based on botanical data are incomplete for much of the northeastern United States. This may be due to inadequate sampling from both archaeological and natural deposits or to poor site depositional conditions (for example, abrasive soil texture, excessive water, or extreme pH values). Consequently, sites in the northeastern United States seldom yield very large quantities of botanical remains or any in very good condition. The level of interpretation for which plant remains may be valuable is thus limited to the types and quantity of data available (Volman, 1981: 2).

The observations made on the preservation of the extant faunal assemblage from Meadowcroft are also applicable to the enormous floral assemblage. Over 97 percent of it was recovered from upper Stratum IIa and above and is therefore of Holocene or modern aspect. Portions of this larger assemblage are discussed elsewhere (Adovasio et al. b, 1977a; Adovasio et al. c, 979-1980b). A moderate amount of floral material, usually charred, was recovered from middle and lower Stratum IIa and does include deciduous forest elements, a finding in keeping with the Holocene character of the fauna.

The dual contribution of macrobotanical and pollen material from Meadowcroft is ideal, since it provides information on both local and regional vegetation. Most types of macrobotanical remains are not designed for long-distance transport. Therefore, their natural presence in sites generally indicates that the plant source was at or near the place of deposition. Taxa not present in a site's cultural assemblage may not necessarily have been absent from the local floral assemblage, however. In contrast to macrobotanical remains, airborne pollen can originate at sources some distance from the final place of deposition.

Thus, most but not all pollen can be considered more of a regional marker for vegetational conditions (Volman, 1981: 4).

Approximately 10 percent of all macrobotanical materials recovered from Meadowcroft have been analyzed. This sample consists of more than 30,000 separate pieces of plant remains. The remaining 90 percent of the material was examined to insure that the studied remains included adequate samples of all types and taxa of data represented at the site. In addition, twelve complete sample columns were taken. Sediment contained in these columns was floated in a hydrogen peroxide solution to separate the heavy (larger seeds and nutshell) from the light (smaller seeds and charcoal) fractions of botanical material. All of the remains recovered from these columns have been analyzed (Volman, 1981: 13).

Obviously, much of the interest in the Meadowcroft floral remains has centered around the interpretation of the materials from Stratum IIa (Table 13.4). Collectively, the flora listed in Table 13.4 are characteristic of temperate deciduous forests. Some might argue that conditions favorable to the development of deciduous forests could not have existed in such relative proximity to the glacial margin. Two prevailing and polarized theories on Pleistocene climates marginal to the large continental glacier have dominated paleoenvironmental research during the past several decades. One theory, presented most aggressively by Deevey (1939), proposes that during glacial advances all major vegetation zones shifted southward without any appreciable mixing or overlapping of plant communities. Braun (1950), on the other hand, suggests that during glacial advances no major forest migrations occurred in unglaciated eastern North America. In this schema, vegetation established during the Tertiary era endured the cooler and wetter conditions of the Pleistocene with minimal change (Volman, 1981: 18-19).

Considerable evidence exists that lends credence to Braun's hypothesis. The extensive floral assemblages recovered from proglacial Lake Monongahela deposits (Gillespie and Clendening, 1968) are very similar to the contemporary floral composition of the area. Important for the interpretation of the Stratum IIa flora at Meadowcroft is the fact that *Fagus* sp., *Tsuga* sp., and *Quercus* sp. are in abundance in the Lake Monongahela sample. The floral remains from proglacial Lake Monongahela include both leaves and pollen. The former should reflect arboreal vegetation present in the immediate vicinity of the lake more accurately than pollen, which can be transported considerable distances by wind action.

While the proglacial Lake Monongahela deposits and associated floral remains are considerably older than the Stratum IIa deposits at Meadowcroft, they do demonstrate the existence of deciduous communities in relative proximity to glacial margins. Stingelin's (1966) analysis of bog

data from West Virginia to Massachusetts also supports the idea of mixed deciduous/boreal forest conditions during the glacial times. This research has pointed to elevation as an important parameter affecting the presence of boreal elements south of the ice front (Volman, 1981: 25). Other data, too, have pointed to the presence of deciduous trees near glacial margins (Grüger, 1972a). Martin (1958), however, has suggested that taiga/tundra and boreal savanna conditions represent the floral response to glacial ice in southeastern Pennsylvania, and prefers to consider the *Quercus* sp., *Tsuga* sp., *Carya* sp., and other deciduous forest elements present in his Marsh Creek sediments as an "anamalous mixture" (Volman, 1981: 26). Thus, there are opposing data sets and varying interpretations of the information in paleoenvironmental reconstruction in the east. Unfortunately, the pollen preservation at Meadowcroft, particularly in the deepest strata, is not good. Only two samples have total grain counts of at least 200, the minimum number sufficient for statistical validity (Barkley, 1934). There is a comparative increase in more recent times, however, in the pollen of weedy, herbaceous annuals (*Chenopodiaceae, Compositae,* and *Gramineae*) that probably reflects an increase in open, disturbed lands.

In specimens of wood and charcoal, the chronological range and diversity of taxa at Meadowcroft from the earliest levels onward suggest that vegetation surrounding the site was of a mixed conifer-hardwood nature. The two genera from the oldest plant-containing sediments, approximately 14,500 years ago, are *Quercus* sp. and *Carya* sp. Both genera remain in evidence to the present day (Volman, 1981: 90).

Two genera that are abundant in the fossil record (*Celtis* sp. and *Pinus* sp.) are no longer extant with any frequency and decrease in numbers from earliest to more recent times. *Celtis* sp. could have been a relatively common species in the prehistoric forests around Meadowcroft. Present data suggest that this plant source may have provided food to both the human and animal populations of the area.

Pinus sp. appears in the prehistoric macrobotanical record from about 11,000 years ago to the present. It becomes particularly abundant from about 3,000 years ago to Historic times, when it was apparently decimated by logging activities. *Pinus* sp. is a pioneer species intolerant of shade. Its presence in relatively large quantities might suggest that the forest surrounding Meadowcroft about 10,000 years ago to the present was in the process of regeneration following some disturbance such as fire, storm damage, or land clearance (Volman, 1981: 91). *Juglans* sp., though a very shade tolerant species (Harlow and Harrar, 1969), persists from about 9,000 years ago to recent times in relatively large amounts in the fossil record. It is therefore likely that *Juglans* sp. retained a dominant or co-dominant position in the forest canopy during its occupancy of the Meadowcroft area.

The only genera represented through time with greater frequency than *Juglans* sp. are *Quercus* sp. and *Tsuga* sp., both of which are tolerant of a variety of light as well as moisture conditions. The presence of *Quercus* sp. from every time period at Meadowcroft intimates that it was (as it is presently) a major component of the mixed conifer-hardwood forest in the vicinity of the site. Evidence based on the presence of *Tsuga* sp. suggests the onset of possibly cooler and moister conditions, although its tolerance of conditions marginal to its preference makes this conjectural. Its co-representation with *Pinus* sp. in comparatively high amounts (circa A.D. 1025 and 1775) suggests that the forest canopy at these times may have been comprised partly or mainly of *Pinus* sp., with *Tsuga* sp. a possible understory component.

Carya sp., *Ulmus* sp., *Fraxinus* sp., and *Fagus* sp. parallel each other in comparative amounts and frequency of representation through time. These genera are mesophytic and tolerant, though *Fagus* sp. is not usually found on dry soils (Harlow and Harrar, 1969). The greatest amounts of *Fagus* sp. recovered from fossil evidence correspond with the greatest amounts recovered of *Tsuga* sp., a genus that also prefers moist habitats. The periods of A.D. 1025 and 1775 may thus have been slightly wetter than previous times, based on the presence and apparent relative abundance of these two genera (Volman, 1981: 93).

Meadowcroft has produced nutshells from two deciduous genera (*Quercus* sp. and *Carya* sp.) that date to at least 9,000 years ago, and *Juglans* sp. from 16,000 years ago. This supports the wood and charcoal data, indicating that mixed conifer-hardwood forests surrounded Meadowcroft at least since this time. Walnut trees were probably present in some abundance for long periods of time in the prehistoric forest. This is also reflected in the wood and charcoal remains to some extent where *Juglans* sp. is recovered in small amounts scattered through time and is present in larger amounts in Strata VIII-XI.

Juglans sp. nutshell is found in every time period at Meadowcroft, but wood and charcoal of this genus are absent from the earliest strata at the site. The greatest amounts of *Juglans* sp. nutshell parallel the greatest amounts of *Juglans* sp. wood and charcoal in most of the recent strata. *Carya* sp. nutshell occurs in greater relative frequency in the fossil record than does *Carya* sp. wood or charcoal.

Quercus sp. acorn shell is not present from earliest times at Meadowcroft, although wood and charcoal remains are present. The lack of acorns from lower levels can probably be attributed to the failure of the aboriginal inhabitants to collect them. Most of the recorded acorns are noncarbonized, and their presence and quantity increase from Stratum V upward.

Domesticates recovered at the site include *Cucurbita pepo* and *Zea mays*. Maize, initially represented by a small, carbonized cob of what seems to be 16-row popcorn, first appears in the Meadowcroft sequence in Stratum IV with two directly associated dates of 340 ± 90 and 375 ± 75 B.C.; squash first occurs in Middle Stratum IV deposits with associated dates of 870 ± 75 B.C. and 865 ± 80 B.C. Presently, these remains constitute the earliest occurrence of either cultigen in the Upper Ohio Valley (Adovasio and Johnson, 1981).

Fruits and seeds (other than nutshell) recovered from Meadowcroft increase through time in both numbers and diversity, though the numbers recovered per stratum are low. The relative increase in weedy annuals since about 1,000 B.C., especially *Amaranthus* sp., suggests some increase in land clearance and/or disturbance. Pollen data from the same period corroborate this phenomenon.

Fruit and seed remains from earlier time periods are unfortunately very scant. However, *Nyssa* sp. stones recovered from at least 13,000 years ago suggest that the environment in the vicinity of Meadowcroft at that time was at least as warm as today, if not slightly warmer. Meadowcroft lies at the extreme margin of this plant's northernmost modern range (Volman, 1981: 95; Fowells, 1965).

Data from pollen, wood, charcoal, fruits, and seeds all suggest that vegetation in the proximity of Meadowcroft the 16,000 years documented. The presence in earliest times of *Quercus* sp., *Juglans* sp., and *Carya* sp. argues against the prevalence of boreal or tundra conditions near the site during late glacial times. All species present in the fossil record are also found in the extant vegetation of the area. The prehistoric composition of the forests around Meadowcroft coincides closely with that of Küchler's (1964) classification of the Appalachian Oak Forest. Only one major taxon associated with the Appalachian Oak Forest continuum, yellow poplar (*Liriodendron tulipifera*), is not represented in the fossil record from Meadowcroft.

The recovery of the remains of deciduous tree species from archaeological levels dating to 16,000 years ago has prompted some investigators to assert that the radiocarbon dates for the site are suspect (C. Haynes, 1980b; MacDonald, this volume). It has been commonly assumed that sites as old as Meadowcroft and as close to the Wisconsinan ice margin should contain a record showing a dominant boreal forest or tundra vegetation. The fact that there is no sound botanical evidence to support a cold, glacial condition at Meadowcroft during late Wisconsinan times has led some analysts to assume that the radiocarbon dates for the site's human occupation must be in error. Other aspects of this supposition have already been discussed.

Much of the apparent misunderstanding that surrounds the interpretation of the Meadowcroft data seems to originate in the thought that Pleistocene continental glaciers exerted tremendous influence on the climate and vegetation of areas to the south of the glacial front. If this is not the case, then there is no reason to conclude that the Meadowcroft dates are in error, since the botanical data have indicated that mixed coniferous-hardwood forests were present during Late Wisconsinan times.

The nature of periglacial vegetation in the northeastern United States is still poorly known. Relatively few well-dated sites have been studied, and vast geographic areas are as yet uninvestigated. Though not in complete agreement with evidence from other sites at similar time periods in contiguous geographic areas, the data from Meadowcroft are informative because they imply a stability in the composition of the vegetation that is not generally acknowledged or accepted for periglacial sites. Paleoenvironmental studies in Pennsylvania especially continue to yield conflicting data.

Assuming the archaeological integrity of the data and the corresponding radiocarbon dates, there are at least two interpretations of the vegetation surrounding the rockshelter during the past 16,000 years:

(1) vegetation in southwestern Pennsylvania remained unchanged by the proximity of the Wisconsin glacier; or
(2) vegetation in southwestern Pennsylvania underwent a period of rapid change from forest tundra to mixed conifer-hardwood forest, documented in the lowest levels at Meadowcroft.

Paleoenvironmental evidence from Pennsylvania is insufficient, to date, to warrant the total support of either of these hypotheses. Most sites known south of the glacial margin contain pollen remains only. Macrobotanical remains are rare and often do not occur at the same sites (or under the same conditions) as pollen. Consequently, pollen and macrobotanical remains are seldom preserved together. This is unfortunate, since macrobotanical data may corroborate or enhance pollen data, providing substantive evidence for the local presence of represented taxa.

Overview

All of the recovered data suggest that throughout its history, Meadowcroft served primarily as a locus or station for hunting, collecting, and food-processing activities. The predominance of projectile points, knives, and scrapers in the lithic assemblage; the relative abundance of food bone; and the remains of edible plants, as well as the general absence of evidence for extensive in situ manufacture of lithic, ceramic, or shell artifacts, strongly support this conclusion.

The archaeological assemblage from Meadowcroft Rockshelter exhibits a number of basic affinities to complexes elsewhere in the eastern United States specifically, and in North America generally. These affinities vary in time, and they are predicated on stylistic and morphological resemblances of one or another of the Meadowcroft artifact classes or their constituents to similar materials from other sites. The lower Stratum IIa assemblage also constitutes the best evidence to date of the pre-Clovis occupation *anywhere* in the hemisphere. While MacNeish (1976), Bryan (1969), and Krieger (1964) enumerate a host of localities in North, Middle, and South America where putatively and potentially early materials occur, the simple fact remains that few, if any, of these localities fulfill the minimum standards of evidence necessary for "proof positive." Poorly substantiated data will not suffice to document pre-Clovis occupation in this hemisphere (Wendorf, 1966; Haynes, 1969b). Proper documentation must include excellent stratigraphy coupled with multiple radiocarbon determinations of artifacts of *indisputable* human manufacture in direct association (Figure 13.11). When these criteria are applied to the vast majority of allegedly pre-Clovis sites, one or another deficiency is inevitably apparent. Most of these sites possess either questionable or nonexistent stratigraphy, few (1-3) or no radiocarbon dates, "artifacts" of doubtful origin, poor stratigraphic or faunal associations, or any combination of these faults. An inherent difficulty therefore exists in *effectively* comparing the early Meadowcroft materials to early assemblages from elsewhere.

The Meadowcroft lower Stratum IIa assemblage does share a number of technological and morphological features with other, possibly related assemblages in both eastern and western North America. Though fluted points are absent from the site, if not from the Cross Creek drainage, the bifacial lanceolate point from the surface of middle Stratum IIa morphologically similar to points recovered in the basal strata of Fort Rock Cave, Oregon (Bedwell, 1973); Ventana Cave, Arizona (Haury, 1950); Levi, Texas (Alexander, 1963); and Bonfire Shelter, Texas (Dibble and Lorrain, 1968). The point is also superficially similar to the Plainview and Milnesand types of the Great Plains region. The Plenge site in New Jersey (Kraft, 1973), the St. Albans site in West Virginia (Broyles, 1971), and numerous surface finds attest to the presence of unfluted lanceolate points in the eastern to the presence of unfluted lanceolate points in the eastern United States. The lanceolate point from Meadowcroft appears to antedate all of these specimens and may, in fact, represent the ancestral form for both fluted and unfluted Planolike points. Tools similar to the Mungai "knives" from Meadowcroft appear at the Shoop site in eastern Pennsylvania (Witthoft, 1971: 29, Plate 4.3), Kellogg Farm, western Pennsylvania (McConaughy et al., 1977), and Lindenmeier, Colorado (Wilmsen, 1974: 64, Fig. 5.1g). The blades, bifaces, graver, and retouched flakes are more-or-less duplicated at Shoop (Witthoft, 1952, 1971); Debert, Nova Scotia (MacDonald, 1968); Williamson, Virginia (McCary, 1951); Blackwater Draw, New Mexico (Hester, 1972); Lindenmeier (Wilmsen, 1974); and many other fluted point localities. Some general

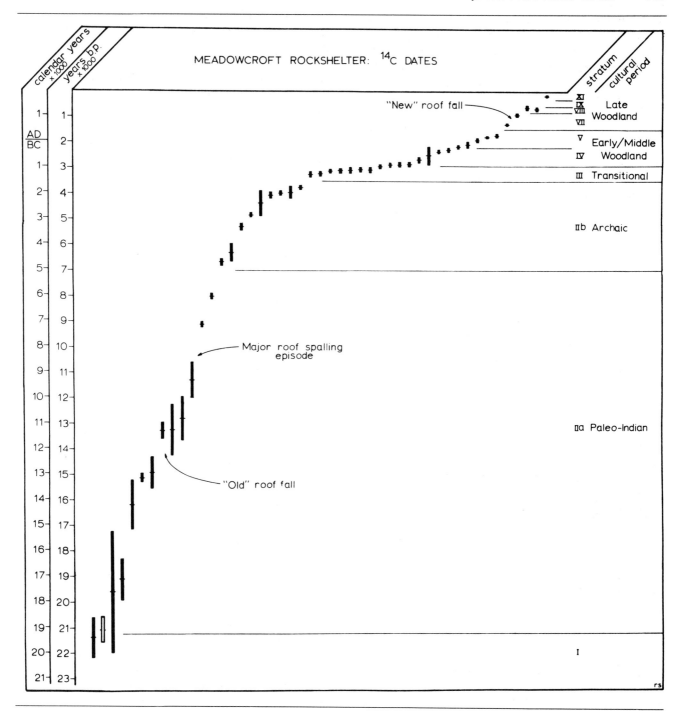

Figure 13.11 Plot of the Meadowcroft Rockshelter Radiocarbon Dates Showing One Standard Deviation

resemblances can be seen to the unfortunately scant basal assemblages from Fort Rock Cave, Oregon (Bedwell, 1973) and Wilson Butte Cave, Idaho (Gruhn, 1961), and to the extensive though undated lithic materials from Wells Creek, Tennessee (Dragoo, 1973).

Since the Stratum IIa Meadowcroft assemblage clearly combines bifacial thinning tecniques with blade tool manufacture, industries like this may have provided the genesis for or represent the substratum of the widely dispersed fluted point industries of North America. Indeed, a "new" site in the Cross Creek drainage, 36WH351, has recently produced unifacially fluted but otherwise morphological *duplicates* of the lanceolate point from Meadowcroft, as well as microblade cores and microblades strongly reminiscent of those from middle and lower Stratum IIa at the rockshelter. The materials from 36WH351 are undated, but their presence does indicate that the basal Stratum IIa diagnostic lithics are neither unique to the widespread fluted point industries of North America.

The basic affinities of the Early/Middle Archaic materials at Meadowcroft would appear to be to the south, in the direction of the Carolina Piedmont, while the later Archaic materials are clearly part of the widespread Laurentian tradition.

The Transitional period and Woodland components at the site are essentially local manifestations of complexes with broad eastern affinities. Notable in this context are obvious ceramic and lithic ties to the Upper Ohio Valley and points generally west and southwest of the shelter.

The final report on the Meadowcroft/Cross Creek Project is scheduled for completion in or near June 1982 (Adovasio et al. e, in press). The current data, however, conclusively demonstrate the presence of prefluted projectile point-using populations in the New World. As such, this information clearly indicates that the "late entry" hypothesis, as advanced and championed by Haynes, Martin, and a diminishing contingent of other scholars, is in error. Put succinctly, the data from Meadowcroft appear to confirm at least a "middle entry" date range for the peopling of the New World and place the initial human crossing of Bering Straits no later than 20,000-25,000 years ago.

Addendum

Subsequent to the preparation of this manuscript, certain data became available which are germane to questions raised on the dating of the Stratum IIa deposits at Meadowcroft Rockshelter. In order to underscore the fact that no particulate or nonparticulate contaminents were present in charcoal samples from the lower levels of Stratum IIa, as well as to silence those critics who questioned the wisdom of sending all of the Meadowcroft charcoal samples to a single laboratory, the last remaining sample from lowest Stratum IIa was recently sent to Irene Stehli at Dicarb Radioisotope Company in Gainesville, Florida. The sample was obtained from a locus immediately below dates SI-2062 at 17,150 $\pm$ 810 B.C. (19,100 B.P.) and SI-2060, the cut bark basketry at 17,650 $\pm$ 2400 B.C. (19,600 B.P.) but above sample SI-2121, the charcoal with no cultural associations at 19,430 $\pm$ 800 B.C. (21,380 B.P.). This charcoal was submitted with virtually no

"background" information other than the fact that it was derived from Cross Creek and "was probably older than 9000 years." Irene pretreated the sample with sodium hydroxide and hydrochloric acid – not the nitration pretreatment used by the Smithsonian laboratory. All counting techniques involved liquid scintillation counting of benzene rather than methane gas assay, which is standard practice at the Smithsonian. Despite the different approaches, DIC-2187 provided an age in perfect stratigraphic order of 19,120 $\pm$ 475 B.C. (21,070 B.P.). This appears in Figure 13.11 as the hollow rectangle in the lower left portion of the plot. According to Stehli, there was absolutely no evidence of any contamination of any sort.

Additionally, in order to resolve questions about the sedimentation rate at Meadowcroft raised by Dincauze (1981: 4) and discussed briefly above, sedimentation rates for the various strata were recently calculated using the present radiocarbon chronology and the average thickness of each depositional unit. The results of this simple exercise are presented in Table 13.5, which clearly demonstrates that significant variation *does* exist in the sedimentation rate.

As Table 13.5 shows, in those strata where attrition is the predominant or only sediment source, sedimentation accumulation is, as Dincauze (1981: 4) has put it, "exquisitely slow." Conversely, in strata where sheet wash from one or both major roof fall reentrants is operative, sedimentation is quite rapid.

To ascertain approximately how slow sedimentation can be in areas affected by attrition alone, the samples collected from the 5m² attrition on the roof of the excavations from 1974 through 1978 were scrutinized again. These samples generally yielded *total* weights ranging from 0.5 to 10 g per day. Average values measured approximately 2 g per day. The sediment collected in the trap consisted of quartz grains with a mean diameter of about 0.15 mm and a density of 2.65 g/cm³. Using this information, a somewhat "rough" calculation can be made for modern sedimentation rate. With a fall of 2.65 g for one day, a volume of 1 cm³ accrues. Over a 5 m² area, this results in a sediment thickness of 2×10^5 cm. This in turn equals a rate of 7.3 cm/1,000 years. As attrition sediments have porosities of 15 percent-25 percent, the actual sedimentation rate would increase to 8.75 cm/1,000 years. Burial of these same sediments causes compaction and results in an apparent decrease in rate. The significant point here is that the modern rate is perfectly compatible with the

Table 13.5: Calculated Rates of Sedimentation for Strata IIa-XI at Meadowcroft Rockshelter

Stratum	Depth (in radiocarbon years)	Average Thickness	Rate of Sedimentation	Dominant and Subordinate Sources
VIII–XI	925 years	35 cm	38cm/1000 years	sheet wash
VII	365 years	40 cm (average value)	110 cm/1000 years	sheet wash and rockfall
VI	375	100 cm	267 cm/1000 years	rockfall and sheet wash
V	625 years	30 cm	48 cm/1000 years	sheet wash and attrition
IV	760 years	55 cm (average value)	72 cm/1000 years	sheet wash and attrition
III	200 years	50 cm	250 cm/1000 years	attrition, sheet wash, and rockfall
IIb	4,700 years	40 cm	8.5 cm/1000 years	attrition and rockfall
IIa	13,000 years	90 cm	6.7 cm/1000 years	attrition and rockfall
Total	20,950 years	440 cm		
Average sedimentation value			21.0cm/1000 years	

measured rates in lower Stratum IIa, where attrition was the dominant sediment source.

NOTE

1. The excavations at Meadowcroft Rockshelter were conducted under the auspices of the Archaeological research Program (now the Cultural Resource Management Program) of the Department of Anthropology, University of Pittsburgh. Generous financial and logistic support for the 1973-1978 excavations and attendant analyses was provided by the University of Pittsburgh, the Meadowcroft Foundation, the Alcoa Foundation, the Buhl Foundation, the Leon Falk Family Trust, the National Science Foundation, the National Geographic Society, and by John Boyle of Oil City, Pennsylvania. Radiocarbon assays were supplied by R. Stuckenrath, Radiation Biology Laboratory, Smithsonian Institution. Vertebrate faunal remains were studied by J. E. Guilday, Carnegie Museum of Natural History, Pittsburgh, Pennsylvania, and P. W. Parmalee, University of Tennessee, Knoxville. Line drawings for this chapter were drafted by K. and F. Adkins, R. L. Andrews, A. Ferenci, and J. D. Gunn; revisions were by J. Evrard.

H. MARIE WORMINGTON

14 Early Man in the New World: 1970-1980

Had I been asked a decade ago what I thought the principal change in Early Man studies would be by 1980, I would have said: "By then we will have conclusive evidence of the presence of human beings for considerably more than 12,000 years." I would have been wrong. We still lack universally acceptable proof of occupation before Clovis times.

This does not mean, however, that I feel that fully acceptable proof will not be found for the presence of people on earlier time levels. On the contrary, I am convinced that it will be. Although I recognize the problems connected with all of the earlier dates that have been discussed, I cannot believe that all of them are wrong. Some of them, which have come from contaminated specimens may, indeed, be too young. It would be a strange coincidence if all contaminants were older.

Over the years we have learned that radiocarbon dating is not quite the alchemist's stone we once hoped that it might be, although it remains one of the most useful tools for archaeologists trying to date their finds. As Rainer Berger has pointed out, new approaches are being tried. Problems remain, but new techniques show real potential.

Radiocarbon dating with accelerators shows particular promise, although there are still problems relating to contamination. The cost of the equipment is very high, but as George MacDonald has noted, an increasing number of facilities will become available. The advantages of using such a technique are obvious. It will enable us to go still further back in time. The use of small radiation counters also makes it possible to use small samples, and this method provides more accurate dates. The smallness of the samples required for either system of dating will lead to less destruction of specimens and will permit work with materials such as fibers, seeds, and other materials available only in very small quantities.

The possibility of obtaining dates through amino acid racemization is also of interest. It must be recognized, however, how important it is that we know the temperature and the environment to which the samples have been exposed. Uranium-thorium series dating, in addition to serving as a cross-check on dates determined by other means, may take us beyond the time limits of other methods of dating. This will be particularly valuable in coastal areas. It may also be useful when shells are found under circumstances such that the effects of isotopes from the environment are at a minimum. Efforts to use uranium series dating and to study hydration dates of volcanic glass at Valsequillo, Mexico, however, have produced dates totally at variance with those based on archaeological and geological evidence.

Fission-track dating of volcanic ash layers can be used to date associated samples beyond the age limit datable by ^{14}C, and the technique could prove to be quite useful in the circum-Pacific area. It is regrettable that calcite in bones does not lend itself to dating by this method. Nevertheless, the advantages of temperature independence and the lack of an upper limit on dates may allow stratigraphic dating in circumstances where other methods cannot be used.

Knut Fladmark's excellent report makes an important point in stressing that during the last 60,000 years or so, it was only during limited periods of time that human beings, culturally adapted to cold environments, could not have moved through Canada, and that the least desirable time would have been between 18,000 and 15,000 years ago. The most favorable times would have been before or after glacial climax stages. Those who are convinced that our present established archaeological dates are the earliest that will be obtained will think of post-15,000-year migrations, but those of us who believe that man has been in the New World for a far longer period will continue to be concerned with the possibilities of the pre-18,000-period.

The history of the Wisconsinan ice sheets is more complex than had been thought. Reassessment of the magnitude of Late Pleistocene glaciation and of the rate of environmental change thus implied has led to discussion within the field of quaternary geology as to whether undated surficial evidence indicates a single late maximum glaciation or several thin, late glaciations that preserved evidence of earlier, more extensive ones. This uncertainty has important implications for the understanding of man's initial movements through northern North America, in particular with regard to the presence of refugia during the Late Wisconsinan. In any case, the Trans-Canada corridor must have been extremely sterile and inhospitable during initial deglaciation.

The possibility of the Pacific Coast route, which could have been followed by people with boats and a littoral-maritime cultural organization, is an intriguing one, particularly in view of Richard Shutler's discussion of the Australian migrants who had to cross open water at a very early period in order to reach the subcontinent. The land-bridge that linked Siberia and the New World was undoubtedly utilized by some migrants, but even when it was not present, water was not necessarily a barrier. Nor, in the consideration of a Pacific Coast route, or possibly some instances in the "ice free corridor," would the crossing of ice tongues by a cold-adapted people be unreasonable. The west coast of North America north of the Strait of Georgia is archaeologically unknown prior to 10,000 B.P., and it seems quite probable that most if not all evidence of a coastal route followed by people adapted to a maritime-littoral way of life would have been erased by rising sea levels. However, the earliest levels at Namu, located on a rise above the Namu River on the central coast of British Columbia and radiocarbon-dated 9720 $\pm$ 140 B.P., provide evidence of man's capable exploitation of the maritime environment at early times (Carlson, 1979).

Shutler's evaluation of blood group distribution and Christy Turner's study of North Asian and New World dental groups certainly provide evidence of an Asiatic origin of New World populations, long postulated on the basis of many other types of evidence.

The dental evidence that suggests two basic distinct migrations, one ancestral to the Paleoindians and the other to the Aleut-Eskimos, is in accord with typological differentiation between the Paleoindians and the Aleut-Eskimo lithic traditions. The possibility of a third migration of ancestors of Na-Dene-speakers is also of interest. Our ideas of the location in Asia from which movements stemmed may well have to be changed.

I was delighted to learn that the Upper Paleolithic crania from Mal'ta are of basically European rather than Asiatic type. When I first went to the Soviet Union in 1958, I was excited about the possibility of seeing the lithic materials from Mal'ta and Afontavo Gora which, at that time, were the earliest known remains from Siberia. I had great hopes that I would find resemblances between those industries and those that I was familiar with in the United States. This was not the case. I could see strong similarities between these finds and finds of the Upper Paleolithic of Western Europe, but no connections with the New World. It is only in recent years that the studies of J. A. Mochanov and N. N. Dikov have provided evidence of a bifacially flaked industry in Siberia. Earlier, H. Müller-Beck had noted similarities between the lithic industries of Kostienki and the New World, but the Don River is far away.

Among my reasons for thinking of greater antiquity for human occupation in the New World are the presence of early dates and apparently ancient, though not always firmly dated, sites far to the south of Bering Strait, notably in Mexico, Middle America, and South America. I am well aware of the models projected by Paul Martin, yet I cannot believe that the Paleoindians rushed off to the south singing "Patagonia, here we come."

My feeling is that hunters and gatherers need to know the area in which they are working and upon which they are dependent for their livelihood. It takes time for them to build up the familiarity with their environment that they need. Once they have it, they are going to stay as long as possible, although pressure on the resource base as a result of environmental change or expanding human population might make movements of all or part of local groups necessary.

I cannot believe, however, that man is the major causative factor in the extinction of Pleistocene fauna in the New World. We have had records of extinction through millions of years of time. Also, there are animals that became extinct during the Pleistocene that we have no reason to believe were hunted by man. Human predators were almost certainly a contributing factor, but there must have been others, the principal one perhaps being climatic change.

As Richard MacNeish has pointed out, there are intriguing sites in Mesoamerica suggestive of considerable antiquity. I have doubts about the possible artifacts from El Bosque in Nicaragua and about the dates, although the excavation was very well handled. I have great faith, however, in the age of the sites at Valsequillo in the vicinity of Puebla, Mexico, first reported by Juan Armenta and later well excavated by Cynthia Irwin-Williams. Some of Armenta's surface finds may fall in the range of 24,000-35,000 years ago.

At five excavated locations, there were firm associations of artifacts and bones of extinct animals in beds that represent a long stratigraphic sequence. The only radiocarbon date available is one from the site of Caulapan, which is 21,850 ± 850 B.P. Unfortunately, it is on shell. The lower levels of another site, El Horno, would appear to be considerably older, and those from the upper levels of the site at Huayatlaco considerably more recent, probably about 9,000 years old. The fauna are of Late Pleistocene age, and the date of a quarter of a million years ago reported by Virginia Steen-McIntyre and Harold Malde, based on uranium dating and fission track dating, has not won general acceptance among archaeologists and palentologists.

Possible artifacts and bones of extinct animals found at Tlapacoya have produced radiocarbon dates comparable with those of Caulapan. As MacNeish has pointed out, more work remains to be done in a number of localities believed to be old but of a somewhat more recent age. The presence of bifacially flaked leaf-shaped forms, blades, and burins is well established. There are also mammoth kill sites in the Valley of Mexico at least 9,000 years old. MacNeish has outlined four stages of lithic technology for Mesoamerica:

Stage I – hypothetical pebble tool stage
Stage II – bone tools and unifaces
Stage III – blades, burins, and leaf-shaped points
Stage IV – regional traditions of projectile points

While there are no definite dates attached to these categories, MacNeish feels that the hypothetical pebble tool stage, based on analogy and a very few artifacts, would begin as early as 35,000-45,000 B.P. Stage II, based primarily on the assemblages and dates at Tlapacoya and Valsequillo, would begin around 20,000 B.P.

The finding of a fluted point, as well as Lerma points, at Los Tapioles in Guatemala, reported by Ruth Gruhn and dated at between 10,000 and 11,000 years ago, is also of interest. The fishtail points first recognized in South America also appear to have been present in Honduras, Panama, and Belize.

Turning to South America, we learn from Alan Bryan's fine summary that there are various hypotheses concerning earlier traditions characterized by bifacially flaked lanceolate points. Much work remains to be done before these can be adequately evaluated. The variety of environments they represent and the resources they provide must be taken into consideration.

The distinctive, almost cylindrical leaf-shaped points of the El Jobo Complex of Venezuela appear to have been made some 12,000-14,000 years ago and used in the hunting of large game, mainly probocidians. Farther to the south, in Patagonia, a tradition of fishtailed points had developed by about 11,000 B.P., and horses, ground sloths, and guanacos were being hunted.

Using Willey's (1971) hypothesis on the early prehistory of South America as a framework, and examining new evidence, Bryan has concluded that the earliest people to pass through Panama and hence into South America were users of unspecialized core and flake tools. Additionally, he proposes that three major bifacial point traditions, willow leaf-shaped, fishtail, and tanged, developed from this early flake tradition with no evidence of external stimuli. While Bryan does not rule out the independent invention of fluted points in South America, he currently views the fluted fishtail point as a fusion of styles of the North American Fluted Point tradition as it diffused southward, and the South American Fishtail Point tradition as it diffused northward. At the same time, he cautions that additional fieldwork is necessary to clarify this. Bryan also notes that a generalized hunting, gathering, and fishing economy analogous to the North American Archaic was present in South America from the earliest time of occupation. For a time it coexisted with a Paleoindian game-hunting economy, but the Archaic had the greater time range, lasting until the time of European contact in some areas.

In South (as well as North) America, I feel sure that there was a greater dependence on vegetal foods than can be proven on the basis of the present evidence. Also, it seems highly probable that the use of hard woods for tools may have been important.

Richard MacNeish's investigations at Pikimachay Cave in northern Peru are suggestive of early occupation of the New World. I cannot evaluate specimens from the lower level, which may date back as much as 20,000 years, but those from higher, but still very ancient strata attributed to the Ayacucho Complex, with dates of 14,000-12,000 years ago, are certainly connected with human occupation. There may be questions about the dates, but artifacts are definitely present, and the presence of human bones certainly indicates the presence of man.

We may now turn to areas far to the north. Richard Morlan and K. R. Fladmark have made an important point in stressing the need for adaption to cold before people could move through the north. No one can question the artifactual nature of the flesher made of a caribou tibia found at Old Crow and discussed by Morlan. I am convinced that other tools and cores and flakes of bone and ivory derived from long-extinct animals are products of human workmanship, and I think it possible that these materials were fractured while green and that the radiocarbon dates may be of the right order of magnitude. There have been many problems because of the fact that specimens had been redeposited, but the geologic, taphonomic, and paleoecological studies that have been discussed provide some new approaches to these problems.

To the south, stemmed points, fluted points, and bones of extinct animals have been found by Emma Lou Davis in the China Lake area of California under circumstances strongly suggesting (but not proving) great age. In California and in the Pinacate area of Northern Mexico, studies by Julian Hayden of differential rates of the patination of artifacts also suggest great antiquity for some cultural manifestations.

In considering some of the sites discussed by Dennis Stanford, I concur with his opinion that the Lewisville site is probably of Clovis age, and that the early dates obtained by radiocarbon assay may have resulted from contamination by lignite burned in hearths. I also agree that, due to the complexity of the stratigraphic pattern at the Levi site, it is impossible to be certain of the validity of claims for pre-Clovis occupation. Friesenhahn Cave may be eliminated from consideration. However, I believe that some of the bones excavated by Stanford at the Dutton, Selby and Lamb Spring sites may have been modified by man and that the boulder that could have served as a bone-processing tool may have been associated with the mammoth bones. Obviously, though, there is no fully acceptable proof. I have strong reservations concerning the artifactual nature of the materials found in the Texas Street area and at Calico Hills, as do Stanford and Roy Carlson. It would be highly desirable to conduct further investigations in the Channel Islands.

The investigations of Meadowcroft Rockshelter undertaken by James Adovasio and his colleagues are very impressive. The nature of the artifacts does not disturb me, and on that basis the dates do not appear to be unreasonable. At the time of the San Diego Symposium, I noted that I lacked the expertise to evaluate the judgments of two of the individuals who know a great deal about radiocarbon dating techniques and who have taken diametrically opposed positions – Vance Haynes and Robert Sturtevant – and I stated that further tests would be desirable. As noted in the addendum to the chapter on Meadowcroft, another sample has been dated, using different techniques, in an effort to determine if there had been contamination. On this basis, it seems probable that the early dates for the lowest strata are correct, but problems remain concerning the presence of modern fauna and of deciduous trees.

Roy Carlson's excellent evaluation of four different basal cultural traditions in northwestern North America is of great interest. He is correct in pointing out the nondiagnostic character of the biface, flakes, and bone tools found in Stratum C at Wilson Butte Cave, which produced a date of 14,500 ± 500, but it is an important find. The idea of a tradition of stemmed or weakly shouldered points with a northern (Lind Coulee) and a southern (Lake Mohave) variant is of special interest. A fluted point tradition is not very well represented in the Pacific Northwest but, as has been previously noted, in California Emma Lou Davis has found fluted points around Lake Mohave under circumstances suggesting great age. The early occupation of the California dry lake sites, as well as the occupation of the Great Basin, is keyed to pluvial lakes. The Lind Coulee tradition, with stemmed points, is of special importance and is better understood as the result of investigations during the last decade. Of particular interest is the great variety

in Lind Coulee tradition material dating just after 10,000 B.P., including bolas stones, barbed bone harpoon heads, bone needles, atlatl hooks, shell beads and pendants, antler bevel faces, chipped stone crescents, and various scrapers and choppers. The earliest find of a point of the Lind Coulee tradition is dated at 13,500 at Fort Rock Cave. A concave base point reminiscent of fluted point forms is of the same age. Many questions remain about the early presence of the Pebble Tool tradition, but it may well be quite ancient, and there is clear evidence for it in later times.

The use of microblades in the northwest, dating back some 11,000 years, provides clear evidence of ties with Asia, and of movements south during and after deglaciation. The association of fluted points with microblades in the Alaskan Arctic may represent the meeting of New World and Old World traditions.

If the Manis mastodon find in Western Washington is a kill site, we then have evidence of the hunting of these browsing animals and of the use of bone points in northwest North America

There has been tremendous progress in Early Man studies in the Plains area of the west. Much of this has resulted from investigations by George Frison. It is of interest to know that Paleoindian sites are to be found not only in the Plains, but also in the foothills and mountainous areas. The movements of the Paleoindians in western North America were not random, but rather systematic and predictable.

The finding of cylindrical bone and ivory objects of Clovis age is important, as is the evidence from the Colby site, which suggests that efforts were made to store meat. An exceptional number of Folsom sites have been found, and sites first investigated earlier – notably Lindenmeier, Agate Basin, and Horner – have been reevaluated. It is interesting to note that Folsom points have been found as far to the east as North Dakota. The Hanson site is notable for establishing the association of Folsom points and unfluted specimens, and investigations at Lubbock Lake have cast new light on the Plainview problem. Alberta points, first known only from surface finds, have now been found in a well-excavated site, the Hudson-Meng site, and similar forms were found in the course of new excavations at the Horner site. More information concerning the terminal Paleoindian period is now available, but much more work is needed to increase our imperfect understanding of the transition from Paleoindian to altithermal cultures.

George McDonald (personal communication) has stated that in the eastern United States he could find no evidence for predecessors of the makers of early fluted points other than Clovis people, and added: "I eagerly await your rebuttal." Meadowcroft is probably the answer.

A great many new fluted point sites have been found in all parts of the eastern area, and there have been important reinvestigations of sites studied at an earlier time.

Some exceptionally large sites have been reported, and much information has been obtained concerning tools and implements other than projectile points. It has become increasingly apparent that there is a far greater range of variation in forms of fluted points in the east than in the west. More information has been obtained relating to the Dalton Complex. Underwater investigations in sink holes in southern Florida have provided spectacular data due to the finding of human bones and those of extinct animals and artifacts of normally perishable materials. One wooden stake has been dated at about 12,000 years.

Conclusions

During the past ten years, one can see that there have been important changes. There has been marked improvement in techniques of excavation and recording. There is much greater use of power equipment for the removal of overburden, and water screening and flotation have become increasingly important. Multidisciplinary studies have increased in importance. Archaeologists no longer work alone as they did many years ago. They have the invaluable assistance of geologists, paleontologists, paleobotanists, and specialists in dating techniques. Paleoecologists have made major contributions, and archaeologists are now more concerned with environmental systems that affect human lives to such a great extent. We try to determine how animals were taken, and by determining the age and sex of bones, it has been possible to obtain information relating to the seasons during which the hunts took place. The extreme scarcity of ancient human bones in this hemisphere has made it difficult for physical anthropologists to give much direct aid to archaeologists, but as we have seen, studies of dental patterns of more recent age and prehistoric specimens from other areas provide valuable insights.

There has been great progress in the realm of typology. Projectile points continue to be of major importance, but we now know a great deal more about other types of stone implements and much more about those made of bone.

Due in large measure to the influence of the late Don Crabtree and his students, there has been increasing emphasis on lithic technology and the replication of ancient stone tools and experimental use. Studies with microscopes have provided valuable information relating to edge-wear patterns, thus permitting inferences as to their use. More attention has been focused on the location of source beds for particular types of stone, and there has been increasing emphasis on quarrying activities. Experiments in penetrating and butchering the carcasses of present-day bison and elephants have provided important insights into the manner in which the Paleoindian may have killed and processed extinct forms of bison and mammoths.

Most important of all, archaeologists are increasingly functioning as anthropologists, with a greater emphasis on the ways of life among prehistoric peoples. New questions are being asked about the nature of sites and the activities represented.

Although I question some of the conclusions reached in the preceding reports, all of which are of very high quality, there are two statements with which I am in complete accord. One is George Frison's comment that: "In the Paleoindian field, the unknown far exceeds the known." The other is Richard MacNeish's statement that: "The best is yet to come." This I believe implicitly.

If I were to be asked what the main change would be ten years from now, I would again say that we would have generally acceptable evidence of human occupation considerably earlier than we have now. Once again, I might be completely wrong.

Certain things I am sure of, however. During the next decade, some questions will be answered but, more important still, new questions will be being asked, and there will be new techniques available to help find solutions to problems. Undoubtedly, we will make great progress in our Early Man studies in the future as we have in the past.

GLOSSARY

adiabatic: process that occurs without gain or loss of heat

allochthonous: not indigenous to area

alluvial: deposited by flowing water

altithermal: a warmer, drier climatic period postulated to have occurred 4,000-8,000 years ago

amino acid racemization: cumulative changes in the form of amino acids beginning at the death of an organism. The measure of the changes may be used as a method of absolute dating of bone tissue. *Aspartic acid* is one of several amino acids.

anadramous: saltwater fish such as salmon which swim upstream into freshwater areas to spawn

apatite fraction: the mineral, inorganic portion of bone

archaeomagnetic dating: an absolute age determination by the comparison of magnetic alignments within undisturbed hearths or kilns to known past magnetic alignments for the region

atlatl: a throwing stick or board with a handle at one end and a groove or peg on the other, used to propel darts or lances with greater speed and force than with the arm alone due to increased leverage

autochthonous: indigenous to a given area

Beringia, Bering Land-Bridge: land area exposed in region of present Bering Strait when sea-levels were lowered as ocean water was taken up by glaciation during the Ice Age; a dry-land link between Siberia and the New World

biocoenoses: reconstruction of life assemblages

biome: ecological unit of plant and animal life

blade: a long, narrow prismatic flake with parallel sides, at least twice as long as wide

B.P.: "before present"– the notation used on radiometric dates (present is taken as 1950 A.D.).

bulb of percussion: the raised area directly below the striking platform on the ventral surface of a conchoidal flake

burin: flake or blade tool with a sharp chiseled or beaked point, thought to have been used as a graver

calcined bone: bone reduced through burning to its mineral constituents

Carabelli's cusp: an extra cusp on the anterolingual portion of a maxillary molar (under genetic control)

chert: fine-grained siliceous rock composed of micro-organisms or precipitated silica grains

chopper: tool manufactured by the removal of flakes in such a manner as to create a steep cutting edge

Clovis: refers to earliest undisputed human cultural activities in North America, the fluted point/mammoth hunting tradition – sometimes called *Llano*

collagen: the nonmineral, noncarbonate, organic fraction of bone

colluvium: material deposited at the base of a slope through gravitational action

conchoidal flake: flake taken from a cryptocrystalline or fine-grained rock – characterized by a bulb of percussion, striking platform remnant, concentric rings, and lines of force on the ventral portion

coniferous: having cones as a reproductive structure

Cordilleran: ice sheets west of the Rocky Mountains during the Late Pleistocene in North America

core: rock or bone from which flakes or blades have been struck

cortex: weathered outer layer of an unmodified stone

cortical spall: flake that retains cortex on its dorsal surface

cryoturbation: mixing due to freezing and thawing

cryptocrystalline: term for glassy rocks (such as obsidian) that break with a conchoidal fracture

cultigen: a cultivated organism, especially plant, for which a wild ancestor is unknown

debitage: lithic waste from tool manufacture (also called detritus)

deflecting wrinkle: ridge or wrinkle on the mesiolingual cusp of a lower molar (under genetic control)

dendrochronology: the study and linking of tree ring patterns with the object of developing regional chronologies in absolute dates

diaphysis: the shaft of a long bone between the *epiphyses*

disconformity: an irregular erosion surface, a variety of unconformity in which no disturbance of the lower beds other than the surface erosion has occurred

drumlin: a teardrop-shaped mound or hill of ground moraine molded by an advancing glacier, with the "tail" in the direction of glacier flow

epiphysis: secondary ossification center at the end of a long bone – fuses to long bone at specific time in an animal's development

erratics: large water-worn boulders transported by glacial or floating ice, scattered over the higher and middle latitudes of the northern hemisphere

eustatic: relating to worldwide changes in sea-levels

flake: piece removed from a stone or bone core by percussion or pressure – may be used unmodified or modified as a tool, or may be waste

flesher: tool used for scraping hides

flintknapping: the craft of flaking or chipping stone into a predetermined shape

fluted point: a lanceolate point which has had one or more thinning flakes removed longitudinally from the base of one or both faces, examples being Clovis, Sandia, and Folsom points

glacial lake: lake formed by glacial meltwater or by the damming of a drainage by a glacier

glaciolacustrine deposits: glacial lake sediments

gleysol: clay formed under waterlogged soils

hinge fracture: a flake that was broken away from the core before reaching a thin tapered end is said to be "hinge-fractured"

Holocene: recent geological period, beginning at the end of the Pleistocene glaciation around 10,000 years ago

humates, humic acid: nonspecific weak acids formed during the decomposition of organic material

ice wedge: a wedge-shaped vertical vein of ground ice found in permafrost areas – may cause *cryoturbation*

indirect percussion: the use of a punch struck by a hammerstone to remove flakes during tool manufacture – allows greater control of flake size and direction than direct percussion

interstadial: period between glacial advances

isostatic: refers to equilibrium of earth's crust in relation to sea-levels

kame: a short irregular ridge or conical hill of sand or gravel deposited in contact with glacier ice

katabatic: relative to the downward motion of air as induced by surface cooling

kill site: place where game animals were killed and butchered

lacustrine deposits: lake sediments

lanceolate: long, slender point, pointed at one or both ends

lithic: pertaining to stone

littoral: inhabiting or occurring on or near the shore

Llano: Clovis

loess: wind-deposited silt, homogeneous and widespread

macroblade: a blade greater than 5 cm in length

mandibular torus: bilateral mounding of bone on lingual surface of mandible

mesic: an environment having a moderate amount of moisture

mesophytic: plant life adapted to a middle range of moisture

microblade: a small blade, probably used end-to-end in a prepared channel to provide a continuous cutting surface

moraine: rock debris "deposited chiefly by direct glacial action, and having constructional topography independent of control by the surface on which the debris lies" (Dictionary of Geological Terms)

naiad: aquatic nymphal stage of any of several flies, such as mayfly or dragonfly

nunatuk: hill or mountain completely surrounded by glacial ice

ochre: reddish brown-to-yellow natural pigment (iron oxide or hematite)

paleosol: old soil indicative of differing past climatic conditions

palynology: the study of pollen grains and spores and the application of this study in the reconstruction of past local climatic conditions

patination: change in surface composition of an artifact by chemical alteration or accretion

pedoturbation: mixing of soil

percussion flaking: the removal of flakes by the direct blows of a hammer or billet

phytogeography: the study of the geographic distribution of plants

phytolith: "a stony or mineral structure secreted by a living plant" (Dictionary of Geological Terms)

pièces esquilles: stone artifacts manufactured by the placing of a core on an anvil and striking with a hammerstone

playa: shallow dry lake bed or basin that collects rain or runoff

Pleistocene: geological epoch, the earlier part of the Quaternary period, characterized by glacial advance and retreat (approximately 2 million to 10,000 B.P.)

pluvial: referring to the action of rain, deposits of rainwater, or ephemeral streams

pressure flaking: the controlled removal of small conchoidal flakes by pressure using a pointed antler or bone tool

prostylid: extra cusp located on the anterobuccal portion of a mandibular molar (under genetic control)

pseudomorph: the replacement of original matter by mineral matter from ground water, preserving the outer shape of the original object

quartzite: grainy stone formed from fused quartz grains

quarry site: place where stone suitable for the manufacture of tools has been mined

Quaternary: the Pleistocene and Holocene epochs, from circa 2 million years ago to the present

radiometric: refers to the measurement of radiant energy, as in radiometric dating – the calculation of an absolute age of materials by means of the detection and measurement of radioactive decay

retouch: the removal of small flakes from the edge of a tool or flake in order to alter the cutting properties of the edge

rockshelter: a shallow cave or overhang used by people as a shelter or habitation

Sangamon: interglacial stage between the Illinoian glacial stage and the Wisconsinan glacial stage (duration, 135,000 years)

sinkhole: surface depression formed by the collapse of the ground over an underground cavern

solifluction: the slow downslope flow of saturated surface sediments

spall: a flake of rock produced by exfoliation (geol.) or by striking (arch.)

spokeshave: artifact with a concave notch in an edge, presumed to have been used to scrape arrowshafts or other cylindrical objects

steppe: treeless level land subject to dry conditions and extremes of temperature

strandline: shore or beach line

striae: surface scores or scratches

striking platform: the portion of a flake on which the blow or pressure that removed it from the core was applied

swale: a shallow marshy depression in generally level ground

tanged point: a projectile point or knife with a notched corner or side, presumably to facilitate hafting

taphocoenoses: reconstruction of primary burial assemblages

taphonomy: the study of the processes of deposition of faunal and paleontological assemblages

terrace: remnant of an old floodplain isolated by lowered water levels

tephra: volcanic ash

thanatocoenoses: reconstruction of death assemblages

thermoluminescence: the property of many minerals of emitting visible light when heated. Thermoluminescence (TL) dating is an age determination technique in which the measurement of the light released during heating gives a measure of the time elapsed since the material was last heated to a critical temperature

till: sediments laid down by glacial ice

travertine: calcium carbonate deposited from solution in ground or surface waters

tufa: chemical sedimentary rock composed of calcium carbonate or silica, deposited from solution in the water of a spring or of a lake or from percolating groundwater (Dictionary of Geological Terms)

unconformity: a buried erosion surface on which erosion took place before another deposition – the geological information for the time between the youngest rocks below and the oldest rocks above is missing

ungulate: a hoofed mammal

use-wear: changes on the working edge of a tool caused by use. Microscopic examination of use-wear may indicate the use to which the tool was put

varve: paired layers of winter and summer sediments from glacial lakes. By coring and counting, the number of years of deposition may be determined

xerophytic: plant life adapted to a dry environment

REFERENCES

Ackerman, R. E.
1968 "Archaeology of the Glacier Bay Region, southeastern Alaska." Report of Investigations No. 44. Laboratory of Anthropology. Washington State University:
1974 "Post-Pleistocene cultural adaptations on the northern Northwest Coast," pp. 1-20 in S. Raymond and P. Schlederman (eds.) Proceedings of the International Conference on the Prehistory and Paleoecology of the Western Arctic and Sub-Arctic. University of Calgary Archaeological Association.
1979 "Observations on prehistory: Gulf of Alaska, Bering Sea, and Asia during the late Pleistocene-early Holocene epochs." Presented at Pacific Science Congress XVI, Khabarovsk, USSR.
1980a "Microblades and prehistory: technological and cultural considerations for the North Pacific coast," pp. 189-197 in D. L. Browman (ed.) Early Native Americans: Prehistoric Demography, Economy, and Technology. The Hague: Mouton.
1980b Southwestern Alaska Archaeological Survey: Kagati Lake Kisaralik-Kwethluk Rivers. Final research report to the National Geographic Society.

Adovasio, J. M.
1981 "Multidisciplinary research in the Northeast: one view from Meadowcroft Rockshelter." Pennsylvania Archaeologist.

Adovasio, J. M. and W. C. Johnson
1981 "The appearance of cultigens in the Upper Ohio Valley: a view from Meadowcroft Rockshelter." Pennsylvania Archaeologist 51: 63-80.

Adovasio, J. M., J. Donahue, R. Stuckenrath, and J. D. Gunn (a)
1981 "A response to Dincauze." Quarterly Review of Archaeology 2: 14-15.

Adovasio, J. M., D. Gunn, J. Donahue, and R. Stuckenrath (b)
1975 "Excavations at Meadowcroft Rockshelter, 1973-1974: a progress report." Pennsylvania Archaeologist 45: 1-30.
1977a "Meadowcroft Rockshelter: retrospect 1976." Pennsylvania Archaeologist 47: 1-93.
1977b "Progress report on the Meadowcroft Rockshelter – a 16,000 year chronicle," in W. S. Newman and B. Salwen (eds.) Amerinds and Their Paleoenvironments in Northeastern North America. Annals of the New York Academy of Sciences 228: 37-159.
1978 "Meadowcroft Rockshelter, 1977: an overview." American Antiquity 43: 632-651.

Adovasio, J. M., J. D. Gunn, J. Donahue, R. Stuckenrath, J. Guilday, and K. Lord (c)
1978 "Meadowcroft Rockshelter," pp. 140-180 in A. L. Bryan (ed.) Early Man in America from a Circumpolar Perspective. Occasional Papers No. 1, Department of Anthropology, University of Alberta, Edmonton.
1979-1980a "Meadowcroft Rockshelter – retrospect 1977 (part 1)." North American Archaeologist 1: 3-44.
1979-1980b "Meadowcroft Rockshelter – retrospect 1977 (part 2)." North American Archaeologist 1: 99-137.

Adovasio, J. M., J. D. Gunn, J. Donahue, R. Stuckenrath, J. E. Guilday, and K. Volman (d)
in press "Yes, Virginia, it really is that old: a reply to Haynes and Mead." American Antiquity 45: 588-596.

Adovasio, J. M. et al. (e)
1981 Meadowcroft Rockshelter and the Archaeology of the Cross Creek Drainage. Pittsburgh: University of Pittsburgh Press.

Agenbroad, L.
1978 The Hudson-Meng Site: An Alberta Bison Kill in the Nebraska High Plains. Washington, DC: University Press of America.

Ager, Thomas A.
1975 "Late Quaternary environmental history of the Tanana Valley, Alaska." Institute of Polar Studies Report 54.
1980 "A 16,000 year pollen record from St. Michael Island, Norton Sound, Western Alaska." Abstracts of the Sixth Conference of the American Quaternary Association, Orono, Maine.
1982 "The Beringian 'Arctic-steppe' – a view from the Yukon delta, Alaska," pp. 75-93 in D. Hopkins et al. (eds.) The Paleoecology of Beringia. New York: Academic Press.

Agogino, G. A. and A. Parrish
1971 "The Fowler-Parrish Site: a Folsom Campsite in eastern Colorado." Plains Anthropologist 16 (52): 111-114.

Aigner, Jean S.
1973 "Pleistocene archaeological remains from south China." Asian Perspective 16.
1976 "Early Holocene evidence for the Aleut maritime adaptations." Arctic Anthropology 13: 32-45.
1978 "The paleolithic of China," pp. 25-41 in A. L. Bryan (ed.) Early Man in America from a Circum-Pacific Perspective. Occasional Paper No. 1, Department of Anthropology, University of Alberta, Edmonton.

Aikens, C. M., D. L. Cole, and R. Stuckenrath
1977 "Excavations at Dirty Shame Rockshelter, southeastern Oregon." Tebiwa 4: 1-29.

Aikens, C. M. and T. Higuchi
1982 Prehistory of Japan. New York: Academic Press.

Alam, S. and D.J.W. Piper
1977 "Pre-Wisconsin stratigraphy and paleoclimates of Atlantic Canada and its bearing on glaciation in Quebec." Geographie Physique et Quaternaire 31: 15-23.

Albanese, John
1974 "Geology of the Casper Archaeological Site," pp. 173-190 in G. C. Frison (ed.) The Casper Site: A Hell Gap Bison Kill on the High Plains. New York: Academic Press.

Alekseeva, Z. V. and I. A. Volkov
1969 Stoianka drevnego cheloveka v Barabinskoi Stepi (Volch'ia Griva) (Settlement of ancient man in the Barabainskaya steppe [Volch'ia Griva], pp. 142-150 in Problemy Chetvertichnoi Geologii Sibiri: KVIII Kongressy. INQUA Parizh. Moscow: Nauka.

Alexander, Herbert L.
1963 "The Levi Site: a Paleo-Indian campsite in central Texas." American Antiquity 28: 510-528.
1973 "The association of Aurignacoid elements with fluted point complexes in North America," pp. 21-31 in S. Raymond and P. Schledermann (eds.) International Conference on the Prehistory and Paleoecology of the Western North American Arctic and Sub-Arctic. University of Calgary Archaeological Association.

Allely, S.
1975 "A Clovis point from the Mohawk River Valley, Western Oregon," pp. 549-552 in C. M. Aikens (ed.) Archaeological Studies in the Willamette Valley, Oregon. Anthropological papers, University of Oregon, No. 8. Eugene.

Alley, N. F.
1979 "Middle Wisconsin stratigraphy and climatic reconstruction, southern Vancouver Island, British Columbia." Quaternary Research 11: 213-237.

Alley, N. F. and S. C. Chatwin
1979 "Late Pleistocene history and geomorphology, southwestern Vancouver Island, British Columbia." Canadian Journal of Earth Sciences 16: 1645-1657.

Alley, N. F. and S. A. Harris
  1974   "Pleistocene glacial lake sequences in the foothills of southwestern Alberta, Canada." Canadian Journal of Earth Sciences 11: 1220-1235.

Ames, K. M., J. P. Green, and M. Pfoertner
  1981   "Hatwai (10NP143): Interim Report." Archaeological Reports No. 9. Boise State University.

Amsden, C. A.
  1937   "The Lake Mohave artifacts," pp. 51-97 in the Archaeology of Pleistocene Lake Mohave: A Symposium. Southwest Museum Papers No. 11. Los Angeles.

Anderson, A. D.
  1975   "The Cooperton mammoth: an early man bone quarry." Great Plains Journal 14: 130-173.

Anderson, Douglas D.
  1978   "Western Arctic and Sub-Arctic," pp. 29-50 in R. S. Taylor and C. W. Meighan (eds.) Chronologies in New World Archaeology. New York: Academic Press.
  1980   "Continuity and change in the prehistoric record from North Alaska." Senri Ethnological Studies 4: 233-251. Osaka.

Anderson, R. S. and R. B. Davis
  1980   "Late and postglacial vegetational history at Upper South Branch Post in northern Maine." Abstracts of the Sixth Conference of the American Quaternary Association, Orono, Maine.

Andrews, J. T.
  1973   "The Wisconsin Laurentide Ice Sheet: dispersal centers, problems of rates and retreat, and climatic implications." Arctic and Alpine Research 5: 185-199.
  1974   "Cenozoic glaciation and crustal movements of the Arctic," pp. 277-317 in J. D. Ives and R. G. Barry (eds.) Arctic and Alpine Environments. New York: Methuen.
  1980   "Growth and disintegration of ice sheets." Abstracts of the Sixth Conference of the American Quaternary Association, Orono, Maine.

Andrews, J. T. and J. D. Ives
  1978   "Cockburn nomenclature and the late Quaternary history of the eastern Canadian Arctic." Arctic and Alpine Research 10: 617-633.

Andrews, J. T. and M. A. Mahaffy
  1975   "Growth rate of the Laurentide Ice Sheet and sea level lowering (with emphasis on the 115,000 B.P. sea level low)." Quaternary Research 6: 167-183.

Andrews, J. T. and R. M. Retherford
  1978   "A reconnaissance survey of Late Quaternary sea levels, Bella Bella/Bella Coola Region, central British Columbia coast." Canadian Journal of Earth Sciences 15: 341-350.

Anonymous
  1979   "Near St. Louis, archaeologists finally confirm a man-mastodon relationship in Eastern America." Early Man (Summer) 1, 25.

Antevs, E.
  1937   "Age of the Lake Mohave Culture," pp. 45-49 in The Archaeology of Pleistocene Lake Mohave: A Symposium. Southwest Museum Papers, No. 11.

Apland, B.
  1977   "Early chipped stone industries of the central coast of British Columbia." M.A. thesis, Department of Archaeology, Simon Fraser University.

Armenta Camacho, Juan
  1978   Vestigios de Labor Humana en Hueso de Animales Extintos de Valsequillo, Puebla. Mexico Consejo Editorial del Gobierno del Estado de Puebla, Mexico.

Armstrong, J. E.
  1981   "Post-Vashon Wisconsin glaciation, Fraser lowland, British Columbia." Geological Survey of Canada, Bulletin 322.

Ashworth, A. C., L. Clayton, and W. B. Bickley
  1972   "The Mosbeck site: a paleoenvironmental interpretation of the late Quaternary history of Lake Agassiz based on fossil insect and mollusk remains." Quaternary Research 2: 176-188.

Aveleyra, L. and M. Maldonado-Koerdell
  1953   "Association of artifacts with mammoth in the Valley of Mexico." American Antiquity 18: 332-341.

Bada, J. L. and P. M. Helfman
  1975   "Amino acid racemization dating of fossil bones." World Archaeology 7: 160-173.

Bada, J. L., R. A. Schroeder, and G. F. Carter (a)
  1974   "New evidence for the antiquity of man in North America deduced from aspartic acid racemization." Science 184: 791-793.

Bada, J. L., R. A. Schroeder, R. Protsch, and R. Berger (b)
  1974   "Concordance of collagen-based radiocarbon and aspartic acid racemization ages." Proceedings of the National Academy of Sciences, Vol. 71: 914-917.

Barkley, F. A.
  1934   "The statistical theory of pollen analysis." Ecology 15: 283-289.

Barry, R. G., J. T. Andrews, and M. A. Mahaffy
  1975   "Continental ice sheets: conditions for growth." Science 190: 979-981.

Beckett, P. H.
  1980   "The AKE site: collections and excavations of LA 13423, Catron County, New Mexico." Report 357, Department of Sociology and Anthropology, New Mexico State University, Las Cruces.

Bedwell, S. F.
  1970   "Prehistory and environment of the pluvial Fort Rock Lake area of south central Oregon." Ph.D. dissertation, University of Oregon.
  1973   Fort Rock Basin Prehistory and Environment. Eugene: University of Oregon Books.

Behrensmeyer, A. and A. Hill (eds.)
  1980   Fossils in the Making. Chicago: University of Chicago Press.

Beiswenger, Jane
  1974   "Pollen report on the Casper Site," pp. 247-249 in G. C. Frison (ed.) The Casper Site: A Hell Gap Bison Kill on the High Plains. New York: Academic Press.
  1982   "Pollen report for the Agate Basin site," pp. 349-352 in G. Frison and D. Stanford (eds.) The Agate Basin Site: Paleoindian Occupation in Eastern Wyoming. New York: Academic Press.

Beltrão, M. C. de M. C.
  1974   "Datacões arqueológicas mais antigas do Brasil." Anais da Academia Brasileira de Ciencias 46: 211-251.

Beltrão, M. C. de M. C., J. Danon, C. R. Enriquez, E. Zuleta, and G. Poupeau
  1983   "Thermoluminescence studies of archaeological heated cherts from the Alice Boër Site," in A. L. Bryan (ed.) New Evidence for the Pleistocene Peopling of the Americas. Orono: Center for Early Man Studies. (In press)

Benmouyal, J.
  1976   "Archaeological research in the Gaspé Peninsula, preliminary report." Current Research Reports, Department of Archaeology, Simon Fraser University, Publication No. 3.

Bennett, C. L., R. P. Benkens, M. R. Clover, H. E. Gove, R. B. Liebert, A. E. Litherland, K. H. Purser, and W. E. Sondheim
  1977   "Radiocarbon dating using electrostatic accelerators: negative ions provide the key." Science 198: 508-510.

Berger, R.
  1978   "Thoughts on the first peopling of America and Australia," pp. 23-25 in A. L. Bryan (ed.) Early Man in America from a Circum-Pacific Perspective. Occasional Paper No. 1, Department of Anthropology, University of Alberta, Edmonton.
  1979   "Radiocarbon dating with accelerators." Journal of Archaeological Science 6: 101-104.
  1981   "Early man on the California Channel Islands," p. 46 in Evidencia Arqueológica de Ocupación Humana en America anterior 11,500 años a. p. Comisión XII, X Congreso, Union Internacional de Ciencias Prehistoricas y Protohistoricas, Mexico.

Berger, R., A. G. Horney, and W. F. Libby
  1964   "Radiocarbon dating of bone and shell from their organic components." Science 144: 999-1001.

Berger, R., R. Protsch, R. Reynolds, C. Rozaire, and J. Sackett
  1971   "New radiocarbon dates based on bone collagen of California paleoindians." Contributions of the Archaeological Research Facility, University of California, No. 12. Berkeley.

Berman, D. I., N. Vinokurov, and B. A. Korotjaev
  1979   "On the Beringian connections of Curculionidal, Carabidal and Heteroptera faunas." Abstracts, 14th Pacific Science Congress, Khabarovsk, USSR.

Berti, A. A.
1975 "Paleobotany of Wisconsinan interstades, eastern Great Lakes region, North America." Quaternary Research 5: 591-619.

Beynon, D. E.
in press "Geoarchaeology of Meadowcroft Rockshelter and the Cross Creek Drainage," in J. M. Adovasio et al. (eds.) Meadowcroft Rockshelter and the Archaeology of the Cross Creek Drainage. Pittsburgh: University of Pittsburgh Press.

Binford, L. S.
1981 Bones: Ancient Men and Modern Myths. New York: Academic Press.

Bird, J. B.
1938 "Antiquity and migrations of the early inhabitants of Patagonia." Geographical Review 28: 250-275.
1946 "The archaeology of Patagonia, pp. 17-24 in J. Steward (ed.) Handbook of South American Indians, Bureau of American Ethnology Bulletin 143, vol. 1. Washington, D.C.
1970 "Paleo-Indian discoidal stones from southern South America." American Antiquity 35: 205-209.
1973 "The Wisconsin deglaciation of Canada." Arctic and Alpine Research 5: 165-168.

Bird, J. B. and Richard Cooke
1978 "The occurrence in Panama of two types of Paleo-Indian projectile ponts," pp. 263-272 in A. L. Bryan (ed.) Early Man in America from a Circum-Pacific Perspective. Occasional Papers No. 1, Department of Anthropology, University of Alberta, Edmonton.

Bischoff, J. L. and R. J. Rosenbauer
1981 "Uranium series dating of human skeletal remains from the Del Mar and Sunnyvale Sites." California Science 213: 1003-1005.

Black, C. [ed.]
1974 "History and prehistory of the Lubbock Lake Site." Texas Tech University Museum Journal, Vol. XV. Lubbock.

Black, R. F.
1973 "Late Quaternary sea-level changes, Umnak Island, Aleutians – their effects on ancient Aleuts, and their causes." Quaternary Research 4: 264-281.

Black, R. F.
1980 "Valders-Two Creeks-Wisconsin revisited: the Valders till is most likely post-Twocreekan." Geological Society of America Bulletin 91(1): 713-723.

Blackwelder, R. W., O. H. Pilkey, and J. D. Howard
1979 "Late Wisconsinan sea levels on the southeast United States Atlantic Shelf based on in-place shoreline indicators." Science 204: 618-620.

Blake, W., Jr.
1980 "Mid-Wisconsinan interstadial deposits beneath Holocene beaches, Cape Storm, Ellesmere Island, Arctic Canada." Abstracts of the Sixth Conference of the American Quaternary Association, Orono, Maine.

Bleuer, N. K.
1980 "Growth and disintegration of ice sheets." Abstracts of the Sixth Conference of the American Quaternary Association, Orono, Maine.

Bluemel, J. P.
1974 "Early history of Lake Agassiz in southeast North Dakota." Geological Society of America Bulletin 85: 811-814.

Bombin, M. and A. L. Bryan
1978 "New perspectives on early man in southwestern Rio Grande do Sul, Brazil," pp. 301-302 in A. L. Bryan (ed.) Early Man in America from a Circum-Pacific Perspective. Occasional Papers No. 1, Department of Anthropology, University of Alberta, Edmonton.

Bonnichsen, Robson
1978a "Critical arguments for Pleistocene artifacts from the Old Crow Basin, Yukon: a preliminary statement," pp. 102-118 in A. L. Bryan (ed.) Early Man in America from a Circum-Pacific Perspective. Occasional Papers No. 1, Department of Anthropology, University of Alberta, Edmonton.
1978b "Clovis: migration or in situ development?" Abstracts of the Fifth Conference of the American Quaternary Association, Edmonton.
1979 "Pleistocene bone technology in the Beringian Refugium." National Museum of Man Mercury Series, Archaeological Survey of Canada, Paper No. 89, Ottawa.
1981 "Late Pleistocene colonization of Northern New England," pp. 28-29 in Evidencia Arqueológica de Ocupación Humana en America anterior 11,500 años a.p. Comisión XII, X Congreso, Union Internacional de Ciencias Prehistoricas y Protohistoricas, Mexico, D.F.

Bonnichsen, Robson, Victor Konrad, Vickie Clay, Terry Gibson, and Douglas Schnurrenberger
1980 "Archaeological research at Munsungen Lake: 1980." Preliminary Technical Report of Activities, Institute for Quaternary Studies, Orono, Maine.

Borden, C. E.
1950 "Preliminary report on archaeological investigations in the Fraser Delta region." Anthropology in British Columbia 1: 13-27. Victoria.
1952 "Results of archaeological investigations in central B. C." Anthropology in British Columbia 3: 31-43. Victoria.
1968 "Prehistory of the Lower Mainland (British Columbia)," pp. 9-26 in A. H. Siemen (ed.) Lower Fraser Valley: Evolution of a Cultural Landscape, B. C. Geographical Series 9. Vancouver: University of British Columbia.
1969 "Early population movements from Asia into western North America." Syesis 2: 1-13.
1975 "Origins and development of early Northwest Coast culture to about 3,000 B.C." National Museum of Man Mercury Series, Archaeological Survey of Canada, Paper No. 45, Ottawa.

Bordes, F.
1968 The Old Stone Age. New York: McGraw-Hill.

Bordes, F. and C. Thibault
1977 "Thoughts on the initial adaptation of hominids to European glacial climates." Quaternary Research 8: 115-127.

Borns, H. W. and P. E. Calkin
1977 "Quaternary glaciation, west-central Maine." Geological Society of America Bulletin 88: 1773-1784.

Borns, H. W. and T. J. Hughes
1977 "The implications of the Pineo Ridge readvance in Maine." Geographie Physique et Quaternaire 31: 203-206.

Bothner, M. H. and E. C. Spiker
1980 "Upper Wisconsinan till recovered on the continental shelf southeast of New England." Science 210: 423-425.

Bowdler, Sandra
1977 "The coastal colonization of Australia," pp. 205-246 in J. Allen et al. (eds.) Sunda and Sahul: Prehistoric Studies in Southeast Asia, Melanesia and Australia. London: Academic Press.

Bradley, B. A.
1977 "Comments on the lithic technology of the Casper Site materials," pp. 191-197 in G. C. Frison (ed.) The Casper Site: A Hell Gap Bison Kill on the High Plains. New York: Academic Press.
1982 "Flaked stone technology and typology at the Agate Basin Site," pp. 181-208 in G. Frison and D. Stanford (eds.) The Agate Basin Site: Paleoindian occupation in eastern Wyoming. New York: Academic Press.

Brainerd, G. W.
1953 "A re-examination of the dating evidence for the Lake Mohave artifact assemblage." American Antiquity 18: 270-271.

Braun, E. L.
1950 Deciduous Forests of Eastern North America. Philadelphia: Blakiston.

Briggs, Nancy D. and John A. Westgate
1978 "Fission track age of tephra marker beds in Beringia." Abstracts of the Fifth Conference of the American Quaternary Association. Edmonton.

Broecker, W. S.
1965 "Isotope geochemistry and the Pleistocene climatic record," pp. 737-753 in H. E. Wright and D. G. Frey (eds.) The Quaternary of the United States. Princeton, NJ: Princeton University Press.

Brooks, I. A.
1977 "Geomorphology and Quaternary geology of Codrey Lowland and adjacent plateaus, southwest Newfoundland." Canadian Journal of Earth Sciences 14: 2101-2119.

Brown, K. L.
1980 "A brief report on Paleoindian archaic occupations in the Basin, Guatemala." American Antiquity 45: 313-324.

Brown, R.J.E.
1960 "The distribution of permafrost and its relation to air temperature in Canada and the USSR." Arctic 13: 163-177.

Broyles, B.
1971   The St. Albans Site, Kanawha County, West Virginia: Second Preliminary Report. Morgantown: West Virginia Geological and Economic Survey.

Bryan, A. L.
1965   "Paleo-American prehistory," Occasional Papers of the Idaho State University Museum, No. 16, Pocatello.
1969   "Early man in America and the late Pleistocene chronology of western Canada and Alaska." Current Anthropology 10: 339-365.
1973   "Paleoenvironments and cultural diversity in Late Pleistocene South America." Quaternary Research 3: 237-256.
1978   "An overview of Paleo-American prehistory from a circum-Pacific Perspective, pp. 306-327 in A. L. Bryan (ed.) Early Man in America from a Circum-Pacific Perspective. Occasional Papers No. 1, Department of Anthropology, University of Alberta, Edmonton.
1979   "Smith Creek Cave," in D. R. Tuohy and D. Rendall (eds.) The Archaeology of Smith Creek Canyon, Eastern Nevada. Anthropological Papers of the Nevada State Museum, No. 17.
1980   "The stemmed point tradition: an early technological tradition in western North America," pp. 77-107 in L. B. Harten et al. (eds.) Anthropological Papers in Memory of Earl H. Swanson, Jr. Special publication of the Idaho Museum of Natural History. Pocatello.
n. d.   "Prehistoric cultural development at Forte Marechal Luz: a technological study of Sambaqui artifacts." Unpublished manuscript.

Bryan, A. L. and M. C. de M. C. Beltrão
1978   "An early stratified sequence near Rio Claro, east central São Paulo State, Brazil," in Early Man in America from a Circum-Pacific Perspective. Occasional Papers No. 1, Department of Anthropology, University of Alberta, Edmonton.

Bryan, A. L. and R. Gruhn
1978   "Results of a test excavation at Lapa Pequena, MG, Brazil." Universidad Federal de Minas Gerais, Museu de Historia Natural, Arquivos III: 261-325. Belo Horizonte.

Bryan, A. L., Douglas Schnurrenberger, and Ruth Gruhn
1980   "An early postglacial lithic industry in east-central New York State." AMQUA Handbook.

Bryan, A. L., R. M. Casamiquila, J. M. Cruxent, R. Gruhn, and C. Ochsenius
1978   "An El Jobo mastodon kill at Taima-taima, Venezuela." Science 200: 1275-1277.

Bryson, R. A., W. M. Wendland, J. D. Ives, and J. T. Andrews
1969   "Radiocarbon isochrons on the disintegration of the Laurentide Ice Sheet." Arctic and Alpine Research 1: 1-14.

Bullen, R. P. and W. W. Plowden
1963   "Preceramic archaic site in the highlands of Honduras." American Antiquity 28: 382-385.

Burk, C. A.
1965   "Geology of the Alaska peninsula-island arc and continental margin." Geological Society of America Memoir 99.

Butler, B. Robert
1961   "The Old Cordilleran culture in the Pacific northwest." Occasional Papers of the Idaho State College Museum, No. 5, Pocatello.
1965   "A report on investigations of an early man site near Lake Channel, southern Idaho." Tebiwa 8: 1-20.
1968   "An introduction to archaeological investigations in the Pioneer Basin locality of eastern Idaho." Tebiwa 11: 1-30.
1969   "The earlier cultural remains at Cooper's Ferry." Tebiwa 12: 35-50.
1978   A Guide to Understanding Idaho Archaeology. The Upper Snake and Salmon River County (3rd ed.). Pocatello: Idaho State University.

Calkin, P. E. and J. H. McAndrews
1980   "Geology and paleontology of two late Wisconsinan sites in western New York State." Geological Society of America Bulletin 91: 295-306.

Calkin, P. E. and K. E. Miller
1977   "Late Quaternary environment and man in western New York," in W. S. Newman and B. Salwen (eds.) Amerinds and Their

Paleoenvironments in Northeastern North America. Annals of the New York Academy of Sciences 228: 297-315.

Campbell, E. W.
1949   "Two ancient archaeological sites in the Great Basin." Science 109: 340.

Campbell, E. W. and W. H. Campbell
1937   "The Lake Mohave site," pp. 9-43 in The Archaeology of Pleistocene Lake Mohave: A Symposium. Southwest Museum Papers, No. 11. Los Angeles.

Cardich, A.
1978   "Recent excavations at Lauricocha (central Andes) and Los Toldos (Patagonia)," pp. 296-302 in A. L. Bryan (ed.) Early Man in America from a Circum-Pacific Perspective. Occasional Papers No. 1, Department of Anthropology, University of Alberta, Edmonton.

Carlisle, R. C.
in press   "The Cross Creek drainage in the historic time period," in J. M. Adovasio et al. (eds.) Meadowcroft Rockshelter and the Archaeology of the Cross Creek Drainage. Pittsburgh: University of Pittsburgh Press.

Carlson, C.
1979   "The early component at Bear Cove." Canadian Journal of Archaeology 3: 177-209.

Carlson, R. L.
1960   "Chronology and culture change in the San Juan Islands." American Antiquity 25: 562-586.
1970   "Excavations at Helen Point on Mayne Island." Archaeology in British Columbia, New Discoveries. B.C. Studies No. 6-7: 113-125.
1979   "The early period on the central coast of British Columbia." Canadian Journal of Archaeology 3: 211-228.

Carlson, R. L. and P. M. Hobler
1976   "Archaeological survey of Seymour Inlet, Quatsino Sound, and adjacent localities," pp. 115-141 in R. L. Carlson (ed.) Current Research Reports. Department of Archaeology Publication No. 3, Simon Fraser University.

Carter, George
1957   Pleistocene Man at San Diego. Baltimore, MD: Johns Hopkins Press.
1980   Earlier Than You Think. College Station: Texas A&M Press.

Carter, L.
1973   "Surficial sediments of Barkley Sound and the adjacent continental shelf, west coast Vancouver Island." Canadian Journal of Earth Sciences 10: 441-459.

Chard, C. S.
1974   Northeast Asia in Prehistory. Madison: University of Wisconsin Press.

Chauchat, C. and J. M. Dricot
1979   "Un nouveau type humain fossile en Amerique du Sud: l'homme de Paijan (Perou)." Compte Rendus, Academie des Sciences, Paris 289, Serie D: 387-389.

Chmielewski, Waldemar and Henryk Kubiak
1962   "The find of mammoth bones at Skaratki in the Lowicz district." Folia Quaternaria 9: 27.

Choquette, W.
1982   "Archaeological survey in the Purcell Mountains." Presented at the 35th Northwest Anthropological Conference, Simon Fraser University.

Christiansen, E. A.
1979   "The Wisconsinan deglaciation of southern Saskatchewan and adjacent areas." Canadian Journal of Earth Sciences 16: 913-938.
1980   "The Wisconsinan deglaciation of southern Saskatchewan and adjacent areas: reply to Teller et al." Canadian Journal of Earth Sciences 17: 541.

Churcher, C. J. and A. V. Morgan
1976   "A grizzly bear from the middle Wisconsin of Woodbridge, Ontario." Canadian Journal of Earth Sciences 13: 341-347.

Cinq-Mars, Jacques
1973   "Preliminary archaeological survey, Mackenzie Corridor." Task Force on Northern Oil Development Report No. 73-11, Ottawa.
1974   "Preliminary archaeological survey, Mackenzie Corridor (second report)." Task Force on Northern Oil Development Report No. 74-11, Ottawa.

1975 "Preliminary archaeological survey, Mackenzie Corridor (final report)." Arctic Land Use Research Program 74-75-92, Ottawa.

1978 "Northern Yukon research programme: survey and excavation." Abstracts of the Fifth Conference of the American Quaternary Association. Edmonton.

1979 "Bluefish Cave I: a late Pleistocene eastern Beringian cave deposit in the northern Yukon." Canadian Journal of Archaeology 3: 1-32.

Clague, J. J.
1976 "Quadra sand and its relation to the late Wisconsinan glaciation of southwest British Columbia." Canadian Journal of Earth Sciences 13: 803-815.

1978 "Mid-Wisconsinan climates of the Pacific Northwest." Geological Survey of Canada Paper 78-1B, Current Research, Part B.

1980 "Late Quaternary geology and geochronology of British Columbia, Part 1: radiocarbon dates." Geological Survey of Canada Paper 80-3.

1981 "Late Quaternary geology and geochronology of British Columbia, Part 2: summary and discussion of radiocarbon dated Quaternary history." Geological Survey of Canada Paper 80-35

Clague, J. J., J. E. Armstrong, and W. H. Mathews
1980 "Advance of the Late Wisconsin Cordilleran ice in southern British Columbia since 22,000 B.P." Quaternary Research 13: 322-326.

Clark, Donald W.
1972 "Archaeology of the Batza Téna obsidian source, west-central Alaska." Anthropological Papers of the University of Alaska 15: 1-21.

1973 "Technological continuity and change within a persistent maritime adaptation, Kodiak Island, Alaska." 9th ICAES Preprint.

1979 "Ocean Bay: an early North Pacific maritime culture." National Museum of Man Mercury Series, Archaeological Survey of Canada, Paper No. 86, Ottawa.

Clark, D. W. and A. MacFayden Clark
1975 "Fluted points from the Batza Téna obsidian source of the Koyukuk River region, Alaska." Anthropological Papers of the University of Alaska 17: 31-38.

1980 "Fluted points from the Batza Téna obsidian source, northwestern Interior Alaska," pp. 141-159 in D. L. Browman (ed.) Early Native Americans. The Hague: Mouton.

Clark, John and Kenneth R. Kietzke
1967 "Paleoecology of the Lower Nodular Zone, Brule formation, in the Big Badlands of South Dakota." Fieldiana: Geology Memoirs 5: 111-137.

Clayton, L.
1980 "Review of the Late Wisconsinan chronology of the southwestern margin of the Laurentide Ice Sheet." Abstracts and Program of the Sixth Conference of the American Quaternary Association, Orono, Maine.

Clayton, L. and S. R. Moran
1980 "Styles of glaciation at the southwestern margin of the Laurentide Ice Sheet in Late Wisconsinan time." Abstracts and Program of the Sixth Conference of the American Quaternary Association, Orono, Maine.

CLIMAP
1976 "The surface of the Ice Age Earth." Science 191: 1131-1137.

Cockfield, W. E.
1921 "Sixtymile and Ladue Rivers area, Yukon." Geological Survey of Canada Memoir 123.

Cockrell, W. A. and L. Murphy
1978 "Pleistocene man in Florida." Archaeology of Eastern North America 6: 1-12.

Cole, D. L.
1968 Archaeological Excavations in Area 6 of Site 35GM9, the Wildcat Canyon Site. Eugene: University of Oregon, Museum of Natural History.

Cole, John R. and Laurie R. Godfrey
1977 "On 'Some paleolithic tools from Northeast North America.' " Current Anthropology 18: 541-543.

Cole, John R., Robert E. Funk, Laurie R. Godfrey, and William Starna
1978 "Criticisms of 'Some paleolithic tools from Northeast North America': a rejoinder." Current Anthropology 19: 665-669.

Colinvaux, P. A.
1967 "Quaternary vegetational history of arctic Alaska," pp. 47-90 in D. M. Hopkins (ed.) The Bering Land Bridge. Stanford, CA: Stanford University Press.

1981 "Historical ecology in Beringia: the south Land Bridge coast at St. Paul Island." Quarternary Research 16: 8-36.

Conover, K.
1978 "Matrix analysis," pp. 67-99 in J. J. Hester and S. M. Nelson (eds.) Studies in Bella Bella Prehistory. Publication No. 5 Department of Archaeology, Simon Fraser University.

Cook, John P.
1969 "The early prehistory of Healy Lake, Alaska." Ph.D. dissertation, Department of Anthropology, University of Wisconsin.

1975 "Archaeology of interior Alaska." Western Canadian Journal of Anthropology 5: 125-133.

Cook, John P. (Ed.)
1970 Report of Archaeological Survey and Excavations Along the Alyeska Pipeline Service Company Haulroad and Pipeline Alignments. College: University of Alaska.

1977 Pipeline Archaeology. College: University of Alaska.

Cormie, A. B.
1981 "Chemical correlation of volcanic ashes for use as stratigraphic markers in archaeology." Master's thesis, Simon Fraser University, Burnaby, British Columbia.

Correal Urrego, Gonzalo
1981 Evidencias culturales y megafauna Pleistocénica en Colombia. Banco de la Republica, Bogotá.

1983 Apuntes sobre el medio ambiente Pleistocénico y el hombre prehistórico en Colombia. In A. L. Bryan (ed.) New Evidence for the Pleistocene Peopling of the Americas. Orono: Center for Early Man Studies.

Cowles, John
1959 "Cougar Mountain Cave in south central Oregon." Daily News Press, Rainier, Oregon.

Crabtree, Don E.
1971 "Experiments in flintworking." Reprinted from Tebiwa, the Journal of the Idaho State University Museum, Pocatello.

Cressman, L. S.
1978 Prehistory of the Far West. Salt Lake City: University of Utah Press.

Cressman, L. S., D. L. Cole, W. A. Davis, T. M. Newman, and D. J. Scheans
1960 "Cultural sequences at the Dalles, Oregon." Transactions of the American Philosophical Society 50.

Cronin, T. M.
1977 "Late Wisconsin marine environments of the Champlain Valley (New York, Quebec)." Quaternary Research 7: 238-253.

Cronin, T. M., B. J. Szabo, T. A. Ager, J. E. Hazel, and J. P. Owens
1981 "Quaternary climates and sea levels of the United States Atlantic coastal plain." Science 211: 233-240.

Crook, W. W. and R. K. Harris
1957 Hearths and Artifacts of Early Man near Lewisville, Texas, and Associated Faunal Material. Bulletin of the Texas Archaeological Society 28: 7-97.

1962 "Significance of a new radio-carbon date from the Lewisville Site." Bulletin of the Texas Archaeological Society 32: 327-330.

Curran, M. L. and D. F. Dincauze
1977 "Paleoindians and paleo-lakes: new data from the Connecticut Drainage," in W. S. Newman and B. Salwen (eds.) Amerinds and Their Paleoenvironments in Northeastern North America. Annals of the New York Academy of Sciences 288: 333-348.

Cwynar, L. S. and J. C. Ritchie
1980 "Arctic steppe-tundra: a Yukon perspective." Science 208: 1375-1377.

Dansgaard, W., S. J. Johnson, H. B. Clausen, and C. C. Langway
1971 "Climatic record revealed by the Camp Century ice core," pp. 370-456 in K. K. Turekian (ed.) The Late Cenozoic Glacial Ages. New Haven, CT: Yale University Press.

Daugherty, Richard D.
1956 "Archaeology of the Lind Coulee Site, Washington." Proceedings of the American Philosophical Society 100: 233-278.

Davis, E. L.
1967 "Men and water at Pleistocene Lake Mohave." American Antiquity 32: 345-353.

1978 "The ancient Californians." Science Series 29, Natural History Museum, Los Angeles.

Davis, E. L. and R. Shutler
1969 "Recent discoveries of fluted points in California and Nevada." Nevada State Museum Papers, Vol. 14: 154-169. Carson City.

Davis, E. L., G. Jefferson, and C. McKinney
1981 "Notes on a Mid-Wisconsin date for man and mammoth, China Lake, California," pp. 36-40 in Evidencia de Ocupación Humana en America anterior a 11,500 años a. p. Comisión XII, X Congreso, Union Internacional de Ciencias Prehistoricas y Protohistoricas, Mexico.

Davis, R., T. E. Bradstreet, R. Stuckenrath, and H. W. Borns
1975 "Vegetation and associated environments during the past 14,000 years near Moulton Pond, Maine." Quaternary Research 5: 435-465.

Davis, Stanley
1979 "The Hidden Falls Site." Presented at the Northwest Anthropology Conference, Eugene, Oregon.

Deevey, E. S.
1939 "Studies on Connecticut lake sediments I: a postglacial climatic chronology for southern New England." American Journal of Science 237: 691-724

Deller, Brian D.
1976 "Paleo-Indian locations on late Pleistocene shorelines, Middlesex County, Ontario." Ontario Archaeology 26: 3-7.

Denton, G. H.
1974 "Quaternary glaciations of the White River Valley, Alaska, with a regional synthesis for the northern St. Elias Mountains, Alaska and Yukon Territory." Geological Society of America Bulletin 85: 871-892.

Detterman, R. L. and B. L. Reed
1973 "Surficial deposits of the Iliamna Quadrangle, Alaska." U.S. Geological Survey Bulletin 1365-A.
1980 "Stratification, structure and economic geology of the Iliamna Quadrangle, Alaska." U. S. Geological Survey Bulletin 1368-B.

Dibble, D. S. and D. Lorrain
1968 "Bonfire Shelter: a stratified bison kill site, Val Verde County, Texas." Texas Memorial Museum Miscellaneous Papers 1, Austin.

Dikov, N. N.
1977 Archaeologic Monuments in Kamchatka, Chukotka, and the Upper Reaches of the Kolyma. Moscow: Nauka.
1979 Ancient Cultures of the Northeastern Asia. Moscow: Nauka.

Dillehay, Thomas
1983 "The cultural relationships of Monte Verde: A Late Pleistocene site in the subantarctic forest of south-central Chile," in A. L. Bryan (ed.) New Evidence for the Pleistocene Peopling of the Americas. Orono: Center for Early Man Studies.

Dincauze, D. F.
1981 "The Meadowcroft papers (Adovasio, Gunn, Donahue, Stuckenrath, Guilday, Lord, Volman; Haynes, Mead)." Quarterly Review of Archaeology 2: 3-4.

Dixon, E. James
1976 "The Pleistocene prehistory of Arctic North America." IX Congrès, Union Internationale des Sciences Préhistoriques et Protohistoriques, Colloque XVII: 168-198. Nice.

Dixon, E. James, David C. Plaskett, and Robert M. Thorson
1980 "Report of 1979 archaeological and geological reconnaissance and testing of cave deposits, Porcupine River, Alaska." Report to the Committee for Research and Exploration, National Geographic Society.

Domning, D. P.
1972 "Steller's sea-cow and the origin of North Pacific aboriginal whaling." Syesis 5: 187-189.

Donahue, J., J. M. Adovasio, and D. E. Beynon
1979 "Geological investigations at Meadowcroft Rockshelter." Presented at the 44th Annual Meeting of the Society for American Archaeology, Vancouver.

Donahue, J., P. I.. Storck, J. M. Adovasio, J. D. Gunn, and R. Stuckenrath
1978 "Archaeological sites: Pittsburgh to Toronto," pp. 65-72 in A. L. Currie and W. O. Mackasey (eds.) Toronto '78: Field Trips Guidebook. Geological Association of Canada.

Dragoo, D. W.
1973 "Wells Creek: an early man site in Stewart County, Tennessee." Archaeology of Eastern North America 1: 1-55.
1980 "The trimmed-core tradition in Asiatic-American contacts," pp. 69-81 in D. L. Browman (ed.) Early Native Americans. The Hague: Mouton.

Dreimanis, A.
1977a "Late Wisconsin glacial retreat in the Great Lakes region North America," in W. S. Newman and B. Salwen (eds.) Amerinds and Their Paleoenvironments in Northeastern North America. Annals of the New York Academy of Sciences 288: 70-89.
1977b "Correlation of Wisconsin glacial events between the eastern Great Lakes and the St. Lawrence lowlands." Geographie Physique et Quaternaire 31: 37-52.

Dreimanis, A. and R. P. Goldthwait
1973 "Wisconsin glaciation in the Huron, Erie and Ontario lobes," in R. F. Black et al. (eds.) The Wisconsinan Stage. Geological Society of America Memoir 136: 71-106.

Dreimanis, A. and A. Raukus
1975 "Did middle Wisconsin, middle Weichselian and their equivalents represent an interglacial or an interstadial complex in the Northern Hemisphere?" pp. 109-120 in Quaternary Studies, Selected Papers from the 9th INQUA Congress, Christchurch, New Zealand.

Dumond, Don E.
1969 "Toward a prehistory of the Na-Dene." American Anthropologist 71: 857-863.
1977 The Eskimos and Aleuts. London: Thames and Hudson.
1980 "The archaeology of Alaska and the peopling of America." Science 209: 984-991.

Dumond, Don E., Winfield Henn, and Robert Stuckenrath
1976 "Archaeology and prehistory on the Alaska Peninsula." Anthropological Papers of the University of Alaska 18: 17-29.

Duvall, J. G. and W. T. Venner
1979 "A statistical analysis of lithics from the Calico Site (SBCM 1500A), California." Journal of Field Archaeology 6: 455-462.

Dyke, A. S.
1978 "Glacial history of and marine limits on southern Somerset Island, District of Franklin." Geological Survey of Canada, Paper 78-1B. Current Research Pt. B: 218-223.
1979 "Glacial and sea-level history of southwestern Cumberland Peninsula, Baffin Island, Northwest Territories, Canada." Arctic and Alpine Research 11: 179-202.

Easterbrook, D. J.
1976 "Quaternary geology of the Pacific Northwest, pp. 441-462 in W. C. Mahaney (ed.) Quaternary Stratigraphy of North America. New York: Halstead Press.

Efremov, I.
1940 "Taphonomy: a new branch of paleontology." Pan-American Geologist 74: 81-93.

Elson, J. A.
1967 "Geology of glacial Lake Agassiz," pp. 37-96 in W. J. Mayer-Oakes (ed.) Life, Land, and Water. University of Manitoba Press.

England, J.
1976 "Late Quaternary glaciation of the eastern Queen Elizabeth Islands, Northwest Territories, Canada – alternative models." Quaternary Research 6: 185-202.

England, J. and R. S. Bradley
1978 "Past glacial activity in the Canadian High Arctic." Science 200: 265-270.

Epstein, J. F.
1969 "The San Isidro site: an early man campsite in Nuevo Leon, Mexico." Anthropological Papers of the University of Texas, No. 1.

Eschman, D. F.
1980 "Middle Wisconsinan ice frontal positions in Michigan." Abstracts and Program of the Sixth Conference of the American Quarternary Association, Orono, Maine.

Espinosa, Jorge
1976 "Excavaciónes arqueológicas en El Bosque informe." Instituto Geografico Nacional, Informe No. 1. Managua, Nicaragua.
1982 El reclamo Nicaragüense, síntesis histórica de la evolución antropologica en America. Banco Central de Nicaragua, Managua.

Evans, G. L.
1961 The Friesenhahn Cave. Austin: Texas Museum Bulletin No. 2: 7-22.

Evenson, E. B., W. R. Farrad, and D. F. Eschman
1976 "Great Lakean substage: a replacement for Valderan substage in the Lake Michigan basin." Quaternary Research 6: 411-424.

Fagan, B. M.
1980 People of the Earth: An Introduction to World Prehistory (Third edition). Boston: Little, Brown.

Fagan, M. and B. Suge
1973 Some Windust Points from Oregon." Tebiwa 16: 66-71.

Fairbridge, R. W.
1977 "Discussion paper: Late Quaternary environments in northeastern coastal North America," in W. S. Newman and B. Salwen (eds.) Amerinds and Their Paleoenvironments in Northeastern North America. Annals of the New York Academy of Sciences 288: 90-92.

Farquhar, R. M. and E. Badone
1979 "Neutron activation analysis of fossil bone from Old Crow Flats, northern Yukon." Abstracts of the Twelfth Annual Meeting of the Canadian Archaeological Association.

Farquhar, R. M., N. Bregman, E. Badone, and B. Beebe
1978 "Element concentrations in fossil bones using neutron activation analysis." Presented to the 1978 symposium on Archaeolmetry and Archaeological Prospecting, Bonn, Germany.

Fidalgo, Francisco et al.
1983 "Investigaciones arqueológicas en el sitio 2 de Arroyo Seco," in A. L. Bryan (ed.) New Evidence for the Pleistocene Peopling of the Americas. Orono: Center for Early Man Studies.

Field, M. E., E. P. Meisburger, E. A. Stanley, and S. J. Williams
1979 "Upper Quaternary peat deposits on the Atlantic inner shelf of the United States." Geological Society of America Bulletin 90, Pt. 1: 618-628.

Fillon, R. H.
1980 "A marine viewpoint on late Wisconsin ice sheet growth and disintegration in eastern North America." Abstracts and Program of the Sixth Conference of the American Quaternary Association, Orono, Maine.

Fisher, Daniel C.
1981 "Mastodon butcher site in southeastern Michigan." Unpublished manuscript.

Fitting, James E.
1975 "Climatic change and cultural frontiers in eastern North America." Michigan Archaeologist 21: 25-39.

Fladmark, K. R.
1970 "Preliminary report on the archaeology of the Queen Charlotte Islands," in R. L. Carlson (ed.) Archaeology in British Columbia: New Discoveries. B. C. Studies No. 6-7: 18-45.
1975 "A paleoecological model for northwest coast prehistory," National Museum of Man Mercury Series, Archaeological Survey of Canada, Paper 43.
1978 "The feasibility of the northwest coast as a migration route for early man," in A. L. Bryan (ed.) Early Man in America from a Circum-Pacific Perspective. Occasional Papers No. 1, Department of Anthropology, University of Alberta, Edmonton.
1979 "Routes: alternate migration corridors for early man in North America." American Antiquity 44: 55-69.
1980 "Paleo-Indian artifacts from the Peace River District," in K. R. Fladmark (ed.) Fragments of the Past: B. C. Archaeology in the 1970's. B. C. Studies No. 48: 124-135.
1981 "Microdebitage analysis: initial considerations." Journal of Archaeological Science.

Flannery, Kent V.
1969 "Preliminary archaeological investigation in the valley of Oaxaca, Mexico." Report to the National Science Foundation.

Fleischer, R. L.
1975 "Advances in fission track dating." World Archaeology 7: 136-150.

Fleischer, R. L., P. B. Price, R. M. Walker, and L.S.B. Leakey
1965 "Fission-track dating of Bed I, Olduvai Gorge." Science 148: 72-74.

Flenniken, J. J.
1980 "Systems analysis of the lithic artifacts," in D. R. Croes and E. Blinman (eds.) Hoko River. Reports of Investigations, No. 58.
Pullman: Washington State University Laboratory of Anthropology.
1981 "Replicative systems analysis: the Dyuktai technique, blades and cores." Presented at the 46th SAA, San Diego.

Flint, N. K.
1955 "Geology and mineral resources of Somerset County, Pennsylvania." Pennsylvania Geological Survey County Report C56A.

Flint, R. F.
1971 Glacial and Quaternary Geology. New York: John Wiley and Sons.

Flohn, H.
1979 "On time scales and causes of abrupt paleoclimatic events." Quaternary Research 12: 135-149.

Florer, L. E.
1972 "Quaternary paleoecology and stratigraphy of the sea cliffs, western Olympic Peninsula, Washington." Quaternary Research 2: 202-216.

Florer-Heusser, L. E.
1975 "Late Cenozoic marine palynology of northeast Pacific Ocean cores," in Quaternary Studies: Selected Papers of the 9th IN-QUA Congress, Christchurch, New Zealand.

Foster, Helen L.
1969 "Reconnaissance geology of the Eagle A-land A-2 quadrangles, Alaska." U.S. Geological Survey Bulletin 1271-G.

Foster, J. B.
1965 "The evolution of the mammals of the Queen Charlotte Islands, British Columbia." B.C. Provincial Museum Occasional Paper 14, Victoria.

Fowells, H. A.
1965 "Silvics of forest trees of the United States." U.S. Department of Agriculture Handbook 271.

Frison, George C.
1974 The Casper Site: A Hell Gap Bison Kill on the High Plains. New York: Academic Press.
1976a "The chronology of Paleo-Indian and altithermal cultures in the Bighorn Basin, Wyoming," in Charles E. Cleland (ed.) Cultural Change and Continuity: Essays in Honor of James Bennett Griffin. New York: Academic Press.
1976b "Cultural activity associated with prehistoric mammoth butchering and processing." Science 194: 728-730.
1977 "The Paleo-Indian in the Powder River Basin." Presented at the 35th Plains Anthropological Conference, Lincoln.
1978 Prehistoric Hunters of the High Plains. New York: Academic Press.
1980 "Pryor Stemmed: a specialized late Paleo-Indian ecological adaptation." Plains Anthropologist 25: 27-46.

Frison, George C. and Bruce A. Bradley
1980 Folsom Tools and Technology of the Hanson Site, Wyoming. Albuquerque: University of New Mexico Press.
1981 "Fluting of Folsom points, archaeological evidence." Lithic Technology 10: 13-16.

Frison, G. C. and D. Stanford (eds.)
1982 "The Agate Basin Site: Paleoindian Occupation in Eastern Wyoming." New York: Academic Press.

Frison, George C., M. Wilson, and D. Wilson
1976 "Fossil bison and artifacts from an early altithermal period arroyo trap in Wyoming." American Antiquity 41: 28-57.

Frison, George C. and George Zeimens
1980 "Bone projectile points: an addition to the Folsom cultural complex." American Antiquity 45: 231-237.

Frison, George C., Danny N. Walker, S. D. Webb, and G. Zeimens
1978 "Paleo-Indian procurement of Camelops on the northwestern plains." Quaternary Research 10: 385-400.

Frye, J. C. and H. B. Willman
1973 "Wisconsinan climatic history inferred from Lake Michigan lobe deposits and soils," in R. F. Black et al. (eds.) The Wisconsinan Stage. Geological Society of America, Memoir 136.

Fryxell, R., T. Bielicki, R. Daugherty, C. Gustafson, H. Irwin, and B. Keel
1968 "A human skeleton from sediments of Mid-Pinedale age in southeastern Washington." American Antiquity 33: 511-514.

Fullerton, D. S.
1980 "Preliminary correlation of post-Erie interstadial events (16,000-10,000 radiocarbon years before present), central and

eastern Great Lakes region, and Hudson, Champlain and St. Lawrence lowlands, United States and Canada." U.S. Geological Survey Professional Paper 1089.

Fulton, R. J.
1967   "Deglaciation in the Kamloops region, British Columbia." Geological Survey of Canada Bulletin 154.
1971   "Radiocarbon geochronology of southern British Columbia." Geological Survey of Canada Paper 71-37.
1975   "Quaternary geology and geomorphology Nicola-Vernon area, British Columbia." Geological Survey of Canada, Memoir 380.

Fulton, R. J. and D. A. Hodgson
1979   "Wisconsin glacial retreat, southern Labrador." Geological Survey of Canada Paper 79-1A.

Fulton, R. J. and G. W. Smith
1978   "Pleistocene stratigraphy of south central British Columbia." Canadian Journal of Earth Sciences 15: 971-980.

Gadd, N. R.
1971   "Pleistocene geology of the central St. Lawrence lowlands." Geological Survey of Canada, Memoir 359.

Gal, Robert
1976   "Paleo-Indians of the Brooks Range: a tradition of uncontrolled comparison." Presented to the 41st Annual Meeting of the Society for American Archaeology, St. Louis.

Garcia C., Angel
1973   "Una Punta acanalada en El Estado de Tlaxcala, México." Comunicaciónes 9, Fundación Alemana para la Investigacion Científica. Puebla, Mexico.

Garcia, Joaquin, Diana Santamaria, Ticul Alvarez, Manuel Reyes, and Fernando Sanchez
1976   "Excavaciones en El Abrigo de Santa Mera, Chiapas." INAH Dept. de Prehistora Informes No. 1, México.

Gard, L. M.
1980   "The Pleistocene geology of Amchitka Island, Aleutian Islands, Alaska." U.S. Geological Survey Bulletin 1478.

Gardner, William M.
1974   "The Flint Run Paleo-Indian complex: a preliminary report 1971-1973 seasons." Department of Anthropology, Catholic University of America, Occasional Paper No. 1.
1976   "Paleo-Indian to early Archaic: continuity and change in eastern North America during the Late Pleistocene and early Holocene." IX Congrès, Union Internationale des Sciences Préhistoriques et Protohistoriques, Colloque XVII: 19-46. Nice.
1977   "Flint Run Paleo-Indian complex and its implications for eastern North American prehistory," in W. S. Newman and B. Salwen (eds.) Amerinds and Their Paleoenvironments in Northeastern North America. Annals of the New York Academy of Sciences 288: 257-263.
1979   "The Thunderbird Paleo-Indian Site and the Middle Shenandoah Valley Research Program," pp. 165-175 in National Geographic Research Reports, 1970 Projects. Washington, D.C.

Gaston, J. and G. F. Grabert
1975   Salvage Archaeology at Birch Bay, Washington. Bellingham: Western Washington State University.

Gibbard, P. L. and A. Dreimanis
1978   "Trace fossils from Late Pleistocene glacial lake sediments in southwestern Ontario, Canada." Canadian Journal of Earth Sciences 15: 1967-1976.

Giddings, J. Louis
1954   "Early man in the Arctic." Scientific American 190: 82-88.
1960   "The archaelogy of Bering Strait." Current Anthropology 1: 121-138.

Gillespie, W. H. and J. A. Clendening
1968   "A flora from proglacial Lake Monongahela." Castanea 33: 267-300.

Glennan, W. S.
1976   "The Manix Lake lithic industry: early lithic tradition or workshop refuse." Journal of New World Archaelogy 1: 43-62.

Goldthwait, R. P.
1978   "Glacier Bay refugium – continued access .to early man." Abstracts of the Fifth Conference of the American Quaternary Association, Edmonton.

Goldthwait, R. P., G. W. White, and J. L. Forsythe
1967   Glacial map of Ohio (revised). Washington, DC: Department of the Interior.

Grabert, G. F.
1968   "North-central Washington prehistory." University of Washington Department of Anthropology, Reports in Archaelogy No. 1, Seattle.
1979   "Pebble tools and time factoring." Canadian Journal of Archaelogy 3: 165-175.

Graham, Russell W.
1976   "Pleistocene and Holocene mammals, taphonomy, and paleoecology of the Friesenhahn Cave local fauna, Bexar County, Texas." Ph.D. dissertation, University of Texas Austin.
1981   "Preliminary report on late Pleistocene vertebrates from the Selby and Dutton archaeological/paleontological sites, Yuma County, Colorado." Contributions to Geology, University of Wyoming 20: 33-56.

Graham, R. W., C. V. Haynes, D. L. Johnson, and M. Kay
1981   "Kimmswick: a Clovis-mastodon association in eastern Missouri." Science 213: 1115-1117.

Gramley, Richard M. and Kerry Rutledge
1981   "A new Paleo-Indian site in the state of Maine." American Antiquity 46: 354-360.

Grant, D. R.
1977   "Glacial style and ice limits, the Quaternary stratigraphic record, and changes of land and ocean level in the Atlantic provinces, Canada." Geographie Physique et Quaternaire 31: 247-260.
1980   "Quaternary sea-level change in Atlantic Canada as an indication of crustal delevelling," pp. 201-214 in N. A. Morner (ed.) Earth Rheology, Isostasy and Eustasy. London: John Wiley and Sons.

Greene, Anne Monseth
1967   "The Betty Greene Site: a late Paleo-Indian site in eastern Wyoming." Master's thesis, University of Pennsylvania.

Griffin, James B.
1978   "The midlands and northeastern United States," pp. 221-280 in J. D. Jennings (ed.) Ancient Native Americans. San Francisco: W. H. Freeman.
1979   "The origin and dispersion of American Indians in North America," pp. 43-55 in W. S. Laughlin and A. B. Harper (eds.) The First Americans: Origins, Affinities, and Adaptations. New York: Fischer.

Grimes, John R.
1979   "A new look at Bull Brook." Anthropology 3: 109-130.

Grosswald, M. G.
1980   "Late Weichselian ice sheet of northern Eurasia." Quaternary Research 13: 1-31.

Grüger, E.
1972a   "Late Quaternary vegetation development in south central Illinois." Quaternary Research 2: 217-231.
1972b   "Pollen and seed studies of Wisconsinan vegetation in Illinois, U.S.A." Geological Society of America Bulletin 83: 2715-2734.

Gruhn, Ruth
1961   "The archaeology of Wilson Butte Cave, south-central Idaho." Occasional Papers of the Idaho State College Museum, No. 6.
1965   "Two early radiocarbon dates from the lower levels of Wilson Butte Cave, south-central Idaho." Tebiwa 8: 57.
1978   "A note on excavations at El Bosque, Nicaragua," pp. 261-262 in Al L. Bryan (ed.) Early Man in America from a Circum-Pacific Perspective. Occasional Papers No. 1, Department of Anthropology, University of Alberta, Edmonton.

Gruhn, R., A. L. Bryan, and J. D. Nance
1977   "Los Tapiales: a Paleo-Indian campsite in the Guatemalan Highlands." American Philosophical Society Proceedings 121: 235-273.

Gryba, E. M.
1981   "A fluted point culture tradition component discovered in southwestern Alberta." Calgary Archaeologist 8-9: 18-20.

Guidon, N.
1983   "Las unidades culturales de São Raimundo Nonato, sudeste del Estado de Piaui," in A. L. Bryan (ed.) New Evidence for the Pleistocene Peopling of the Americas. Orono: Center for Early Man Studies.

Gustafson, Carl, Richard Daugherty, and Delbert Gilbow
1979 "The Manis Mastodon Site: early man on the Olympic Peninsula." Canadian Journal of Archaeology 3: 157-164.

Guthrie, R. Dale
1980 "The first Americans? The elusive Arctic bone culture (review of Bonnichsen, 1979)." Quarterly Review of Archaelogy 1: 2.

Haag, W. G.
1962 "The Bering Strait land bridge." Scientific American 206: 112-120.

Haley, S.
1982 "A second look at the Pasika Complex." Presented at the 35th Northwest Anthropological Conference, Simon Fraser University.

Hallam, Sylvia J.
1977 "The relevance of Old World archaeology to the first entry of man into New Worlds: colonization seen from the Antipodes." Quaternary Research 8: 128-148.

Hansen, B. S. and D. J. Easterbrook
1974 "Stratigraphy and palynology of late Quaternary sediments in the Puget lowland, Washington." Geological Society of America Bulletin 85: 587-602.

Hanson, C. Bruce
1980 "Fluvial taphonomic processes: models and experiments," pp. 156-181 in A. Behrensmeyer and A. Hill (eds.) Fossils in the Making. Chicago: University of Chicago Press.

Harington, C. R.
1975 "Pleistocene muskoxen (symbos) from Alberta and British Columbia." Canadian Journal of Earth Sciences 12: 903-919.
1977 "Pleistocene mammals of the Yukon Territory." Ph.D. dissertation, University of Alberta, Edmonton.
1978 "Quaternary vertebrate faunas of Canada and Alaska and their suggested chronological sequence." National Museum of Natural Sciences, Syllogeus 15. Ottawa.
1980a "Radiocarbon dates on some Quaternary mammals and artifacts from northern North America." Arctic 33: 815-832.
1980b "Pleistocene mammals from Lost Chicken Creek, Alaska." Canadian Journal of Earth Sciences 17: 168-198.

Harington, C. R., Robson Bonnichsen, and Richard E. Morlan
1975 "Bones say man lived in Yukon 27,000 years ago." Canadian Geographical Journal 91: 42-48.

Harington, C. R., H. W. Tipper, and R. J. Mott
1974 "Mammoth from Babine Lake, British Columbia." Canadian Journal of Earth Sciences 11: 285-303.

Harlow, W. M. and E. S. Harrar
1969 Textbook of Dendrology. New York: McGraw-Hill.

Haron, R. S., P. Thompson, H. P. Schwarcz, and D. Ford
1978 "Late Pleistocene paleoclimates of North America as inferred from stable isotope studies of speleothems." Quaternary Research 9: 54-70.

Harrington, M. R.
1948 "An ancient site at Borax Lake, California." Southwest Museum Papers, No. 16, Los Angeles.

Harrison, B. and K. Killen
1978 "Lake Theo: a stratified, early man bison butchering and camp site, Briscoe County, Texas." Panhandle Plains Historic Museum, Special Archaeological Report 1, Canyon, Texas.

Haury, E. W.
1950 The Stratigraphy and Archaeology of Ventana Cave, Arizona. Albuquerque and Tucson: The University of New Mexico and University of Arizona Presses.

Hayden, Brian (ed.)
1979 Lithic Use-Wear Analysis. New York: Academic Press.

Haynes, C. Vance, Jr.
1968 "Geochronology of late Quaternary alluvium," pp. 591-631 in R. B. Morrison and H. E. Wright, Jr. (eds.) Means of Correlation of Quaternary Successions. Salt Lake City: University of Utah Press.
1969a "Comment on Early Man in America and the Late Pleistocene Chronology of Western Canada and Alaska, by A. L. Bryan." Current Anthropology 10: 353-354.
1969b "The earliest Americans." Science 166: 709-715.
1970 "Geochronology of man-mammoth sites and their bearing on the origin of the Llano Complex," pp. 72-92 in Wakefield Dort,

Jr., and J. Knox Jones, Jr. (eds.) Pleistocene and Recent Environments of the Central Great Plains. University of Kansas Special Publication No. 3.
1971 "Time, environment, and early man." Arctic Anthropology 8 3-14.
1973 "The Calico Site: artifacts or geofacts?" Science 181: 305-310.
1977 "When and from where did man arrive in northeastern North America? A discussion," pp. 137-160 in W. S. Newman and B. Salwen (eds.) Amerinds and Their Paleoenvironments in Northeastern North America. Annals of the New York Academy of Sciences.
1980a "The Clovis culture." Canadian Journal of Anthropology 1: 115-121.
1980b "Paleo-Indian charcoal from Meadowcroft Rockshelter: Is contamination a problem?" American Antiquity 45: 582-588.
1982 "Were Clovis progenitors in Beringia?" pp. 383-398 D. M. Hopkins et al. (eds.) The Paleoecology of Beringia. New York: Academic Press.

Haynes, Gary
1978 "Morphological damage and alteration to bone: laboratory experiments, field studies, and zoo studies." Abstracts of the Fifth Conference of the American Quaternary Association, Edmonton.
1980a "Evidence of carnivore gnawing of Pleistocene and recent mammalian bones." Paleobiology 6: 341-351.
1980b "Taphonomic studies in North America: analogues for paleoecology." Abstracts of the Sixth Conference of the American Quaternary Association, Orono, Maine.
1981a "Utilization of megafaunal prey carcasses." Abstracts of the Seventh Conference of the American Quaternary Association, Seattle.
1981b "Prey bones and predators: potential ecologic information from analysis of bone sites." Ossa 7.
1981c "Utilization and skeletal disturbances of North American prey carcasses." Arctic 25.
1983 "Frequencies of spiral and green-bone fractures on ungulate limb bones in modern surface assemblages." American Antiquity 48: 102-114.

Heizer, Robert, and Richard Brooks
1965 "Lewisville – ancient campsite or wood rat houses?" Southwestern Journal of Anthropology 21: 155-165.

Henn, W.
1978 "Archaeology of the Alaska peninsula, 1973-1975." Anthropological Papers of the University of Oregon, Eugene.

Hershey, Salley
1979 "The Denver elephant project: bone breaking experiments." Megafauna Punchers Review 1: 28-30.

Herzer, R. H.
1978 "Submarine canyons and slumps on the continental shelf off southern Vancouver Island." Geological Survey of Canada Paper 78-1A. Ottawa.

Hester, J. J.
1972 "Blackwater, Locality No. 1." Publications of the Fort Burgwin Research Center 8. Dallas: Southern Methodist University.

Hester, J. J. and S. M. Nelson (eds.)
1978 "Studies in Bella Bella prehistory." Department of Archaeology Publication No. 5, Simon Fraser University.

Hester, T. R.
1973 "Chronological ordering of Great Basin prehistory." Contributions of the University of California Archaeological Research Facility No. 17, Berkeley.

Hester, T. R., Thomas C. Kelly and Giancarlo Ligabue
1981 "A fluted Paleo-Indian projectile point from Belize, Central America." Center for Archaeological Research, Working Papers No. 1. San Antonio: University of Texas.

Heusser, C. J.
1960 "Late Pleistocene environments of Pacific North America." American Geographical Society Special Publication 35.
1972 "Palynology and phytogeographical significance of a late Pleistocene refugium near Kalaloch, Washington." Quaternary Research 2: 189-201.

1973 "Environmental sequence following the Fraser advance of the Juan de Fuca lobe, Washington." Quaternary Research 3: 284-306.

1974 "Quaternary vegetation, climate and glaciation of the Hoh River Valley, Washington." Geological Society of America Bulletin 85: 1547-1560.

1977 "Quaternary palynology of the Pacific slope of Washington." Quaternary Research 8: 282-306.

Hobler, P. M.
1978 "The relationship of archaeological sites to sea levels on Moresby Island, Queen Charlotte Islands." Canadian Journal of Archaeology 2: 1-14.

Hoffecker, John Frank
n.d. "Activity areas and functional analysis of the Dry Creek site," in W. R. Powers et al., "The Dry Creek site." Unpublished report to the National Park Service.

Holmes, Charles E.
1974 "New evidence for a Late Pleistocene culture in central Alaska: preliminary investigations at Dry Creek." Presented to the 7th Annual Meeting of the Canadian Archaeological Association, Whitehorse.

Hopkins, D. M. (ed.)
1967a The Bering Land Bridge. Stanford, CA: Stanford University Press.

Hopkins, D. M.
1967b "Quaternary marine transgressions in Alaska," pp. 47-90 in D. M. Hopkins (ed.) The Bering Land Bridge. Stanford, CA: Stanford University Press.

1973 "Sea level history in Beringia during the past 250,000 years." Quaternary Research 3: 520-540.

1979 "Landscape and climate of Beringia during Late Pleistocene and Holocene time," pp. 15-41 in W. S. Laughlin and A. B. Harper (eds.) The First Americans: Origins, Affinities and Adaptations. New York: Fischer.

n.d. "Development of the northern hemisphere ice sheets during the past 120,000 years: an aspect of the paleogeography of the Arctic Steppe biome." Presented to the Wenner-Gren Symposium No. 81, Burg Wartenstein.

Hopkins, D. M., P. A. Smith, and J. V. Matthews
1981 "Dated wood from Alaska and the Yukon: implications for Forest Refugium Beringia." Quaternary Research 15: 217-249.

Hopkins, D. M., J. V. Matthews, Jr., C. E. Schweger, and S. B. Young (eds.)
1982 The Paleoecology of Beringia. New York: Academic Press.

Hughes, Jack T.
1949 "Investigations in western South Dakota and northeastern Wyoming." American Antiquity 14: 266-277.

Hughes, O. L.
1972 "Surficial geology of northern Yukon Territory and northwestern District of Mackenzie, Northwest Territories." Geological Survey of Canada, Paper 69-36.

Hughes, O. L., C. R. Harington, J. A. Janssens, J. V. Mathews, Jr., R. E. Morlan, N. W. Rutter, and C. E. Schweger.
1981 "Upper Pleistocene stratigraphy, paleoecology, and archaeology of the northern Yukon interior, eastern Beringia, I: Bonnet Plume Basin." Arctic 34: 329-365.

Hultén, Eric
1937 Outline of the History of Arctic and Boreal Biota During the Quaternary Period. Stockholm: Bokforlagsaktiebologet Thule.

Humphrey, R. L.
1966 "The prehistory of the Utokuk River region, arctic Alaska: early fluted point tradition with Old World relationships." Current Anthropology 7: 586-588.

1970 "The prehistory of the Arctic Slope of Alaska: Pleiocene cultural relationships between Eurasia and North America." Ph.D. dissertation, University of New Mexico.

Humphrey, R. L. and Dennis Stanford (eds.)
1979 Pre-Llano Cultures of the Americas: Paradoxes and Possibilities. Washington, DC: Anthropological Society of Washington.

Hunkins, K. A., W. H. Be, N. D. Opdyke, and G. Mathieu
1971 "The late Cenozoic history of the Arctic Ocean," pp. 215-237 in K. K. Turekion (ed.) The Late Cenozoic Glacial Ages. New Haven, CT: Yale University Press.

Hurt, W. R.
1964 "Recent radiocarbon dates for central and southern Brazil." American Antiquity 30: 25-33.

Hurt, W. R. and O. Blasi
1969 "O projeto arqueologico 'Lagoa Santa,' Minas Gerais, Brasil." Arquivos do Museu Parananse, n.s., Arqueologia No. 4, Curitiba.

Hurt, W. R., T. van der Hammen, and G. Correal U.
1976 "The El Abra Rockshelters, Sabana de Bogotá, Colombia, South America." Occasional Papers and Monographs No. 2. Bloomington: Indiana University Museum.

Husted, W.
1969 "Bighorn Canyon archaeology." River Basin Surveys: Publications in Salvage Archaeology No. 12. Washington, DC: Smithsonian Institution.

Irving, W. N.
1971 "Recent early man research in the North." Arctic Anthropology 8: 68-82.

1978 "Pleistocene archaeology in eastern Beringia," pp. 96-101 in A. L. Bryan (ed.) Early Man in America from a Circum-Pacific Perspective. Occasional Papers No. 1, Department of Anthropology, University of Alberta, Edmonton.

Irving, W. N. and C. R. Harington
1973 "Upper Pleistocene radiocarbon dates artifacts from the Northern Yukon." Science 179: 335-340.

Irving, W. N., J. T. Mayhall, F. J. Melbye, and B. F. Beebe
1977 "A human mandible in probable association with a Pleistocene faunal assemblage in eastern Beringia: a preliminary report." Canadian Journal of Archaeology 1: 81-93.

Irwin-Williams, C.
1967 "Association of early man with horse, camel and mastodon at Hueyatlaco, Valsequillo (Puebla, Mexico)," pp. 337-347 in P. S. Martin (ed.) Pleistocene Extinctions. New Haven, CT: Yale University Press.

Irwin-Williams, C. and C. V. Haynes
1970 "Climatic change and early population dynamics in the southwestern United States." Quaternary Research 1: 59-71.

Irwin-Williams, C., H. Irwin, G. Agogino, and C. V. Haynes
1973 "Hell Gap: Paleo-Indian occupation of the High Plains." Plains Anthropologist 18(59): 40-53.

Ives, J. D.
1974 "Biological refugia and the Nunatak hypothesis," pp. 605-636 in J. D. Ives and R. G. Barry (eds.) Arctic and Alpine Environments. New York: Methuen.

1977 "Were parts of the north coast of Labrador ice-free at the Wisconsin glacial maximum?" Geographie Physique et Quaternaire 31: 401-403.

1978 "The maximum extent of the Laurentide ice sheet along the east coast of North America during the last glaciation." Arctic 31: 24-53.

Ives, J. D., H. Nichols, and S. Short
1976 "Glacial history and paleoecology of northeastern Noveau-Quebec and northern Labrador." Arctic 29: 48-53.

Jackson, L. E., Jr.
1979 "New evidence for the existence of an ice-free corridor in the Rocky Mountain foothills near Calgary, Alberta, during late Wisconsin time." Geological Survey of Canada, Paper 79-1A.

1980a "Glacial history and stratigraphy of the Alberta portion of the Kananaskis Lakes map area." Canadian Journal of Earth Sciences 17: 459-477.

1980b "Quaternary stratigraphy and history of the Alberta portion of the Kananaskis Lakes map area and its implications for the existence of an ice-free corridor during Wisconsinan time." Canadian Journal of Anthropology 1: 9-10.

Jelinek, A. J.
1980 "Human actions and reactions – the archaeological record." Abstracts of the Sixth Conference of the American Quaternary Association, Orono, Maine.

Jennings, Jesse D.
1974 Prehistory of North America (Second edition). New York: McGraw-Hill.

Johnson, E. (ed.)
1977 "Paleoindian lifeways." Museum Journal 17.

Johnson, E. and V. Holliday
1980 "A Plainview kill/butchering locale on the Llano Estacado – the Lubbock Lake Site." Plains Anthropologist 25: 89-111.

Johnson, R. G. and J. T. Andrews
1979   "Rapid ice-sheet growth and initiation of the last glaciation."
Quaternary Research 12: 119-134.
Johnson, W. C.
1981   Archaeological Review Activities in Survey Region IV, Northwestern Pennsylvania. Report prepared for the Pennsylvania
Historical and Museum Commission by the Cultural Resource
Management Program, University of Pittsburgh, under the
supervision of J. M. Adovasio.
Jopling, A. V., W. N. Irving, and B. F. Beebe
1981   "Stratigraphic, sedimentological, and faunal evidence for the
occurrence of the Pre-Sangamonian artifacts in northern
Yukon." Arctic 34: 3-33.
Karlstrom, T.N.V.
1964   "Quaternary geology of the Kenai lowlands and glacial geology
of the Cook Inlet region, Alaska." U.S. Geological Survey Professional Paper 443.
1965   "Upper Cook Inlet area and Matanuska River valley," pp.
114-125 in C. B. Schultz and H. Smith (eds.) INQUA
Guidebook for Field Conference F. Lincoln, NE: Fifth INQUA
Congress.
1969   "Regional setting and geology," pp. 20-55 in T.N.V. Karlstrom
and G. E. Ball (eds.) The Kodiak Island Refugium: Its Geology,
Flora, Fauna and History. Edmonton: Ryerson Press.
Karlstrom, T.N.V. and G. E. Ball (eds.)
1969   The Kodiak Island Refugium: Its Geology, Flora, Fauna and
History. Edmonton: Boreal Institute.
Kaufman, A. and W. S. Broecker
1965   "Comparison of Th^{230} - C^{14} ages for carbonate materials, Lakes
Lahontan and Bonneville." Journal of Geophysical Research
70: 4039-4054.
Klein, R. G.
1976   "Cultural adaptations to Pleistocene 'steppe tundras' in the Old
World." Abstracts of the Fourth Conference of the American
Quaternary Association.
Kern, J. P.
1977   "Origin and history of Upper Pleistocene marine terraces, San
Diego, California." Geological Society of America Bulletin 88:
1553-1566.
Knobel, E. W.
1947   Soil Survey, Akron Area, Colorado. U.S. Department of
Agriculture Series 1938, No. 14.
Knudson, R.
1973   "Organizational variability in late Paleo-Indian assemblages."
Ph.D. dissertation, Washington State University.
Kopper, J. S., R. E. Funk, and Lewis Dumont
1980   "Additional Paleo-Indian and Archaic materials from the Dutchess Quarry Cave area, Orange County, New York." Ar-
chaeology of Eastern North America 8: 125-137.
Kraft, H. C.
1973   "The Plenge Site: a Paleo-Indian occupation site in New Jersey."
Archaeology in Eastern North America 1: 56-117.
1977   "Paleo-Indians in New Jersey," in W. S. Newman and B. Salwen
(eds.) Amerinds in Northeastern North America. Annals of the
New York Academy of Sciences 288: 264-281.
Krantz, G. S.
1969   "Examination of human skeletal remains," in R. Fryxell and
B. C. Keel (eds.) Emergency Salvage Excavations for the
Recovery of Early Human Remains and Related Scientific
Materials from the Marmes Rockshelter Archaeological Site,
Southeastern Washington, May 3-December 15, 1968.
Krieger, A. D.
1964   "Early man in the New World," pp. 28-81 in J. D. Jennings
and E. Norbeck (eds.) Prehistoric Man in the New World.
Chicago: University of Chicago Press.
Krinsley, D. H. and J. C. Doornkamp
1973   Atlas of Quartz Sand Surface Textures. Cambridge, Eng.: Cam-
bridge University Press.
Kroeber, A. L.
1939   Cultural and Natural Areas of Native North America. Berkeley:
University of California Press.
Krumbein, W. C.
1942   "Settling-velocity and flume-behavior of nonspherical particles."
Transactions of the American Geophysical Union 23: 621-632.

Ku, T. L. and J. P. Kern
1974   "Uranium-series age of the Upper Pleistocene Nestor Terrace,
San Diego, California." Geological Society of America Bulletin
85: 1713-1716.
Küchler, A. W.
1964   "Potential natural vegetation of the coterminous United States."
American Geographical Society Special Publication 36.
Kurtén, B. and E. Anderson
1980   Pleistocene Mammals of North America. New York: Colum-
bia University Press.
Lahren, L. A.
1976   The Myers-Hindman Site: An Exploratory Study of Human
Occupation Patterns in the Upper Yellowstone Valley from 7000
B.C. to A.D. 1200. Livingston, MT: Anthropologos Researches
International.
Lahren, L. and R. Bonnichsen
1974   "Bone foreshafts from a Clovis burial in southwestern Mon-
tana." Science 186: 147-150.
Lamb, H. H. and A. Woodroffe
1970   "Atmospheric circulation during the last ice age." Quaternary
Research 1: 29-58.
Laming-Emperaire, A., A. Prous, A. Vilhena de Moraes, and
M. Beltrão
1975   "Grottes et abris de la region de Lagoa Santa, Minas Gerais,
Brasil." Cahiers d'Archeologie d'Amerique du Sud.1, Paris.
Larnach, S. L.
1974   "The origin of the Australian Aboriginal." APA 9 (October).
Laughlin, William S.
1963   "Eskimos and Aleuts: their origins and evolution." Science 142:
633-645.
1966   "Genetical and anthropological characteristics of Arctic populations," pp. 469-495 in J. S. Weiner and P. Baker (eds.) The
Biology of Human Adaptability.
1979   "Problems in the physical anthropology of North American Indians, Eskimos and Aleuts." Arctic Anthropology 16: 165-177.
1980   Aleuts: Survivors of the Bering Land Bridge. New York: Holt,
Rinehart & Winston.
Laughlin, William S., Jørgen B. Jørgensen, and Bruno Fröhlich
1979   "Aleuts and Eskimos: survivors of the Bering Land Bridge coast,"
pp. 91-104 in W. S. Laughlin and A. B. Harper (eds.) The First
Americans: Origins, Affinities, and Adaptations. New York:
Gustav Fischer.
Layton, Thomas N.
1972   "Lithic chronology in the Fort Rock Valley, Oregon." Tebiwa
15: 1-21.
Leakey, L.S.B., Ruth D. Simpson, and Thomas Clemento
1968   "Archaeological excavations in the Calico Mountains, California: preliminary report." Science 160: 1022-1023.
Leonhardy, F. C. and D. G. Rice
1970   "A proposed culture typology for the Lower Snake River region,
southeastern Washington." Northwest Anthropological Research
Notes 4: 1-29.
Lewis, R. O.
1978   "Use of opal phytoliths on paleo-environmental reconstruction
at the Hudson-Meng Site," in Larry D. Agenbroad (ed.) The
Hudson-Meng Site: An Alberta Bison Kill in the Nebraska High
Plains. Washington, DC: University Press of America.
Libby, W. F.
1952   Radiocarbon Dating. Chicago: University of Chicago Press.
Lichti-Federovich, S.
1970   "The pollen stratigraphy of a dated section of Late Pleistocene
lake sediments from central Alberta." Canadian Journal of Earth
Sciences 7: 938-945.
Lindroth, C. H.
1969   "The biological importance of Pleistocene refugia," pp. 7-19
in T.N.V. Karlstrom and G. E. Ball (eds.) The Kodiak Island
Refugium: Its Geology, Flora, Fauna and History. Edmonton:
Boreal Institute.
1970   "Survival of animals and plants in ice-free refugia during
Pleistocene glaciations." Endeavour 24: 129-134.
Lord, K.
in press   "Molluscan fauna from Meadowcroft Rockshelter and the
Cross Creek Drainage," in J. M. Adovasio et al. (eds.)

Meadowcroft Rockshelter and the Archaeology of the Cross Creek Drainage. Pittsburgh: University of Pittsburgh Press.

Luebbers, R.
1978   "Excavations: stratigraphy and artifacts," pp. 11-66 in J. J. Hester and S. M. Nelson (eds.) Studies in Bella Bella Prehistory. Department of Archaeology, Simon Fraser University, Publication No. 5

Luternauer, J. L.
1972   "Patterns of sedimentation in Queen Charlotte Sound, B.C." Ph.D. dissertation, Department of Geology and the Institute of Oceanography, University of British Columbia, Vancouver.

Lynch, Thomas F.
1974   "Early man in South America." Quaternary Research 4: 356-377.
1976   "The entry and postglacial adaptation of man in Andean South America," pp. 69-100 in J. B. Griffin (compiler) Habitats Humains anterieurs à L'Holocene en Amerique. Union Internationale des Sciences Prehistoriques et Protohistoriques, IX Congress, Nice.
1978   "The South American Paleo-Indians," pp. 455-489 in J. D. Jennings (ed.) Ancient Native Americans. San Francisco: W. H. Freeman.

MacDonald, G. F.
1968   "Debert: a Paleo-Indian site in central Nova Scotia." Anthropological Papers No. 16, National Museum of Canada.
1971   "A review of research on Paleo-Indian in eastern North America, 1960-1970." Arctic Anthropology 8: 32-42.

MacDougall, D. and P. B. Price
1974   "Attempt to date early South African hominids by using fission tracks in calcite." Science 185: 943-944.

Macgowan, K.
1950   Early Man in the New World. New York: Macmillan.

Macintosh, N.W.G.
1972   "Radiocarbon dating as a pointer in time to the arrival and history of men in Australia and islands to the Northwest." Proceedings: 8th International Conference on Radiocarbon Dating, Wellington, New Zealand.

Macintosh, N.W.G. and S. L. Larnach
1976   "Aboriginal affinities looked at in world context," pp. 113-126 in R. L. Kirk and A. G. Thorne (eds.) The Origin of the Australians. Canberra: Australian Institute of Aboriginal Studies.

MacNeish, Richard S.
1958   "Preliminary archaeological investigations in the Sierra de Tamaulipas, Mexico." Transactions of the American Philosophical Society 48.
1971   "Early man in the Andes." Scientific American 224: 36-46.
1975   "Excavations and reconnaissance." The Prehistory of the Tehuacan Valley, Vol. 5. Austin: University of Texas Press.
1976   "Early man in the New World." American Scientist 63: 316-327.
1978   "Late Pleistocene adaptations: a look at early peopling of the New World as of 1976." Journal of Antropological Research 34: 475-496.
1979a   "Earliest man in the New World and its implications for Soviet-American archaeology." Arctic Anthropology 16: 2-15.
1979b   "The Early Man remains from Pikimachay Cave, Ayacucho Basin, Highland Peru,"pp. 1-47 in R. L. Humphrey and D. Stanford (eds.) Pre-Llano Cultures of the Americas: Paradoxes and Possibilities. Washington, DC: Anthropological Society of Washington.
1981   "The stratigraphy of Pikimachay, Ac Serie," pp. 19-56 in Prehistory of the Ayacucho Basin, Volume 2: Excavations and Chronology. Ann Arbor: University of Michigan Press.

MacNeish, R. S. and Frederick A. Peterson
1962   "The Santa Marta Rock Shelter, Ocozocoautla, Chiapas." Provo, UT: New World Archaeological Foundation, Paper No. 14.

MacNeish, R. S., A. Nelken-Terner, and Irmgard Johnson
1967   The Prehistory of the Tehuacan Valley, Vol. 2. Austin: University of Texas Press.

MacNeish, R. S., S. Jeffrey, K. Wilkerson, and A. Nelken-Terner
1980   First Annual Report of the Belize Archaic Archaeological Reconnaissance. Andover, MA: Robert S. Peabody Foundation.

Maglio, Vincent J.
1973   "Origin and evolution of the Elephantidae." Transactions of the American Philosophical Society 63.

Mall, Roberto Garcia
1977   "Analisis de los materiales arqueológicos de la Cueva del Texcal, Puebla," in Dept. de Prehistoria Colección Cientifica No. 56, Mexico: INAH.

Martin, Paul S.
1958   "Pleistocene ecology and biogeography of North America," pp. 375-405 in C. L. Hubbs (ed.) Zoogeography. American Association for the Advancement of Science Publication 51.
1973   "The discovery of America." Science 179: 969-974.

Martin, P. S. and H. E. Wright, Jr.
1967   Pleistocene Extinctions: The Search for a Cause. New Haven, CT: Yale University Press.

Mathewes, R. W.
1973   "A palynological study of postglacial vegetation changes in the University Research Forest, southwestern British Columbia." Canadian Journal of Botany 51: 2085-2103.
1979   "A paleoecological analysis of Quadra Sand at Point Grey, British Columbia, based on indicator pollen." Canadian Journal of Earth Sciences 16: 847-858.

Mathews, W. H.
1979   "Late Quaternary environmental history affecting human history of the Pacific northwest." Canadian Journal of Archaeology 3: 145-156.
1980   "Retreat of the last ice sheets in northeastern British Columbia and adjacent Alberta." Geological Survey of Canada Bulletin 331.

Mathews, W. H., J. G. Fyles, and H. W. Nasmith
1970   "Postglacial crustal movements in southern British Columbia and adjacent Washington State." Canadian Journal of Earth Sciences 7: 690-702.

Matson, R. G.
1976   "The Glenrose Cannery Site." National Museum of Man Mercury Series, Archaeological Survey of Canada, Paper No. 52, Ottawa.

Matthews, J. V., Jr.
1974   "Wisconsin environment of interior Alaska: pollen and microfossil analysis of a 27 m core from the Isabella Basin, Fairbanks, Alaska." Canadian Journal of Earth Sciences 11: 828-842.
1975   "Insects and plant macrofossils from two Quaternary exposures in the Old Crow-Porcupine region, Yukon Territory, Canada." Arctic and Alpine Research 7: 249-259.
1980   "Possible evidence of Early Wisconsinan warm interstadial in East Beringia." Abstracts of the Sixth Conference of the American Quaternary Association, Orono, Maine.
1982   "East Beringia during late Wisconsinan time: Arctic-steppe or fell-field? A review of the biotic evidence," pp. 127-152 in D. M. Hopkins et al. (eds.) The Paleoecology of Beringia. New York: Academic Press.

Maxwell, J. A. and M. B. Davis
1972   "Pollen evidence of Pleistocene and Holocene vegetation on the Allegheney Plateau, Maryland." Quaternary Research 2: 506-530.

Mayer-Oakes, W. J.
1983   "Early man projectile points and lithic technology in the Ecuadorean Sierra," in A. L. Bryan (ed.) New Evidence for the Pleistocene Peopling of the Americas. Orono: Center for Early Man Studies.

McCary, B. C.
1951   "A workshop of early man in Dinwiddie County, Virginia." American Antiquity 17: 9-17.

McConaughy, M. A., J. D. Applegarth, and D. F. Faignaert
1977   "Fluted points from Slippery Rock, Pennsylvania." Pennsylvania Archaeologist 47: 30-36.

McCracken, Harold (ed.)
1978   The Mummy Cave Project in Northwestern Wyoming. Cody: Buffalo Bill Historical Center.

McDonald, B. C.
1971   "Late Quaternary stratigraphy and deglaciation in eastern Canada," pp. 331-353 in K. K. Turekian (ed.) The Late Cenozoic Glacial Ages. New Haven, CT. Yale University Press.

McGhee, Robert and James A. Tuck
1975   "An archaic sequence from the Strait of Belle Isle, Labrador." National Museum of Man Mercury Series Paper No. 34, Ottawa.

McKennan, R. A. and J. P. Cook
  1968 "Prehistory of Healy Lake, Alaska." Proceedings of the VIIIth International Congress of Anthropological and Ethnological Sciences 3: 182-184. Tokyo.
McKenzie, G. D. and R. P. Goldthwait
  1971 "Glacial history of the last eleven thousand years in Adams Inlet, southeastern Alaska." Geological Society of America Bulletin 82: 1767-1782.
McLaren, P. M. and D. M. Barnett
  1978 "Holocene emergence of the south and east coasts of Melville Island, Queen Elizabeth Islands, Northwest Territories, Canada." Arctic 31: 415-427.
McNett, Charles W., Jr., Barbara A. McMillan, and Sydne B. Marshall
  1977 "The Shawnee-Minisink Site," in W. S. Newman and B. Salwen (eds.) Amerinds and Their Paleoenvironments in Northeastern North America. Annals of the New York Academy of Sciences 288: 282-296.
McPherson, A. H.
  1965 "The origin of diversity in mammals of the Canadian Arctic tundra." Systematic Zoology 14: 153-173.
Mead, J. I.
  1980 "Is it really that old? A comment about the Meadowcroft Rockshelter 'Overview.'" American Antiquity 45: 579-582.
Mehl, Maurice G.
  1966 "The Grundel mastodon." Report of the Investigations of the Missouri Geological Survey and Water Resources 35.
Mercer, J. H.
  1972 "The lower boundary of the Holocene." Quaternary Research 2: 15-24.
Miller, G. H.
  1980 "Late Foxe glaciation of southern Baffin Island, Northwest Territories, Canada." Geological Society of America Bulletin 9: 399-405.
Miller, M. M.
  1976 "Quaternary erosional and stratigraphic sequences in the Alaska-Canada Boundary Range," pp. 463-492 in W. C. Mahaney (ed.) Quaternary Stratigraphy of North America. New York: Halstead Press.
Miller, S. J. and W. Dort
  1978 "Early Man at Owl Cave: current investigations at the Wasden Site, eastern Snake River Plain, Idaho," pp. 129-139 in A. L. Bryan (ed.) Early Man in America from a Circum-Pacific Perspective. Occasional Papers No. 1 of the Department of Anthropology, University of Alberta, Edmonton.
Miller, R. D.
  1973 "Gastineau Channel Formation, a composite glaciomarine deposit near Juneau, Alaska." U.S. Geological Survey Bulletin 1394-C.
  1975 "Surficial geologic map of the Juneau urban area and vicinity, Alaska." Miscellaneous Investigation Series, U.S. Geological Survey.
Minor, R.
  1979 "An early lithic complex near the mouth of the Columbia River." Presented at the 32nd Annual Northwest Anthropological Conference.
Mirambell, Lorena
  1973 "El Hombre en Tlapacoya desde hace unos 20 mil anos." INAH Boletin (epoca II) 4: 3-8. Mexico City.
Mitchell, D.
  1965 "Preliminary excavations at a cobble tool site (DjRl 7) in the Fraser Canyon, British Columbia." Anthropological Papers 10, National Museum of Man, Ottawa.
Mochanov, Yu. A.
  1977 Drevneishie etapy zaseleniia chelovekom Severo-Vostochnoi Azii (Most Ancient Stages of Human Settlement in Northeast Asia). Novosibirsk: Nauka.
  1978 "Stratigraphy and absolute chronology of the Paleolithic of Northeast Asia," pp. 54-66 in A. L. Bryan (ed.) Early Man in America from a Circum-Pacific Perspective. Occasional Papers No. 1, Department of Anthropology, University of Alberta, Edmonton.
  1980 "Early migration to America: Dyuktai culture," pp. 119-132 in D. L. Browman (ed.) Early Native Americans. The Hague: Mouton.
Moeller, Roger W.
  1980 "6LF21: a Paleo-Indian site in western Connecticut." Occasional Paper No. 2, American Indian Archaeological Institute.
Money, D. C.
  1965 Climate, Soils and Vegetation. London: University Tutorial Press.
Montané, Julio
  1968 "Paleo-Indian remains from Laguna de Tagua-Tagua, central Chile." Science 161: 1137-1138.
Moody, U.
  1978 "Microstratigraphy, paleoecology, and tephrochronology of the Lind Coulee Site, central Washington." Ph.D. dissertation, Washington State University.
Moore, T. C.
  1973 "Late Pleistocene-Holocene oceanographic changes in the northeastern Pacific." Quaternary Research 3: 99-109.
Morlan, R. E.
  1974 "Archaeological resource management in Yukon Territory," pp. 142-153 in S. Raymond and P. Schlederman (eds.) Proceedings of the International Conference on the Prehistory and Paleoecology of the Western North American Arctic and Subarctic, Department of Anthropology, University of Calgary.
  1977 "Fluted point makers and the extinction of the Arctic-Steppe biome in eastern Beringia." Canadian Journal of Archaeology 1: 95-108.
  1978 "Early Man in northern Yukon Territory: perspectives of 1977," pp. 78-95 in A. L. Bryan (ed.) Early Man in America from a Circum-Pacific Perspective. Occasional Papers No. 1 of the Department of Anthropology, University of Alberta, Edmonton.
  1979 "A stratigraphic framework for Pleistocene artifacts from Old Crow River, northern Yukon Territory," pp. 125-145 in R. L. Humphrey and D. Stanford (eds.) Pre-Llano Cultures in the Americas: Paradoxes and Possibilities. Washington, DC: Anthropological Society of Washington.
  1980a "Taphonomy and archaeology in the upper Pleistocene of the northern Yukon Territory: a glimpse of the peopling of the New World." Archaeological Survey of Canada, Mercury Series Paper No. 94, National Museum of Man, Ottawa.
  1980b "Taphonomy as an aid to archaeological reconnaissance and interpretation: an example from northern Yukon Territory." Abstracts of the Sixth Conference of the American Quaternary Association, Orono, Maine.
Morlan, R. E. and Jacques Cinq-Mars
  1982 "Ancient Beringians: human occupations in the Late Pleistocene of Alaska and the Yukon Territory," pp. 353-381 in D. M. Hopkins et al. (eds.) The Paleoecology of Beringia. New York: Academic Press.
Morlan, R. E. and J. V. Matthews, Jr.
  1978 "New Dates for Early Man." GEOS Winter 1978: 2-5.
Morner, N. A.
  1973 "The Erie Interstade," pp. 107-134 in R. F. Black et al. (eds.) The Wisconsinan Stage. Geological Society of America Memoir 136.
  1977 "Climatic framework at the end of the Pleistocene and the Holocene: paleo-climatic variations during the last 35,000 years." Geographie Physique et Quaternaire 31: 23-36.
Mott, R. J.
  1975 "Palynological studies of lake sediment profiles from southwestern New Brunswick." Canadian Journal of Earth Sciences 12: 273-288.
  1977 "Late Pleistocene and Holocene palynology in southeastern Quebec." Geographie Physique et Quaternaire 31: 139-150.
Mott, R. J. and L. D. Farley-Gill
  1978 "A late Quaternary pollen profile from Woodstock, Ontario." Canadian Journal of Earth Sciences 15: 1101-1111.
Muller, E. H.
  1963 "Geology of Chautaqua County, New York, Part II: Pleistocene geology." New York State Museum and Science Service Bulletin 392, Albany.

Muller, J. and T. D. Milliman
  1973 "Relict carbonate-rich sediments on southeastern Grand Bank, Newfoundland." Canadian Journal of Earth Sciences 10: 1744-1750.
Muller, R. A.
  1977 "Radioisotope dating with a cyclotron." Science 196: 489-494.
Mullineaux, D. R., R. E. Wilcox, R. Fryxell, and M. Rubin
  1978 "Age of the last major Scabland flood of the Columbia plateau in eastern Washington. Quaternary Research 10: 171-180.
Murray, D. F.
  1980 "Balsam poplar in Arctic Alaska." Canadian Journal of Anthropology 1: 29-32.
Myers, T.
  1979 "Clary Ranch: a late Paleo-Indian site in western Nebraska." Presented at the 37th Plains Conference, Kansas City, MO.
Nelson, A. R.
  1980 "Chronology of Quaternary landforms, Quivitu Peninsula, northern Cumberland Peninsula, Baffin Island, Northwest Territories, Canada." Arctic and Alpine Research 12: 265-286.
Nelson, D. E., R. G. Korteling, and W. F. Stott
  1977 "Carbon-14: direct detection at natural concentrations." Science 198: 507-508.
Nelson, N.
  1937 "Notes on cultural relations between Asia and America." American Antiquity 2: 367-372.
Newman, T. M.
  1966 "Cascadia Cave." Occasional Papers of the Idaho State University Museum, No. 18, Pocatello.
Ochietti, S.
  1977 "Stratigraphie du Wisconsinien de la region de Trois Rivieres-Shawnigan, Quebec. " Geographie Physique et Quaternaire 31: 307-322.
Ochsenius, Claudio and Ruth Gruhn (eds.)
  1981 Taima-Taima: Final Report of the 1976 Excavation. Monografías Científicas, Programa CIPICS, Universidad Francisco de Miranda, Coro, Venezuela.
Ogden, J. G. III
  1977 "The late Quaternary paleoenvironmental record of northeastern North America," in W. S. Newman and B. Salwen (eds.) Amerinds and Their Paleoenvironments in Northeastern North America. Annals of the New York Academy of Sciences 288: 16-34.
Olson, E.
  1980 "Taphonomy: its history and role in community evolution," in A. Behrensmeyer and A. Hill (eds.) Fossils in the Making. Chicago: University of Chicago Press.
Ore, T. H. and C. N. Warren
  1971 "Late Pleistocene-early Holocene geomorphic history of Lake Mojave, California." Geological Society of America Bulletin 82: 2553-2562.
Orr, Phil C.
  1968 Prehistory of Santa Rosa Island. Santa Barbara, CA: Santa Barbara Museum of Natural History.
Osborne, H. D.
  1956 "Early lithic in the Pacific Northwest." Research Studies of the State College of Washington 24: 38-44. Pullman.
Packer, J. G.
  1980 "Paleoecology of the ice-free corridor: the phytopographical evidence." Canadian Journal of Anthropolgy 1: 33-36.
Palanca, F. and G. Politis
  1979 "Los cazadores de fauna extinguida de la Provincia de Buenos Aires," pp. 69-91 in Prehistoria Bonaerense. Olavarria: Municipalidad de Olavarria.
Park, Edward
  1978 "The Ginsberg caper: hacking it as in the Stone Age." Smithsonian 9: 85-96.
Patterson, Leland W.
  1980 "Comments on a statistical analysis of lithics from Calico." Journal of Field Archaeology 7: 374-377.
Paula Couto, Carlos de
  1950 Peter Wilhelm Lund: Memorias sobre a Paleontologia Brasileira. Rio de Janeiro: Instituto Nacional do Livro.
Pearson, R.
  1978 "Image and life: 50,000 years of Japanese prehistory." Museum

Note 5, University of British Columbia. Museum of Anthropology, Vancouver.
Pettigrew, R.
  1975 "Cultural Resources Survey in the Alvord Basin Southeastern Oregon." Unpublished manuscript, Department of Anthropology, University of Oregon.
Péwé, T. L.
  1975a "Quaternary geology of Alaska." U.S. Geological Survey Professional Paper 835.
  1975b "Quaternary stratigraphic nomenclature in unglaciated central Alaska." U.S. Geological Survey Paper 852.
  1976 "Late Cenozoic history of Alaska," pp. 494-506 in W. C. Mahaney (ed.) Quaternary Stratigraphy of North America. New York: Halstead Press.
Péwé, T. L., D. M. Hopkins, and J. L. Giddings
  1965 "The Quaternary geology and archaeology of Alaska," pp. 355-374 in H. E. Wright and D. G. Frey (eds.)The Quaternary of the United States. Princeton, NJ: Princeton University Press.
Porter, Lee
  1979 "Ecology of a Late Pleistocene (Wisconsin) ungulate community near Jack Wade, east central Alaska." MSc. thesis, University of Washington.
Porter, Lee and D. M. Hopkins
  in press "Butchered caribou skulls, Pleistocene and Recent, from eastern Beringia." American Antiquity.
Porter, S. C.
  1978 "Glacier Peak tephra in the North Cascade Range, Washington: stratigraphy, distribution, and relationship to late glacial events." Quaternary Research 10: 30-41.
Post, A.
  1976 "The tilted forest: glaciological-geologic implications of vegetated neoglacial ice at Lituya Bay, Alaska." Quaternary Research 6: 111-117.
Powers, W. R.
  1973 "Paleolithic man in northeast Asia." Arctic Anthropology 10: 1-106.
  1978 "Perspectives on Early Man, pp. 114-122 in Abstracts of the Fifth Conference of the American Quaternary Association, Edmonton.
  n.d. "Dry Creek and its place in the early archaeology of the north," in W. R. Powers et al., "The Dry Creek Site." Unpublished Report.
Powers, W. Roger, R. Dale Guthrie, and John F. Hoffecker
  n.d. "The Dry Creek site." Unpublished report.
Powers, W. R. and Thomas D. Hamilton
  1978 "Dry Creek: a Late Pleistocene human occupation in central Alaska," pp. 72-77 in A. L. Bryan (ed.) Early Man in America from a Circum-Pacific Perspective. Occasional Papers No. 1, Department of Anthropology, University of Alberta, Edmonton.
Prest, V. K.
  1969 "Retreat of Wisconsin and recent ice in North America." Geological Survey of Canada Map 1251A.
  1977 "General stratigraphic framework of the Quaternary in eastern Canada." Geographie Physique et Quaternaire 31: 7-14.
Prest, V. K., D. R. Grant, and V. N. Rampton
  1969 "Glacial map of Canada." Geological Survey of Canada Map 1253A.
Prichonnet, G.
  1977 "La deglaciation de la vallée du Saint-Laurent et l'envasion marine contemporaine." Geographie Physique et Quaternaire 31: 323-346.
Prous, A.
  1983 "Os mais antigos vestígios arqueológicos no Brasil Central (Estados de Minas Gerais, Goiás e Babia)," in A. L. Bryan (ed.) New Evidence for the Pleistocene Peopling of the Americas. Orono: Center for Early Man Studies.
Raemsch, Bruce E. and William W. Vernon
  1977 "Some paleolithic tools from northeast North America." Current Anthropology 18: 97-99.
Rampton, V.
  1971 "Late Quaternary vegetational and climatic history of the Snag-Klutlan area, southwestern Yukon Territory, Canada." Geological Society of America Bulletin 82: 959-978.

Rancier, J., G. Haynes, and D. Stanford
1981   "Investigations of Lamb Spring." Southwestern Lore.
Ranere, A.
1976   "The preceramic of Panama: the view from the interior," pp. 103-137 in Proceedings of the first Puerto Rican Symposium on Archaeology. Fundacion Arqueológica Antropológia e Historia de Puerto Rico, San Juan.
1980   "Human movement in tropical America at the end of the Pleistocene," pp. 41-46 in L. B. Harten et al. (eds.) Anthropological Papers in Memory of Earl H. Swanson, Jr. Pocatello: Idaho Museum of Natural History.
Rannie, W. F.
1977   "A note on the effect of a glacier on the summer thermal climate of an ice-marginal area." Arctic and Alpine Research 9: 301-304.
Reagan, M. S., R. M. Rowlett, E. G. Garrison, W. Dort, V. Bryant, and Chris Johannsen
1978   "Flake tools stratified below Paleo-Indian artifacts." Science 200 1272-1275.
Reeves, B.O.K.
1971   "On the coalescence of the Laurentide and Cordilleran ice-sheets in the western interior of North America with particular reference to the Alberta area," pp. 205-228 in A. H. Stryd and R. H. Smith (eds.) Aboriginal Man and Environments on the Plateau of Northwest America. Calgary: University of Calgary Archaeological Association.
1973   "The nature and age of the contact between the Laurentide and Cordilleran ice sheets in the western interior of North America." Arctic and Alpine Research 5: 1-16.
1975   "Early Holocene (ca. 8,000 to 5,500 B.C.) prehistoric land resource utilization patterns in Waterton Lakes National Park, Alberta." Arctic and Alpine Research 7: 237-248.
1981   "Mission River and the Texas Street question," p. 47 in Evidencia Arqueológica de ocupación humana en America anterior a 11,500 anos a.p. Comisión XII, X Congreso, Union Internacional de Ciencias Prehistoricas y Protohistoricas, Mexico, D.F.
Reher, Charles A.
1974   "Population study of the Casper Site bison," pp. 113-124 in G. C. Frison (ed.) The Casper Site: A Hell Gap Bison Kill on the High Plains. New York: Academic Press.
n.d.   "Paleoecological and archaeological interpretation of a sub-fossil bison population from the Jones-Miller site," in D. Stanford (ed.) The Jones-Miller Site.
Reid, J. R.
1970   "Lake Wisconsin and neoglacial history of the Martin River Glacier, Alaska." Geological Society of America Bulletin 81: 3493-3604.
Reider, R. G.
1980   "Late Pleistocene and Holocene soils of the Carter/Kerr-McGhee Archaeological Site, Powder River Basin, Wyoming." Catena 7: 301-315.
Rice, D. G.
1972   "The Windust Phase in Lower Snake River region prehistory." Washington State University Laboratory of Anthropology, Report of Investigations 50. Pullman.
Richard, P.
1977   "Vegetational tardiglaciare au Quebec merdional et implications paleoclimatiques." Geographie Physique et Quaternaire 31: 161-176.
Ritchie, J. D.
1980   "Towards a late Quaternary paleoecology of the ice-free corridor." Canadian Journal of Anthropology 1: 15-27.
Ritchie, J. D. and Les C. Cwynar
1982   "The Late Quaternary vegetation of the North Yukon," pp. 113-126 in D. Hopkins et al. (eds.) The Paleoecology of Beringia. New York: Academic Press.
Ritchie, J. D. and F. K. Hare
1971   "Late Quaternary vegetation and climate near the Arctic treeline of northwestern North America." Quaternary Research 1: 331-342.
Ritchie, William A. and Robert E. Funk
1973   "Aboriginal settlement patterns in the northeast." Memoir 20 New York State Museum and Science Service.

Roed, M. A.
1975   "Cordilleran and Laurentide multiple glaciation west-central Alberta, Canada." Canadian Journal of Earth Sciences 12: 1493-1515.
Rogers, M. J.
1939   "Early lithic industries of the lower basin of the Colorado River and adjacent desert areas." San Diego Museum Papers, No. 3.
1966   "Ancient hunters of the Far West." San Diego Union Tribune.
Roosa, William B.
1977   "Great Lakes Paleo-Indian: the Parkhill Site, Ontario," in W. S. Newman and B. Salwen (eds.) Amerinds and Their Paleoenvironments in North America. Annals of the New York Academy of Sciences 288: 349-354.
Rouse, Irving
1976   "Peopling of the Americas." Quaternary Research 6: 567-612.
Rouse, I. and J. M. Cruxent
1963   Venezuelan Archaeology. New Haven, CT: Yale University Press.
Ruddiman W. F. and A. MacIntyre
1979   "Warmth of the subpolar north Atlantic Ocean during Northern Hemisphere ice-sheet growth." Science 204: 173-175.
Ruddiman, W. F., A. MacIntyre, V. Niebler-Hurt, and J. T. Durazzi
1980   "Oceanic evidence for the mechanism of rapid northern hemisphere glaciation." Quaternary Research 13: 33-64.
Rutter, N. W.
1976   "Multiple glaciation in the Canadian Rocky Mountains with special emphasis on northeastern British Columbia," pp. 409-439 in W. C. Mahaney (ed.) Quaternary Stratigraphy of North America. New York: Halstead Press.
1980   "Late Pleistocene history of the western Canadian ice-free corridor." Canadian Journal of Anthropology 1: 1-8.
Saarnisto, M.
1974   "The deglaciation history of the Lake Superior region and its climatic implications." Quaternary Research 4: 316-339.
Sanger, D.
1966   "Excavations in the Lochnore-Nesikep Creek locality, British Columbia Interior Report." Anthropological Paper No. 12, National Museum of Canada.
1967   "The southwestern periphery of the Northwest Microblade tradition." Presented at the 32nd Meeting of the Society for American Archaeology, Ann Arbor.
1968   "Prepared core and blade traditions in the Pacific Northwest." Arctic Anthropology 5.
1970   "The archaeology of the Lochnore-Nesikep Creek locality, British Columbia." Syesis 3, Supplement 1.
St. Onge, D. A.
1980   "The Wisconsin deglaciation of southern Saskatchewan and adjacent areas: discussion." Canadian Journal of Earth Sciences 17: 287-288.
Saunders, J.
1977   "Lehner Ranch revisited." pp. 48-64 in E. Johnson (ed.) Paleoindian Lifeways. Texas Tech University Museum Journal 17.
Schmitz, P. I.
1983   Cazadores antiguos en el sudoeste de Goiás, Brasil. In A. L. Bryan (ed.) New Evidence for the Pleistocene Peopling of the Americas. Orono: Center for Early Man Studies.
Schmoll, H. R., D. J. Szabo, M. Rubin, and E. Dubrovolny
1972   "Radiometric dating of marine shells from the Bootlegger Cove Clay, Anchorage area, Alaska." Geological Society of America Bulletin 83: 1107-1114.
Schneider, F.
1975   "The results of archaeological investigation at the Moe Site 32MN101, North Dakota." Unpublished manuscript, University of North Dakota.
Schooler, E. E.
1974   "Pleistocene beach ridges of northwestern Pennsylvania." Pennsylvania Geological Survey, Fourth Series, General Geology Report 64, Harrisburg.
Schweger, C. E.
1982   "Late Pleistocene vegetation of eastern Beringia: pollen analysis of dated alluvium," pp. 95-112 in D. M. Hopkins et al. (eds.) The Paleoecology of Beringia. New York: Academic Press.

Schweger, C. E. and J. A. Janssen
  1980 "Paleoecology of the Boutellier nonglacial interval, St. Elias Mountains, Yukon Territory, Canada." Arctic and Alpine Research 12: 309-317.

Semken, H. A., Jr.
  1980 "Holocene climatic reconstruction derived from the three micromammal bearing cultural horizons at the Cherokee Sewer Site, Northwestern Iowa," in D. C. Anderson and H. A. Semken (eds.) The Cherokee Excavatioins: Holocene Ecology and Human Adaptations in Northwestern Iowa. New York: Academic Press.

Sheets, P. D. and D. K. Grayson (eds.)
  1979 Volcanic Activity and Human Ecology. New York: Academic Press.

Sheppard, J. C. and R. M. Chutters
  1976 "Washington State University natural radiocarbon measurements." Radiocarbon 18: 140-149.

Shepps, V. C., G. W. White, J. B. Droste, and R. F. Sitler
  1959 "Glacial geology of northwestern Pennsylvania." Pennsylvania Geological Survey, Fourth Series, Bulletin G-32.

Sher, A. V.
  1974 "Pleistocene mammals and stratigraphy of the far northeast USSR and North America." International Geological Review 16: 1-284.

Shlemon, R. J. and J. L. Bischoff
  1981 "Soil-geomorphic and uranium-series dating of the Calico Site, San Bernardino County, California," pp. 41-42 in Evidencia Arqueológica de ocupación humana en America anterior a 11,500 años a.p., Comisión XII, X Congreso, Union Internacional de Ciencias Prehistoricas y Protohistoricas, Mexico, D.F.

Shutler, Richard, Jr. (ed.)
  1971 "Papers from a symposium on early man in North America, new developments: 1960-1970." Arctic Anthropology 8: 2.

Simpson, R. D.
  1958 "The Manix Lake archaeological survey." The Masterkey 32: 4-10.
  1978 "The Calico Mountains archaeological site," pp. 219-220 in A. L. Bryan (ed.) Early Man in America from a Circum-Pacific Perspective. Occasional Papers No. 1 of the Department of Anthropology, University of Alberta, Edmonton.

Simpson, R. D., L. W. Patterson, and C. A. Singer
  1981 "Early lithic technology of the Calico Site, Southern California," in Evidencia Arqueológica de ocupación humana en America anterior a 11,000 años a.p., Comisión XII, X Congreso, Union Internacional de Ciencias Prehistoricas y Protohistoricas, México, D.F.

Sirkin, L. A. and R. Stuckenrath
  1975 "The mid-Wisconsinan (Farmdalian) interstadial in the northern Atlantic coastal plain." Geological Society of America 7: 118-119.
  1980 "The Port Washington warm interval in the northern Atlantic coastal plain." Geological Society of America Bulletin 91: 332-336.

Sirkin, L. A., C. S. Denny, and M. Rubin
  1977 "Late Pleistocene environment of the central Delmarva Peninsula, Delaware, Maryland." Geological Society of America Bulletin 88: 139-142.

Slatt, R. M.
  1977 "Late Quaternary terriginous and carbonate sedimentation on Grand Bank of Newfoundland." Geological Society of America Bulletin 88: 1357-1367.

Smith, J.
  1974 "The Northeast Asian-Northwest American microblade tradition (NANAMT)." Journal of Field Archaeology 1: 347-364.

Solecki, Ralph S.
  1951 "Notes on two archaeological discoveries in northern Alaska, 1950." American Antiquity 17: 55-57.

Spiker, E., L. Kelly, C. Oman, and M. Rubin
  1977 "U.S. Geological Survey radiocarbon dates XII." Radiocarbon 19: 332-353.

Spurling, B. E.
  1980 "The Site C heritage resource inventory and assessment, final report: substantive contributions." Report submitted to B.C. Hydro and Power Authority by Department of Archaeology, Simon Fraser University.

Stalker, A. M.
  1980 "The geology of the ice free corridor: the southern half." Canadian Journal of Anthropology 1: 11-13.

Stanford, D.
  1978a "The Jones-Miller Site: an example of Hell Gap bison procurement strategy." Plains Anthropologist, Memoir No. 14, Lincoln,
  1978b "Some Clovis points." Abstracts of the Fifth Conference of the American Quaternary Association, Edmonton.
  1979a "Afterword: resolving the question of New World origins," pp. 147-150 in R. L. Humphrey and D. Stanford (eds.) Pre-Llano Cultures of the Americas: Paradoxes and Possibilities. Washington, DC: Anthropological Society of Washington.
  1979b "The Selby and Dutton sites: evidence for a possible pre-Clovis occupation on the High Plains," pp. 101-125 in R. L. Humphrey and D. Stanford (eds.) Pre-Llano Cultures of the Americas: Paradoxes and Possibilities. Washington, DC: Anthropological Society of Washington.

Stanford, Dennis (ed.)
  n.d. "The Jones-Miller Site." Manuscript in preparation.

Stanford, Dennis, Robson Bonnichsen, and Richard E. Morlan
  1981 "The Ginsberg experiment: modern and prehistoric evidence of a bone-flaking technology." Science 212: 438-440.

Stanford, D., W. Wedel, and G. Scott
  1981 "Archaeological investigations of the Lamb Spring Site." Southwestern Lore 47: 14-27.

Stewart, T. Dale
  1973 The People of America. New York: Charles Scribner's Sons.
  1974 "Perspectives on some problems of Early Man common to America and Australia," pp. 114-135 in A. P. Elkin and N.W.G. Macintosh (eds.) Grafton Elliott Smith: The Man and His Work. Sydney: Sydney University Press.

Stingelin, R. W.
  1966 "Late-glacial and postglacial vegetational history in the north central Appalachian region." Dissertation Abstracts 26: 6650.

Storck, Peter L.
  1979 "A report on the Banting and Hussey Sites: two Paleo-Indian campsites in Simcoe Country, southern Ontario." National Museum of Man Mercury Series No. 93, Archaeological Survey of Canada.

Stravers, L. K.
  1980 "Palynology and deglaciation history of the Labrador-Ungava Peninsula." Abstracts and Program of the Sixth Conference of the American Quaternary Association, Orono, Maine.

Stryd, A. H. and L. V. Hills
  1972 "An archaeological site survey of the Lillooet Big Bar area, British Columbia." Syesis 5: 191-209.

Sugden, D. E.
  1977 "Reconstruction of the morphology, dynamics and thermal characteristics of the Laurentide ice sheet at its maximum." Arctic and Alpine Research 9: 21-47.

Swanson, E. H. and P. G. Sneed
  1966 "The archaeology of the Shoop Rockshelters in east-central Idaho." Occasional Papers of the Idaho State University Museum, No. 17, Pocatello.

Swanston, D. N.
  1969 "A late Pleistocene glacial sequence from Prince of Wales Island, Alaska." Arctic 22: 25-33.

Szathmary, Emöke J.E., and Nancy S. Ossenberg
  1978 "Are the biological differences between North American Indians and Eskimos truly profound?" Current Anthropology 19: 673-701.

Teller, J. T. and M. M. Fenton
  1980 "Late Wisconsinan glacial stratigraphy and history of southeastern Manitoba." Canadian Journal of Earth Sciences 17: 19-35.

Teller, J. T., S. R. Moran, and L. Clayton
  1980 "The Wisconsinan deglaciation of southern Saskatchewan and adjacent areas: discussion." Canadian Journal of Earth Sciences 17: 539-541.

Terasmae, J.
  1980 "Some problems of late Wisconsin history and geochronology in southeastern Ontario." Canadian Journal of Earth Sciences 17: 361-381.

Tesmer, I. H.
1975 "Geology of Cattaraugus County, New York." Buffalo Society of Natural Sciences Bulletin 27.
Thomas, R. H.
1977 "Calving bay dynamics and ice-sheet retreat up the St. Lawrence Valley system." Geographie Physique et Quaternaire 31: 347-356.
Thompson, Raymond M.
1948 "Notes on the archaeology of the Utukok River, northwestern Alaska." American Antiquity 14: 62-65.
Thorson, R. M.
1980 "Ice-sheet glaciation of the Puget lowland, Washington, during the Vashon stade (Late Pleistocene)." Quaternary Research 13: 303-321.
Thorson, R. M. and T. D. Hamilton
1977 "Geology of the Dry Creek site: a stratified Early Man site in interior Alaska." Quaternary Research 7: 149-176.
Tiffin, D. L.
1976 "Continental margin topography and origin off western Canada." Presented at the Conference on Geomorphology of the Canadian Cordillera and its bearing on mineral deposits, Geological Association of Canada, Vancouver, February 6-7.
Tipper, H. W.
1971 "Multiple glaciation in central British Columbia." Canadian Journal of Earth Sciences 8: 743.
Toups, P.
1969 "Early prehistory of the Clearwater Valley." Ph.D. dissertation Tulane University.
Tseitlin, S. M.
1979 Geologiia Paleolita Severnoi Azii (Geology of the Paleolithic of Northern Asia). Moscow: Nauka.
Tucker, C. M. and S. B. McCann
1980 "Quaternary events on the Burin Peninsula, Newfoundland, and the islands of St. Pierre and Miquelon, France." Canadian Journal of Earth Sciences 7: 1462-1479.
Tunnell, J.
1977 "Fluted projectile point production as revealed by lithic specimens from the Adair-Steadman Site in northwest Texas." Texas Tech University Museum Journal 17: 140-168. Lubbock.
Tuohy, D. R.
1968 "Some early lithic sites in western Nevada," in C. Irwin-Williams (ed.) Early Man in Western North America. Eastern New Mexico University Contributions in Anthropology 1: 27-38. Portales.
1969 "Breakage, burin facets and the probable technological linkage among Lake Mohave, Silver Lake, and other varieties of projectile points in the desert west." Nevada State Museum University Paper No. 14: 132-152. Carson City.
1974 "A comparative study of late Paleo-Indian manifestations in the Great Basin." Nevada Archaeological Survey Research Paper No. 5: 91-116. Reno.
Turner, Christy G. II
1971 "Three-rooted mandibular first permanent molars and the question of American Indian origins." American Journal of Physical Anthropology 34: 229-241.
1979a "Sinodonty and Sundadonty: a dental anthropological view of Mongoloid microevolution, origin, and dispersal into the Pacific basin, Siberia, and the Americas." Presented at XIV Pacific Science Congress, Khabarovsk, USSR.
1979b "Dental anthropological indications of agriculture among the Jomon people of central Japan." American Journal of Physical Anthropology 51: 619-635.
1981 'Review of The First Americans: origins, affinities, and adaptations." American Anthropologist 83: 194-196.
Turner, Christy G. II, and Junius Bird
1981 "Dentition of Chilean Paleo-Indians and peopling of the Americas." Science 212: 1053-1055.
Tuthill, S. J.
1967 "Paleozoology and molluskan paleontology of the glacial Lake Agassiz region," pp. 299-312 in W. J. Mayer-Oakes (ed.) Life, Land and Water. Manitoba: University of Manitoba Press.
Valentine, J. W. and H. H. Veeh
1969 "Radiometric ages of Pleistocene terraces from San Nicholas Island, California." Geological Society of America Bulletin 80: 1415-1418.

Van der Hammen, T. and G. Correal U.
1978 "Prehistoric man on the sabana de Bogotá: data for an ecological prehistory." Paleogeography, Paleoclimatology, Paleoecology 25: 179-190.
van der Linden, W. J. and R. H. Fillon
1976 "Hamilton Bank, Labrador margin: origin and evolution of a glaciated shelf." Geological Survey of Canada, Paper 75-40.
Veeh, H. H. and J. W. Valentine
1967 "Radiometric ages of Pleistocene fossils from Cayucos, California." Geological Society of America Bulletin 78: 547-550.
Vilks, G.
1980 "Post glacial basin sedimentation on Labrador Shelf." Geological Survey of Canada Paper 78-28.
Vilks, G. and P. J. Mudie
1978 "Early deglaciation of the Labrador Shelf." Science 202: 1181-1183.
Vincent, J. S.
1978 "Limits of ice advance, glacial lakes, and marine transgressions on Banks Island, District of Franklin: a preliminary interpretation." Geological Survey of Canada Paper 78-1C.
Voegelin, C. F. and F. N. Voegelin
1966 Map of North American Indian Languages. American Ethnological Society.
Volman, K. Cushman
1981 "Paleoenvironmental implications of botanical data from Meadowcroft Rockshelter, Pennsylvania." Ph.D. dissertation, Texas A&M University, College Station, Texas.
Voorhies, M. R.
1969 "Taphonomy and population dynamics of an early Pliocene vertebrate fauna, Knox County, Nebraska." University of Wyoming Contributions to Geology, Special Paper No. 1.
Voss, Jerome A.
1977 "The Barnes Site: functional and stylistic variability in a small Paleo-Indian assemblage." Mid-Continental Journal of Archaeology 2: 253-305.
Wagner, F.J.E.
1977 "Paleoecology of marine Pleistocene mollusca, Nova Scotia." Canadian Journal of Earth Sciences 14: 1305-1321.
Wagner, W. R., L. Heyman, R. E. Gray, D. J. Belz, R. Lund, A. S. Cate, and C. D. Edgerton
1970 "Geology of the Pittsburgh area." Pennsylvania Geological Survey, Fourth Series, General Geology Report G-59, Harrisburg.
Warren, C. N.
1967 "The San Dieguito Complex: a review and hypothesis." American Antiquity 32: 168-187.
1968 "The view from Wenas: a study in Plateau prehistory." Occasional Papers of Idaho State University Museum, No. 24. Pocatello.
Warren, C. N. and J. DeCosta
1964 "Dating Lake Mohave artifacts and beaches." American Antiquity 30: 206-209.
Weber, F. R., T. D. Hamilton, D. M. Hopkins, C. A. Repenning, and H. Haas
1981 "Canyon Creek: a late Pleistocene vertebrate locality in interior Alaska." Quaternary Research 16: 167-180.
Weber, R. H.
1980 "Geology of the AKE Site," in P. H. Beckett, The AKE Site: Collections and Excavations of LA 13423, Catron County, New Mexico. New Mexico State University.
1981 Personal communication.
Weber, R. L. (compiler)
1981 "Current research: Amazon basin and eastern Brazil." American Antiquity 46: 206.
Wedel, Waldo
1965 "Investigations at the Lamb Spring site, Colorado." Manuscript on file at the National Science Foundation, Washington, D.C.
Wedel, Waldo, Wilfred Husted, and John Moss
1968 "Mummy Cave: prehistoric record from the Rock Mountains of Wyoming." Science 160: 184-186.
Wendorf, F.
1966 "Early Man in the New World: problems of migration." American Naturalist 100: 253-270.

West, F. W.
1981   The Archaeology of Beringia. New York: Columbia University Press.

Wheat, Joe Ben
1972   "The Olsen-Chubbuck Site: a Paleo-Indian bison kill." Society for American Archaeology, Memoir No. 26.
1979   "The Jurgens Site." Plains Anthropologist, Memoir 15.

Wheeler, Richard P.
n.d.   "39FA56: Archaeological remains in three reservoir areas in South Dakota and Wyoming." Manuscript on file, Midwest Archaeological Center, National Park Service, Lincoln, Nebraska.

White, G. W., S. M. Totten, and D. L. Gross
1969   "Pleistocene stratigraphy of northwestern Pennsylvania." Pennsylvania Geological Survey, Fourth Series, General Geology Report G-55, Harrisburg.

White, J. M., R. W. Mathewes, and W. H. Mathews
1979   "Radiocarbon dates from Boone Lake and their relation to the ice-free corridor in the Peace River district of Alberta, Canada." Canadian Journal of Earth Sciences 16: 1870-1877.

White, J. P. and J. F. O'Connell
1979   "Australian prehistory: new aspects of antiquity." Science 203: 21-27.

Whitehead, D. R.
1973   "Late Wisconsin vegetational changes in unglaciated eastern North America." Quaternary Research 3: 621-631.
1979   "Late-glacial and postglacial vegetational history of the Berkshires, western Massachusetts." Quaternary Research 12: 333-357.

Willey, G. R.
1971   An Introduction to American Archaeology, Vol. Two: South America. Englewood Cliffs, NJ: Prentice-Hall.

Willey, G. R. and P. Phillips
1958   Method and Theory in American Archaeology. Chicago: University of Chicago Press.

Williams, L. D.
1978   "Ice-sheet initiation and climatic influences of expanded snow cover in Arctic Canada." Quaternary Research 10: 141-149.

Wilmsen, E. N.
1974   Lindenmeier: A Pleistocene Hunting Society. New York: Harper and Row.

Wilmsen, E. N. and F.H.H. Roberts, Jr.
1978   "Lindenmeier, 1934-1974: concluding report on investigations." Smithsonian Contributions to Anthropology 24.

Wilson, M.
1978   "Archaeological kill site populations and the Holocene evolution of the genus Bison." Plains Anthropologist, Memoir 14.

Witthoft, J.
1952   "A Paleo-Indian site in eastern Pennsylvania: an early hunting culture." Proceedings of the American Philosophical Society 96: 464-495.
1971   "A Paleo-Indian site in eastern Pennsylvania," pp. 13-64 in B. C. Kent et al. (eds.) Foundations of Pennsylvania Prehistory. Harrisburg: The Pennsylvania Historical and Museum Commission.

Workman, William B.
1980   "Holocene peopling of the New World: implications of the Arctic and Subarctic data." Canadian Journal of Anthropology 1: 129-139.

Wormington, H. Marie
1957   Ancient Man in North America. Denver: Denver Museum of Natural History Popular Series 4.

Wright, H. E.
1971a   "Late Quaternary vegetational history of North America," pp. 37-56 in K. K. Turekian (ed.) The Late Cenozoic Glacial Ages. New Haven, CT: Yale University Press.
1971b   "Retreat of the Laurentide ice sheet from 14,000 to 9,000 years ago." Quaternary Research 1: 316-330.
1978   "Pollen analyses at Mummy Cave," pp. 43-45 in H. McCracken (ed.) The Mummy Cave Project in Northwestern Wyoming. Cody: Buffalo Bill Historical Center.

Wright, James V.
1972   The Shield Archaic. Ottawa: National Museum of Man Publications in Archaeology No. 3.

Wu, S. and C. A. Jones
1978   "Molluscs from the Hudson-Meng Site," pp. 193-210 in L. D. Agenbroad (ed.) The Hudsen-Meng Site: An Alberta Bison Kill in the Nebraska High Plains. Washington, DC: University Press of America.

Youngman, Phillip M.
1975   Mammals of the Yukon Territory. Ottawa: National Museum of Natural Sciences Publications in Geology 10.

Yurtsev, B. A.
1974   Problemy botanicheskoi geografii Severo-Vostochnoi Azii (Problems of Phytogeography of Northeastern Asia). Leningrad: Nauka.

Zant, K. V.
1979   "Late glacial and postglacial pollen and plant macrofossils from Lake West Okoboji, northwestern Iowa." Quaternary Research 12: 358-380.

Zubov, A. A. and N. E. Kaldiva
1979   Ethnic Odontology. Moscow: Science Press.

SUBJECT INDEX

SITE INDEX

Numbers in boldface refer to end maps.

ABOUT THE CONTRIBUTORS

JAMES M. ADOVASIO is Chairman of the Department of Anthropology and Director of the Cultural Resource Management Program at the University of Pittsburgh. He is a specialist in Paleoindians, archaeological theory and method, primitive technology, and the prehistory of North America, Mesoamerica, and the Near East.

RAINER BERGER, Professor of Geophysics, Geography, and Anthropology, is Chairman of the Interdepartmental Archaeology Program at the University of California, Los Angeles. His research interests include dating methods based on the use of isotopes and other physical evidence.

ALAN L. BRYAN is Professor of Anthropology at the University of Alberta. He is a specialist in Early Man of North, Middle, and South America.

ROY L. CARLSON is a Professor of Archaeology at Simon Fraser University. Research interests include the prehistory and ethnology of the Northwest Coast, Southwest, and Old World Paleolithic, as well as archaeological theory.

KNUT R. FLADMARK is an Associate Professor of Archaeology at Simon Fraser University. He specializes in geoarchaeology, Paleoindians, historical archaeology, North American prehistory, the Northwest Coast, the Interior, the Arctic, and the Plains.

GEORGE C. FRISON is Professor and Head, Department of Anthropology, at the University of Wyoming. He is a specialist in prehistory, primitive technology, and the U.S. Plains.

GEORGE F. MacDONALD is Senior Scientist with the Archaeological Survey of Canada and Acting Director for the National Museum of Man, National Museums of Canada. He is a specialist in the Paleoindian, archaeology of North America, and the Northwest Coast.

RICHARD S. MacNEISH is Director of the Robert S. Peabody Foundation for Archaeology and specializes in New World archaeology.

RICHARD E. MORLAN is an archaeologist with the Archaeological Survey of Canada, National Museum of Man, National Museums of Canada. He is a specialist in the Paleoindian, paleoecology, the Western Boreal Forest, Alaska, and Japan-Northeast Asia.

RICHARD SHUTLER, Jr., is Professor and Chairman of the Department of Archaeology, and Director of the Museum of Archaeology and Ethnology at Simon Fraser University. Research interests include the Paleoindian, Oceanic and Southeast Asian prehistory, and Fossil Man in Asia.

DENNIS STANFORD is Curator at the Department of Anthropology, National Museum of Natural History, Smithsonian Institution. He is a specialist in the Paleoindian and North American archaeology.

CHRISTY G. TURNER II is Professor of Anthropology, Arizona State University, specializing in dental anthropology, skeletal analysis, and cultural relationships; Alaska, the U.S. Southwest, the Pacific Basin, eastern Asia, and Siberia.

H. MARIE WORMINGTON is Adjunct Professor at Colorado College. Research interests include the earliest cultures of the New World and related cultures of eastern Asia, as well as Fremont culture.

DATE DUE

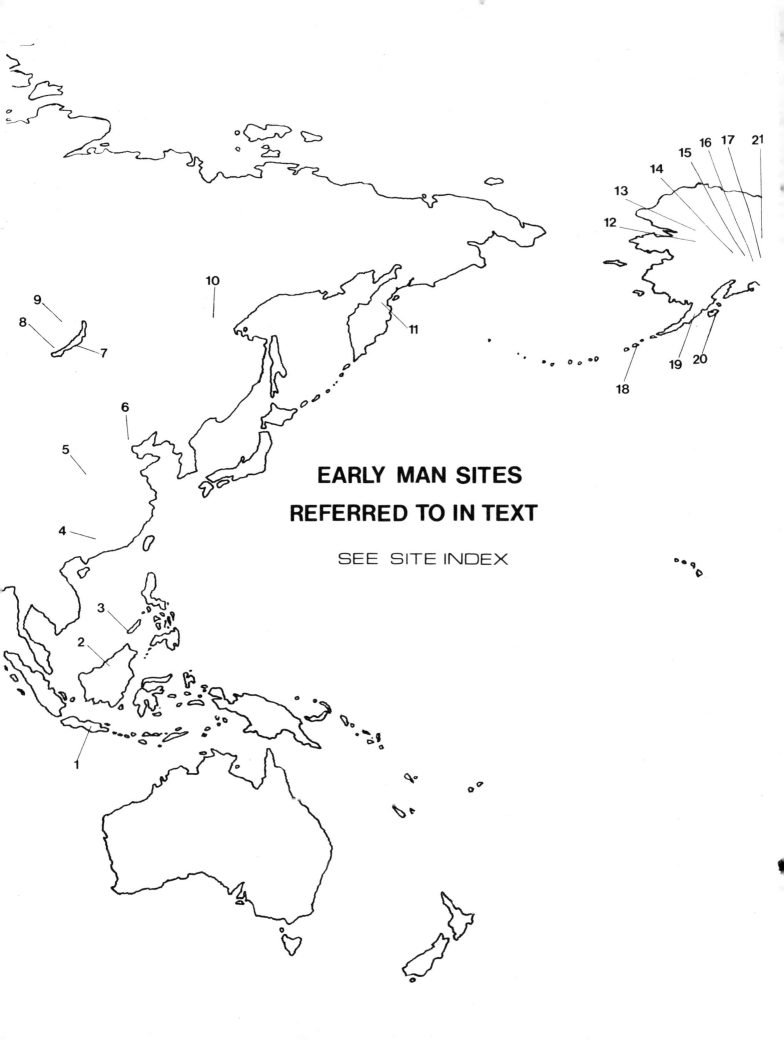

EARLY MAN SITES
REFERRED TO IN TEXT

SEE SITE INDEX